SHONEN JUMP MANGA

## Vol. 24

# YUGI VS. MARIK

### STORY AND ART BY
### KAZUKI TAKAHASHI

# THE STORY SO FAR...

YUGI MUTOU/
YU-GI-OH

When 10th grader Yugi solved the Millennium Puzzle, another spirit took up residence in his body...Yu-Gi-Oh, the King of Games, a dark avenger who challenges evildoers to "Shadow Games" of life and death!

## YUGI FACES DEADLY ENEMIES!

Using his gaming skills, Yugi fights ruthless adversaries like Maximillion Pegasus, multimillionaire creator of the collectible card game "Duel Monsters," and Ryo Bakura, whose friendly personality turns evil when he is possessed by the spirit of the Millennium Ring. But Yugi's greatest rival is Seto Kaiba, the world's second-greatest gamer—and the ruthless teenage president of Kaiba Corporation. At first, Kaiba and Yugi are bitter enemies, but after fighting against a common adversary—Pegasus—they come to respect one another. But for all his powers, there is one thing Yu-Gi-Oh cannot do: remember who he is and where he came from.

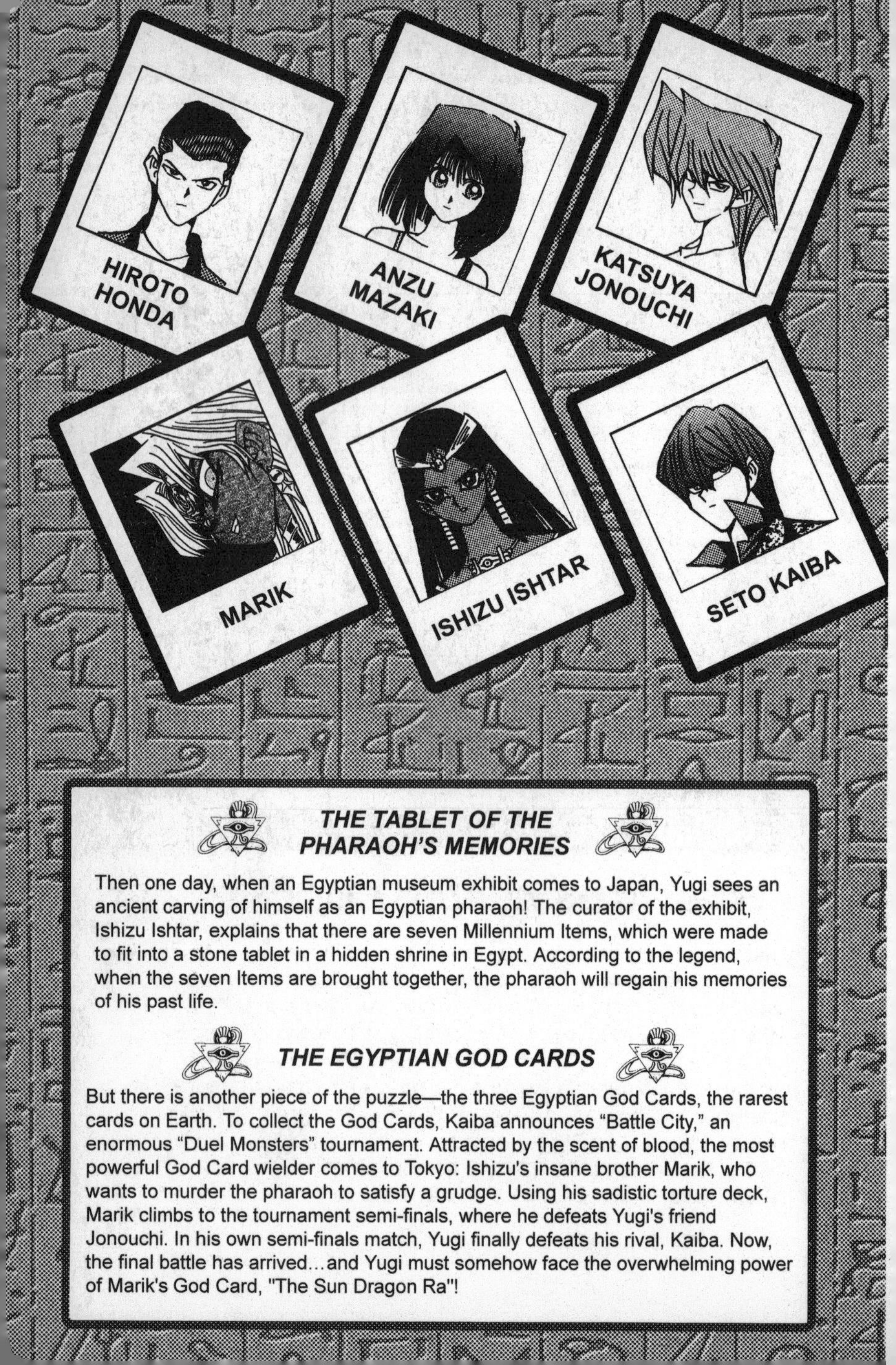
HIROTO HONDA
ANZU MAZAKI
KATSUYA JONOUCHI
MARIK
ISHIZU ISHTAR
SETO KAIBA

## *THE TABLET OF THE PHARAOH'S MEMORIES*

Then one day, when an Egyptian museum exhibit comes to Japan, Yugi sees an ancient carving of himself as an Egyptian pharaoh! The curator of the exhibit, Ishizu Ishtar, explains that there are seven Millennium Items, which were made to fit into a stone tablet in a hidden shrine in Egypt. According to the legend, when the seven Items are brought together, the pharaoh will regain his memories of his past life.

## *THE EGYPTIAN GOD CARDS*

But there is another piece of the puzzle—the three Egyptian God Cards, the rarest cards on Earth. To collect the God Cards, Kaiba announces "Battle City," an enormous "Duel Monsters" tournament. Attracted by the scent of blood, the most powerful God Card wielder comes to Tokyo: Ishizu's insane brother Marik, who wants to murder the pharaoh to satisfy a grudge. Using his sadistic torture deck, Marik climbs to the tournament semi-finals, where he defeats Yugi's friend Jonouchi. In his own semi-finals match, Yugi finally defeats his rival, Kaiba. Now, the final battle has arrived…and Yugi must somehow face the overwhelming power of Marik's God Card, "The Sun Dragon Ra"!

# Yu-Gi-Oh! DUELIST

## Vol. 24

## CONTENTS

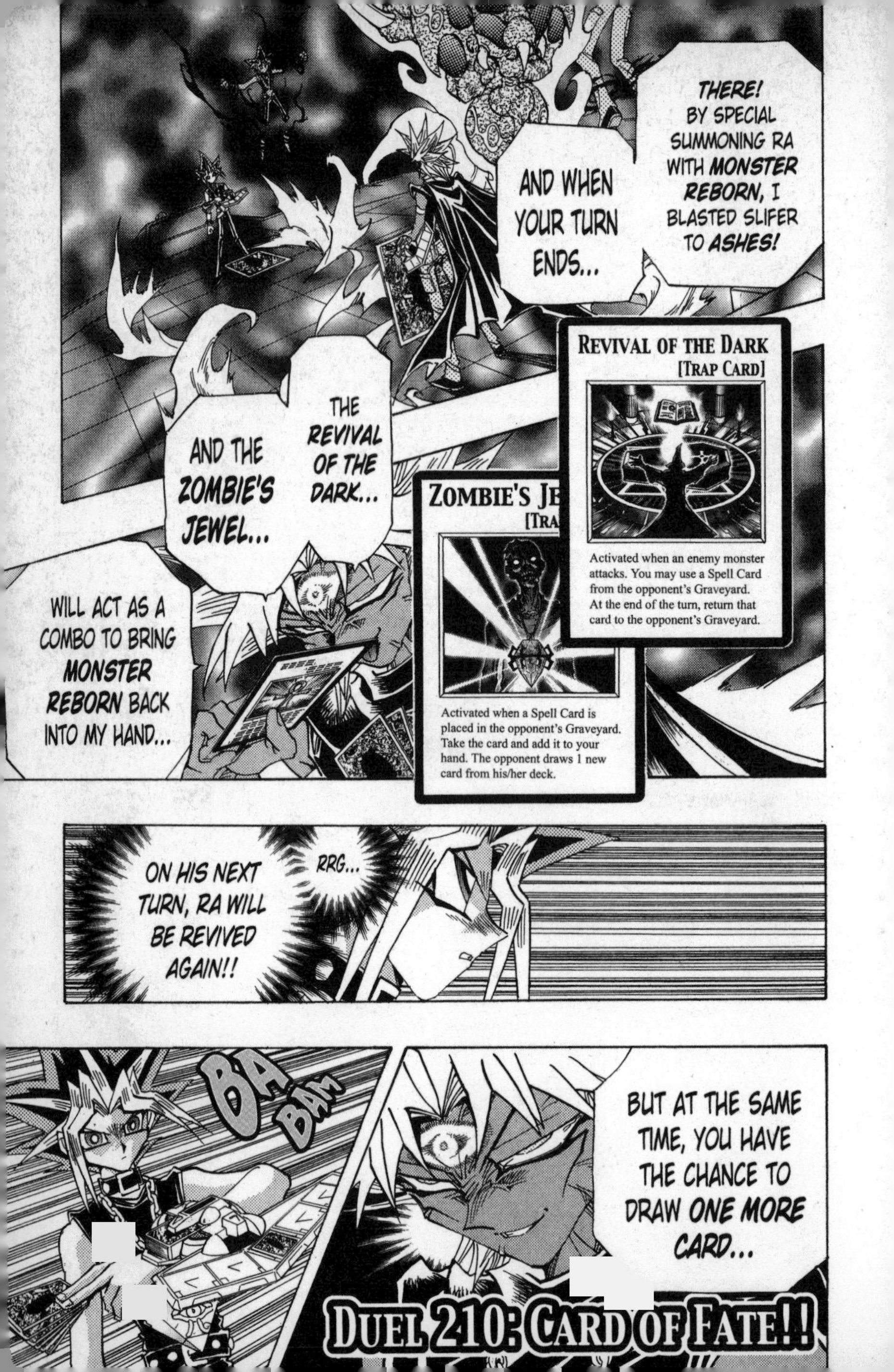
THERE! BY SPECIAL SUMMONING RA WITH MONSTER REBORN, I BLASTED SLIFER TO ASHES!
AND WHEN YOUR TURN ENDS...
REVIVAL OF THE DARK
[TRAP CARD]
Activated when an enemy monster attacks. You may use a Spell Card from the opponent's Graveyard. At the end of the turn, return that card to the opponent's Graveyard.
Activated when a Spell Card is placed in the opponent's Graveyard. Take the card and add it to your hand. The opponent draws 1 new card from his/her deck.
THE REVIVAL OF THE DARK...
AND THE ZOMBIE'S JEWEL...
WILL ACT AS A COMBO TO BRING MONSTER REBORN BACK INTO MY HAND...
RRG...
ON HIS NEXT TURN, RA WILL BE REVIVED AGAIN!!
BUT AT THE SAME TIME, YOU HAVE THE CHANCE TO DRAW ONE MORE CARD...
BA
BAM
DUEL 210: CARD OF FATE!!

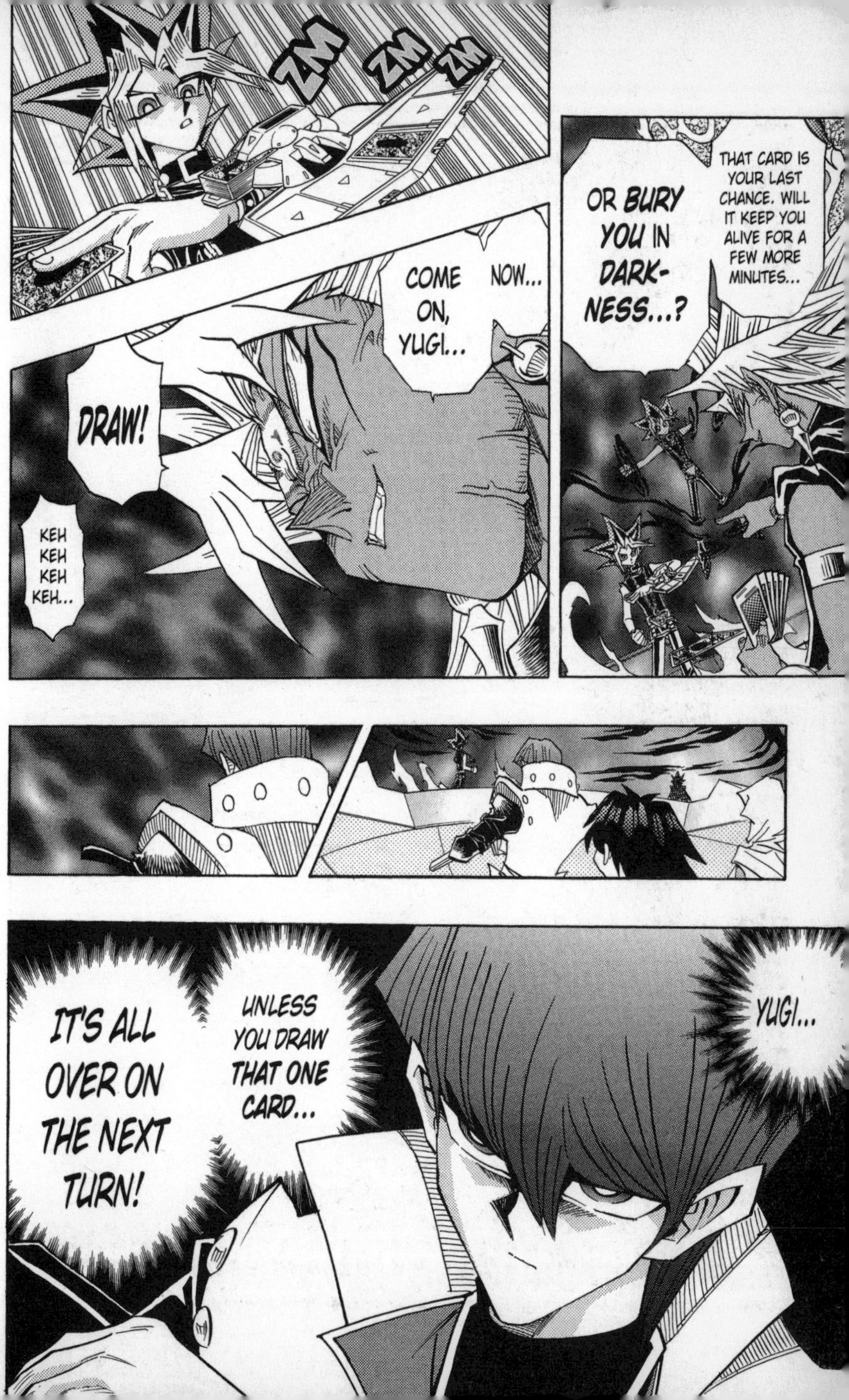
THAT CARD IS YOUR LAST CHANCE. WILL IT KEEP YOU ALIVE FOR A FEW MORE MINUTES...
OR BURY YOU IN DARKNESS...?
ZM ZM ZM
COME ON, YUGI... NOW...
DRAW!
KEH KEH KEH KEH...
YUGI...
UNLESS YOU DRAW THAT ONE CARD...
IT'S ALL OVER ON THE NEXT TURN!

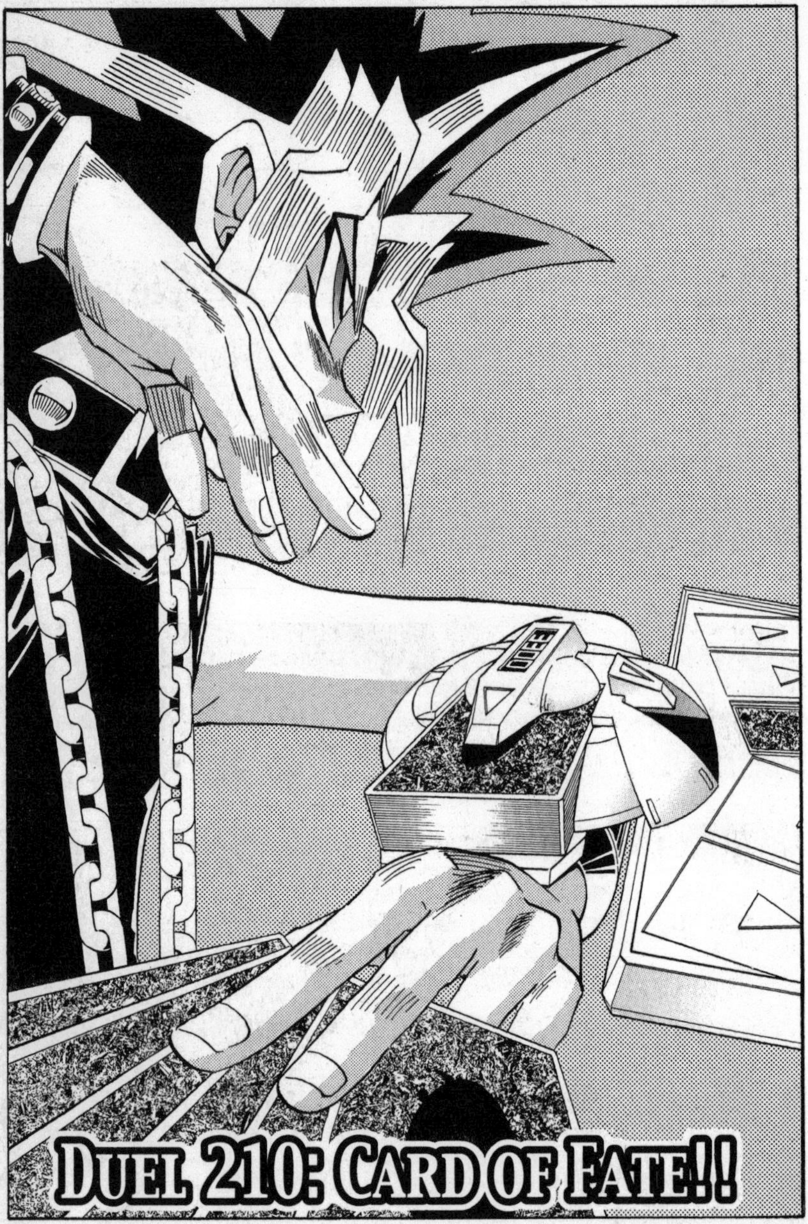
DUEL 210: CARD OF FATE!!

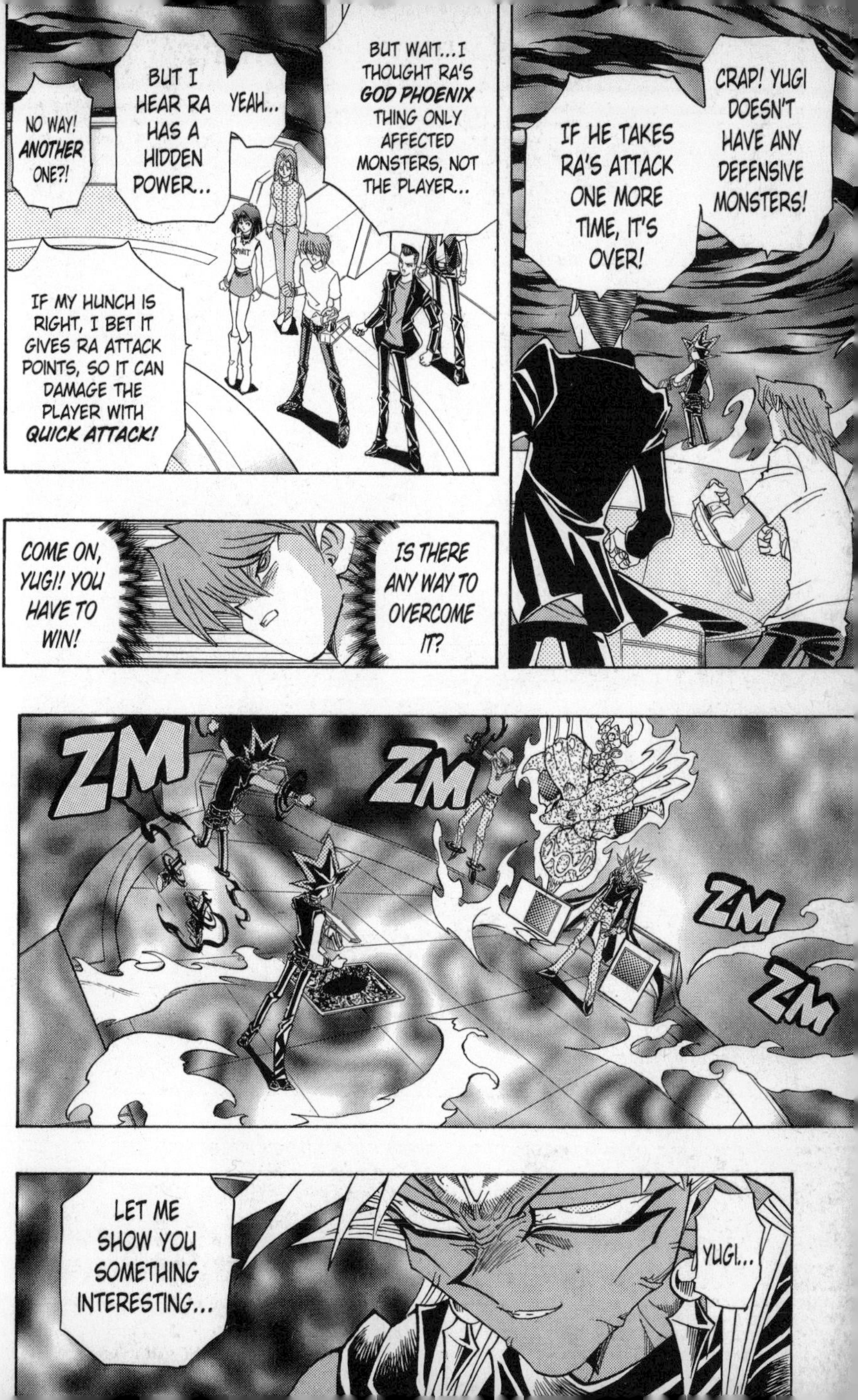

CRAP! YUGI DOESN'T HAVE ANY DEFENSIVE MONSTERS!
IF HE TAKES RA'S ATTACK ONE MORE TIME, IT'S OVER!
BUT WAIT...I THOUGHT RA'S GOD PHOENIX THING ONLY AFFECTED MONSTERS, NOT THE PLAYER...
YEAH...
BUT I HEAR RA HAS A HIDDEN POWER...
NO WAY! ANOTHER ONE?!
IF MY HUNCH IS RIGHT, I BET IT GIVES RA ATTACK POINTS, SO IT CAN DAMAGE THE PLAYER WITH QUICK ATTACK!
IS THERE ANY WAY TO OVERCOME IT?
COME ON, YUGI! YOU HAVE TO WIN!
ZM
ZM
ZM
ZM
YUGI...
LET ME SHOW YOU SOMETHING INTERESTING...

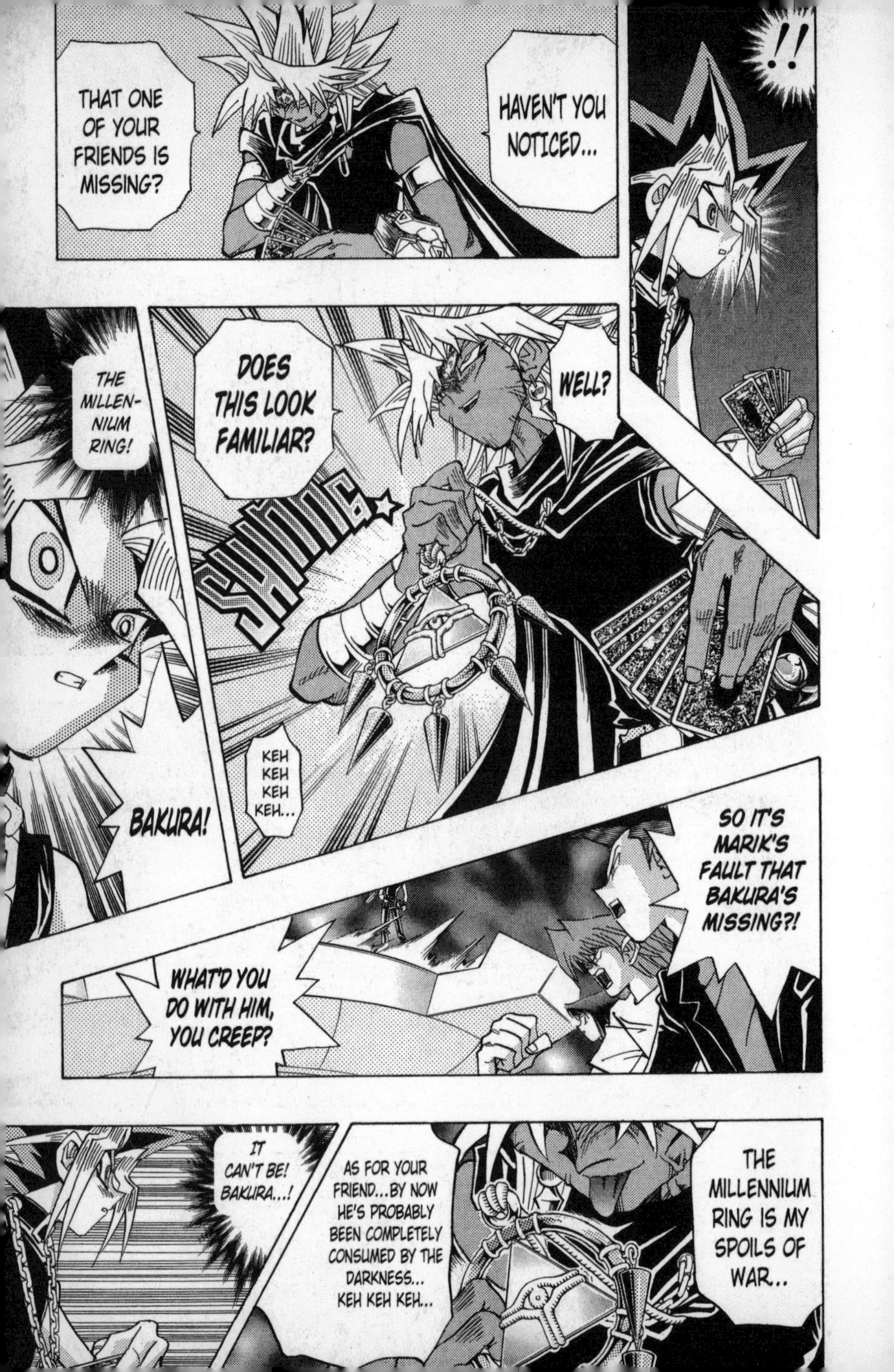
!!
HAVEN'T YOU NOTICED...
THAT ONE OF YOUR FRIENDS IS MISSING?
WELL?
DOES THIS LOOK FAMILIAR?
SHING☆
KEH KEH KEH KEH...
THE MILLENNIUM RING!
BAKURA!
SO IT'S MARIK'S FAULT THAT BAKURA'S MISSING?!
WHAT'D YOU DO WITH HIM, YOU CREEP?
THE MILLENNIUM RING IS MY SPOILS OF WAR...
AS FOR YOUR FRIEND...BY NOW HE'S PROBABLY BEEN COMPLETELY CONSUMED BY THE DARKNESS... KEH KEH KEH...
IT CAN'T BE! BAKURA...!

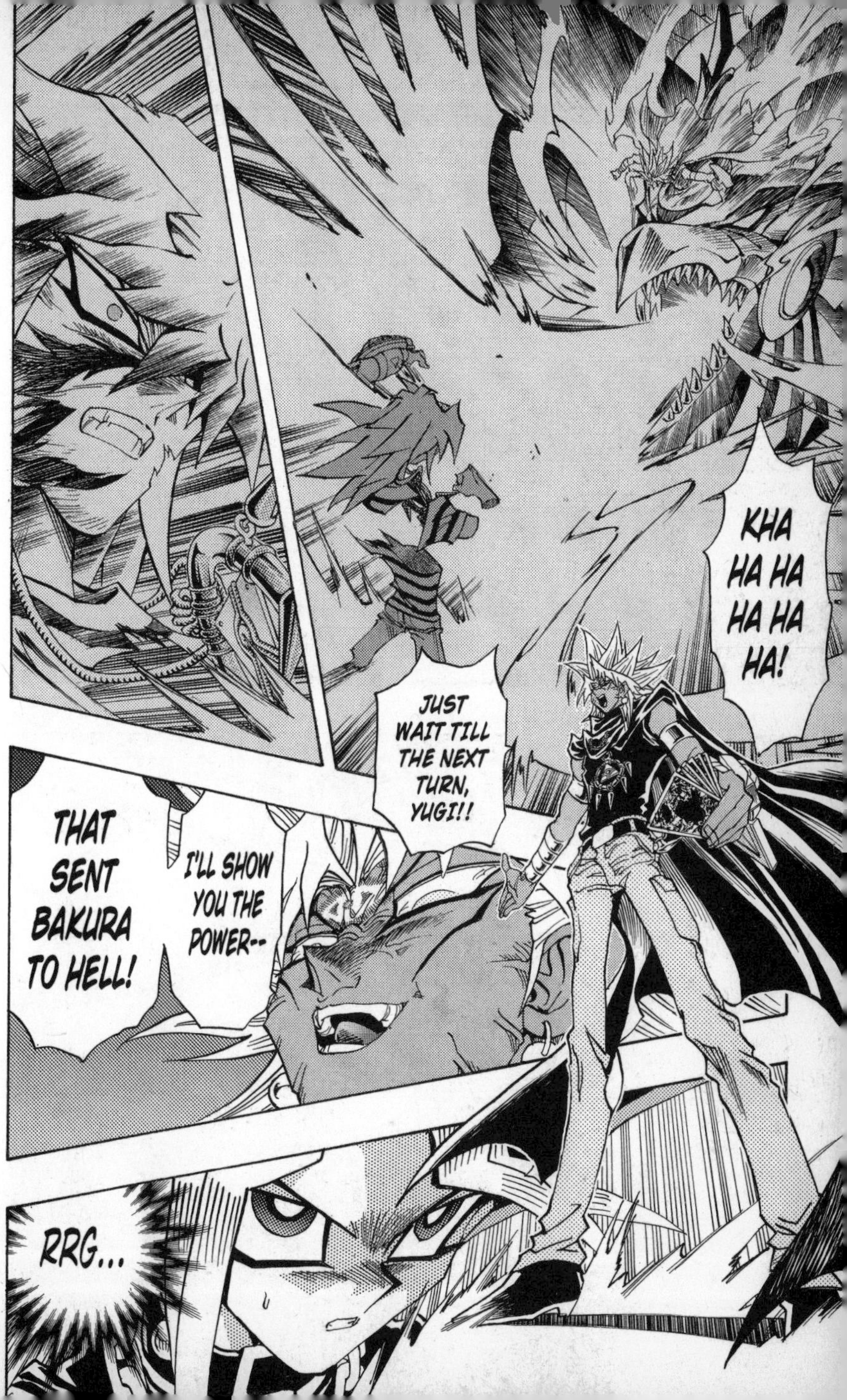
KHA HA HA HA HA HA!
JUST WAIT TILL THE NEXT TURN, YUGI!!
I'LL SHOW YOU THE POWER--
THAT SENT BAKURA TO HELL!
RRG...

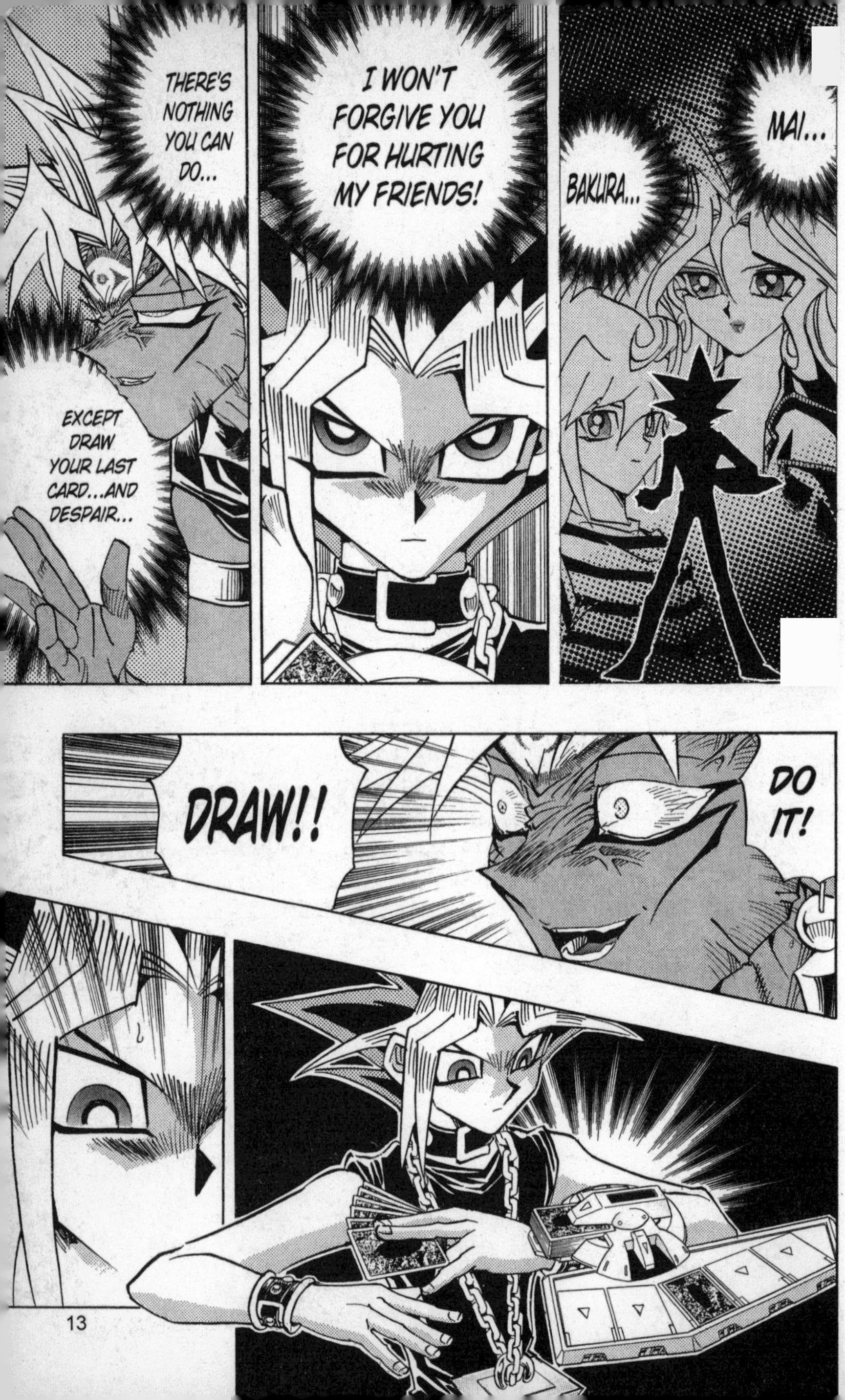
MAI...
BAKURA...
I WON'T FORGIVE YOU FOR HURTING MY FRIENDS!
THERE'S NOTHING YOU CAN DO...
EXCEPT DRAW YOUR LAST CARD...AND DESPAIR...
DO IT!
DRAW!!

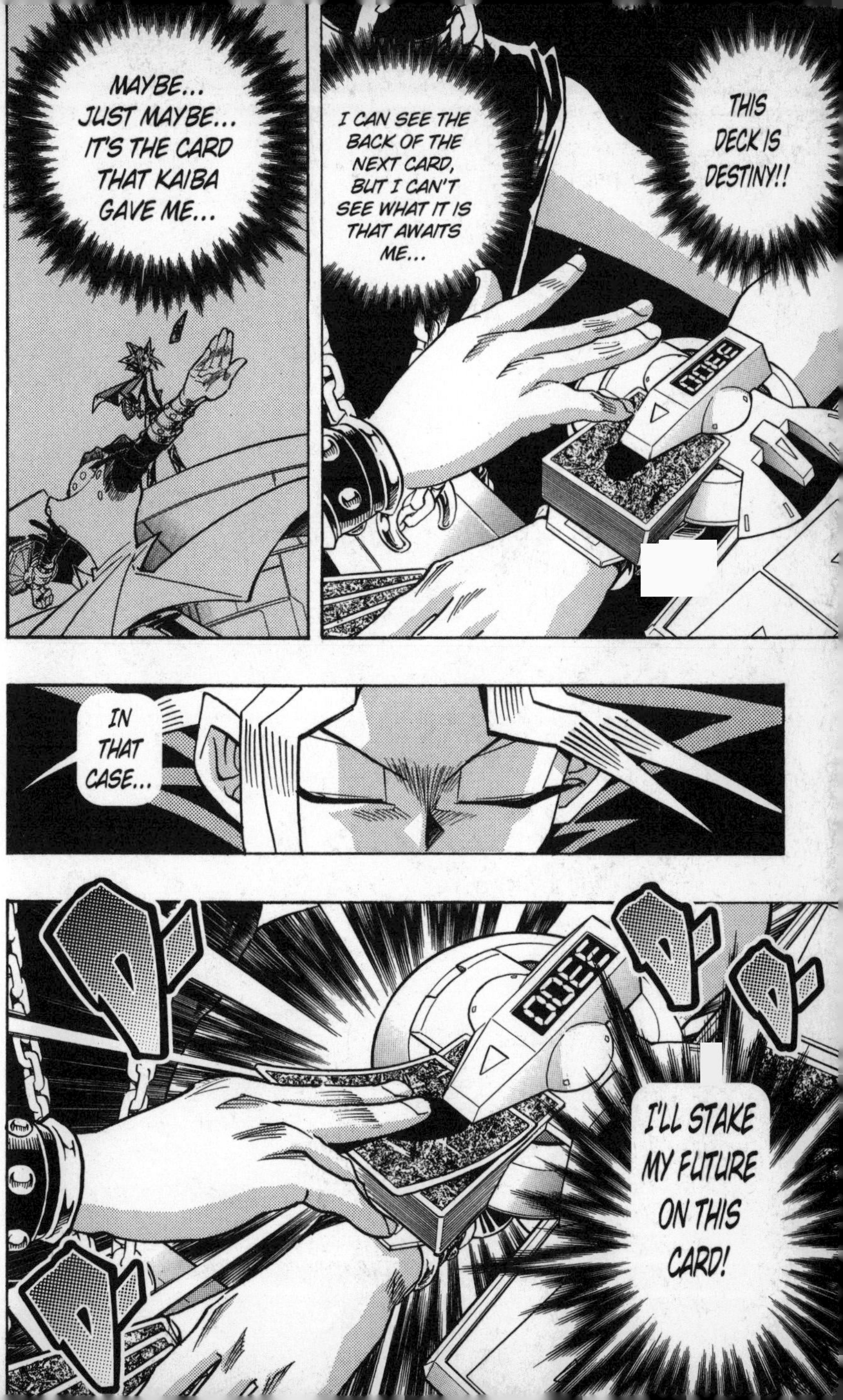
THIS DECK IS DESTINY!!
I CAN SEE THE BACK OF THE NEXT CARD, BUT I CAN'T SEE WHAT IT IS THAT AWAITS ME...
MAYBE... JUST MAYBE... IT'S THE CARD THAT KAIBA GAVE ME...
IN THAT CASE...
I'LL STAKE MY FUTURE ON THIS CARD!

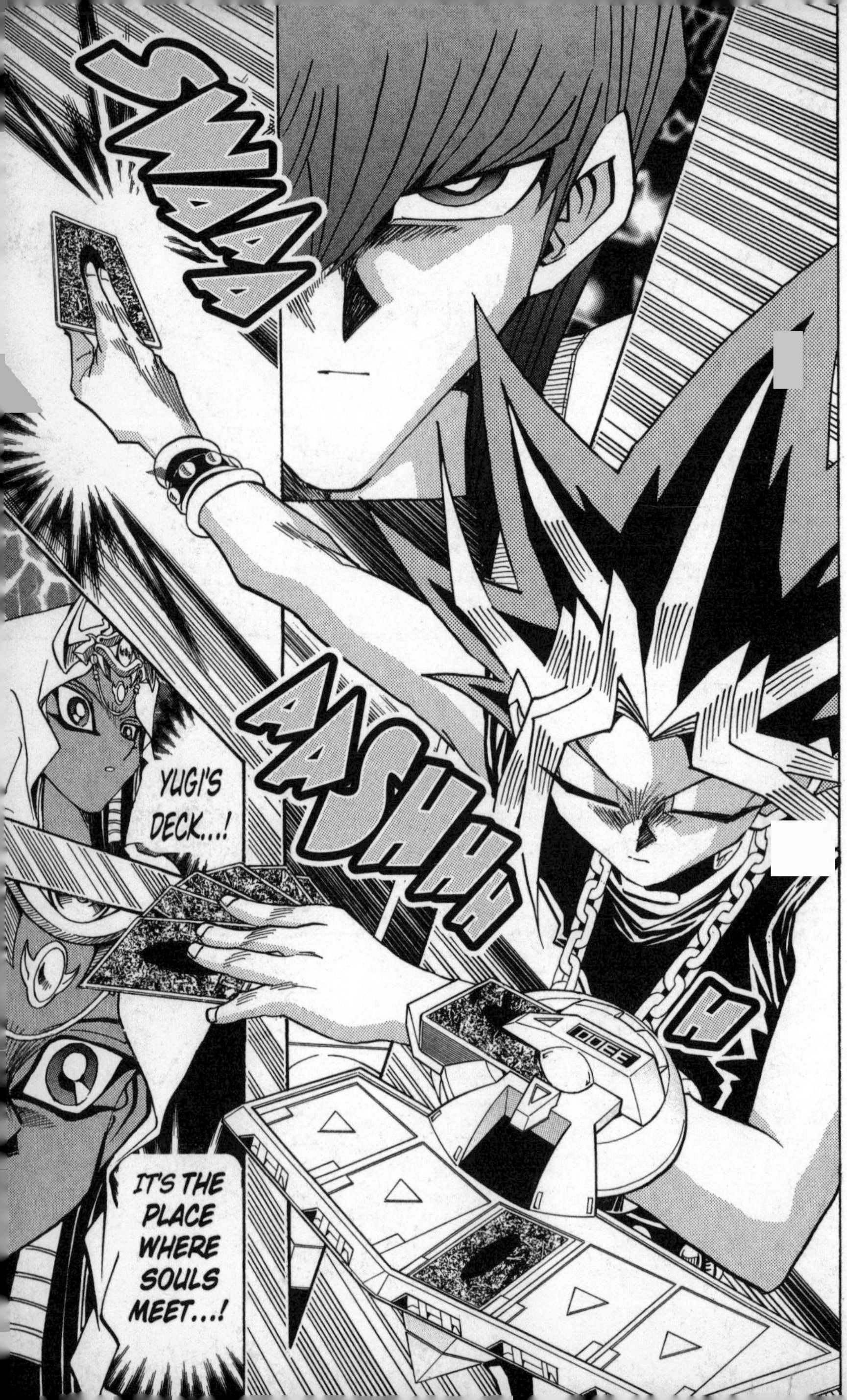
SWAAA
AASHHH
H
YUGI'S DECK...!
IT'S THE PLACE WHERE SOULS MEET...!

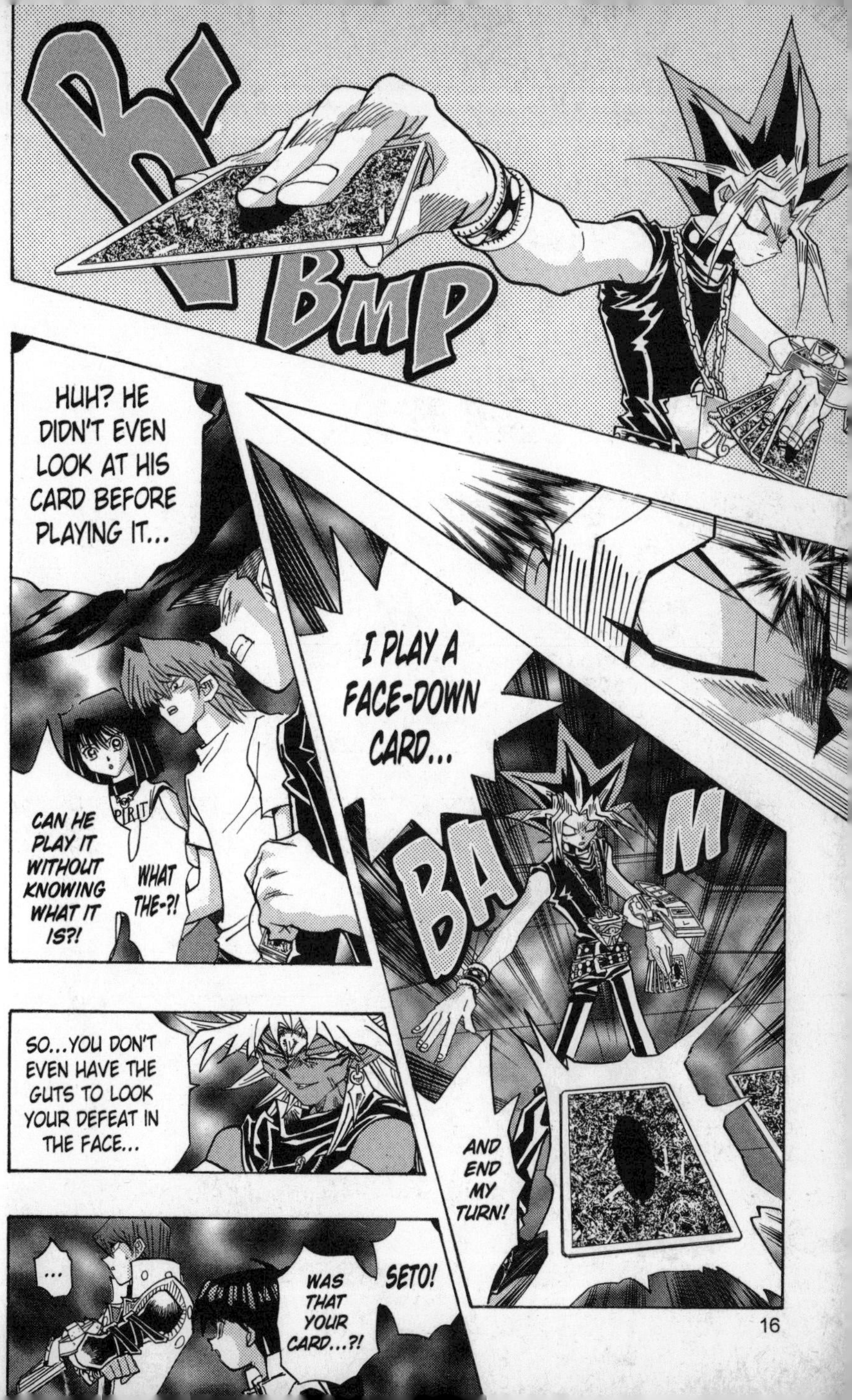
BI
BMP
I PLAY A FACE-DOWN CARD...
BAM
AND END MY TURN!
HUH? HE DIDN'T EVEN LOOK AT HIS CARD BEFORE PLAYING IT...
WHAT THE-?!
CAN HE PLAY IT WITHOUT KNOWING WHAT IT IS?!
SO...YOU DON'T EVEN HAVE THE GUTS TO LOOK YOUR DEFEAT IN THE FACE...
SETO!
WAS THAT YOUR CARD...?!
...

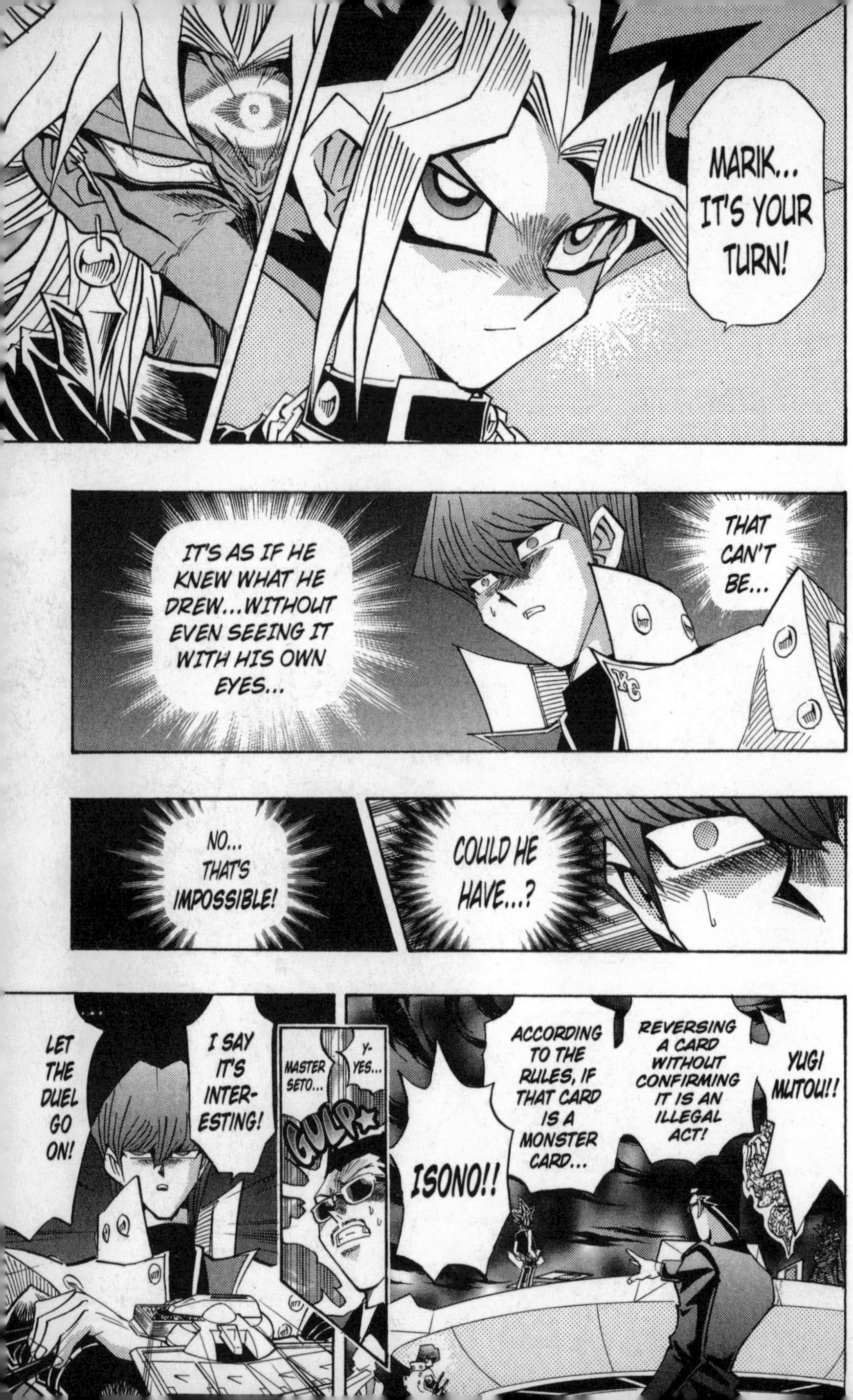
MARIK... IT'S YOUR TURN!
THAT CAN'T BE...
IT'S AS IF HE KNEW WHAT HE DREW...WITHOUT EVEN SEEING IT WITH HIS OWN EYES...
COULD HE HAVE...?
NO... THAT'S IMPOSSIBLE!
YUGI MUTOU!!
REVERSING A CARD WITHOUT CONFIRMING IT IS AN ILLEGAL ACT!
ACCORDING TO THE RULES, IF THAT CARD IS A MONSTER CARD...
ISONO!!
Y-YES...
MASTER SETO...
GULP
...
I SAY IT'S INTERESTING!
LET THE DUEL GO ON!

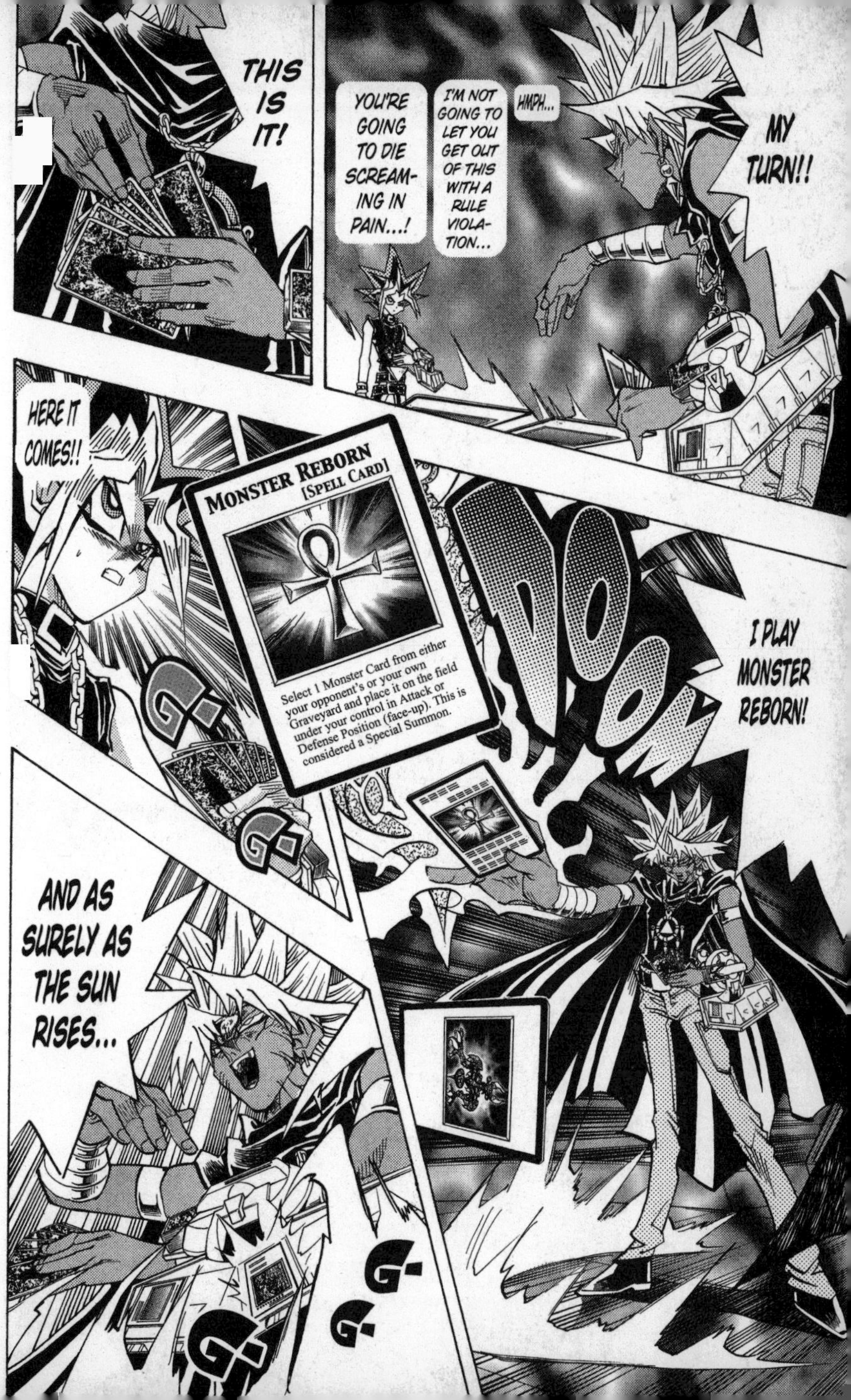
MY TURN!!
HMPH...
I'M NOT GOING TO LET YOU GET OUT OF THIS WITH A RULE VIOLATION...
YOU'RE GOING TO DIE SCREAMING IN PAIN...!
THIS IS IT!
I PLAY MONSTER REBORN!
DOOM
MONSTER REBORN
[SPELL CARD]
Select 1 Monster Card from either your opponent's or your own Graveyard and place it on the field under your control in Attack or Defense Position (face-up). This is considered a Special Summon.
G-
G-
HERE IT COMES!!
G-
G-
AND AS SURELY AS THE SUN RISES...
G-

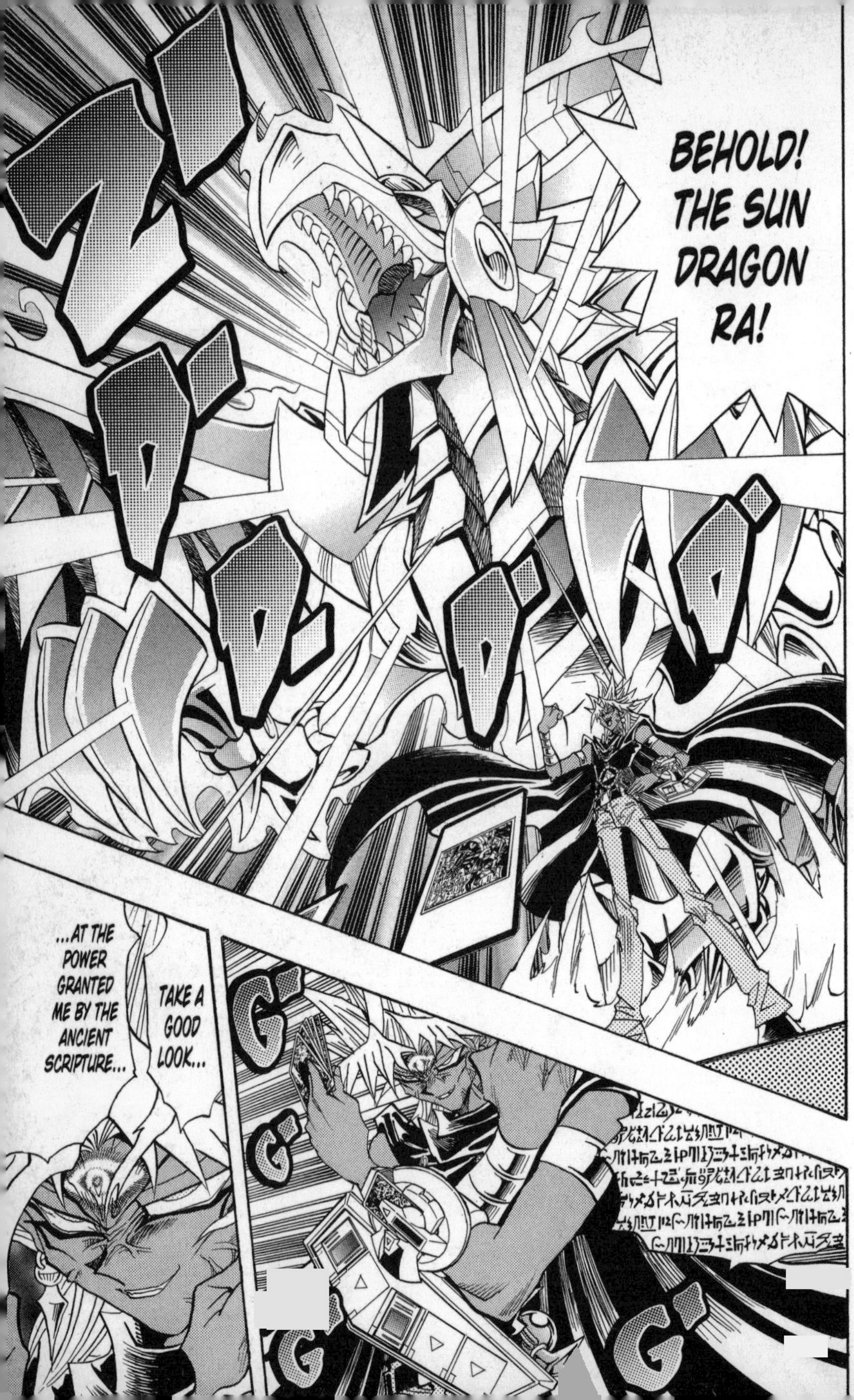
BEHOLD! THE SUN DRAGON RA!
G
G
G
G
TAKE A GOOD LOOK...
...AT THE POWER GRANTED ME BY THE ANCIENT SCRIPTURE...

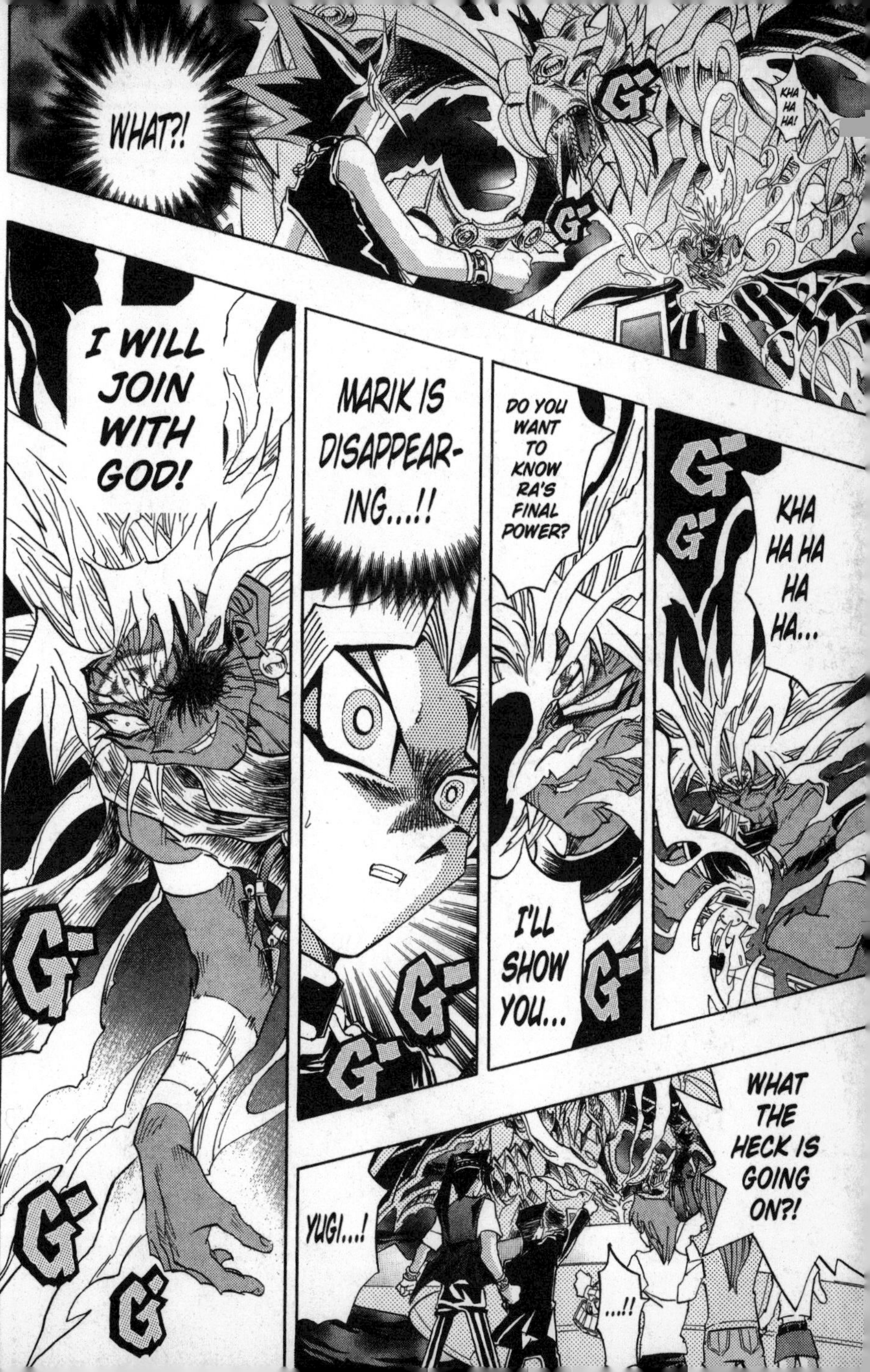
KHA HA HA!
G
G
WHAT?!
KHA HA HA HA HA...
G
G
DO YOU WANT TO KNOW RA'S FINAL POWER?
I'LL SHOW YOU...
G
MARIK IS DISAPPEAR-ING...!!
G
G
WHAT THE HECK IS GOING ON?!
...!!
YUGI...!
I WILL JOIN WITH GOD!
G
G
G

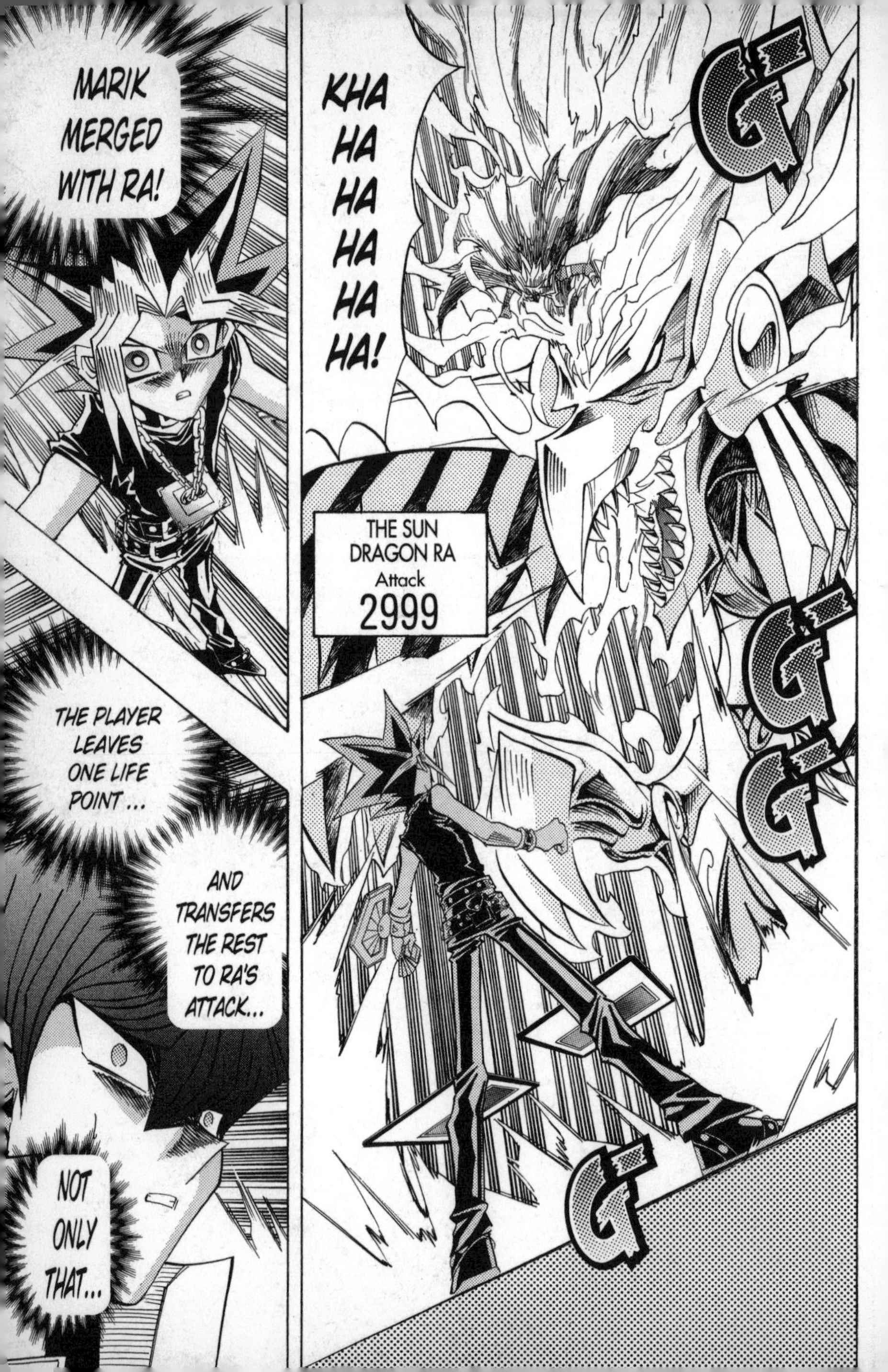
G
KHA HA HA HA HA HA!
THE SUN DRAGON RA Attack 2999
G
G
G
MARIK MERGED WITH RA!
THE PLAYER LEAVES ONE LIFE POINT ...
AND TRANSFERS THE REST TO RA'S ATTACK...
NOT ONLY THAT...

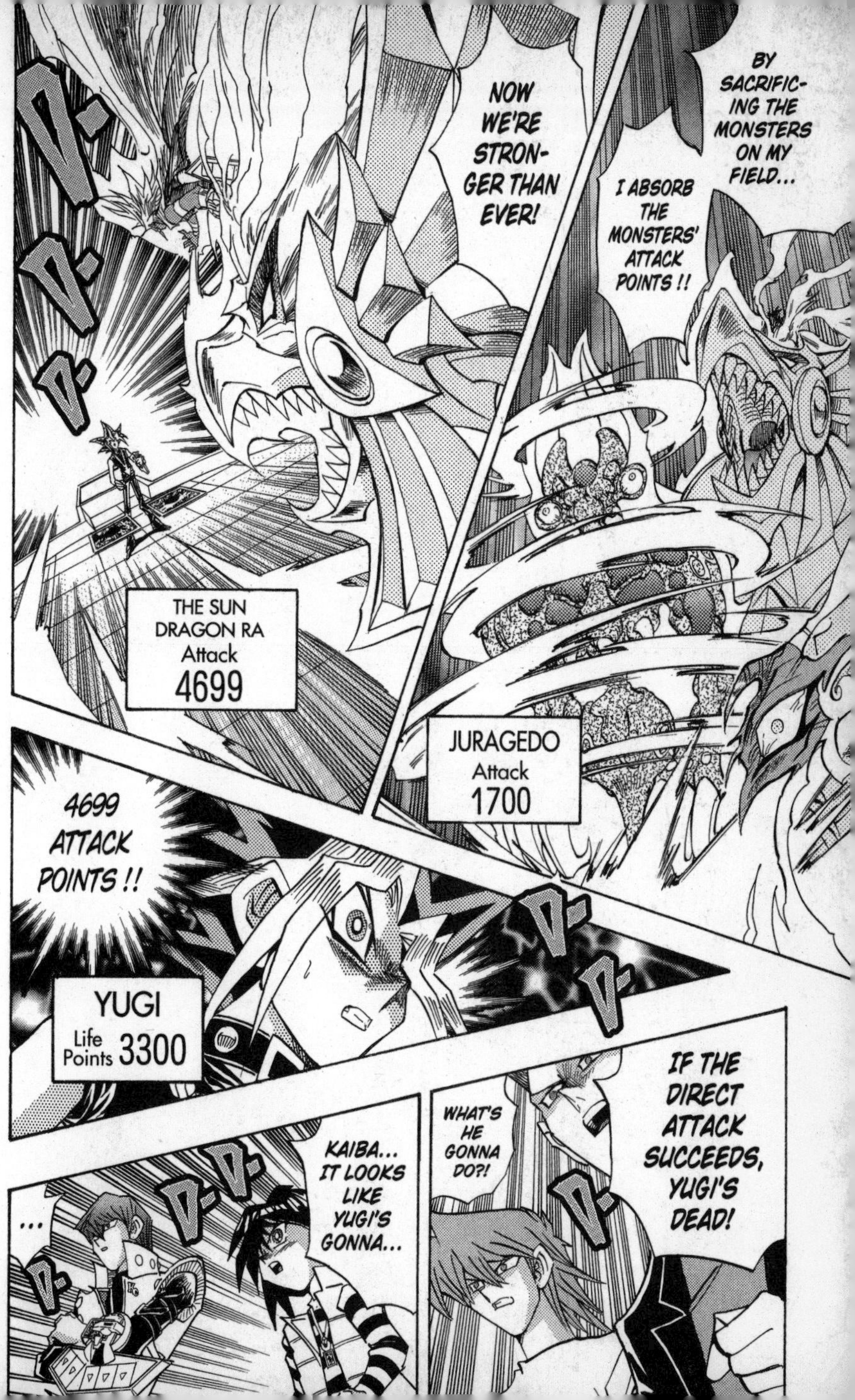
BY SACRIFICING THE MONSTERS ON MY FIELD...
I ABSORB THE MONSTERS' ATTACK POINTS !!
JURAGEDO Attack 1700
NOW WE'RE STRONGER THAN EVER!
THE SUN DRAGON RA Attack 4699
4699 ATTACK POINTS !!
YUGI Life Points 3300
IF THE DIRECT ATTACK SUCCEEDS, YUGI'S DEAD!
WHAT'S HE GONNA DO?!
KAIBA... IT LOOKS LIKE YUGI'S GONNA...
...

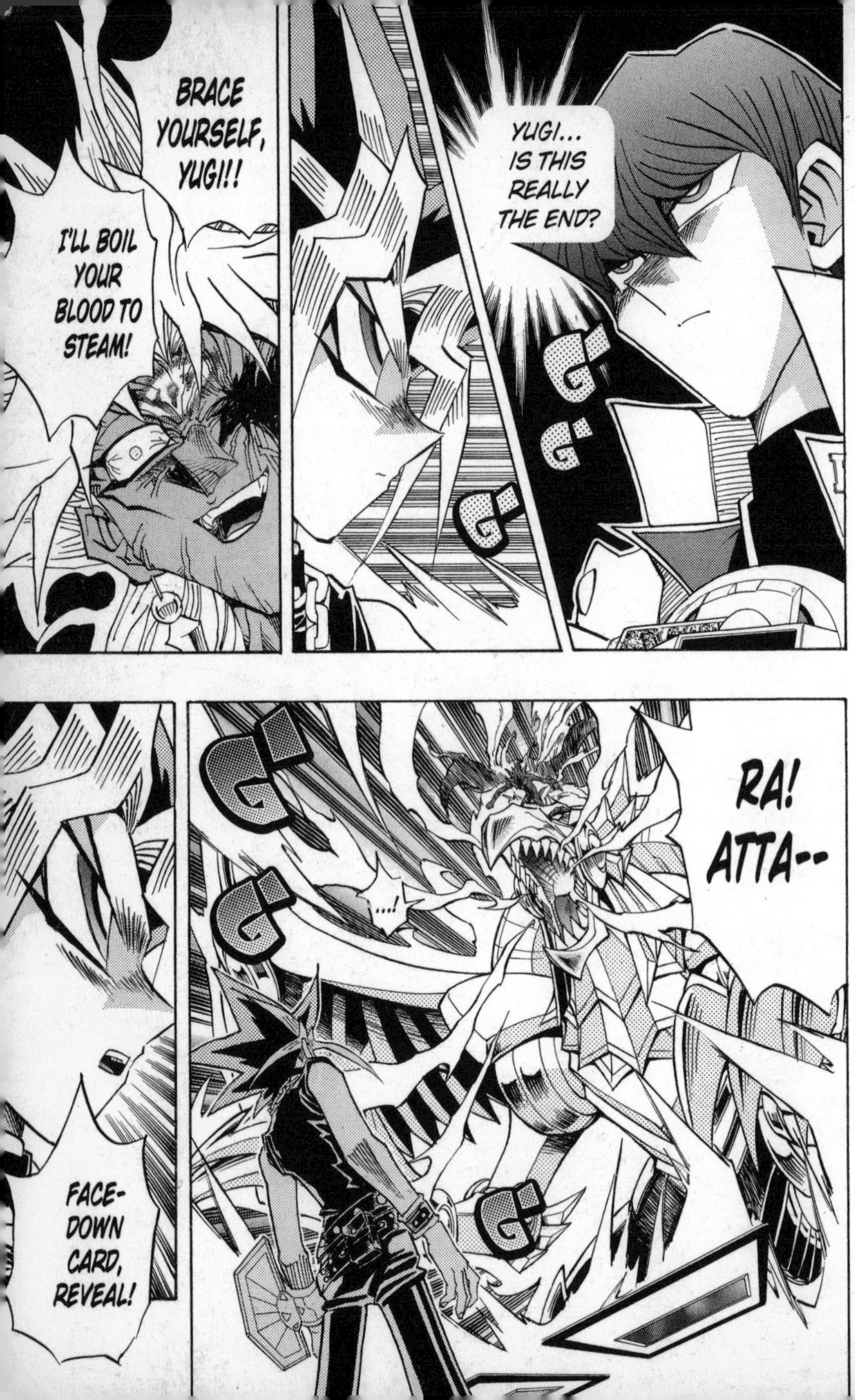
YUGI... IS THIS REALLY THE END?
G
G
G
BRACE YOURSELF, YUGI!!
I'LL BOIL YOUR BLOOD TO STEAM!
RA! ATTA--
G
G
...!
G
FACE-DOWN CARD, REVEAL!

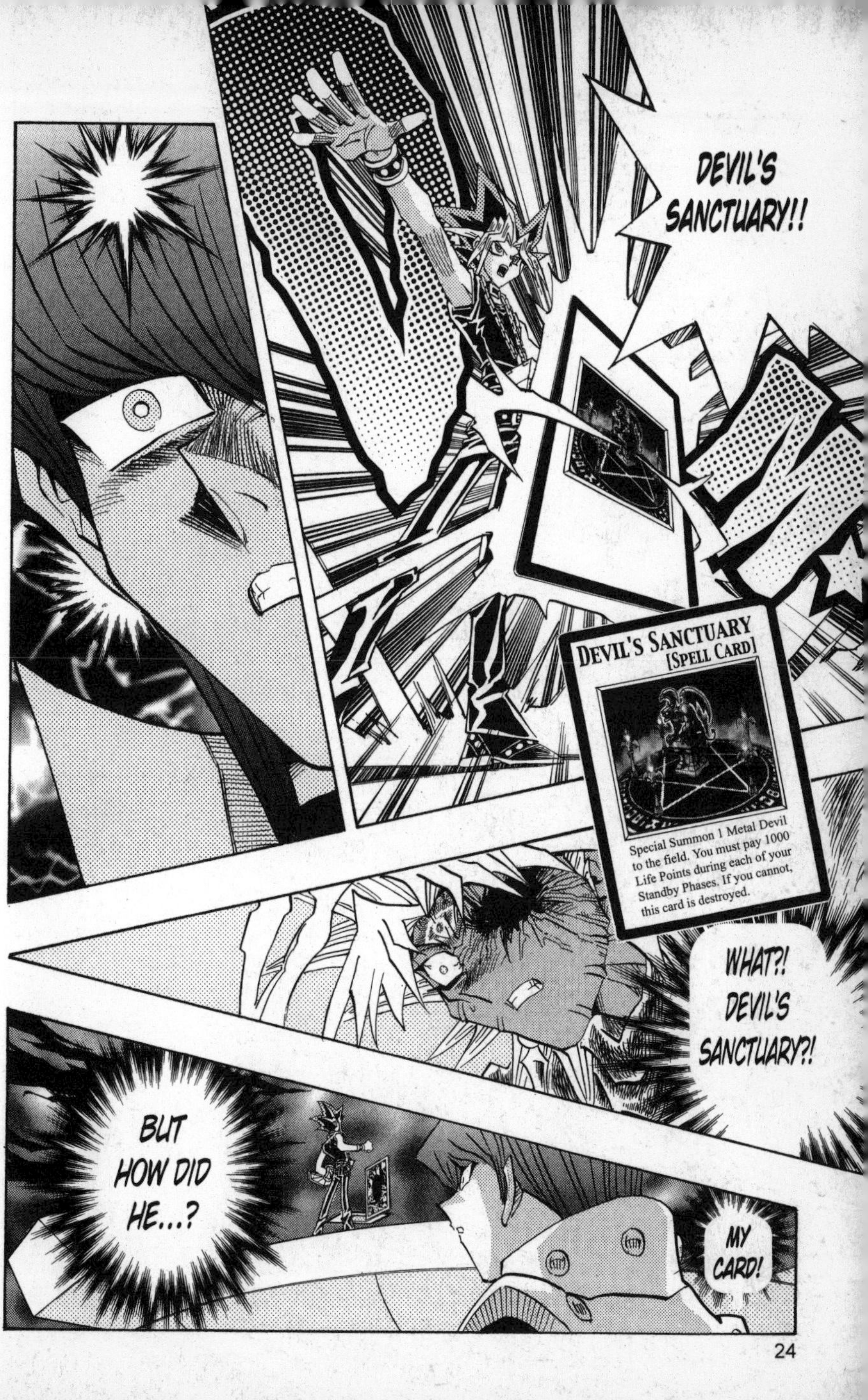
DEVIL'S SANCTUARY!!
DEVIL'S SANCTUARY
[SPELL CARD]
Special Summon 1 Metal Devil to the field. You must pay 1000 Life Points during each of your Standby Phases. If you cannot, this card is destroyed.
WHAT?! DEVIL'S SANCTUARY?!
MY CARD!
BUT HOW DID HE...?

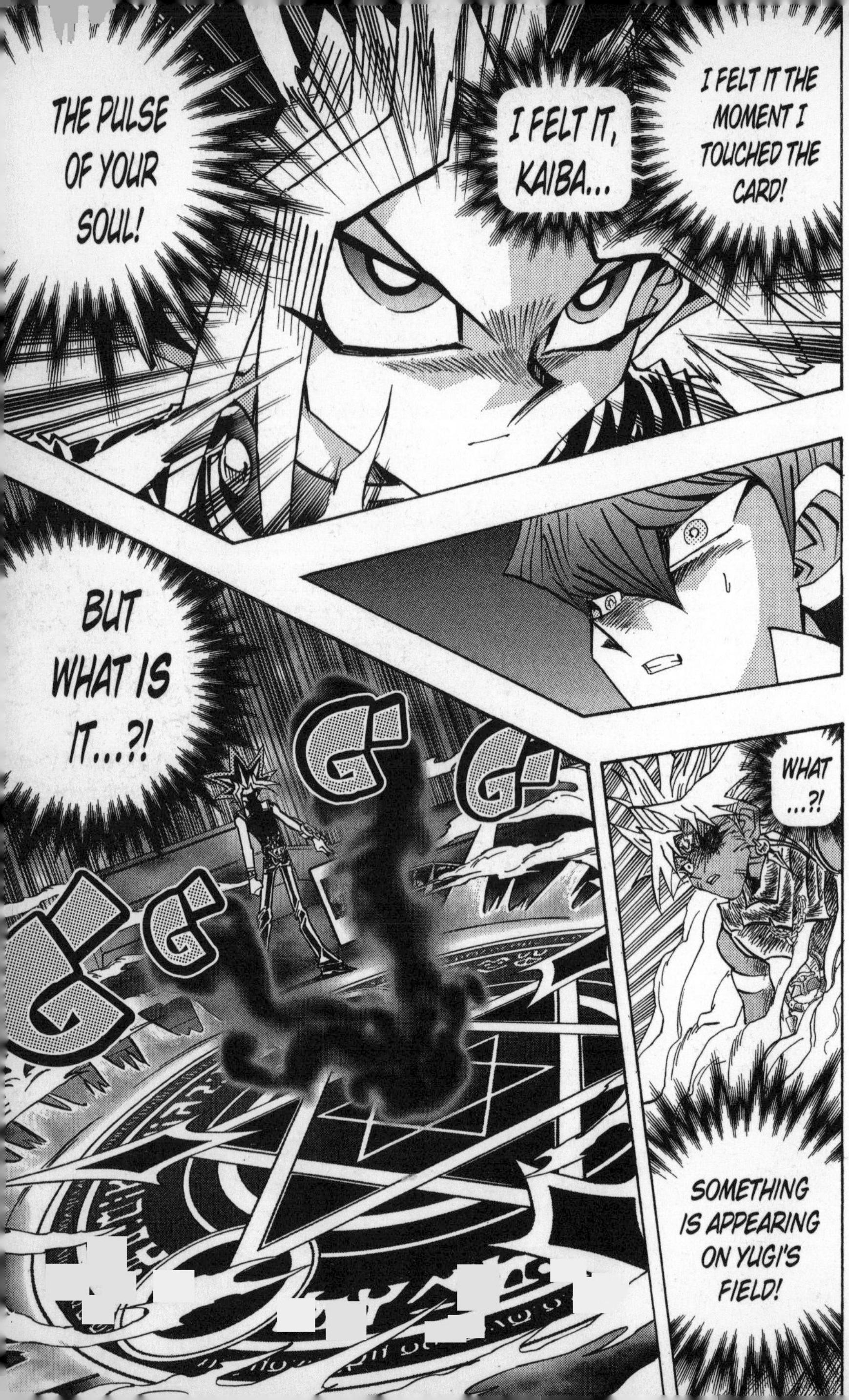
I FELT IT THE MOMENT I TOUCHED THE CARD!
I FELT IT, KAIBA...
THE PULSE OF YOUR SOUL!
WHAT ...?!
SOMETHING IS APPEARING ON YUGI'S FIELD!
BUT WHAT IS IT...?!
G G
G G

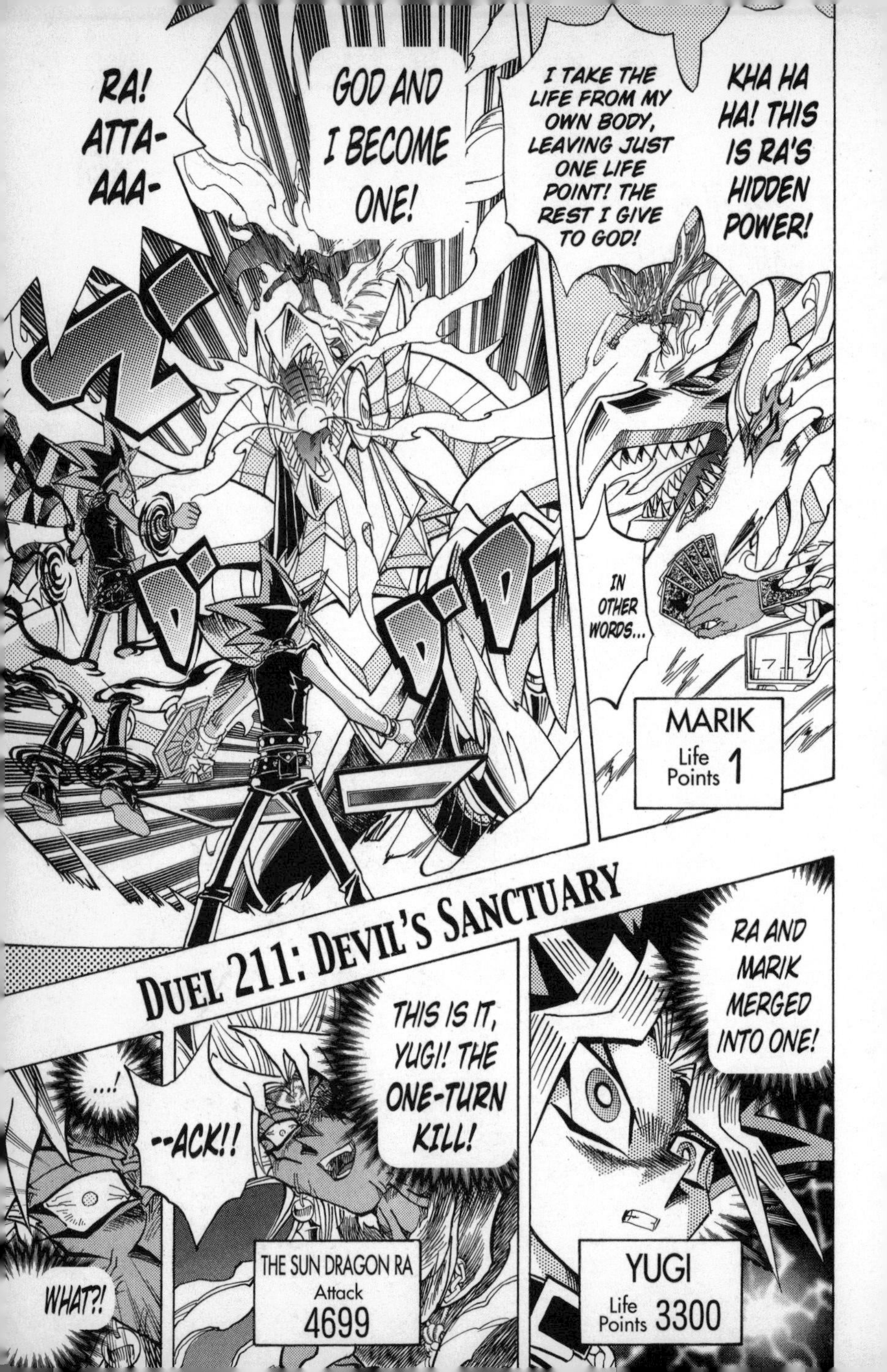
KHA HA HA! THIS IS RA'S HIDDEN POWER!
I TAKE THE LIFE FROM MY OWN BODY, LEAVING JUST ONE LIFE POINT! THE REST I GIVE TO GOD!
IN OTHER WORDS...
MARIK Life Points 1
GOD AND I BECOME ONE!
RA! ATTA-AAA-
DUEL 211: DEVIL'S SANCTUARY
RA AND MARIK MERGED INTO ONE!
YUGI Life Points 3300
THIS IS IT, YUGI! THE ONE-TURN KILL!
THE SUN DRAGON RA Attack 4699
...!
--ACK!!
WHAT?!

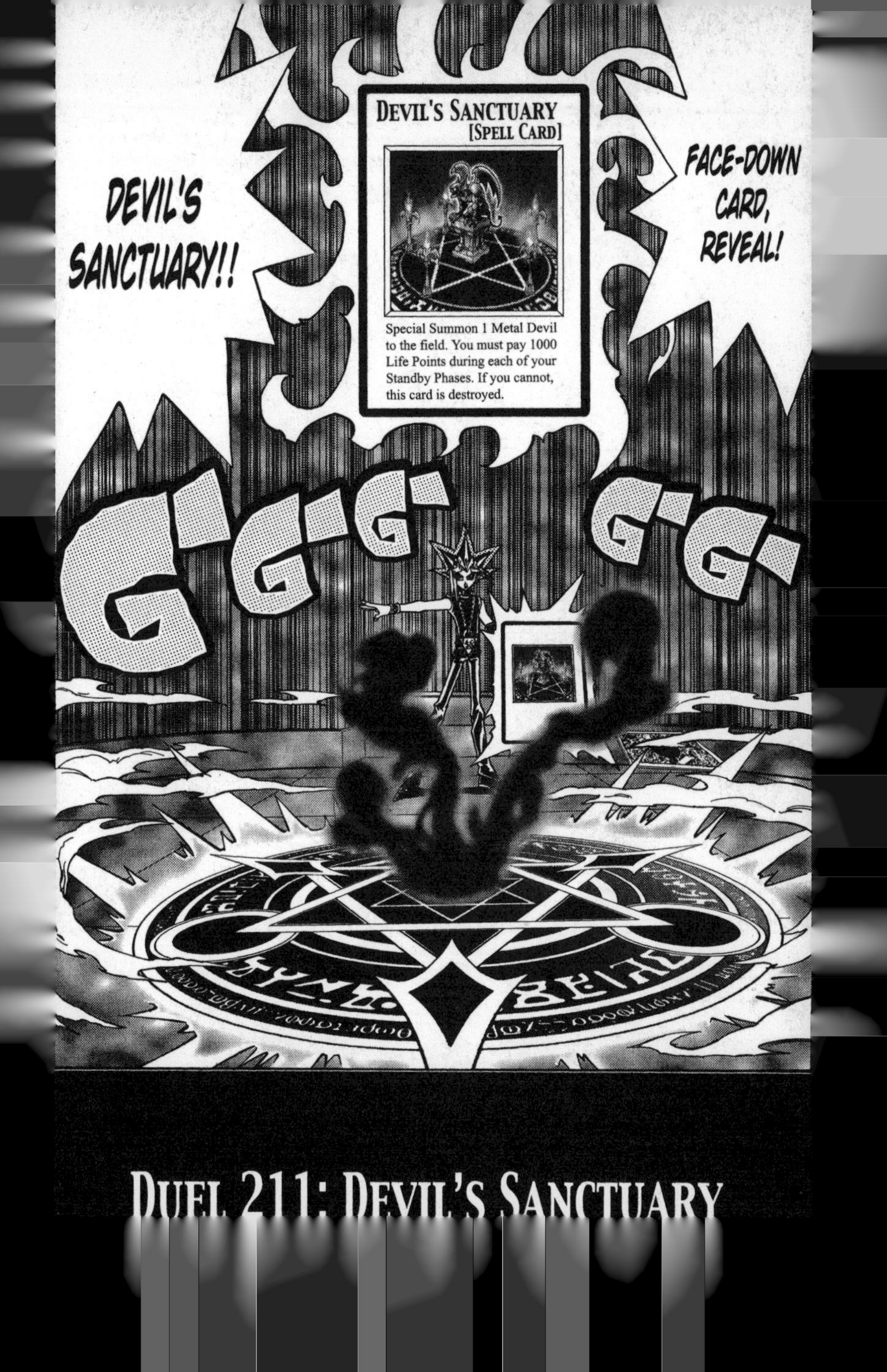
FACE-DOWN CARD, REVEAL!
DEVIL'S SANCTUARY
[SPELL CARD]
Special Summon 1 Metal Devil to the field. You must pay 1000 Life Points during each of your Standby Phases. If you cannot, this card is destroyed.
DEVIL'S SANCTUARY!!
G G G
G G G

# Duel 211: Devil's Sanctuary

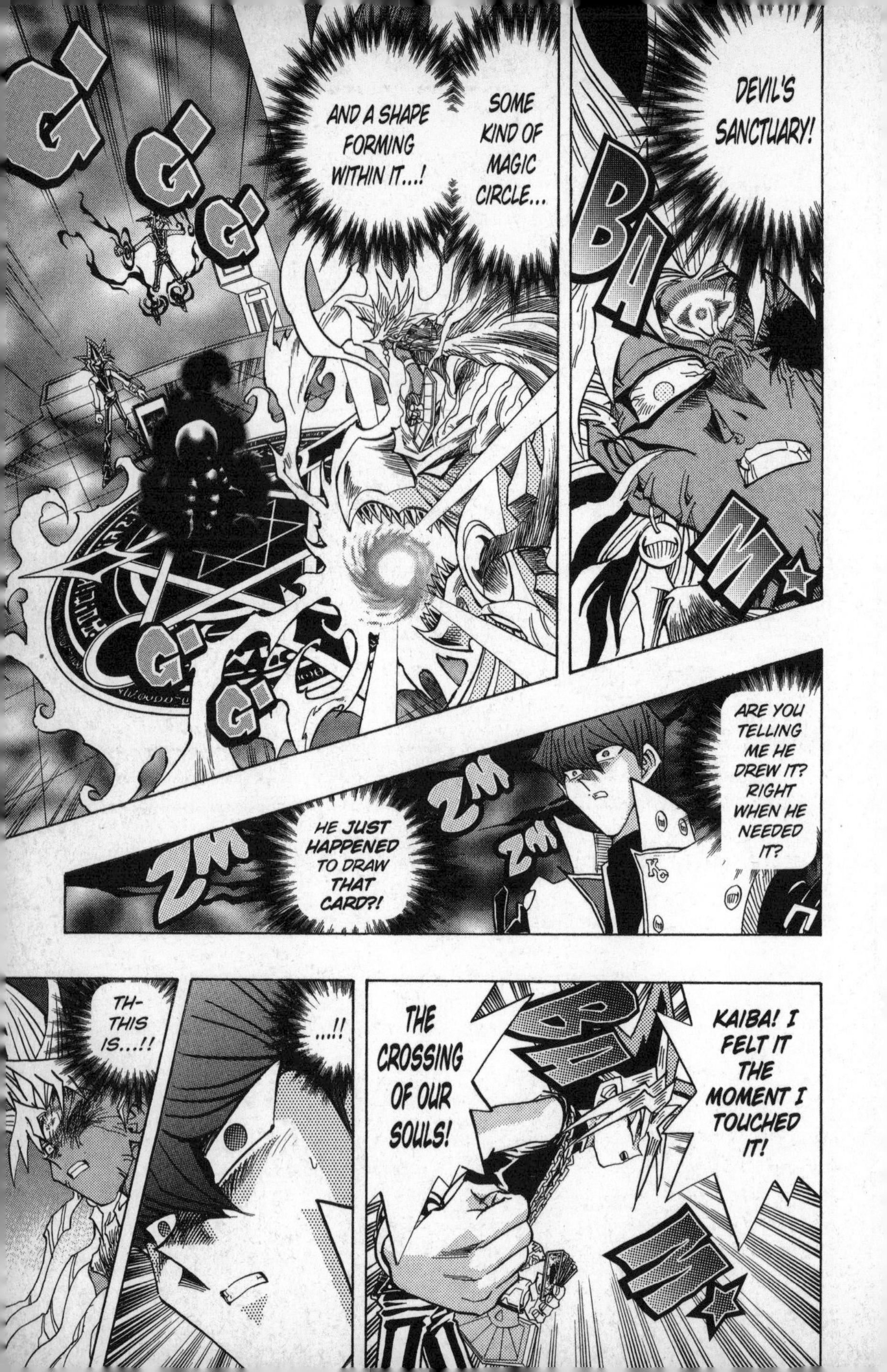
DEVIL'S SANCTUARY!
BA
M☆
SOME KIND OF MAGIC CIRCLE...
AND A SHAPE FORMING WITHIN IT...!
G' G' G'
G' G'
ARE YOU TELLING ME HE DREW IT? RIGHT WHEN HE NEEDED IT?
ZM ZM
HE JUST HAPPENED TO DRAW THAT CARD?!
ZM
KAIBA! I FELT IT THE MOMENT I TOUCHED IT!
BA
M☆
THE CROSSING OF OUR SOULS!
...!!
TH-THIS IS...!!

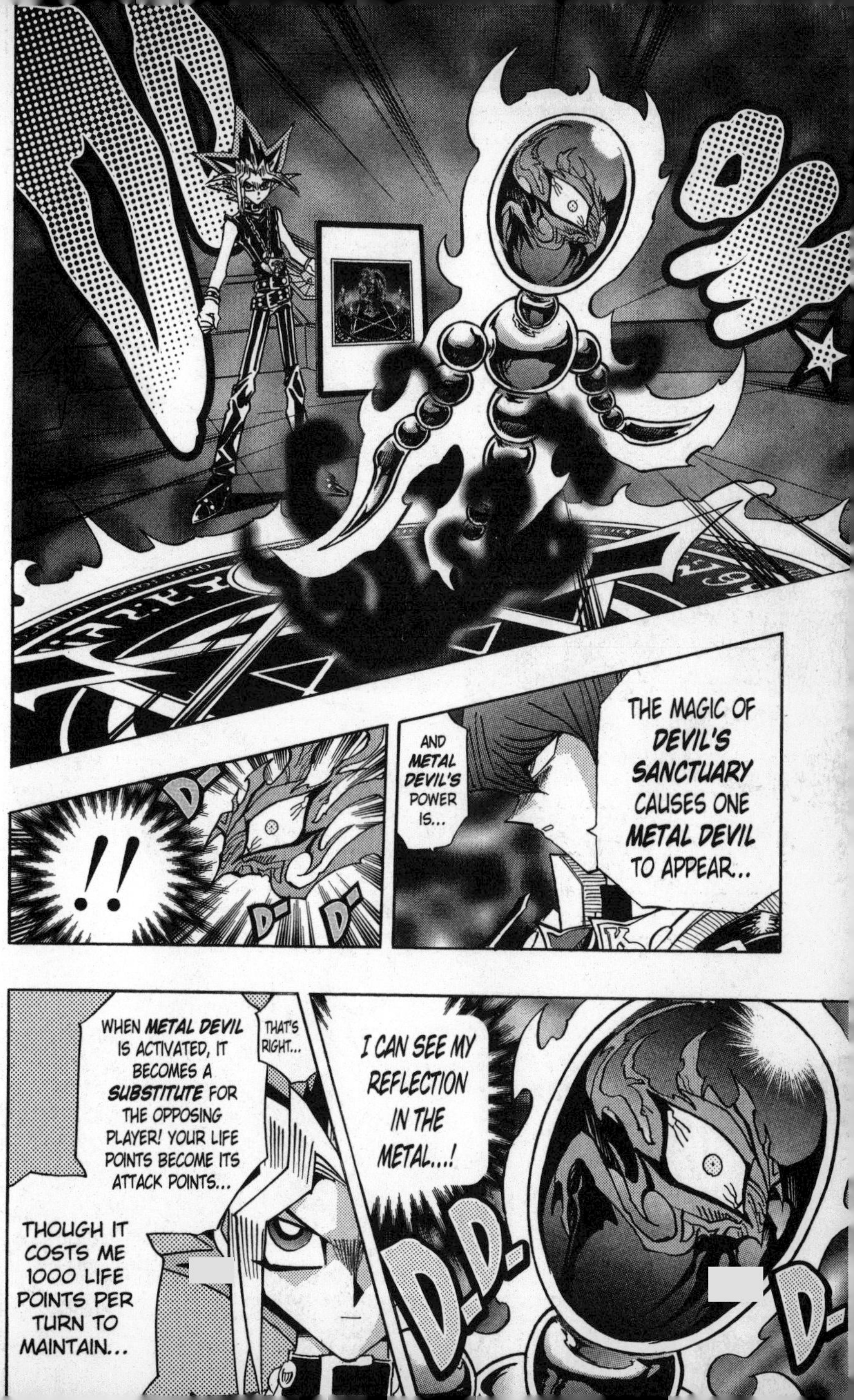
THE MAGIC OF DEVIL'S SANCTUARY CAUSES ONE METAL DEVIL TO APPEAR...
AND METAL DEVIL'S POWER IS...
D-
!!
D-
D-
I CAN SEE MY REFLECTION IN THE METAL...!
D.D.
D-
THAT'S RIGHT...
WHEN METAL DEVIL IS ACTIVATED, IT BECOMES A SUBSTITUTE FOR THE OPPOSING PLAYER! YOUR LIFE POINTS BECOME ITS ATTACK POINTS...
THOUGH IT COSTS ME 1000 LIFE POINTS PER TURN TO MAINTAIN...

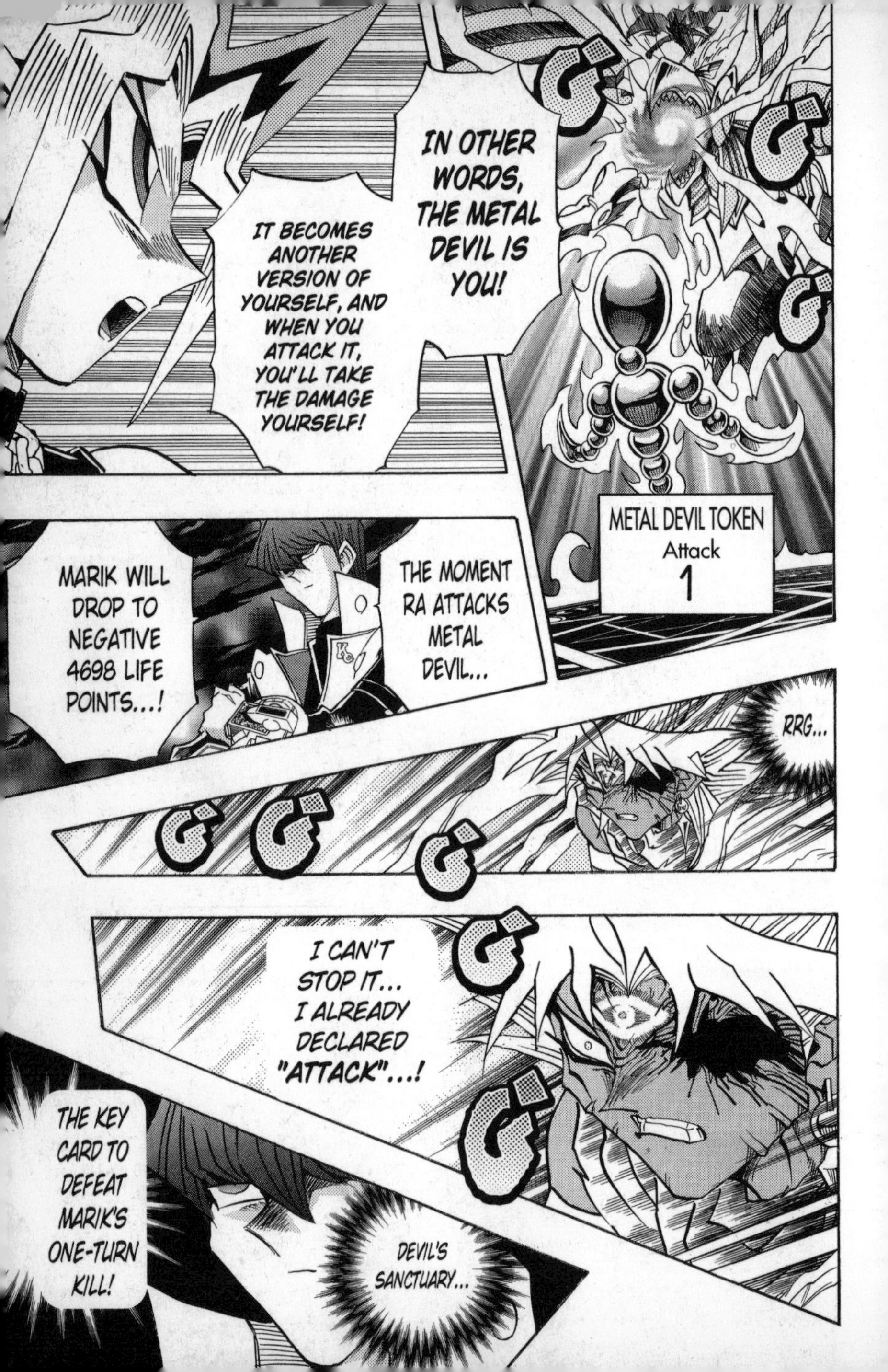

G G G
IN OTHER WORDS, THE METAL DEVIL IS YOU!
METAL DEVIL TOKEN
Attack
1
IT BECOMES ANOTHER VERSION OF YOURSELF, AND WHEN YOU ATTACK IT, YOU'LL TAKE THE DAMAGE YOURSELF!
THE MOMENT RA ATTACKS METAL DEVIL...
MARIK WILL DROP TO NEGATIVE 4698 LIFE POINTS...!
RRG...
G G G
G G
I CAN'T STOP IT... I ALREADY DECLARED "ATTACK"...!
DEVIL'S SANCTUARY...
THE KEY CARD TO DEFEAT MARIK'S ONE-TURN KILL!

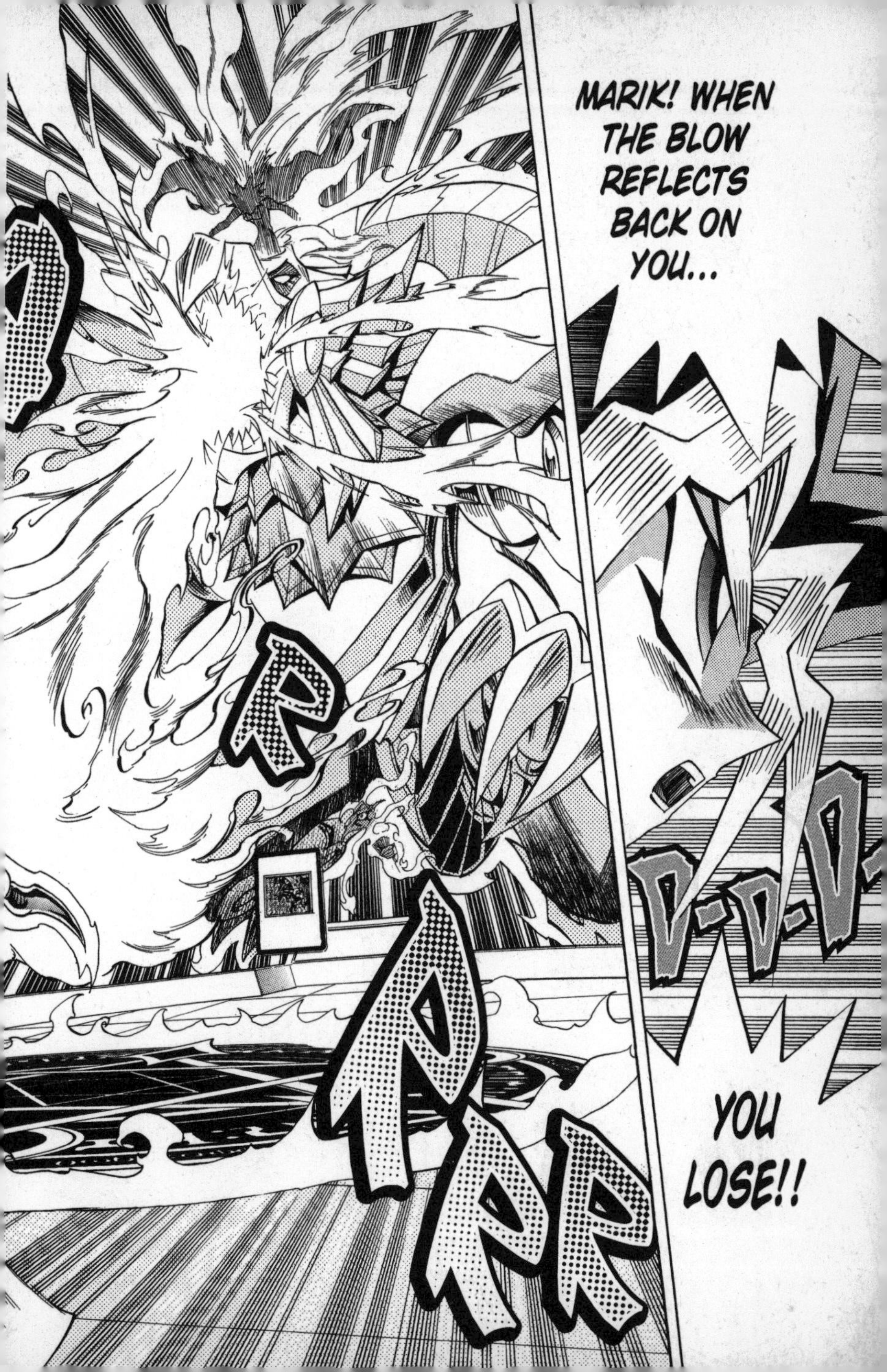
MARIK! WHEN THE BLOW REFLECTS BACK ON YOU...
D-D-D-
YOU LOSE!!
R
RRR

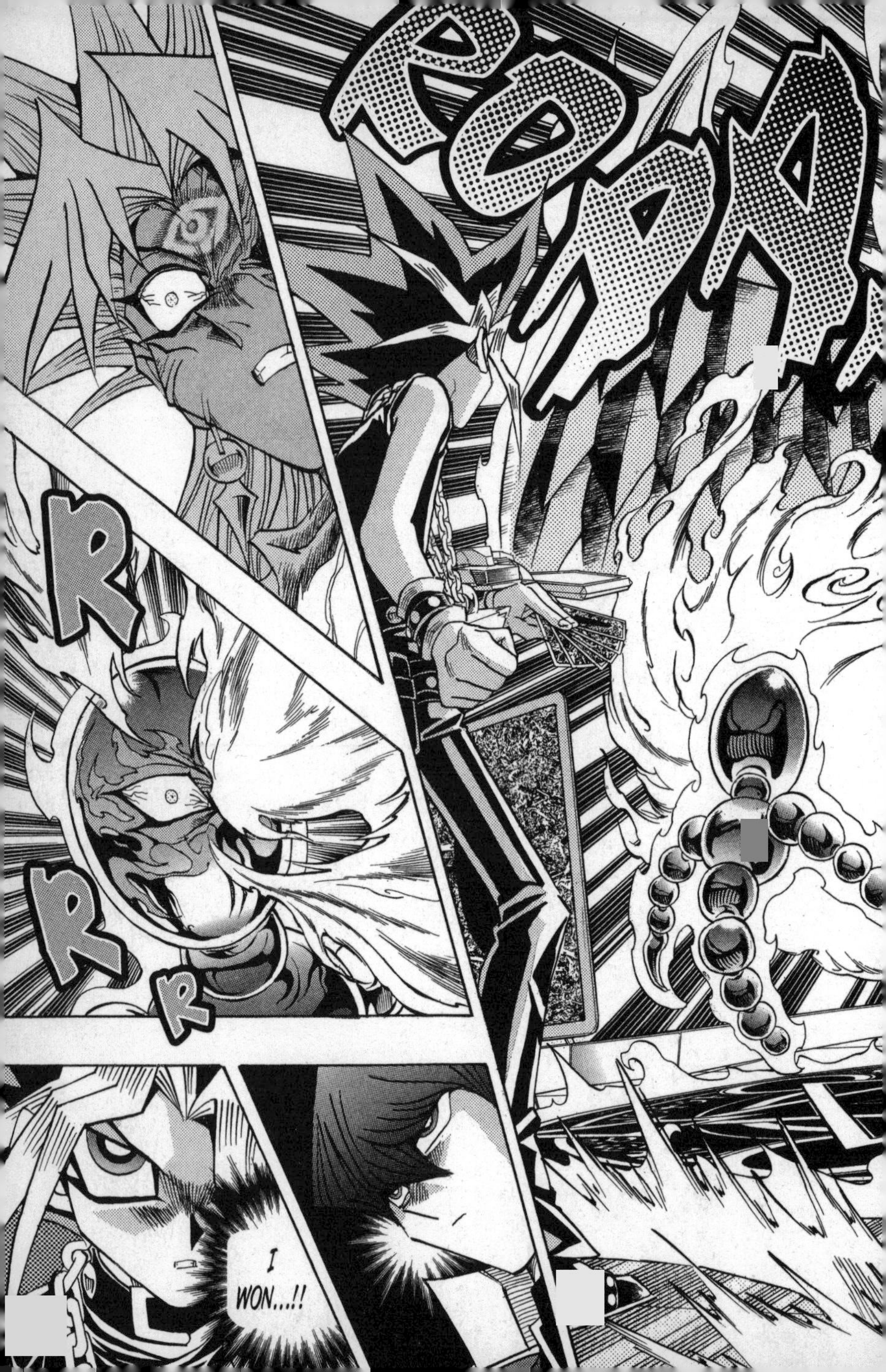
RRR
I WON...!!

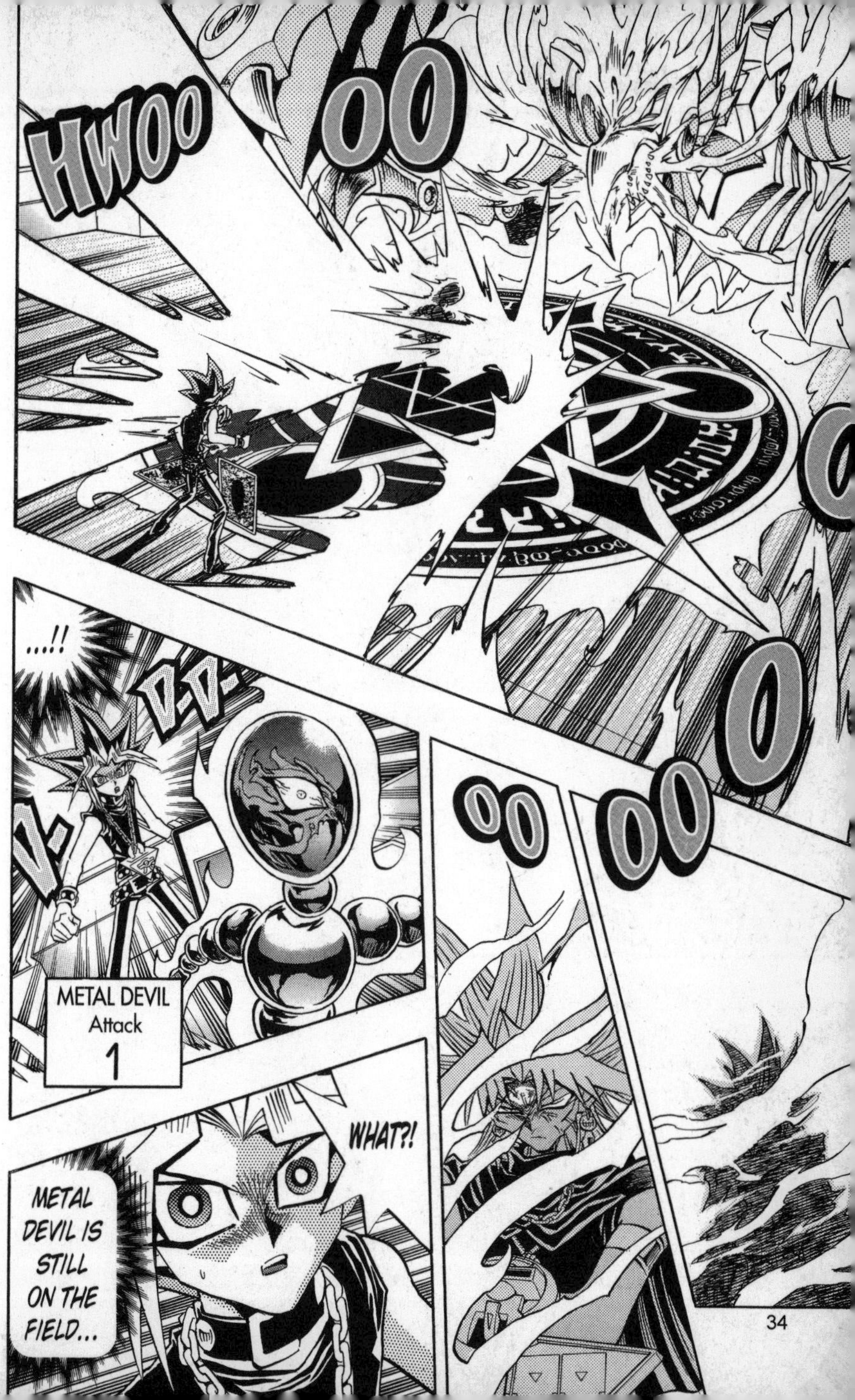
HWOO
OO
O
O
OO
OO
...!!
D.D.
D.
METAL DEVIL
Attack
1
WHAT?!
METAL DEVIL IS STILL ON THE FIELD...

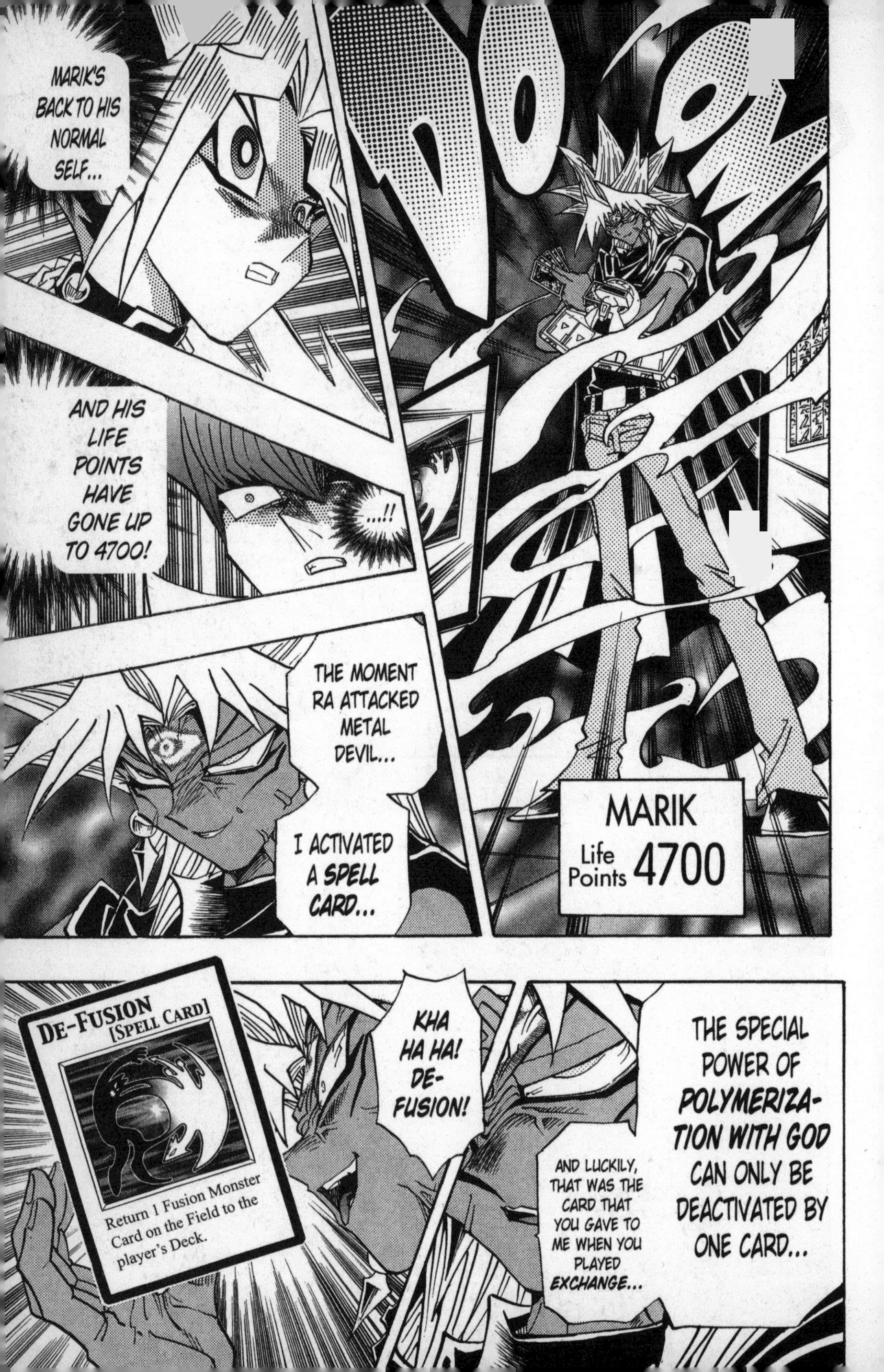
MARIK
Life Points 4700
MARIK'S BACK TO HIS NORMAL SELF...
AND HIS LIFE POINTS HAVE GONE UP TO 4700!
...!!
THE MOMENT RA ATTACKED METAL DEVIL...
I ACTIVATED A SPELL CARD...
THE SPECIAL POWER OF POLYMERIZATION WITH GOD CAN ONLY BE DEACTIVATED BY ONE CARD...
AND LUCKILY, THAT WAS THE CARD THAT YOU GAVE TO ME WHEN YOU PLAYED EXCHANGE...
KHA HA HA! DE-FUSION!
DE-FUSION [SPELL CARD]
Return 1 Fusion Monster Card on the Field to the player's Deck.

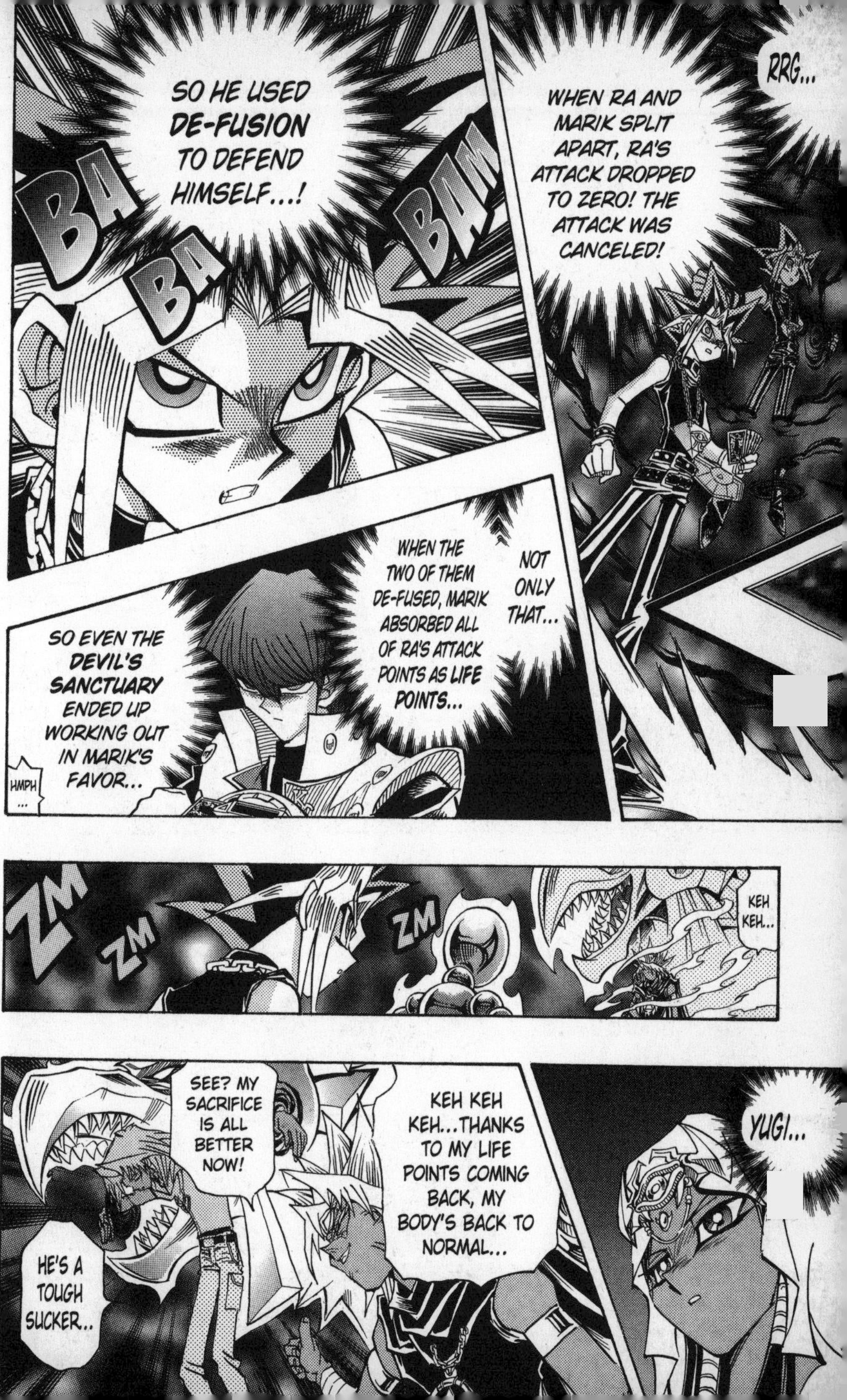
RRG...
WHEN RA AND MARIK SPLIT APART, RA'S ATTACK DROPPED TO ZERO! THE ATTACK WAS CANCELED!
BAM
SO HE USED DE-FUSION TO DEFEND HIMSELF...!
BA
BA
NOT ONLY THAT...
WHEN THE TWO OF THEM DE-FUSED, MARIK ABSORBED ALL OF RA'S ATTACK POINTS AS LIFE POINTS...
SO EVEN THE DEVIL'S SANCTUARY ENDED UP WORKING OUT IN MARIK'S FAVOR...
HMPH...
KEH KEH...
ZM
ZM
ZM
YUGI...
KEH KEH KEH...THANKS TO MY LIFE POINTS COMING BACK, MY BODY'S BACK TO NORMAL...
SEE? MY SACRIFICE IS ALL BETTER NOW!
HE'S A TOUGH SUCKER...

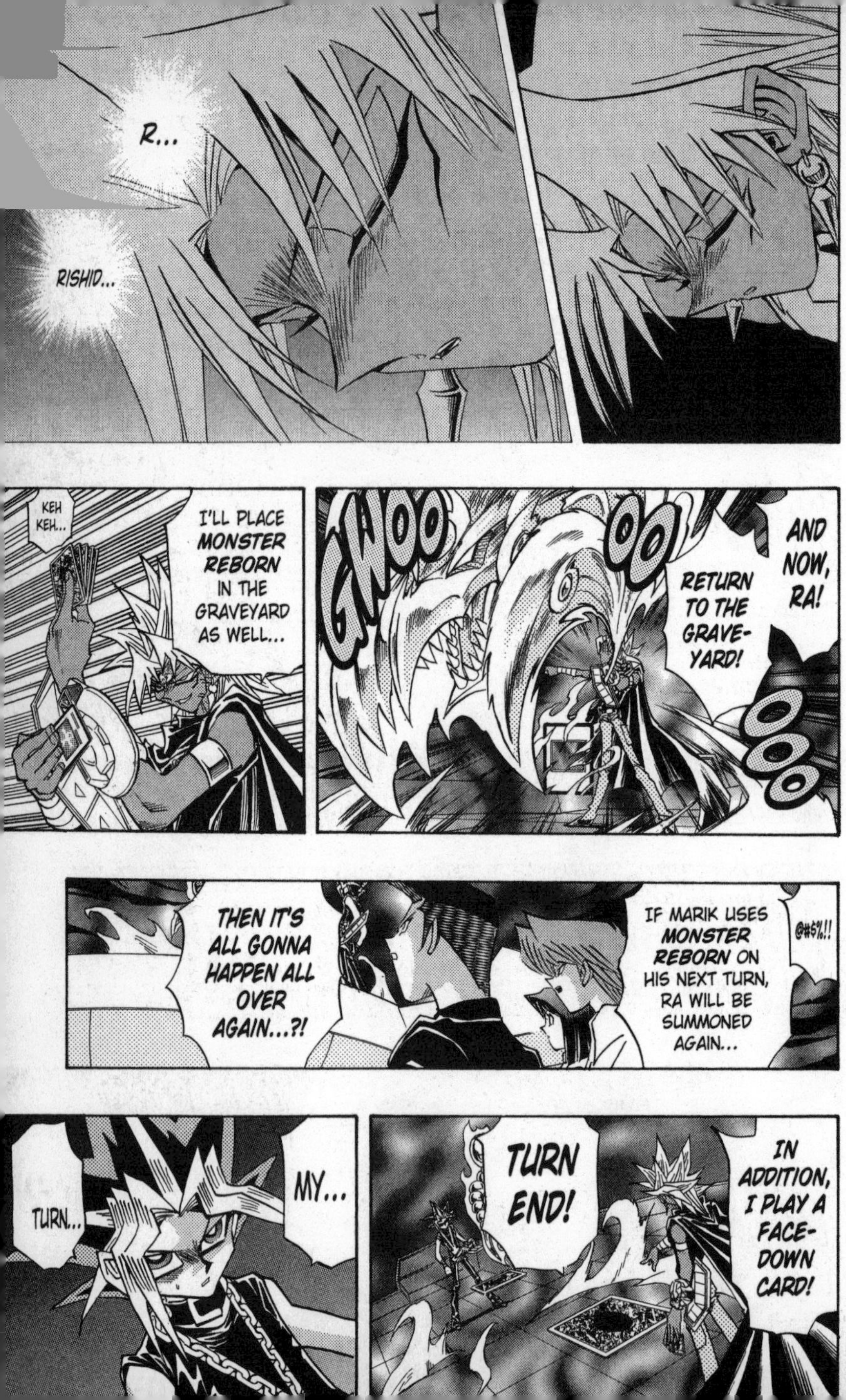
R...
RISHID...
AND NOW, RA!
RETURN TO THE GRAVEYARD!
GWOOOOOOO
KEH KEH...
I'LL PLACE **MONSTER REBORN** IN THE GRAVEYARD AS WELL...
@#$%!!
IF MARIK USES **MONSTER REBORN** ON HIS NEXT TURN, RA WILL BE SUMMONED AGAIN...
THEN IT'S ALL GONNA HAPPEN ALL OVER AGAIN...?!
IN ADDITION, I PLAY A FACE-DOWN CARD!
TURN END!
MY...
TURN...

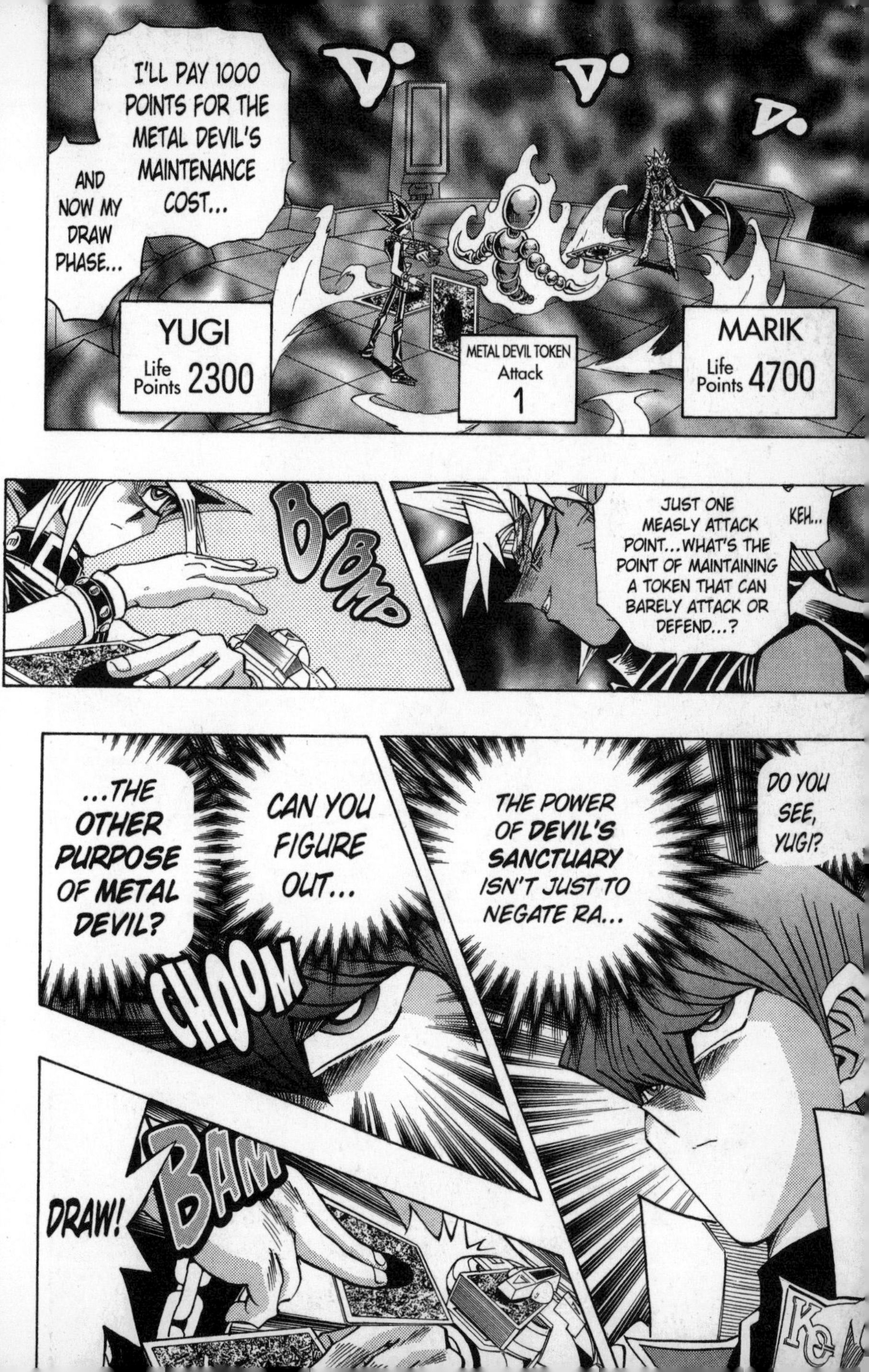
D
D
D
I'LL PAY 1000 POINTS FOR THE METAL DEVIL'S MAINTENANCE COST...
AND NOW MY DRAW PHASE...
MARIK Life Points 4700
METAL DEVIL TOKEN Attack 1
YUGI Life Points 2300
KEH...
JUST ONE MEASLY ATTACK POINT...WHAT'S THE POINT OF MAINTAINING A TOKEN THAT CAN BARELY ATTACK OR DEFEND...?
B'DOMP
DO YOU SEE, YUGI?
THE POWER OF DEVIL'S SANCTUARY ISN'T JUST TO NEGATE RA...
CAN YOU FIGURE OUT...
...THE OTHER PURPOSE OF METAL DEVIL?
CHOOM
BAM
DRAW!

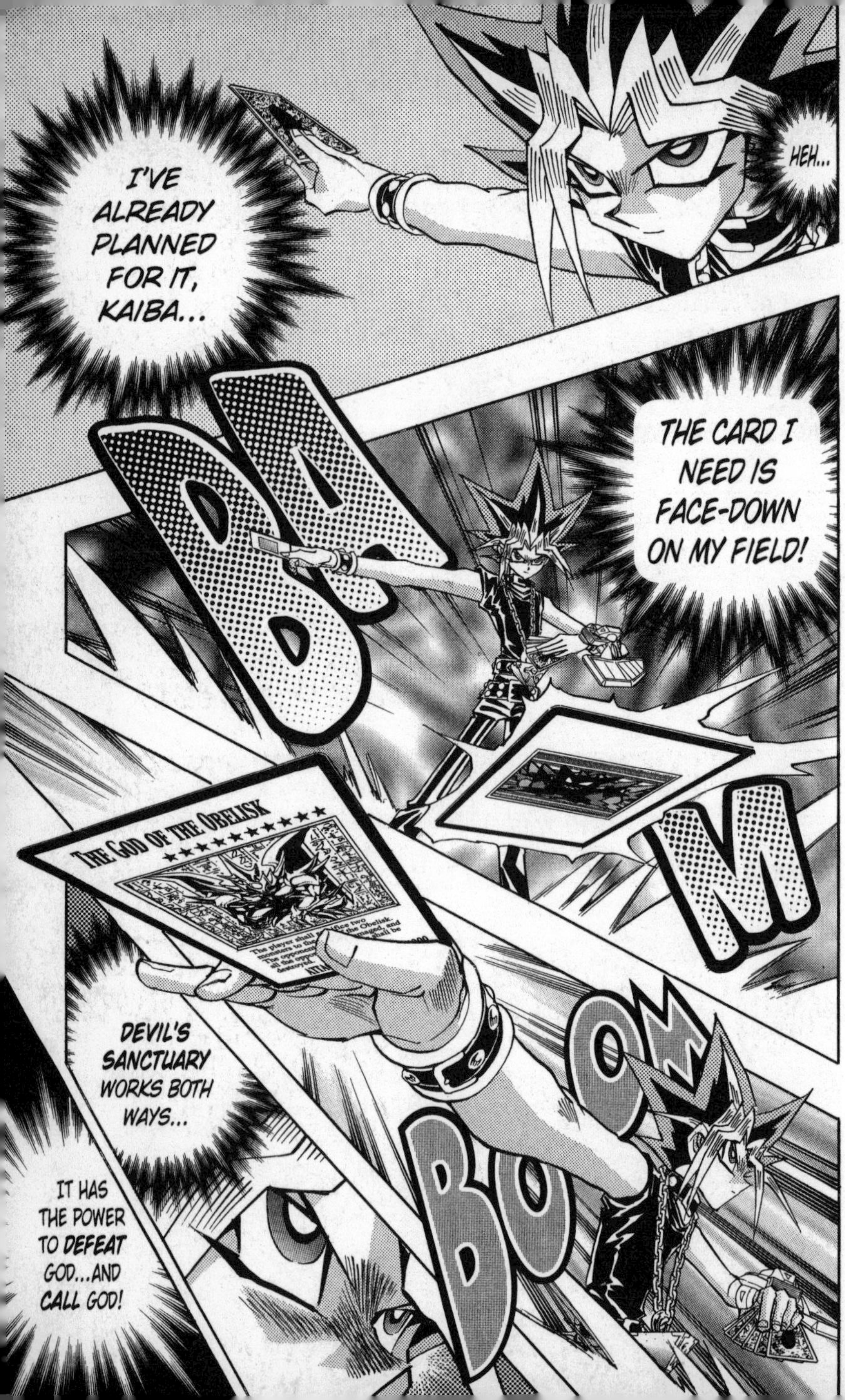
HEH...
I'VE ALREADY PLANNED FOR IT, KAIBA...
THE CARD I NEED IS FACE-DOWN ON MY FIELD!
THE GOD OF THE OBELISK
DEVIL'S SANCTUARY WORKS BOTH WAYS...
IT HAS THE POWER TO DEFEAT GOD...AND CALL GOD!
BOOM

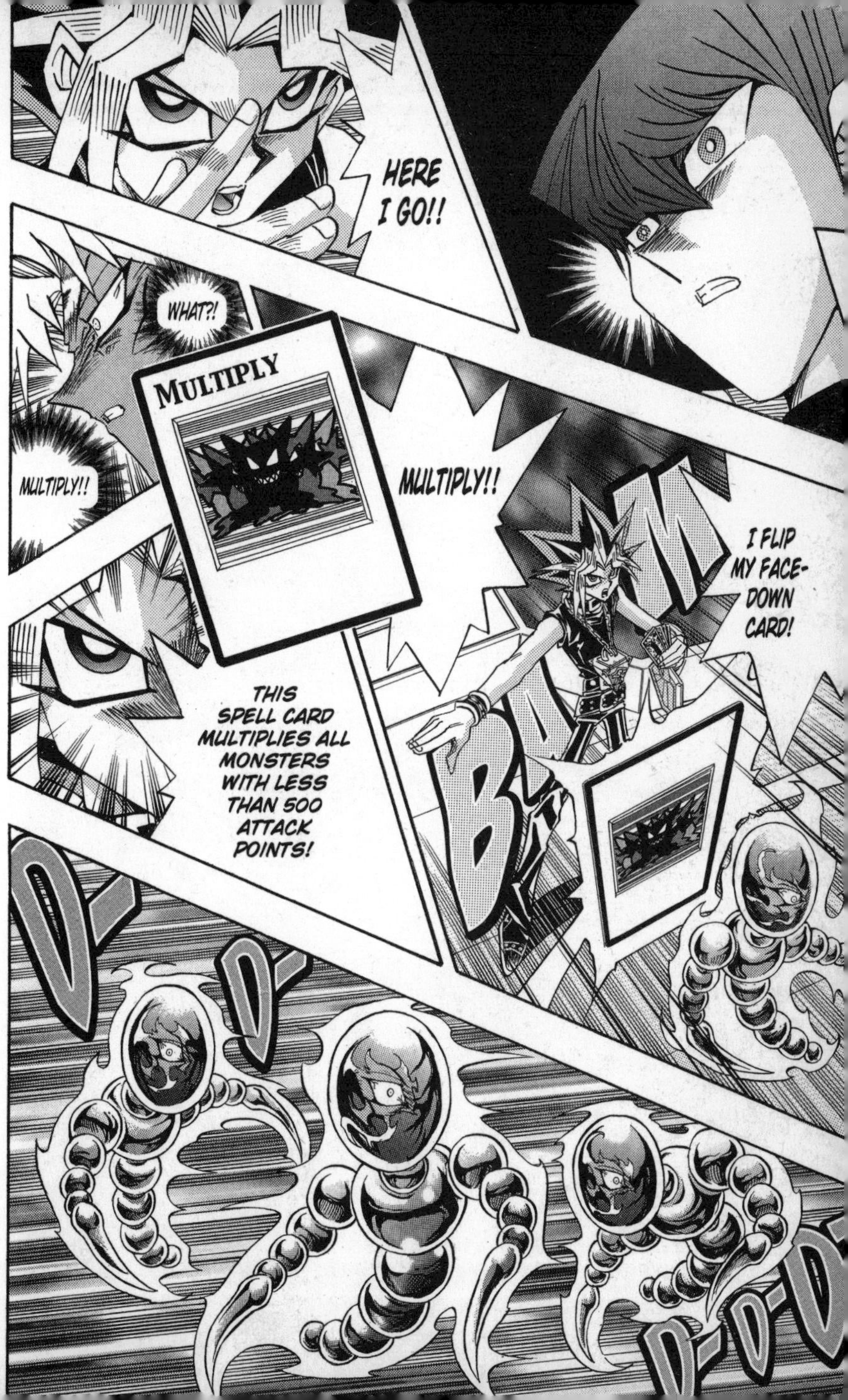
HERE I GO!!
I FLIP MY FACE-DOWN CARD!
BAM
MULTIPLY!!
WHAT?!
MULTIPLY!!
MULTIPLY
THIS SPELL CARD MULTIPLIES ALL MONSTERS WITH LESS THAN 500 ATTACK POINTS!

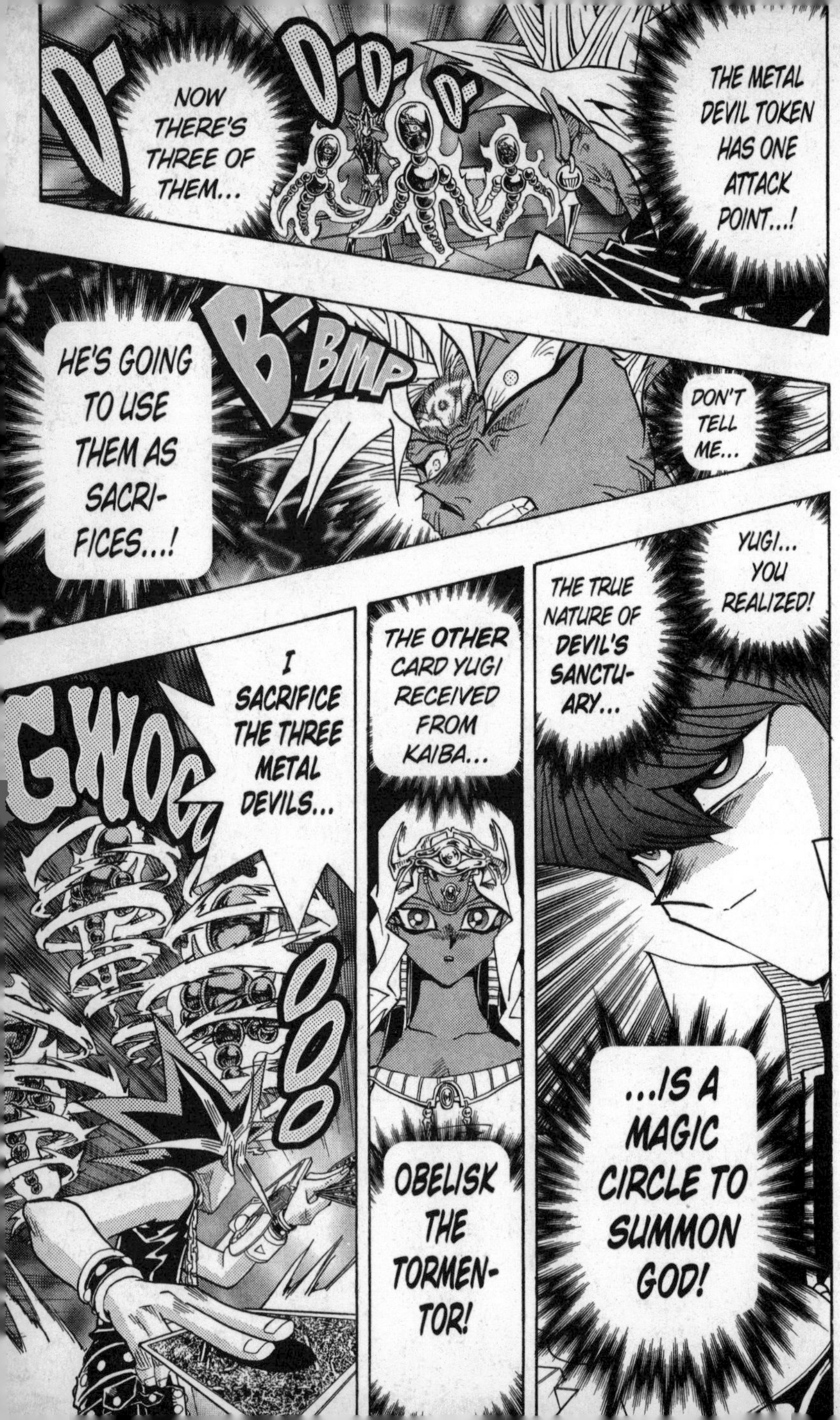
THE METAL DEVIL TOKEN HAS ONE ATTACK POINT...!
D-D-D-
NOW THERE'S THREE OF THEM...
D-
DON'T TELL ME...
B-BMP
HE'S GOING TO USE THEM AS SACRIFICES...!
YUGI... YOU REALIZED!
THE TRUE NATURE OF DEVIL'S SANCTUARY...
...IS A MAGIC CIRCLE TO SUMMON GOD!
THE OTHER CARD YUGI RECEIVED FROM KAIBA...
OBELISK THE TORMENTOR!
I SACRIFICE THE THREE METAL DEVILS...
GHOO
OOOO

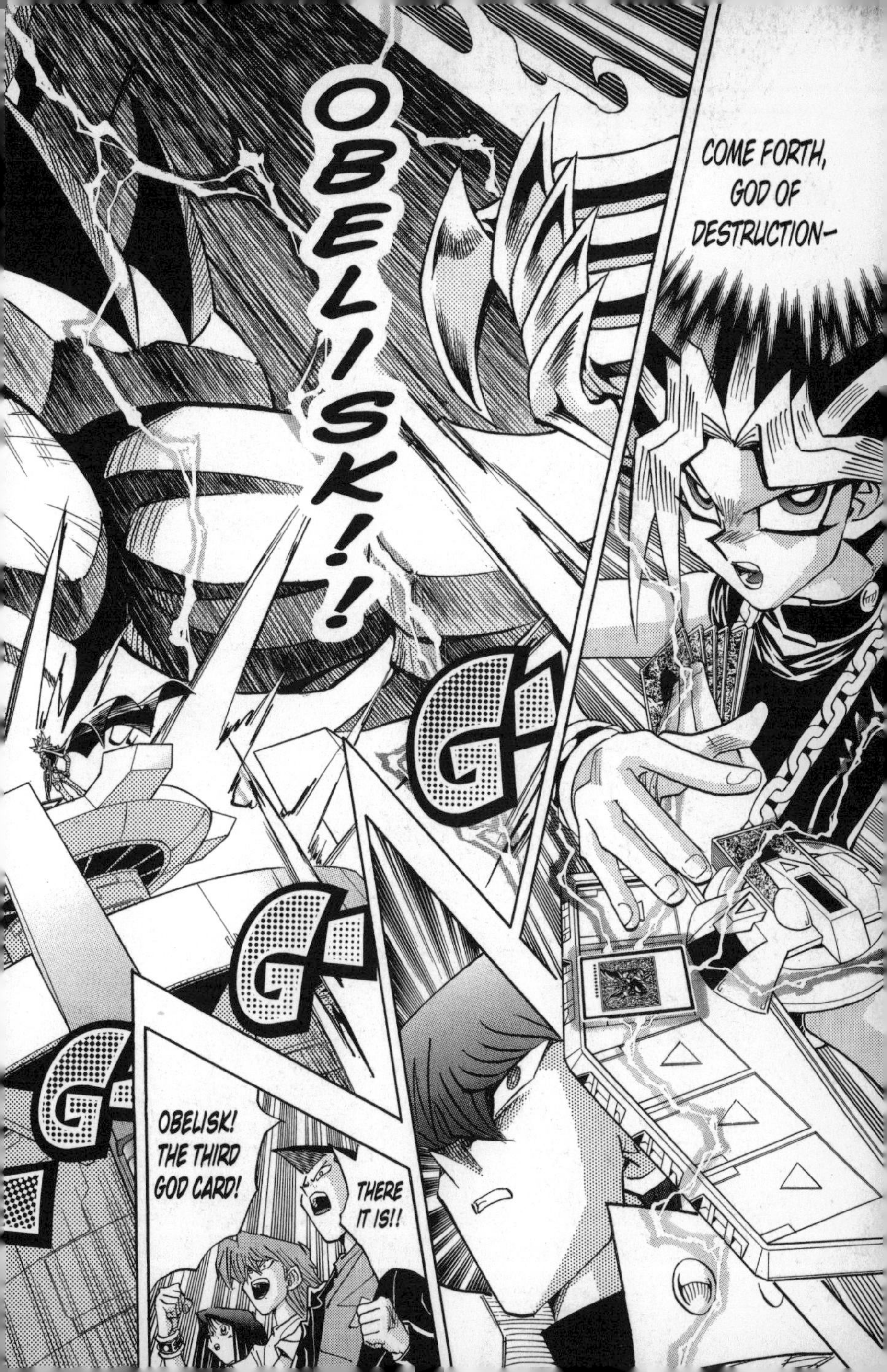
COME FORTH, GOD OF DESTRUCTION—
OBELISK!!
G
G
G
THERE IT IS!!
OBELISK! THE THIRD GOD CARD!

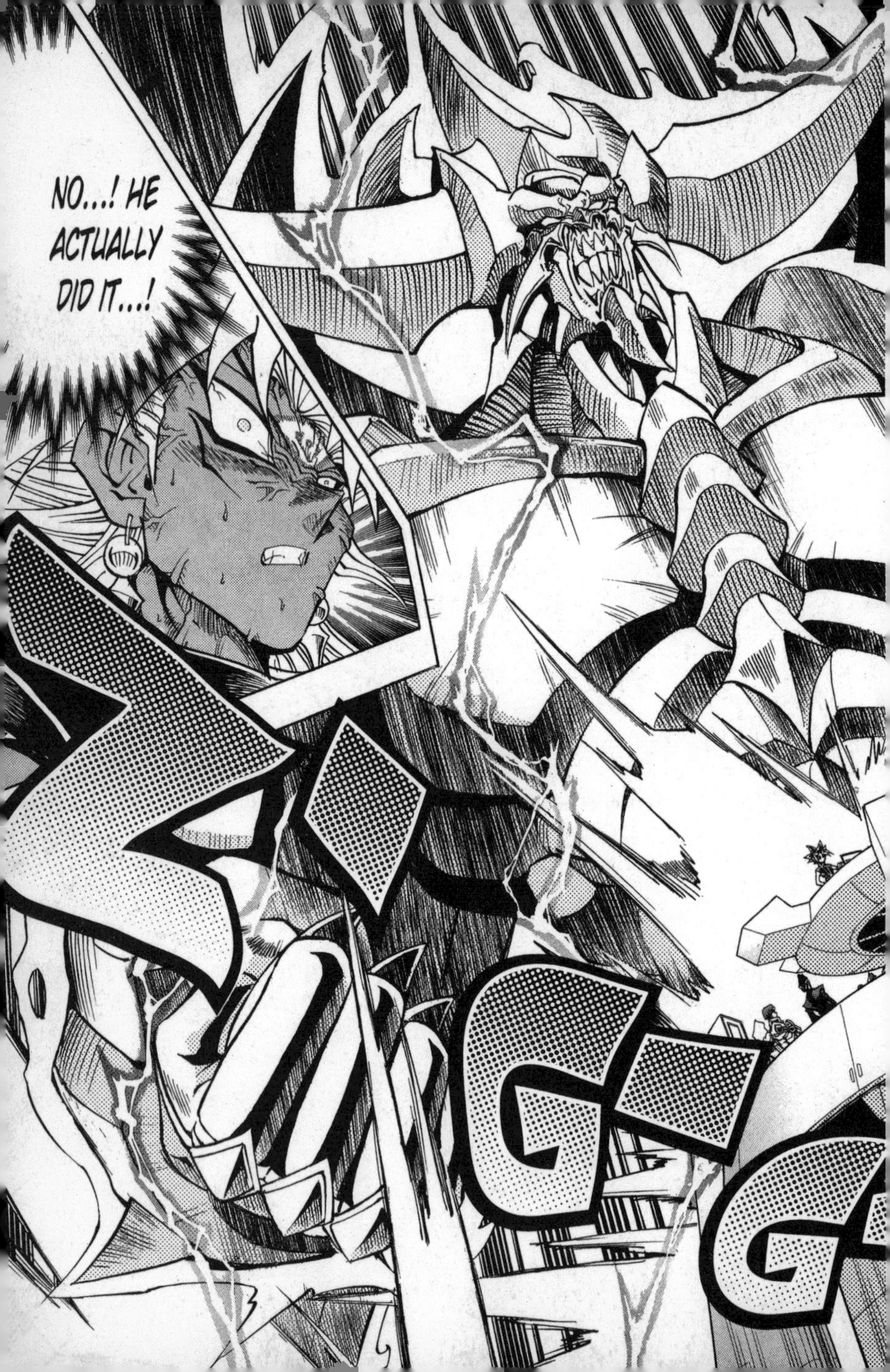
NO...! HE ACTUALLY DID IT...!

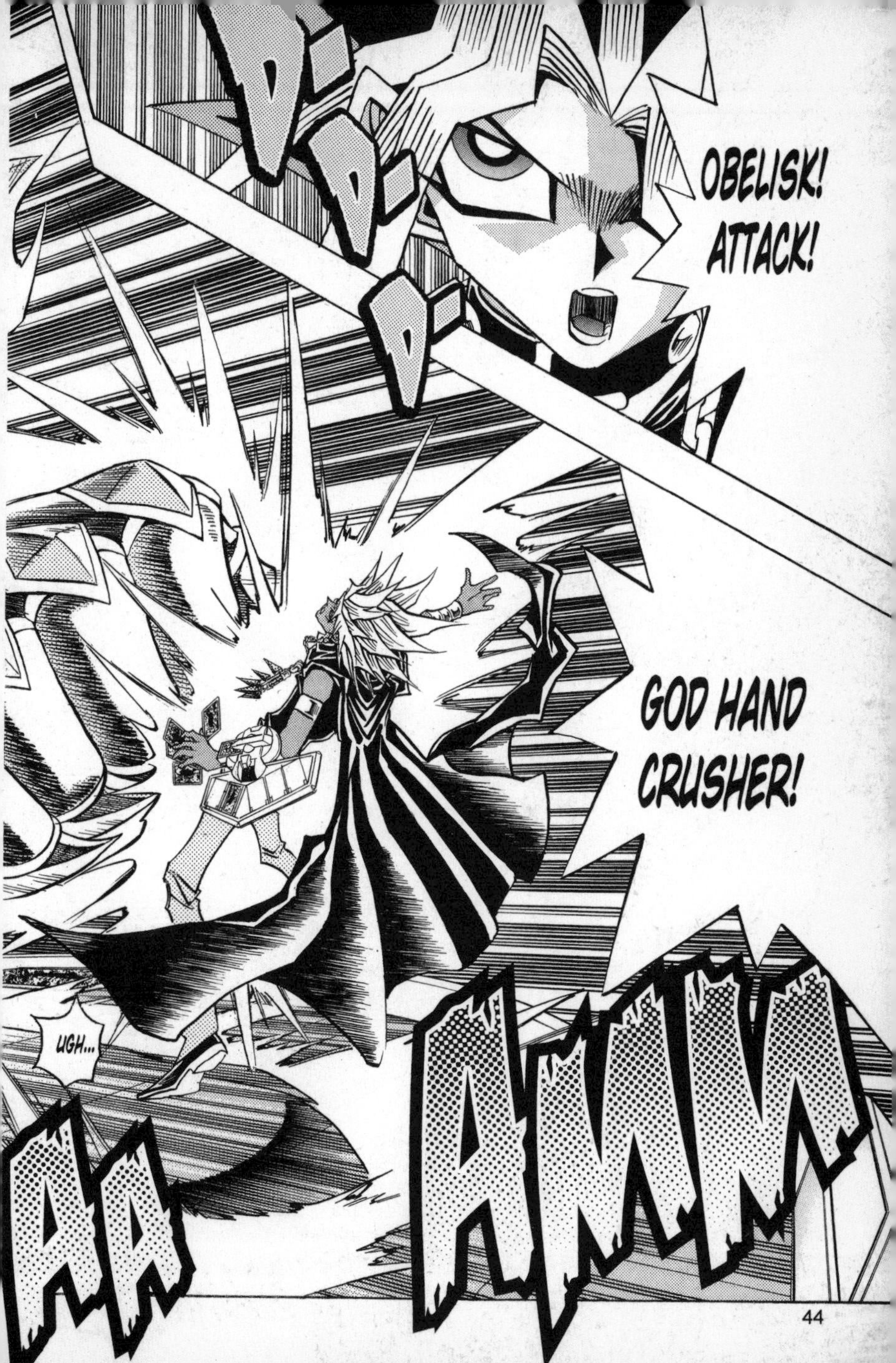
OBELISK! ATTACK!
GOD HAND CRUSHER!
UGH...
AA AMMM

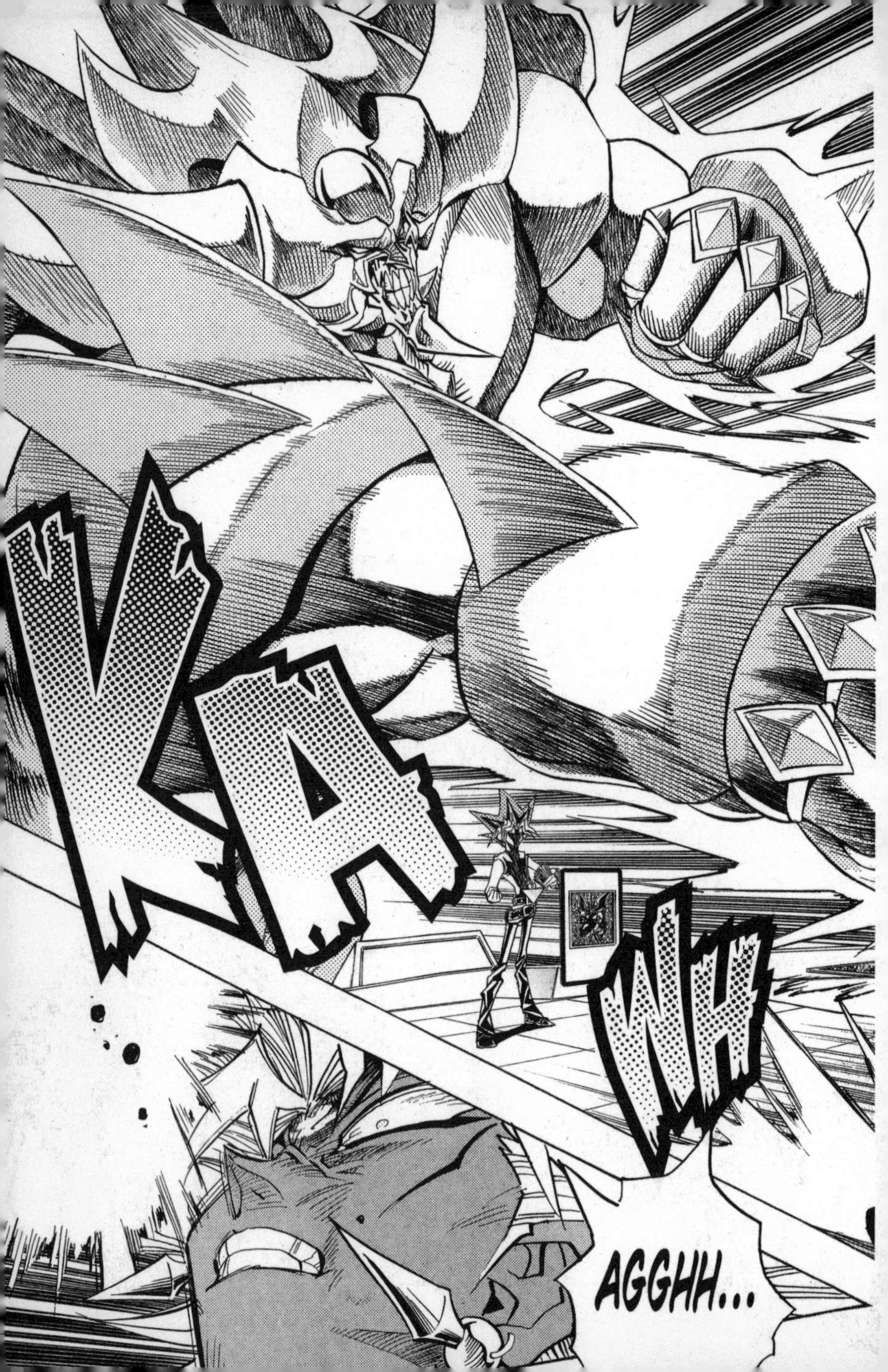
KA
WH
AGGHH...

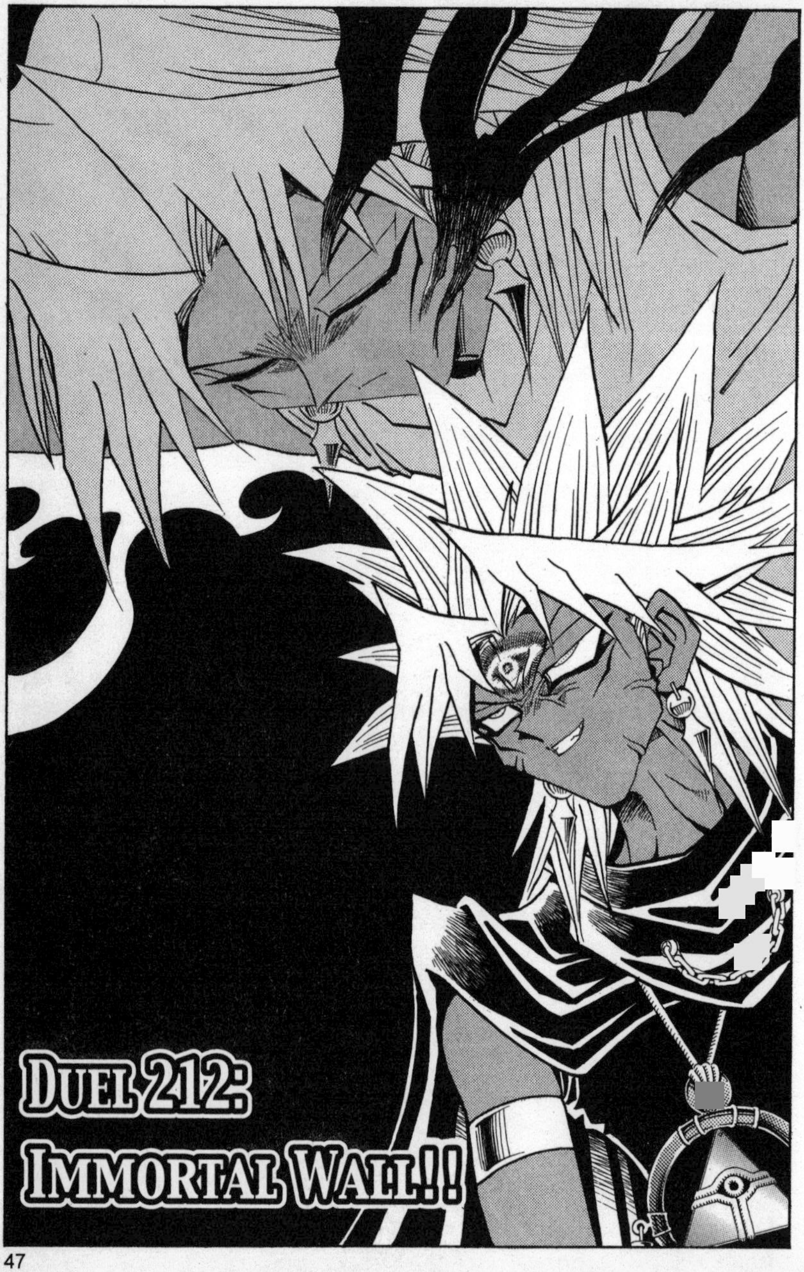
DUEL 212:
IMMORTAL WALL!!

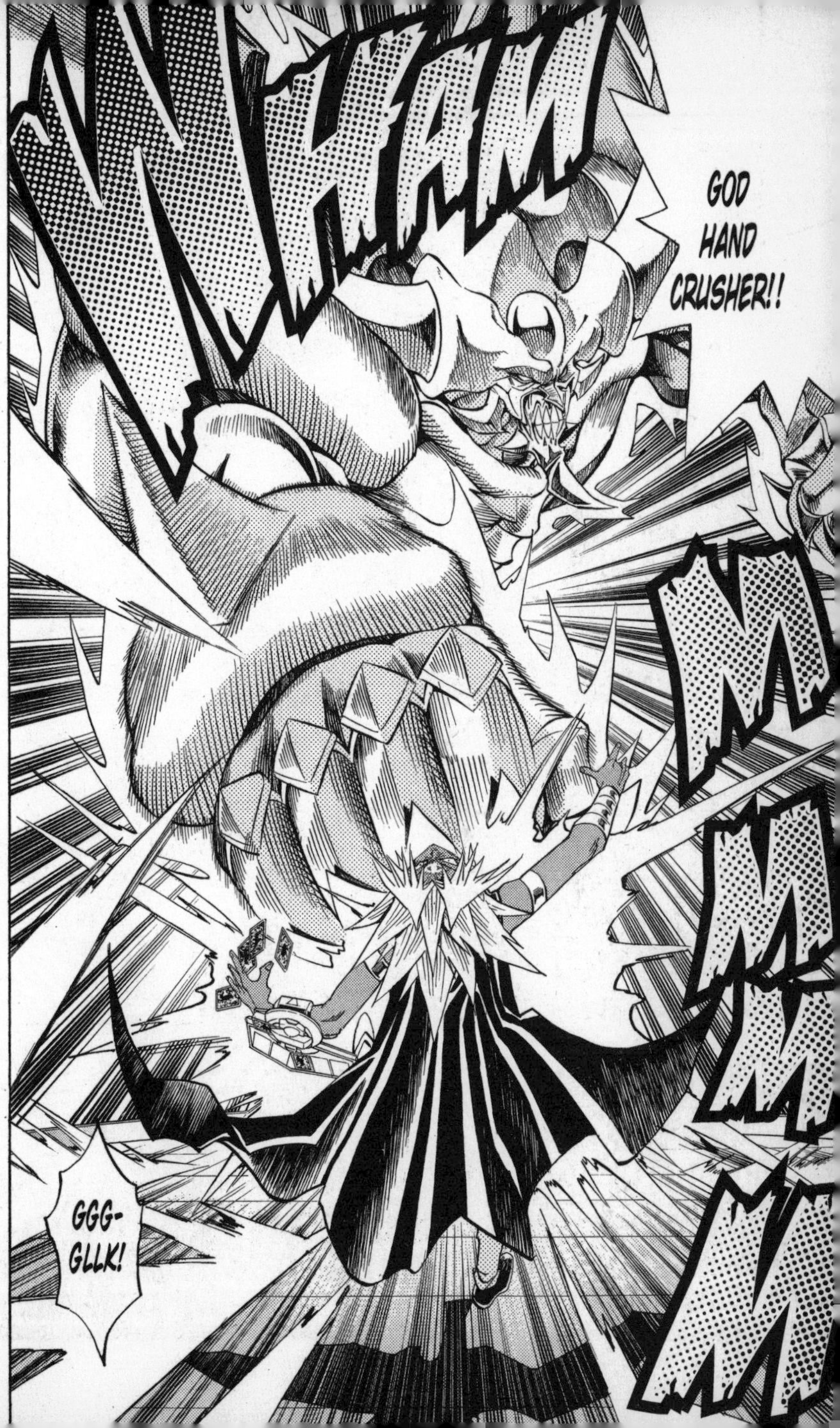
GOD HAND CRUSHER!!
WHAM
GGG-GLLK!

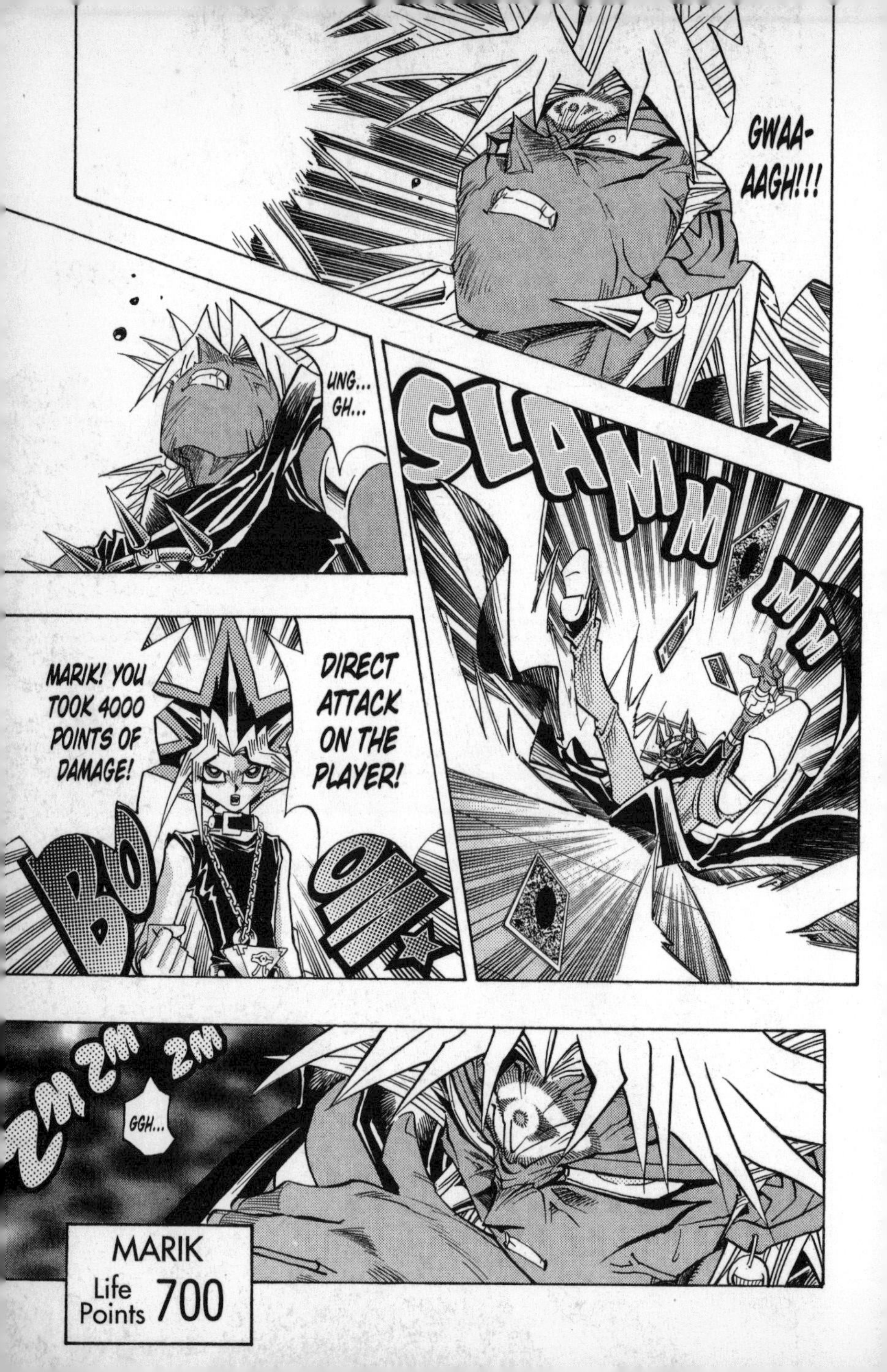
GWAA-AAGH!!!
SLAMMMM
UNG... GH...
DIRECT ATTACK ON THE PLAYER!
MARIK! YOU TOOK 4000 POINTS OF DAMAGE!
BOOM
ZM ZM ZM
GGH...
MARIK Life Points 700

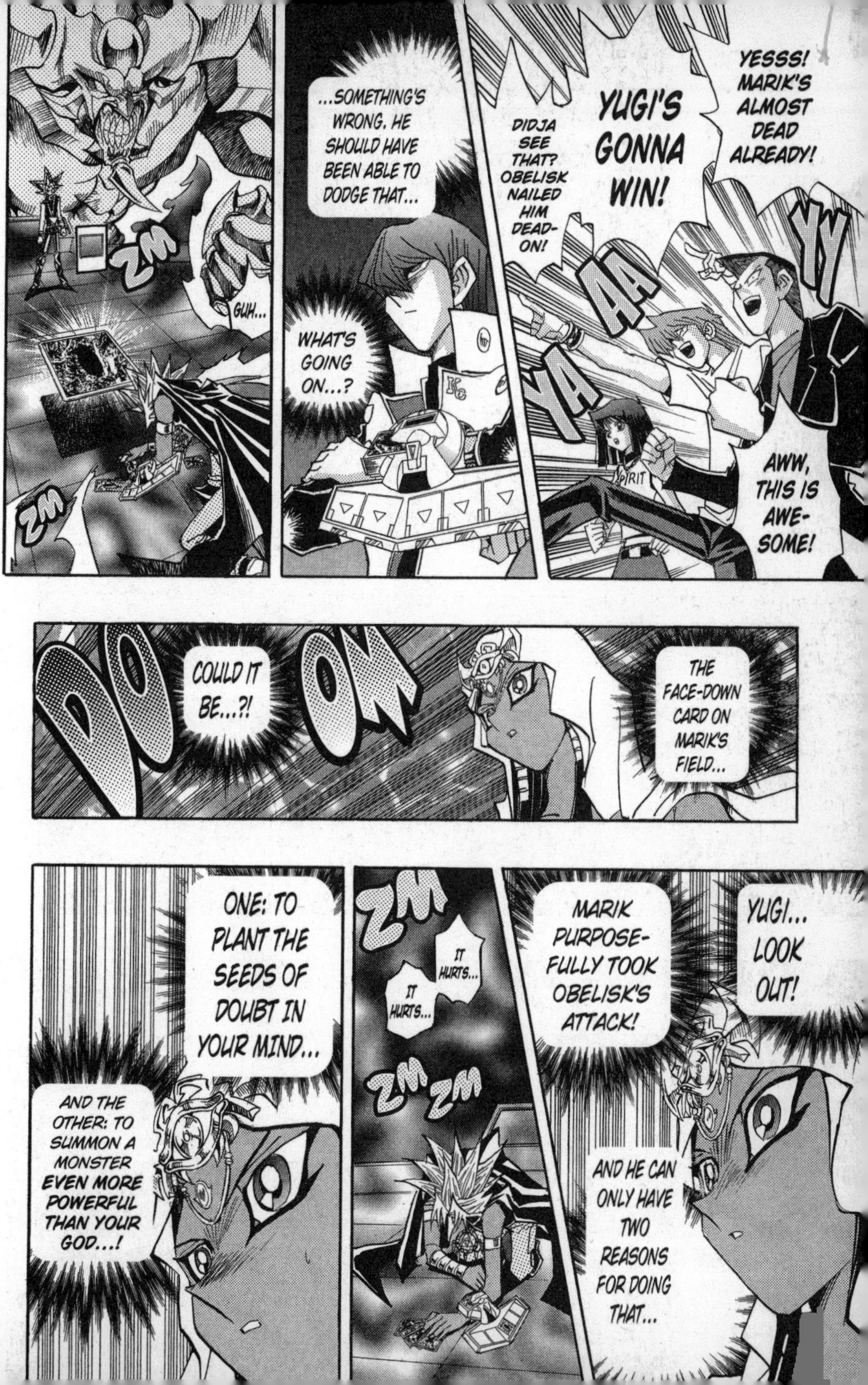
YESSS! MARIK'S ALMOST DEAD ALREADY!
YUGI'S GONNA WIN!
DIDJA SEE THAT? OBELISK NAILED HIM DEAD-ON!
YAAAYY
AWW, THIS IS AWESOME!
...SOMETHING'S WRONG. HE SHOULD HAVE BEEN ABLE TO DODGE THAT...
WHAT'S GOING ON...?
ZM
GUH...
ZM
THE FACE-DOWN CARD ON MARIK'S FIELD...
COULD IT BE...?!
DOOM
YUGI... LOOK OUT!
MARIK PURPOSE-FULLY TOOK OBELISK'S ATTACK!
AND HE CAN ONLY HAVE TWO REASONS FOR DOING THAT...
ZM
IT HURTS...
IT HURTS...
ZM ZM
ONE: TO PLANT THE SEEDS OF DOUBT IN YOUR MIND...
AND THE OTHER: TO SUMMON A MONSTER EVEN MORE POWERFUL THAN YOUR GOD...!

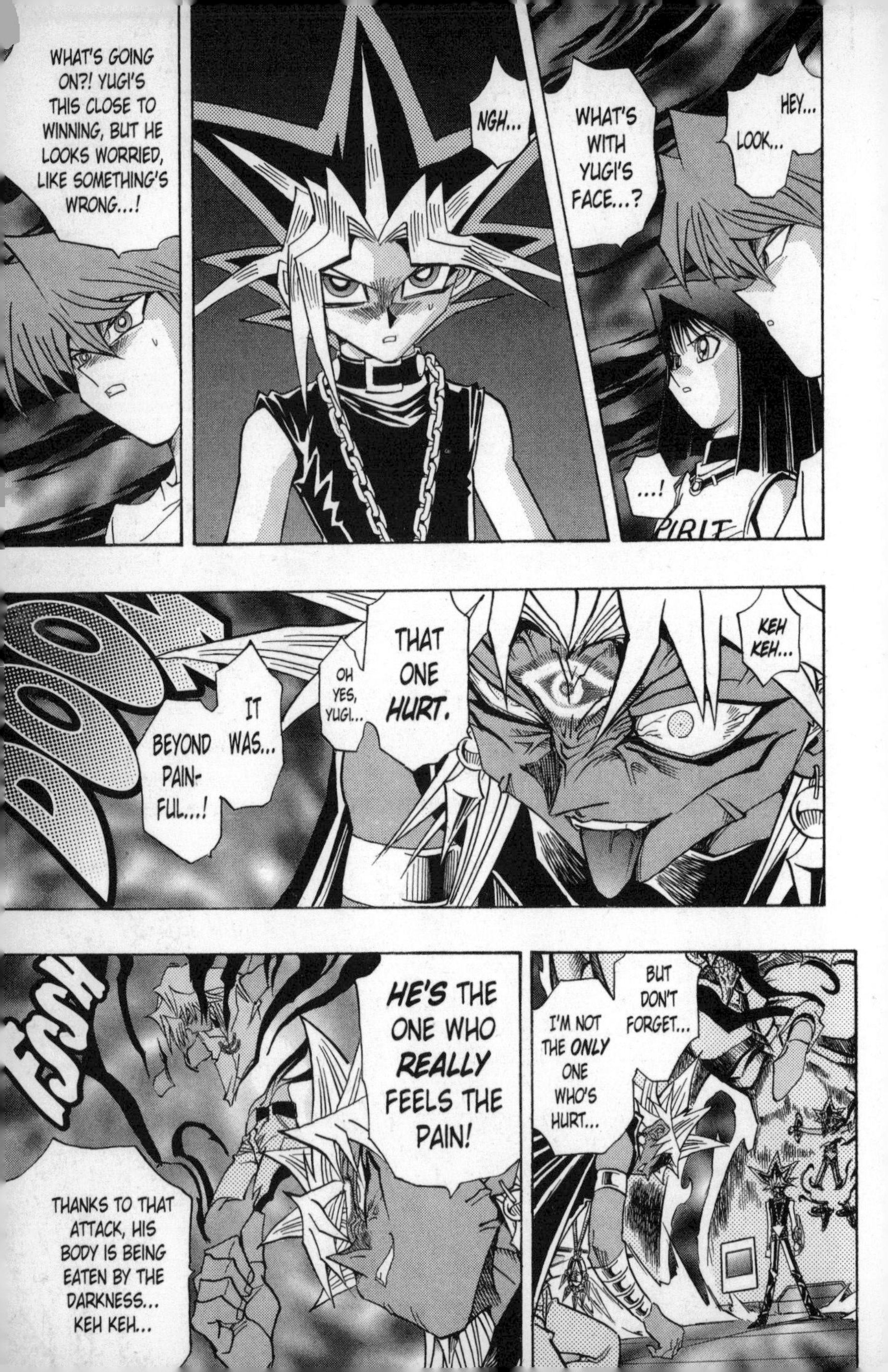

HEY... LOOK...
WHAT'S WITH YUGI'S FACE...?
...!
NGH...
WHAT'S GOING ON?! YUGI'S THIS CLOSE TO WINNING, BUT HE LOOKS WORRIED, LIKE SOMETHING'S WRONG...!
KEH KEH...
THAT ONE HURT.
OH YES, YUGI...
IT WAS...
BEYOND PAINFUL...!
BUT DON'T FORGET...
I'M NOT THE ONLY ONE WHO'S HURT...
HE'S THE ONE WHO REALLY FEELS THE PAIN!
THANKS TO THAT ATTACK, HIS BODY IS BEING EATEN BY THE DARKNESS... KEH KEH...

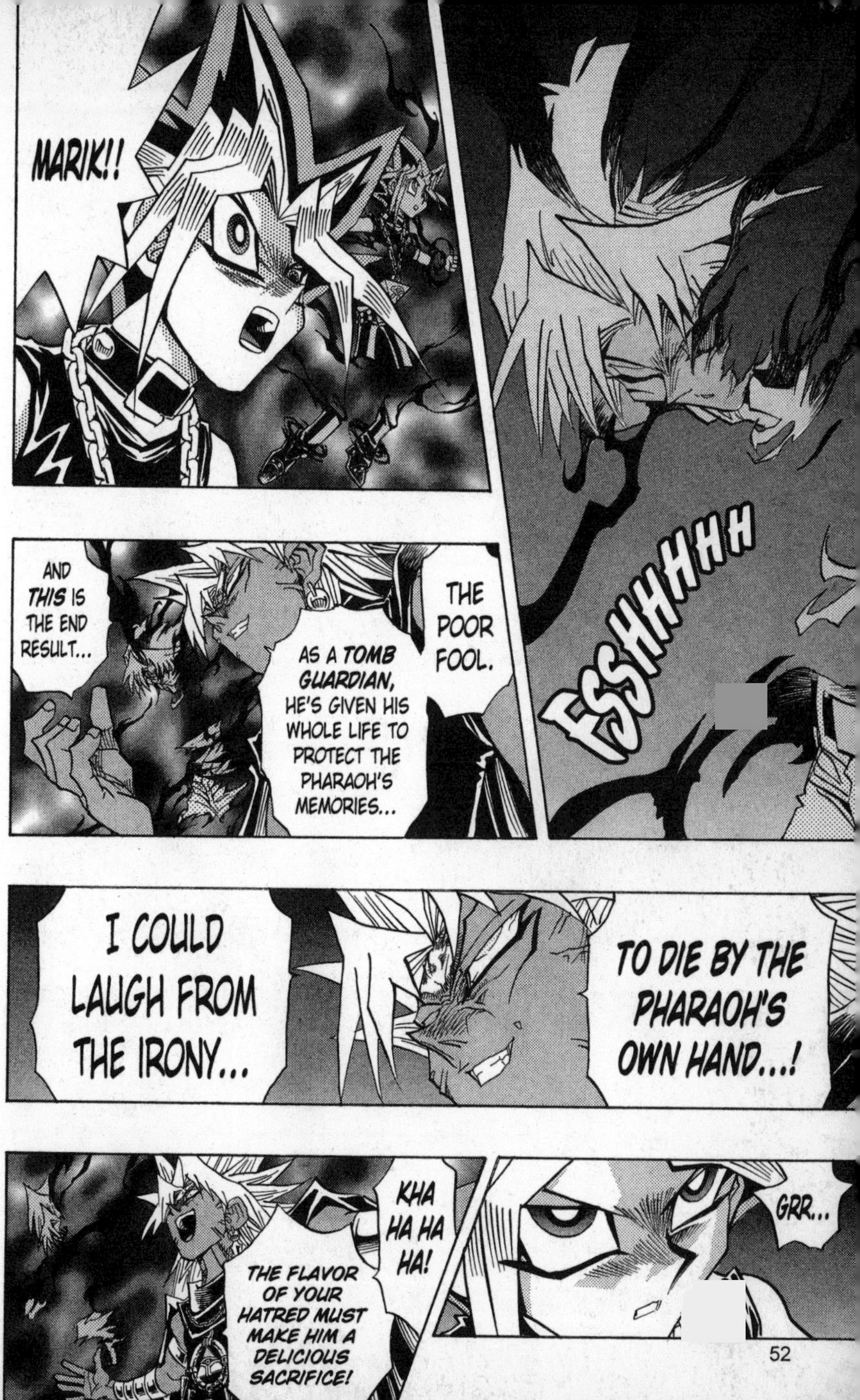
ESSHHHHH
MARIK!!
THE POOR FOOL.
AS A *TOMB GUARDIAN*, HE'S GIVEN HIS WHOLE LIFE TO PROTECT THE PHARAOH'S MEMORIES...
AND *THIS* IS THE END RESULT...
TO DIE BY THE PHARAOH'S OWN HAND...!
I COULD LAUGH FROM THE IRONY...
GRR...
KHA HA HA HA!
THE FLAVOR OF YOUR HATRED MUST MAKE HIM A DELICIOUS SACRIFICE!

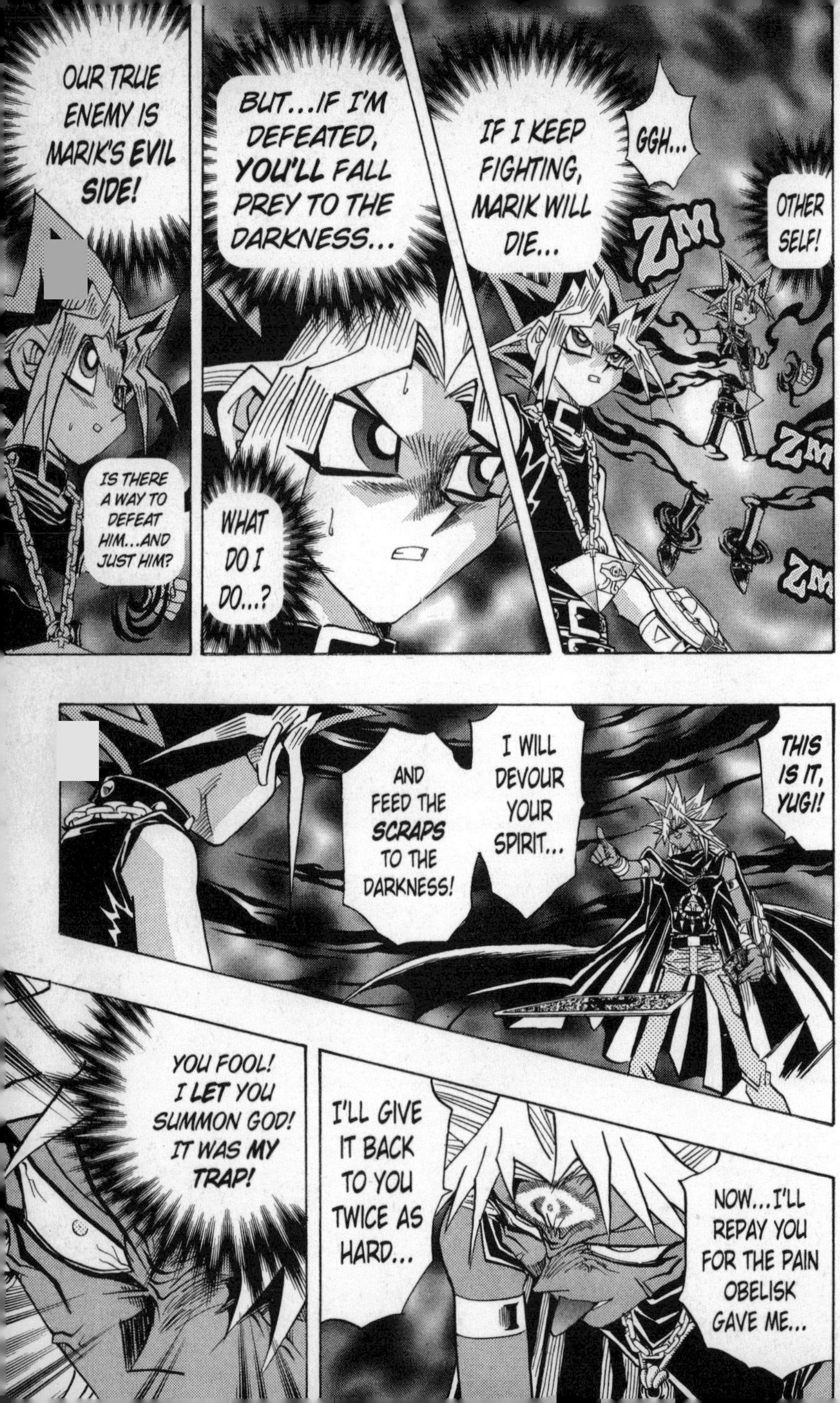
GGH...
OTHER SELF!
ZM
ZM
ZM
IF I KEEP FIGHTING, MARIK WILL DIE...
BUT...IF I'M DEFEATED, **YOU'LL** FALL PREY TO THE DARKNESS...
WHAT DO I DO...?
OUR TRUE ENEMY IS MARIK'S EVIL SIDE!
IS THERE A WAY TO DEFEAT HIM...AND JUST HIM?
THIS IS IT, YUGI!
I WILL DEVOUR YOUR SPIRIT...
AND FEED THE **SCRAPS** TO THE DARKNESS!
NOW...I'LL REPAY YOU FOR THE PAIN OBELISK GAVE ME...
I'LL GIVE IT BACK TO YOU TWICE AS HARD...
YOU FOOL! **I LET** YOU SUMMON GOD! IT WAS **MY** TRAP!

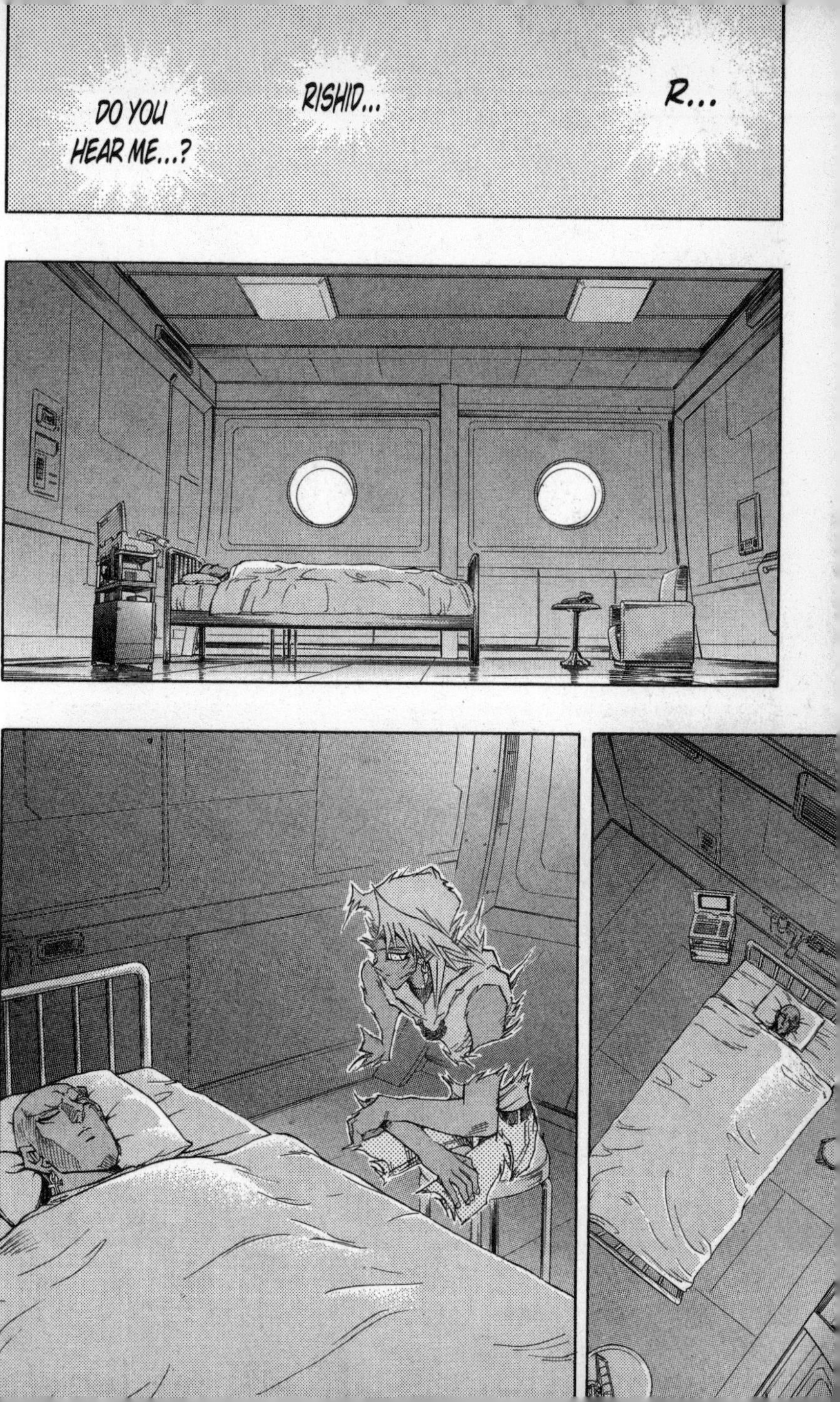
R...
RISHID...
DO YOU HEAR ME...?

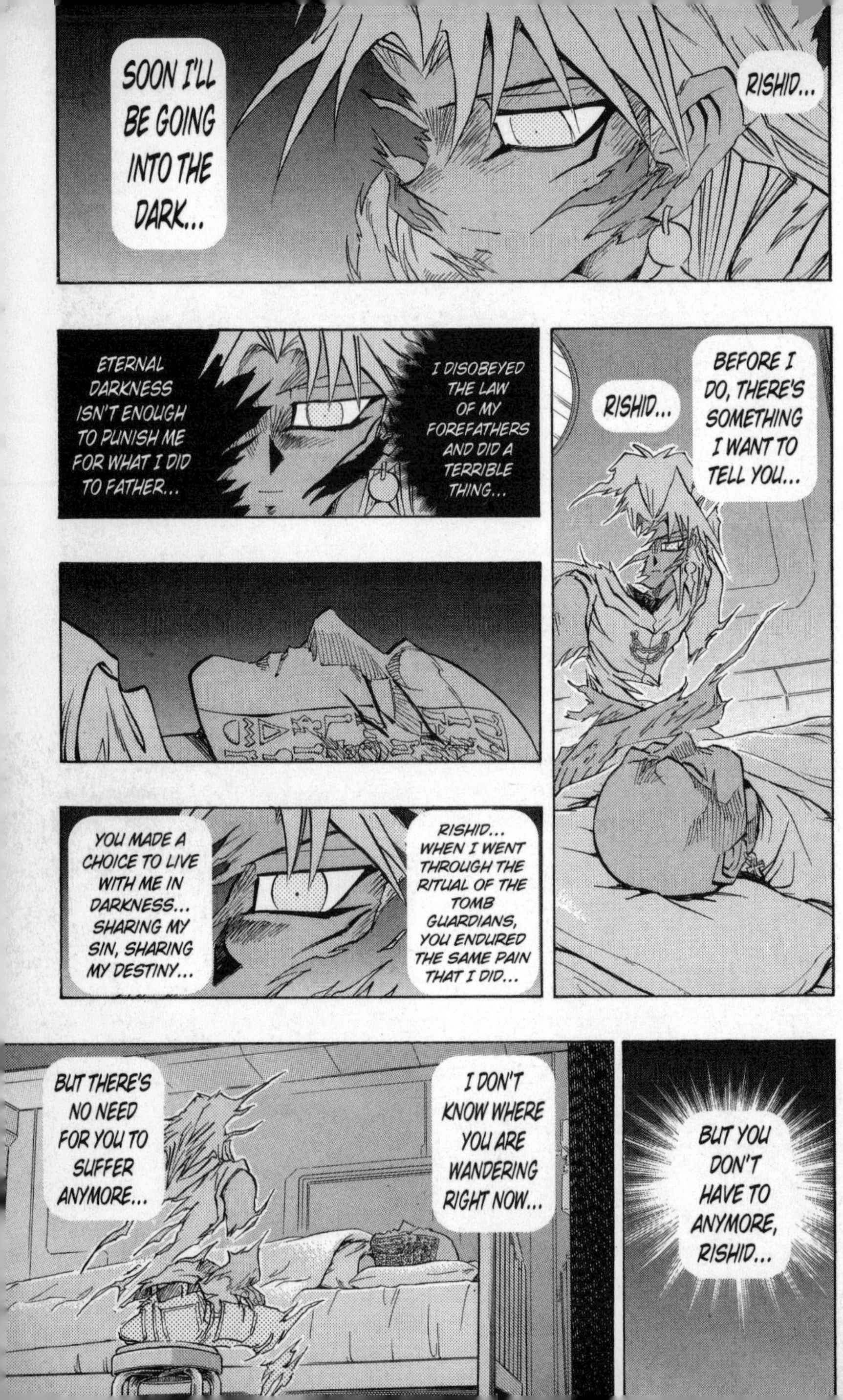
RISHID...
SOON I'LL BE GOING INTO THE DARK...
BEFORE I DO, THERE'S SOMETHING I WANT TO TELL YOU...
RISHID...
I DISOBEYED THE LAW OF MY FOREFATHERS AND DID A TERRIBLE THING...
ETERNAL DARKNESS ISN'T ENOUGH TO PUNISH ME FOR WHAT I DID TO FATHER...
RISHID... WHEN I WENT THROUGH THE RITUAL OF THE TOMB GUARDIANS, YOU ENDURED THE SAME PAIN THAT I DID...
YOU MADE A CHOICE TO LIVE WITH ME IN DARKNESS... SHARING MY SIN, SHARING MY DESTINY...
BUT YOU DON'T HAVE TO ANYMORE, RISHID...
I DON'T KNOW WHERE YOU ARE WANDERING RIGHT NOW...
BUT THERE'S NO NEED FOR YOU TO SUFFER ANYMORE...

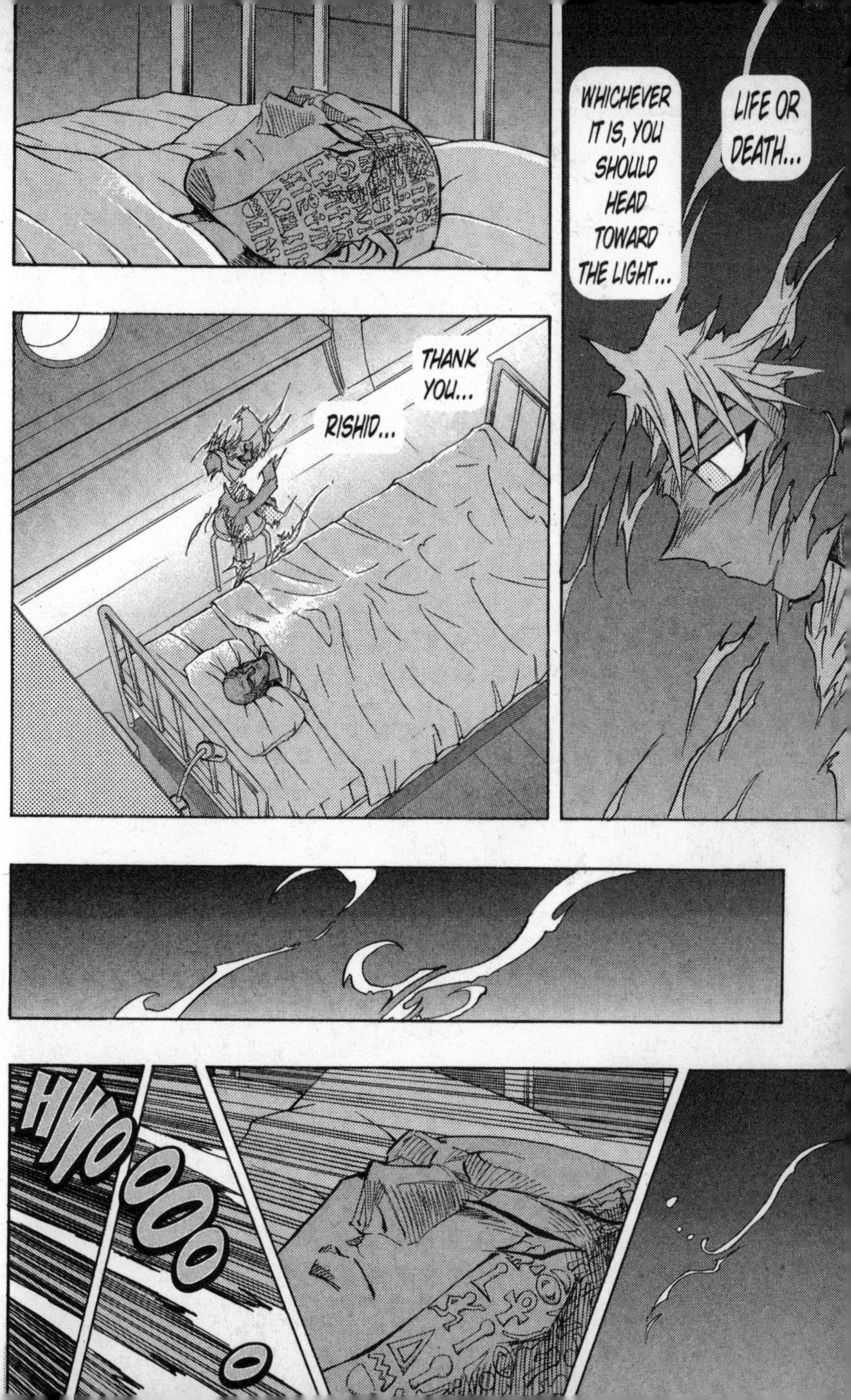
LIFE OR DEATH...
WHICHEVER IT IS, YOU SHOULD HEAD TOWARD THE LIGHT...
THANK YOU...
RISHID...
HWOOOOO O

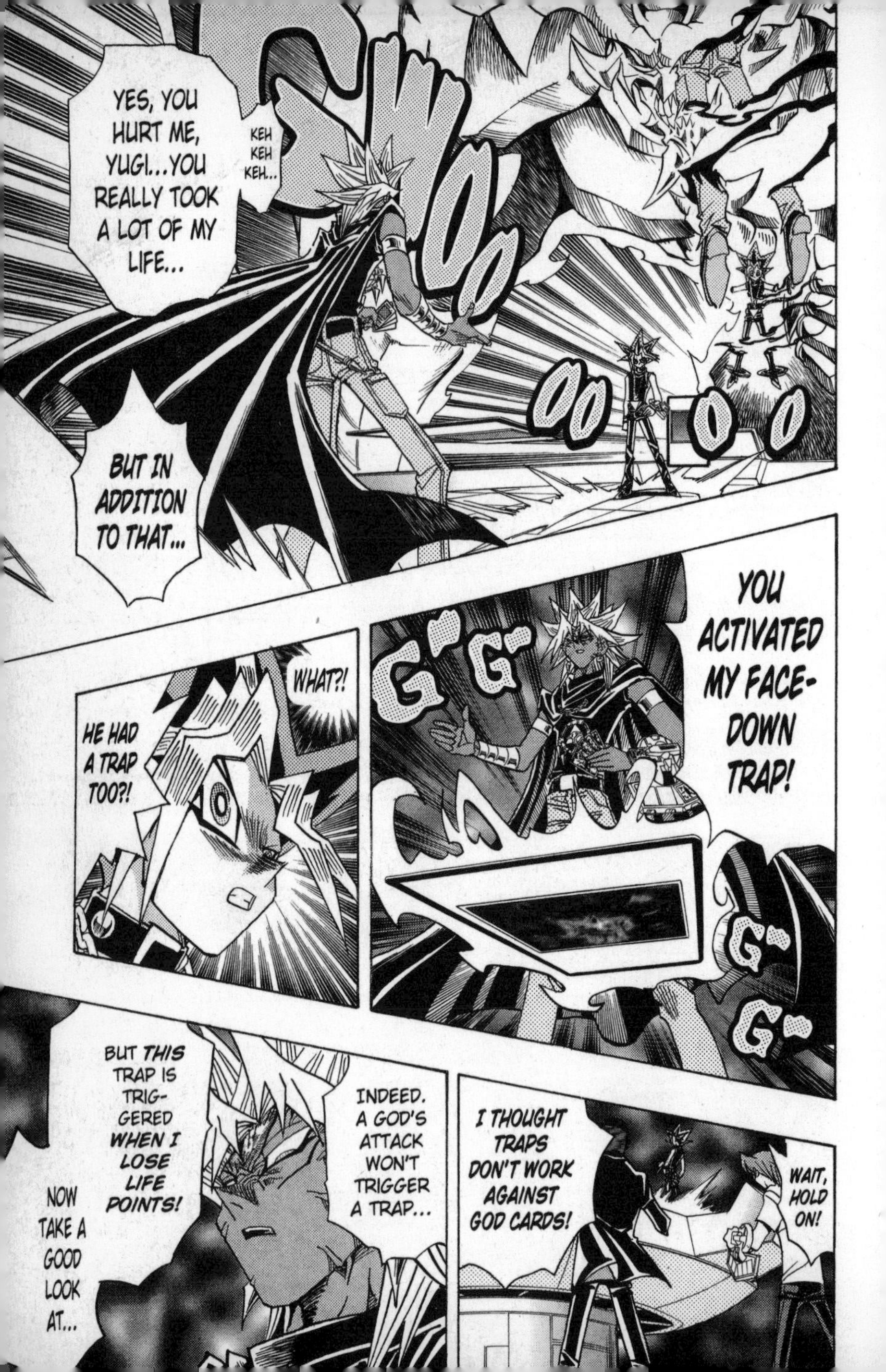
KEH KEH KEH...
YES, YOU HURT ME, YUGI...YOU REALLY TOOK A LOT OF MY LIFE...
BUT IN ADDITION TO THAT...
YOU ACTIVATED MY FACE-DOWN TRAP!
WHAT?!
HE HAD A TRAP TOO?!
WAIT, HOLD ON!
I THOUGHT TRAPS DON'T WORK AGAINST GOD CARDS!
INDEED. A GOD'S ATTACK WON'T TRIGGER A TRAP...
BUT *THIS* TRAP IS TRIG-GERED *WHEN I LOSE LIFE POINTS!*
NOW TAKE A GOOD LOOK AT...

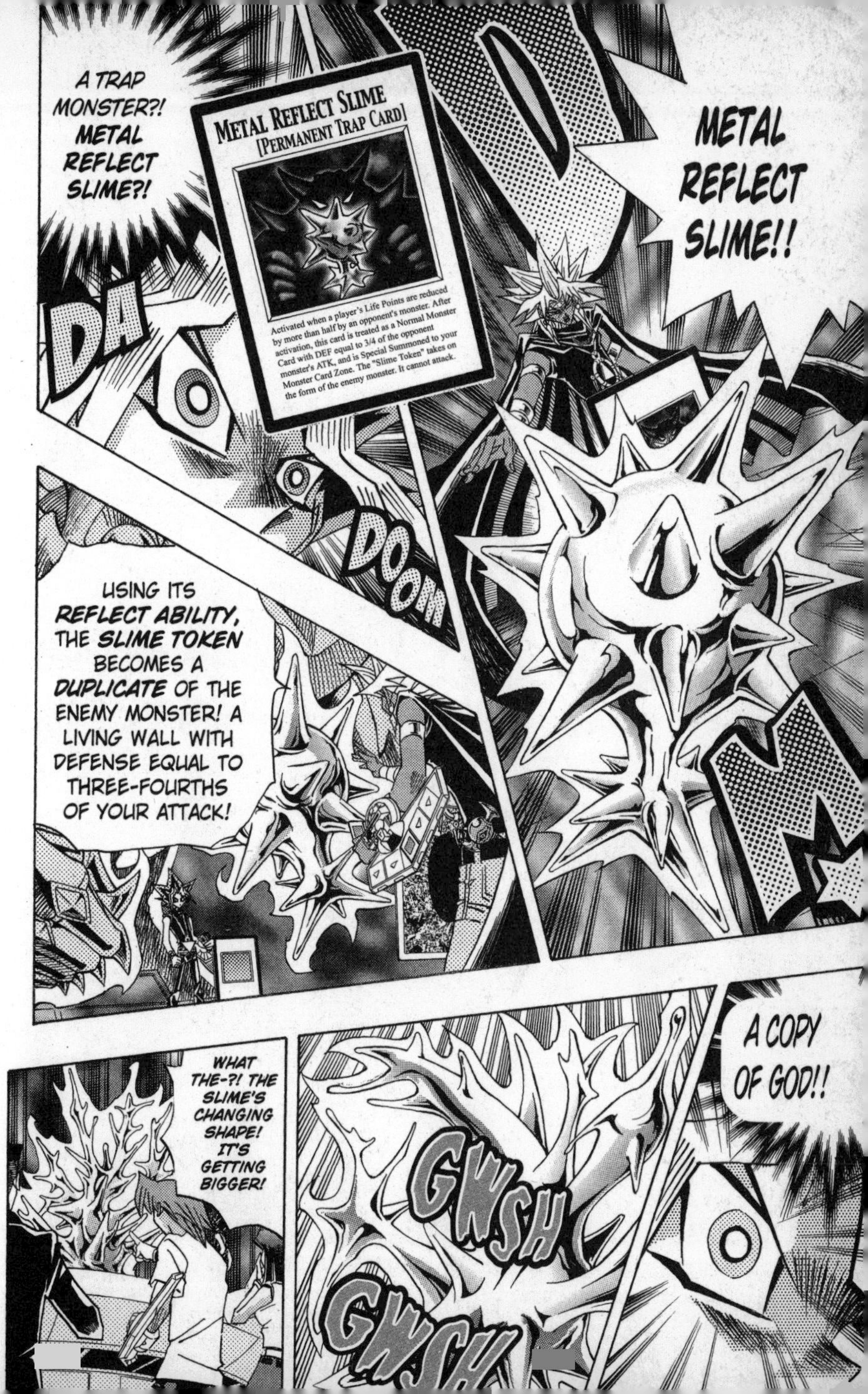
METAL REFLECT SLIME!!
A TRAP MONSTER?! METAL REFLECT SLIME?!
METAL REFLECT SLIME
[PERMANENT TRAP CARD]
Activated when a player's Life Points are reduced by more than half by an opponent's monster. After activation, this card is treated as a Normal Monster Card with DEF equal to 3/4 of the opponent monster's ATK, and is Special Summoned to your Monster Card Zone. The "Slime Token" takes on the form of the enemy monster. It cannot attack.
DA
DOOM
USING ITS REFLECT ABILITY, THE SLIME TOKEN BECOMES A DUPLICATE OF THE ENEMY MONSTER! A LIVING WALL WITH DEFENSE EQUAL TO THREE-FOURTHS OF YOUR ATTACK!
A COPY OF GOD!!
GWSH
GWSH
WHAT THE-?! THE SLIME'S CHANGING SHAPE! IT'S GETTING BIGGER!

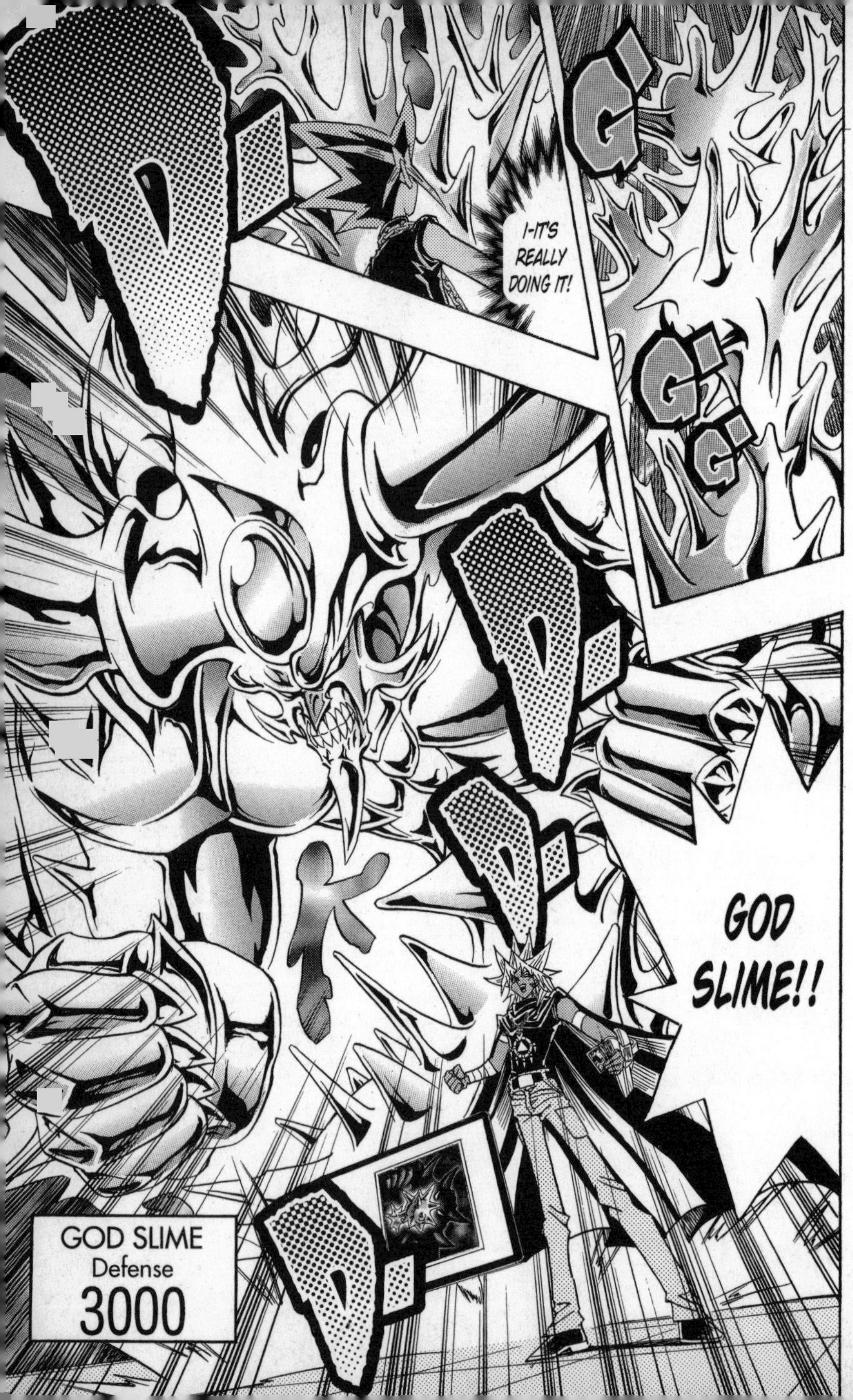
I-IT'S REALLY DOING IT!
GOD SLIME!!
GOD SLIME
Defense
3000

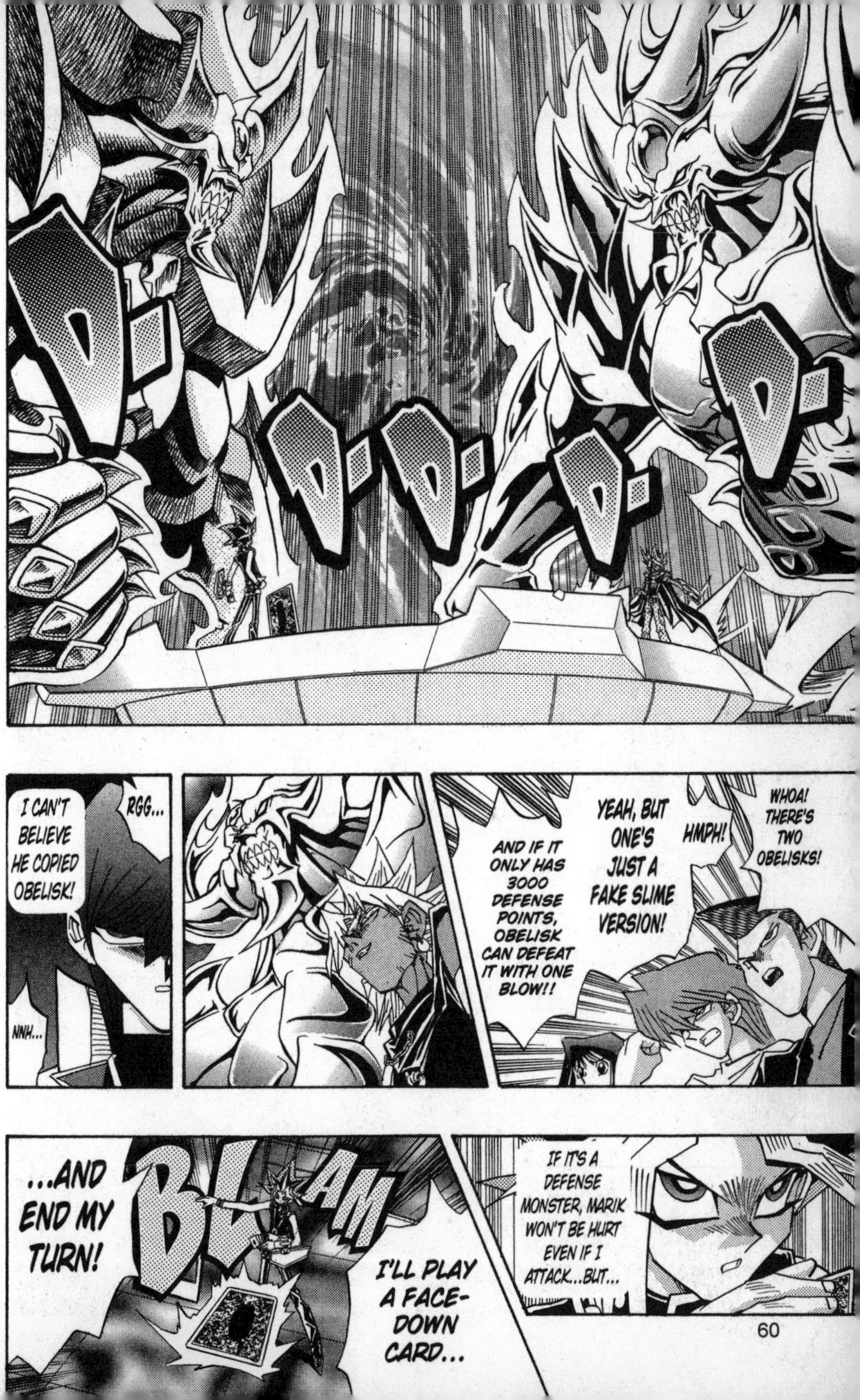
D... D... D... D... D...
WHOA! THERE'S TWO OBELISKS!
HMPH!
YEAH, BUT ONE'S JUST A FAKE SLIME VERSION!
AND IF IT ONLY HAS 3000 DEFENSE POINTS, OBELISK CAN DEFEAT IT WITH ONE BLOW!!
RGG...
I CAN'T BELIEVE HE COPIED OBELISK!
NNH...
IF IT'S A DEFENSE MONSTER, MARIK WON'T BE HURT EVEN IF I ATTACK...BUT...
I'LL PLAY A FACE-DOWN CARD...
BLAM
...AND END MY TURN!

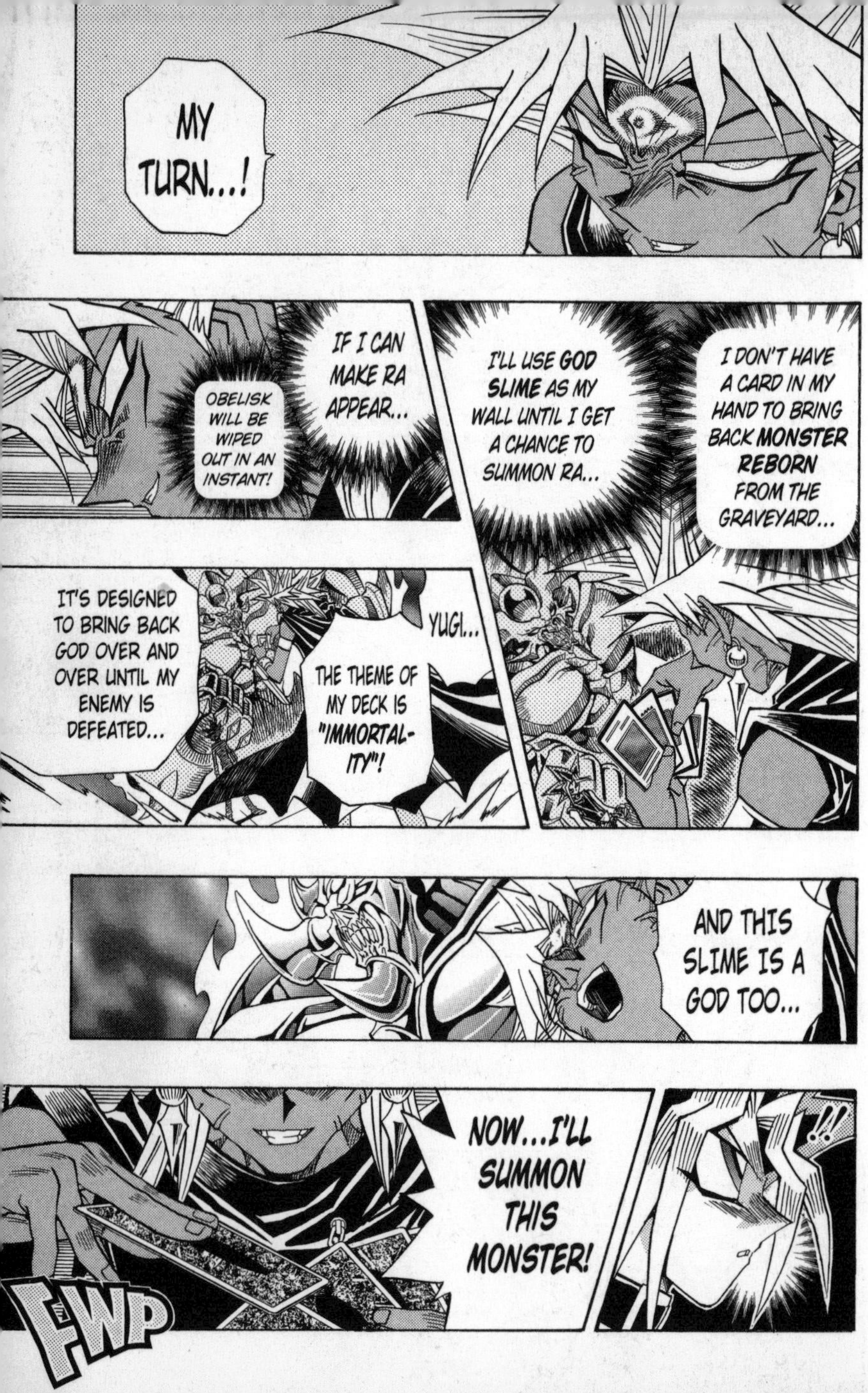
MY TURN...!
I DON'T HAVE A CARD IN MY HAND TO BRING BACK MONSTER REBORN FROM THE GRAVEYARD...
I'LL USE GOD SLIME AS MY WALL UNTIL I GET A CHANCE TO SUMMON RA...
IF I CAN MAKE RA APPEAR...
OBELISK WILL BE WIPED OUT IN AN INSTANT!
YUGI...
THE THEME OF MY DECK IS "IMMORTALITY"!
IT'S DESIGNED TO BRING BACK GOD OVER AND OVER UNTIL MY ENEMY IS DEFEATED...
AND THIS SLIME IS A GOD TOO...
!!
NOW...I'LL SUMMON THIS MONSTER!
FWP

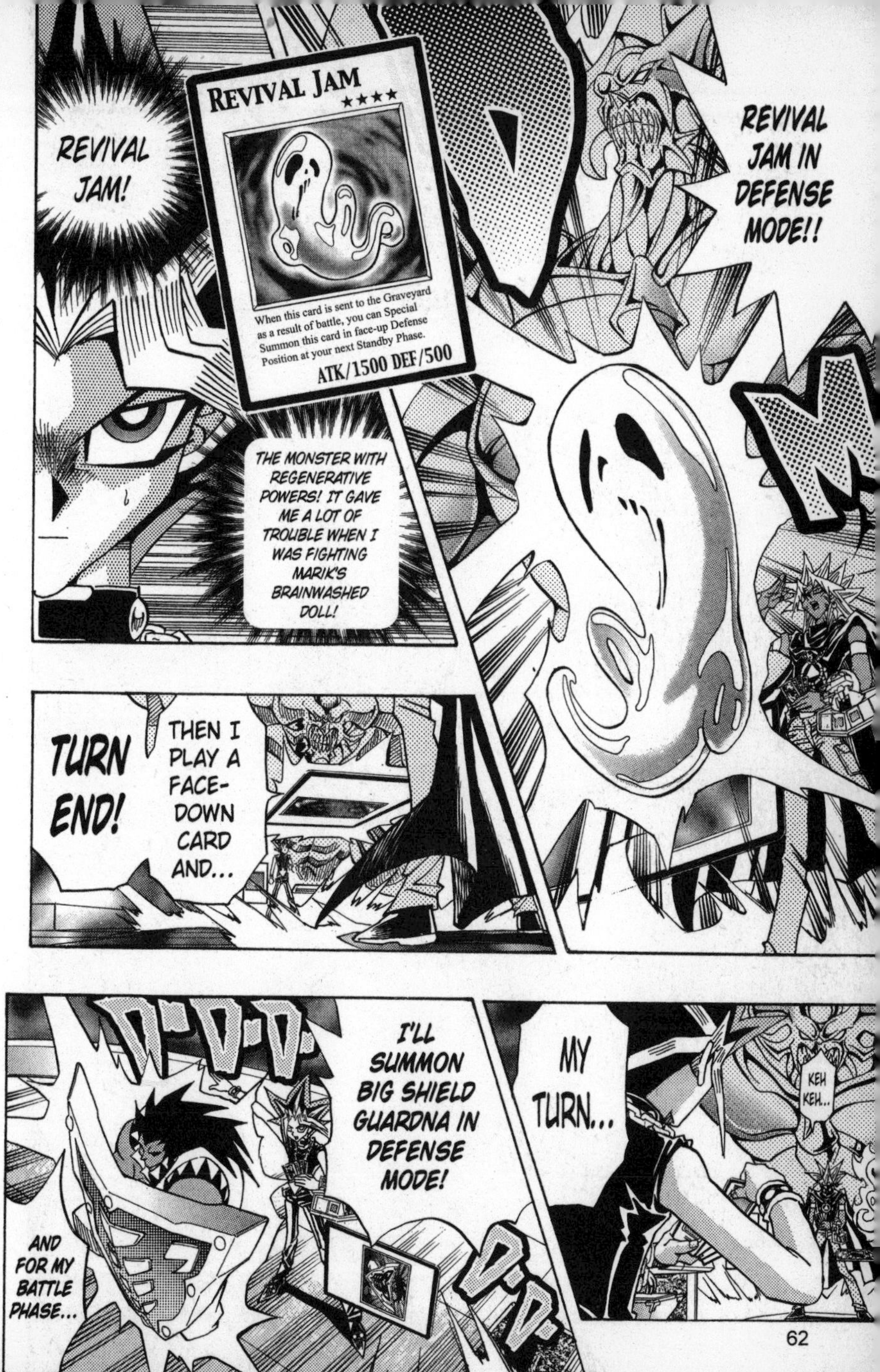
REVIVAL JAM IN DEFENSE MODE!!
REVIVAL JAM ★★★★
When this card is sent to the Graveyard as a result of battle, you can Special Summon this card in face-up Defense Position at your next Standby Phase.
ATK/1500 DEF/500
REVIVAL JAM!
THE MONSTER WITH REGENERATIVE POWERS! IT GAVE ME A LOT OF TROUBLE WHEN I WAS FIGHTING MARIK'S BRAINWASHED DOLL!
THEN I PLAY A FACE-DOWN CARD AND...
TURN END!
KEH KEH...
MY TURN...
D-D-D
I'LL SUMMON BIG SHIELD GUARDNA IN DEFENSE MODE!
D-D
AND FOR MY BATTLE PHASE...

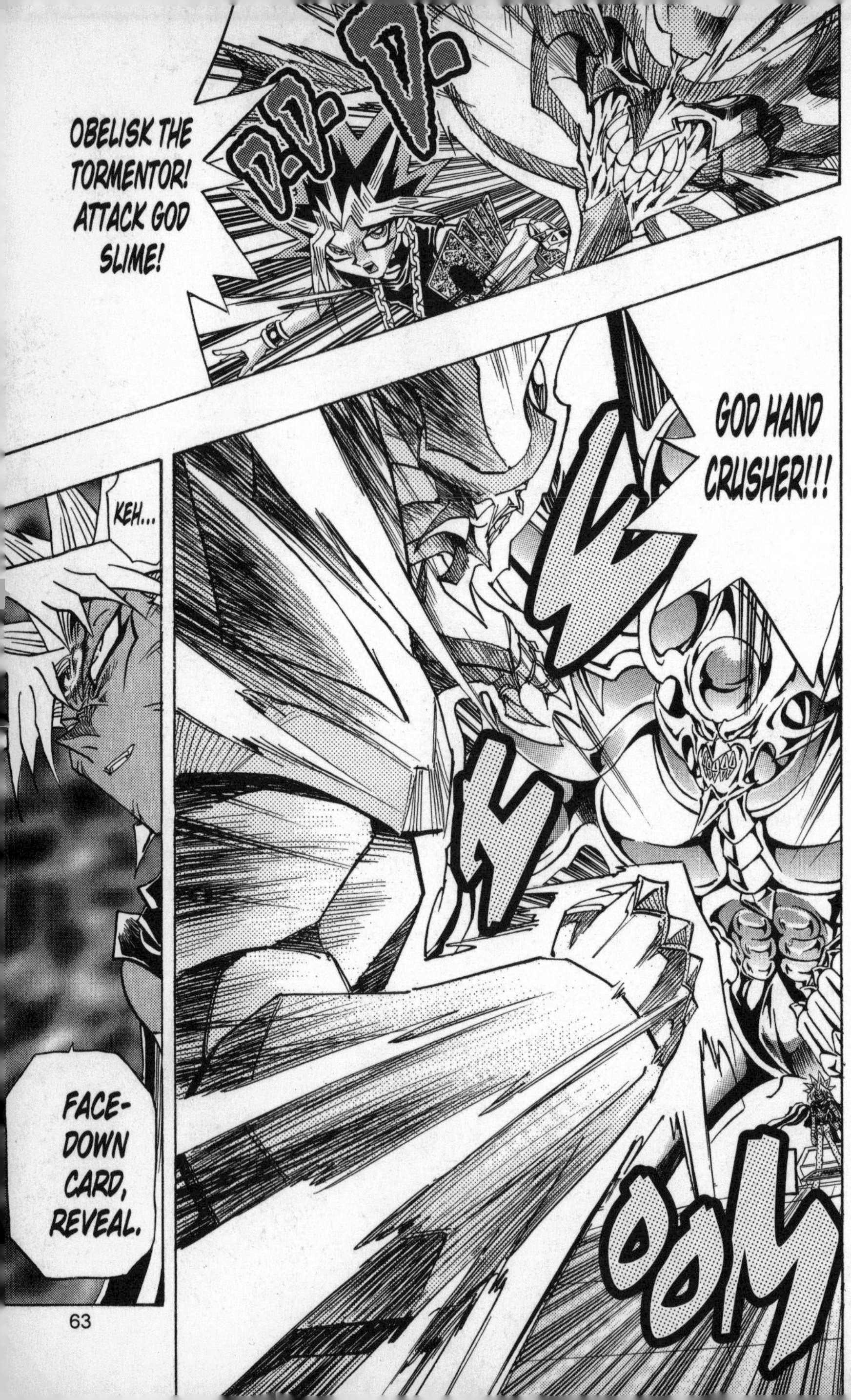
OBELISK THE TORMENTOR! ATTACK GOD SLIME!
GOD HAND CRUSHER!!!
KEH...
FACE-DOWN CARD, REVEAL.

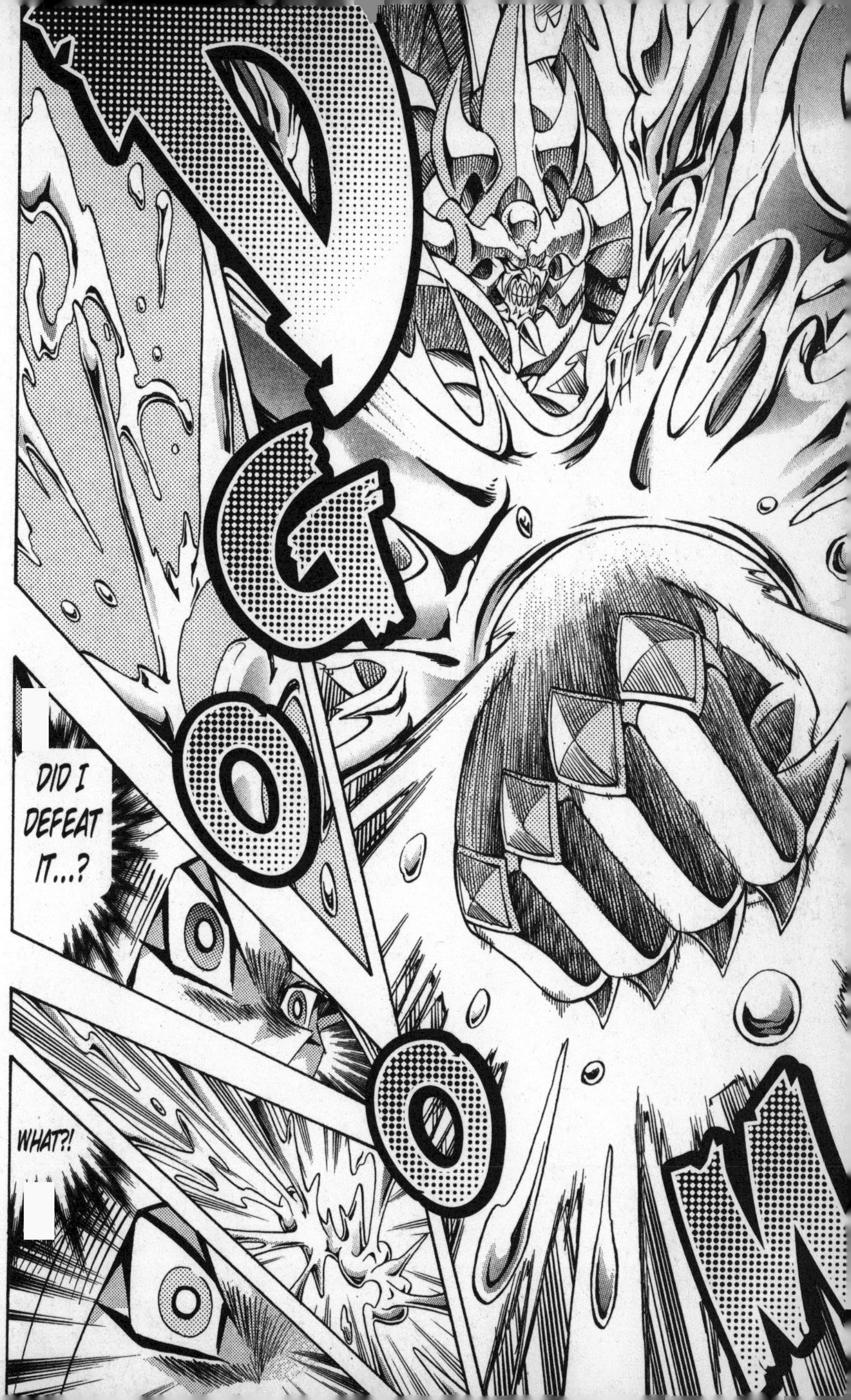
DID I DEFEAT IT...?
WHAT?!

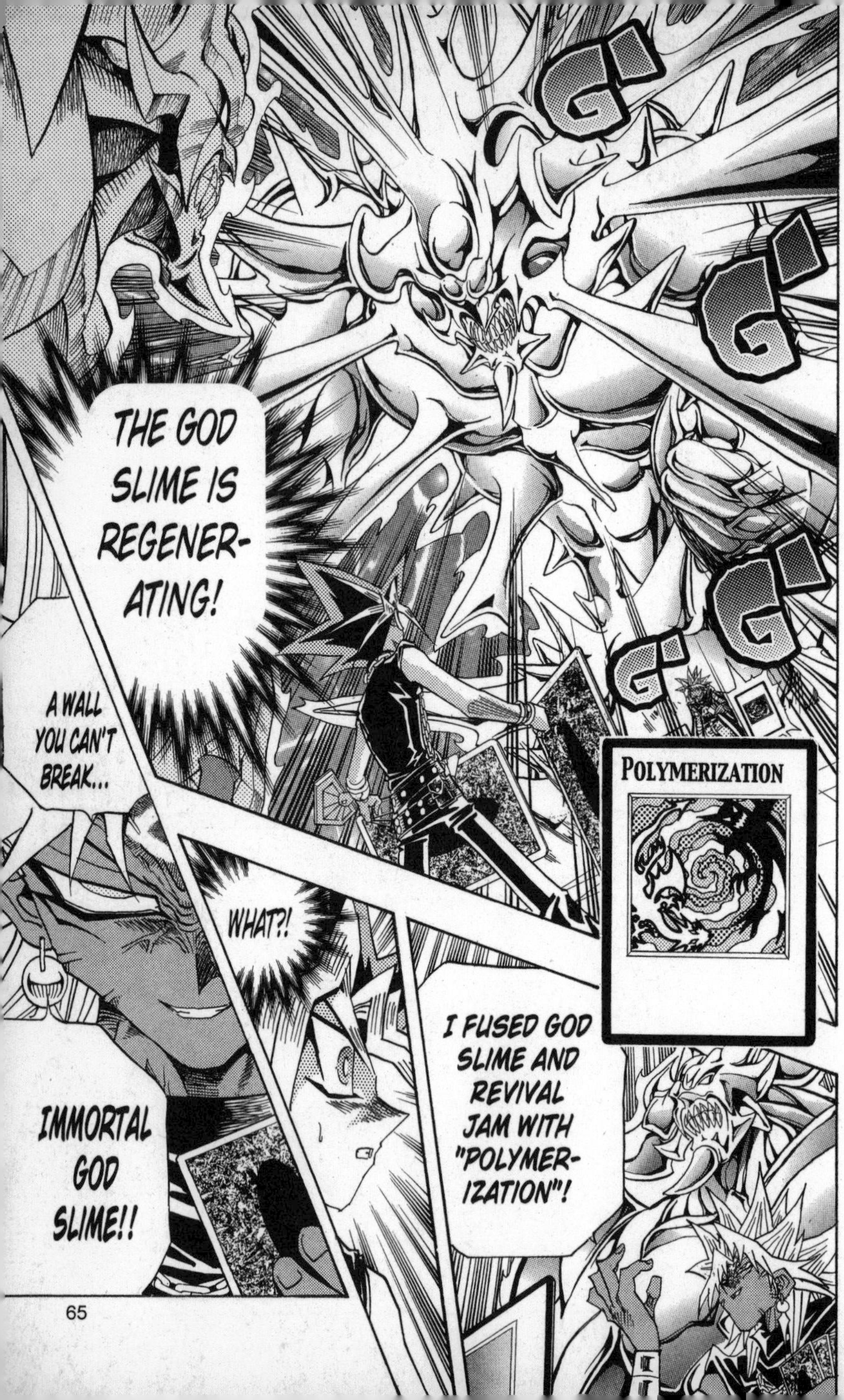
G
G
G
G
G
THE GOD SLIME IS REGENER-ATING!
POLYMERIZATION
I FUSED GOD SLIME AND REVIVAL JAM WITH "POLYMER-IZATION"!
WHAT?!
A WALL YOU CAN'T BREAK...
IMMORTAL GOD SLIME!!

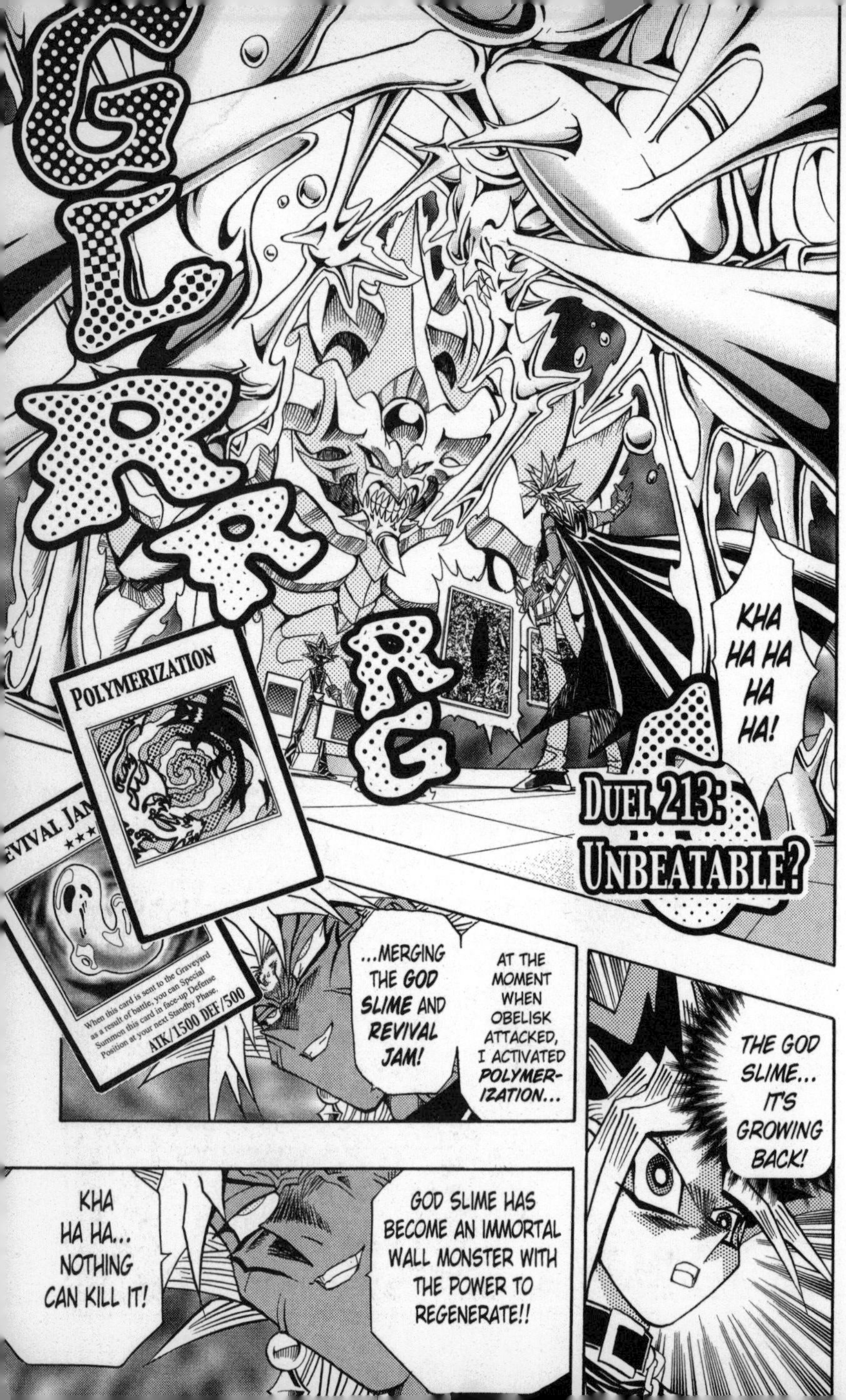
GLRRRG
KHA HA HA HA HA!
DUEL 213: UNBEATABLE?
POLYMERIZATION
EVIVAL JAM
When this card is sent to the Graveyard as a result of battle, you can Special Summon this card in face-up Defense Position at your next Standby Phase.
ATK/1500 DEF/500
THE GOD SLIME... IT'S GROWING BACK!
AT THE MOMENT WHEN OBELISK ATTACKED, I ACTIVATED POLYMERIZATION...
...MERGING THE GOD SLIME AND REVIVAL JAM!
GOD SLIME HAS BECOME AN IMMORTAL WALL MONSTER WITH THE POWER TO REGENERATE!!
KHA HA HA... NOTHING CAN KILL IT!

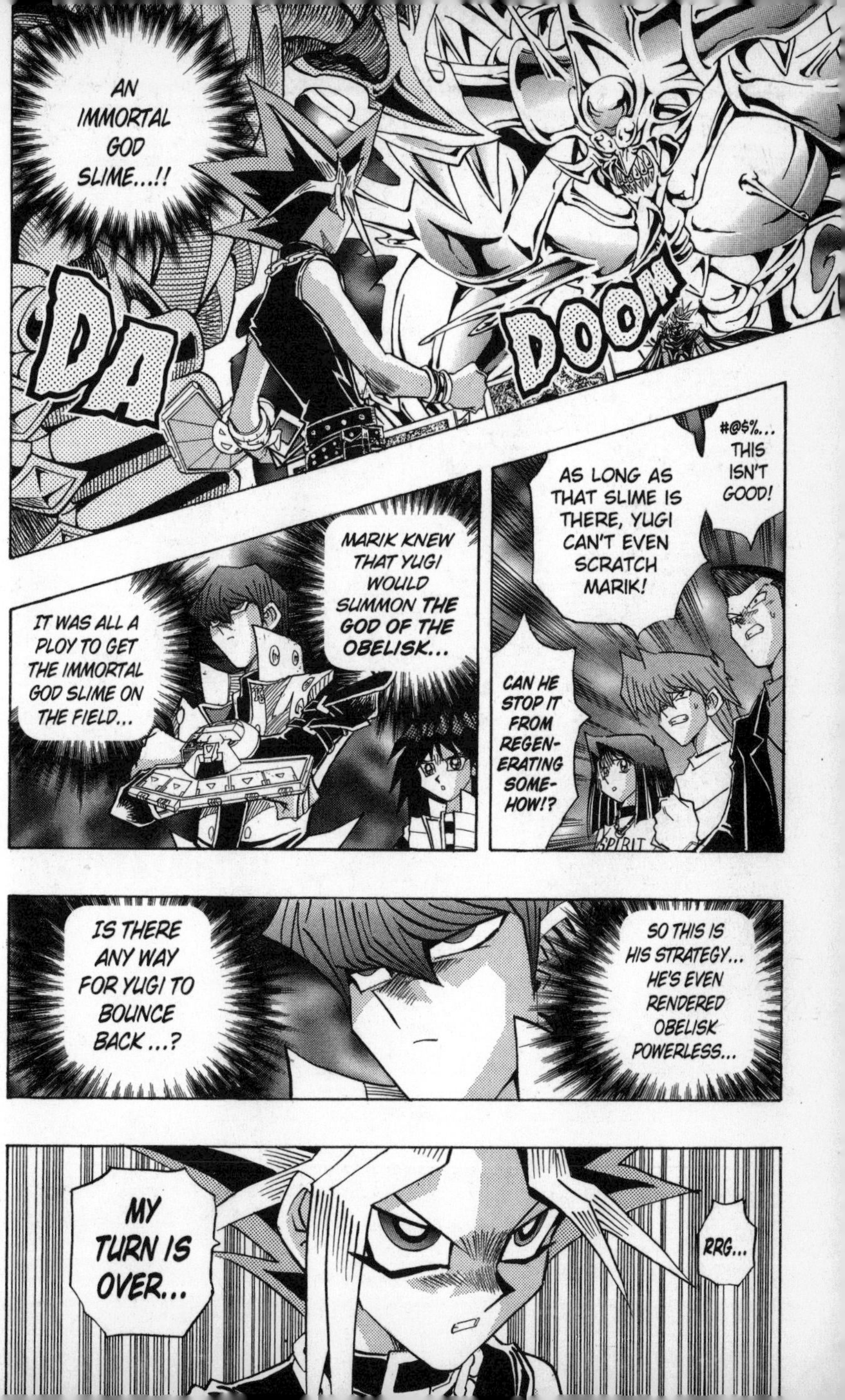
AN IMMORTAL GOD SLIME...!!
DA DOOM
#@$%... THIS ISN'T GOOD!
AS LONG AS THAT SLIME IS THERE, YUGI CAN'T EVEN SCRATCH MARIK!
CAN HE STOP IT FROM REGEN-ERATING SOME-HOW!?
SPIRIT
MARIK KNEW THAT YUGI WOULD SUMMON THE GOD OF THE OBELISK...
IT WAS ALL A PLOY TO GET THE IMMORTAL GOD SLIME ON THE FIELD...
SO THIS IS HIS STRATEGY... HE'S EVEN RENDERED OBELISK POWERLESS...
IS THERE ANY WAY FOR YUGI TO BOUNCE BACK ...?
RRG...
MY TURN IS OVER...

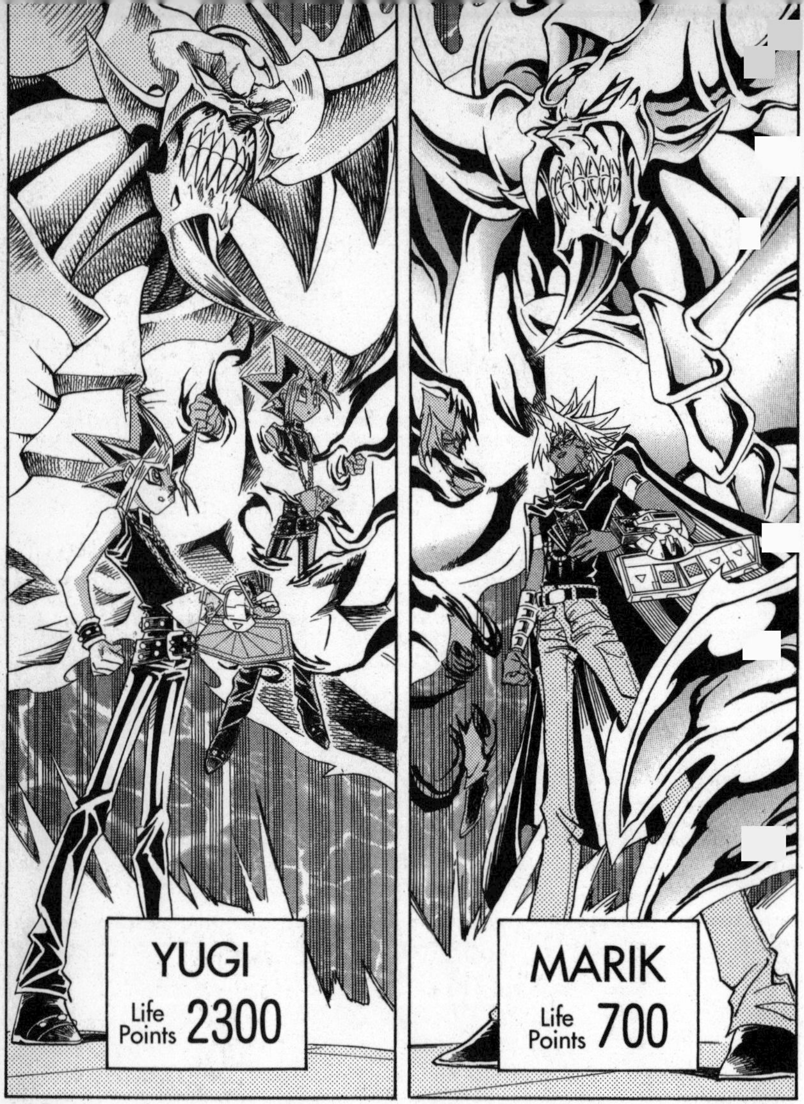
MARIK
Life Points 700
YUGI
Life Points 2300

## DUEL 213: UNBEATABLE?

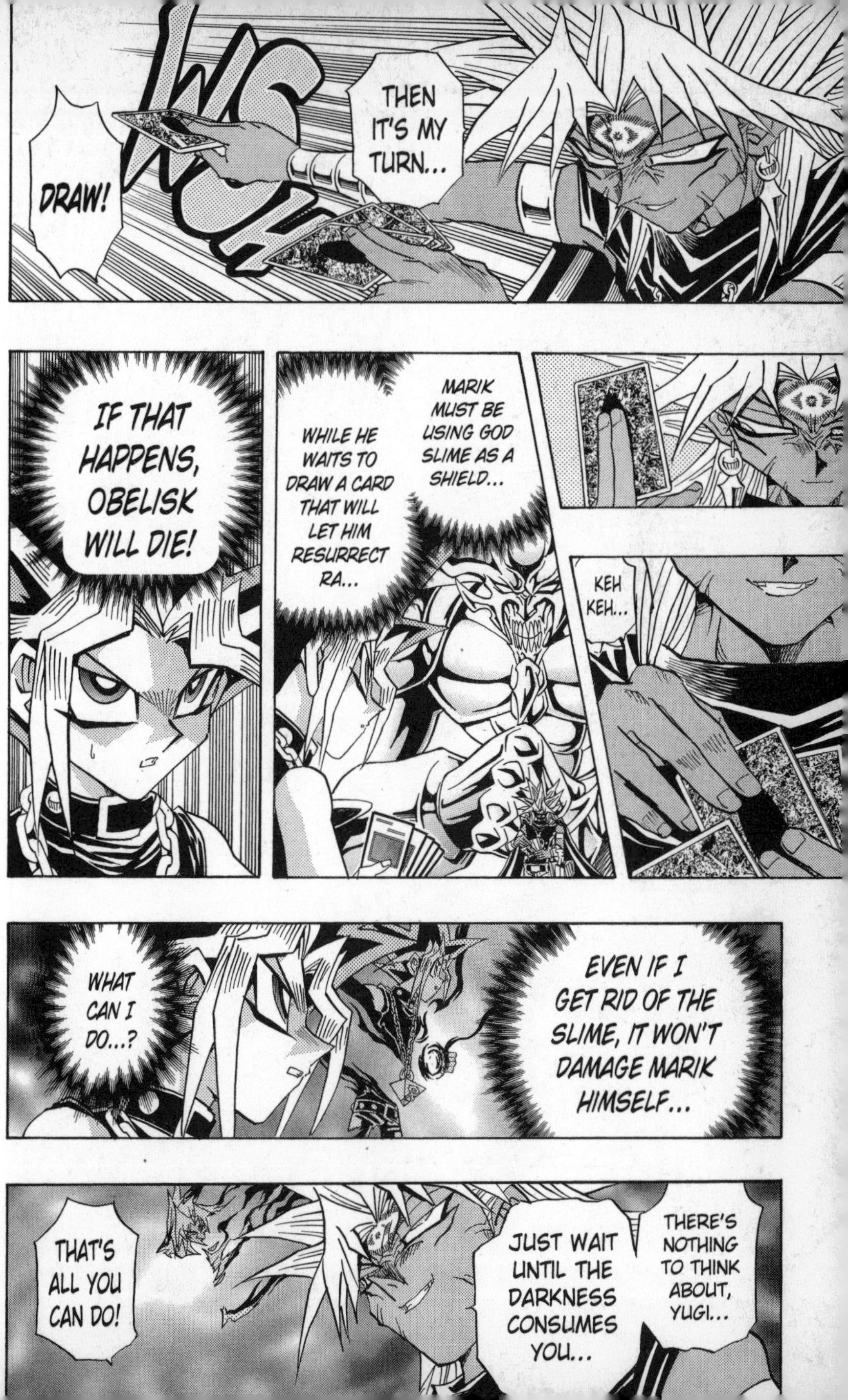
THEN IT'S MY TURN...
DRAW!
KEH KEH...
MARIK MUST BE USING GOD SLIME AS A SHIELD...
WHILE HE WAITS TO DRAW A CARD THAT WILL LET HIM RESURRECT RA...
IF THAT HAPPENS, OBELISK WILL DIE!
EVEN IF I GET RID OF THE SLIME, IT WON'T DAMAGE MARIK HIMSELF...
WHAT CAN I DO...?
THERE'S NOTHING TO THINK ABOUT, YUGI...
JUST WAIT UNTIL THE DARKNESS CONSUMES YOU...
THAT'S ALL YOU CAN DO!

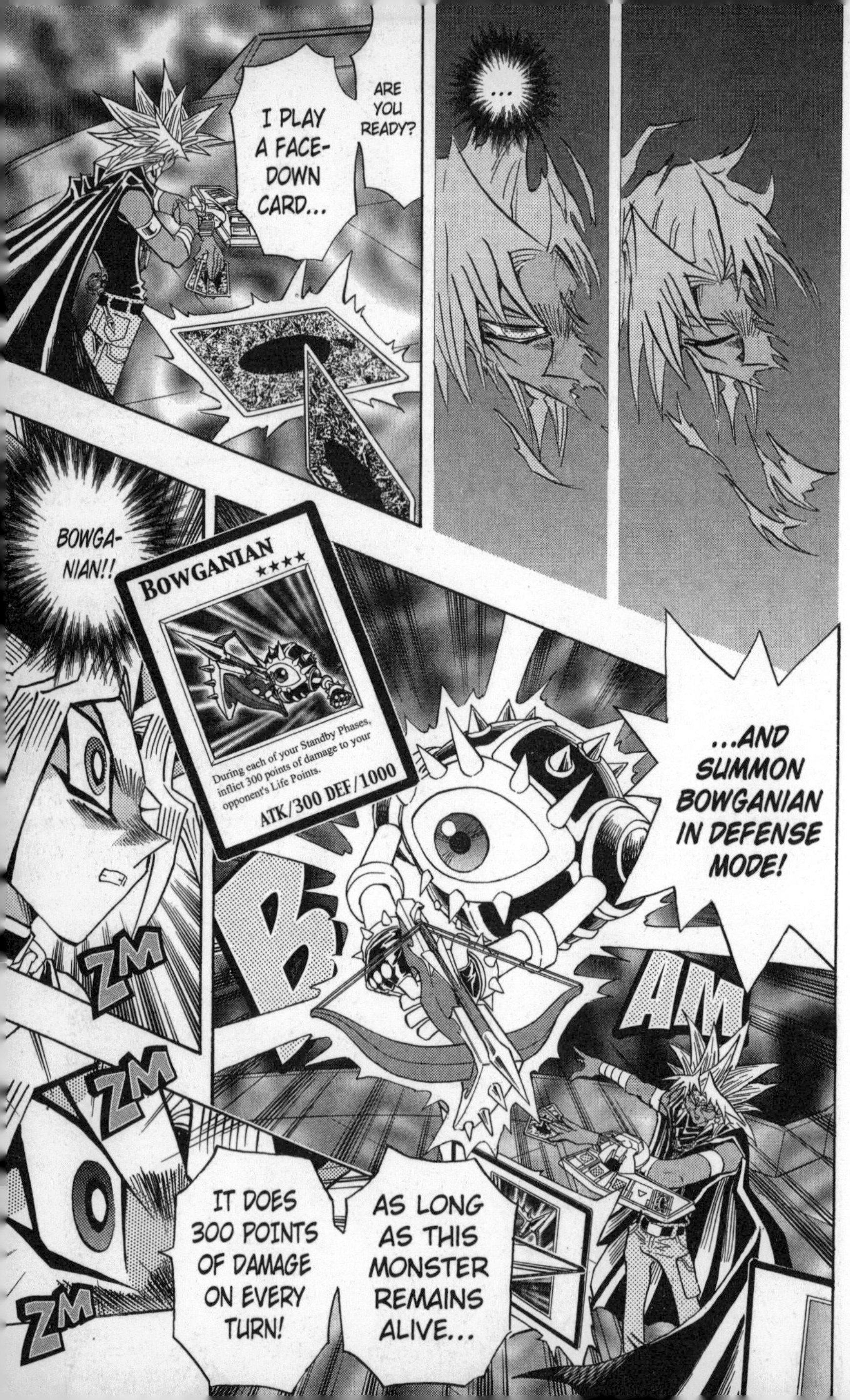
...
ARE YOU READY?
I PLAY A FACE-DOWN CARD...
...AND SUMMON BOWGANIAN IN DEFENSE MODE!
B
AM
BOWGANIAN ★★★★
During each of your Standby Phases, inflict 300 points of damage to your opponent's Life Points.
ATK/300 DEF/1000
BOWGA-NIAN!!
ZM
ZM
ZM
AS LONG AS THIS MONSTER REMAINS ALIVE...
IT DOES 300 POINTS OF DAMAGE ON EVERY TURN!

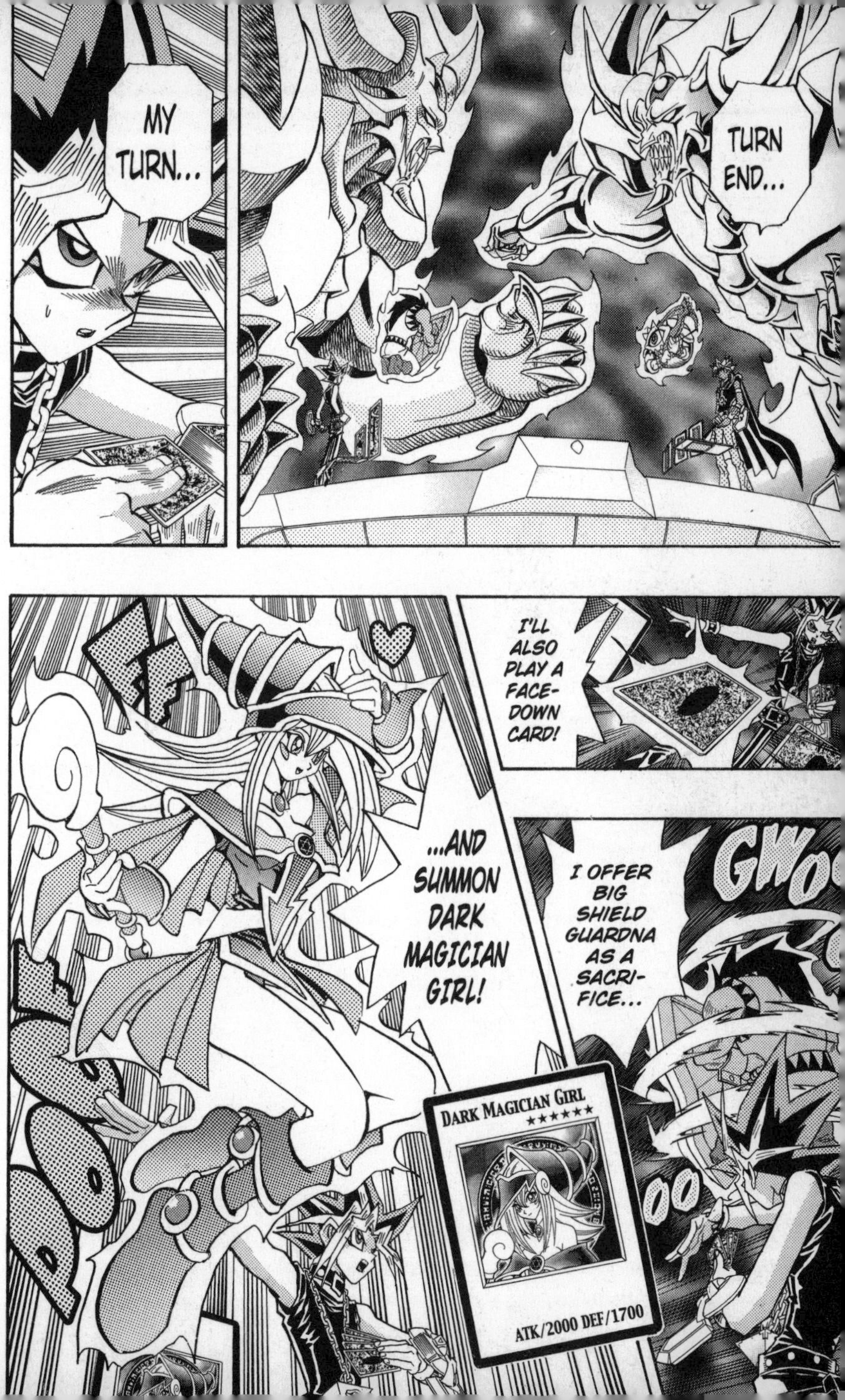
TURN END...
MY TURN...
I'LL ALSO PLAY A FACE-DOWN CARD!
I OFFER BIG SHIELD GUARDNA AS A SACRIFICE...
...AND SUMMON DARK MAGICIAN GIRL!
DARK MAGICIAN GIRL
ATK/2000 DEF/1700

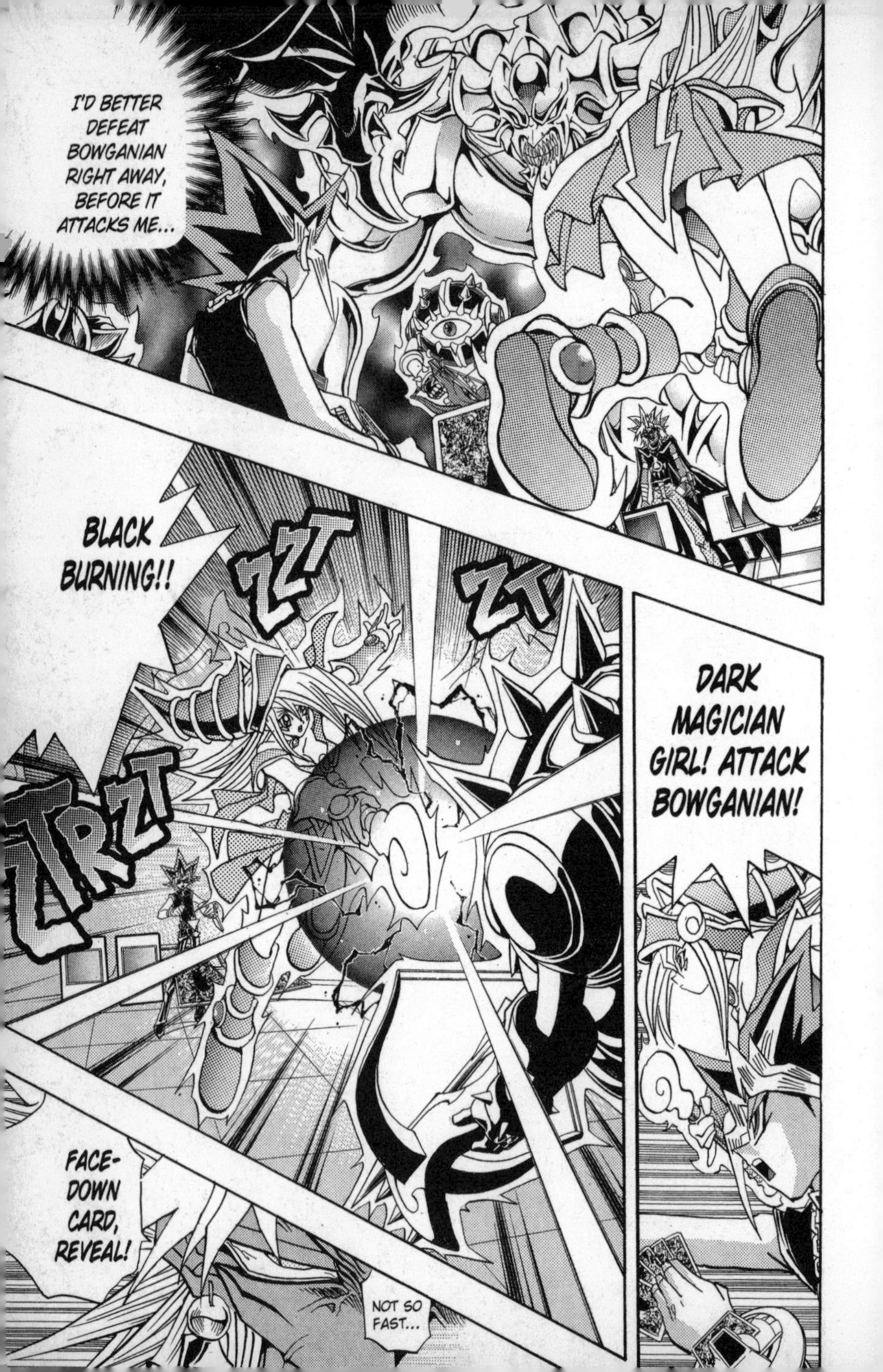
I'D BETTER DEFEAT BOWGANIAN RIGHT AWAY, BEFORE IT ATTACKS ME...
DARK MAGICIAN GIRL! ATTACK BOWGANIAN!
BLACK BURNING!!
ZZT
ZZT
TRZZT
NOT SO FAST...
FACE-DOWN CARD, REVEAL!

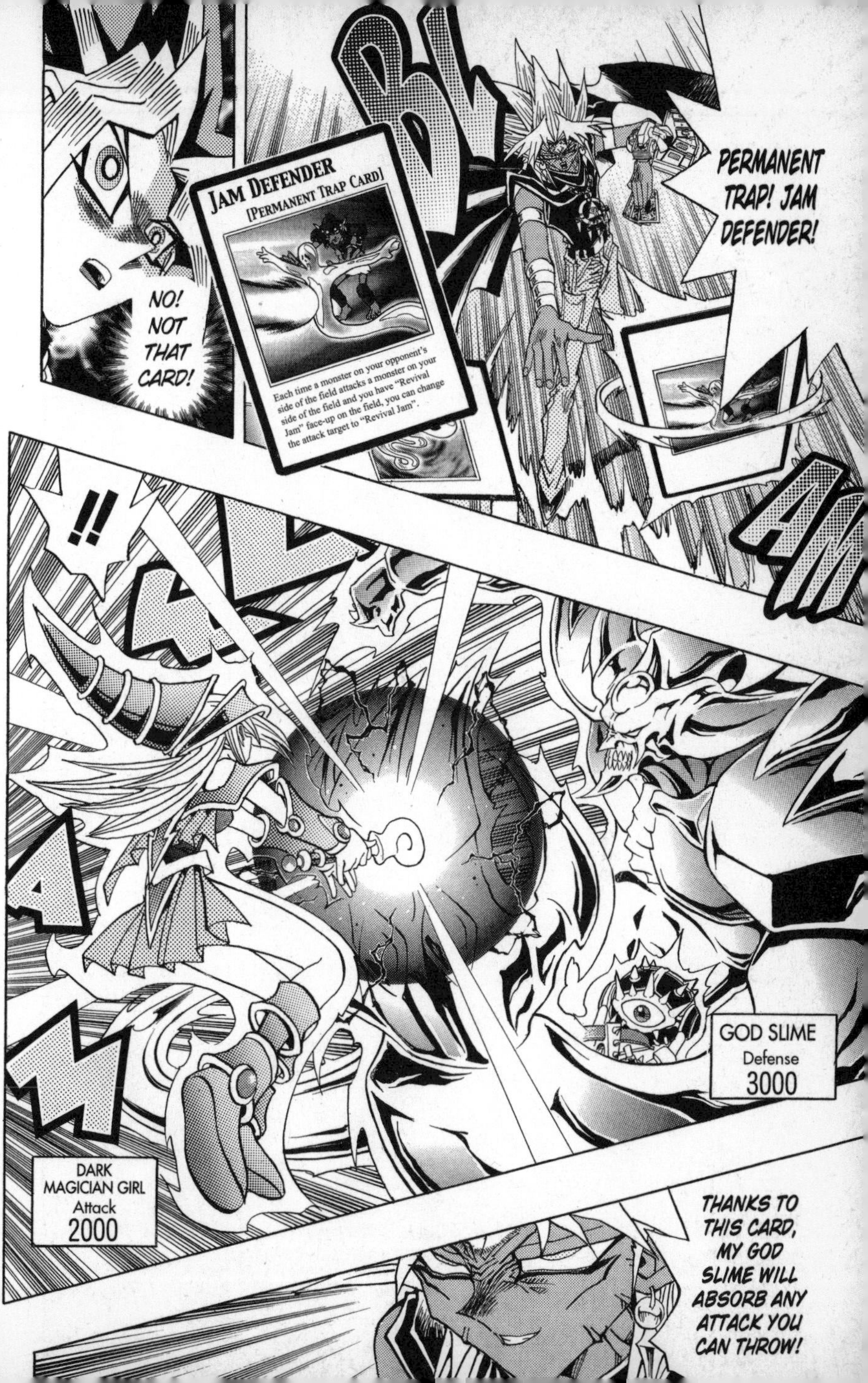
PERMANENT TRAP! JAM DEFENDER!
JAM DEFENDER
[PERMANENT TRAP CARD]
Each time a monster on your opponent's side of the field attacks a monster on your side of the field and you have "Revival Jam" face-up on the field, you can change the attack target to "Revival Jam".
NO! NOT THAT CARD!
!!
GOD SLIME
Defense
3000
DARK MAGICIAN GIRL
Attack
2000
THANKS TO THIS CARD, MY GOD SLIME WILL ABSORB ANY ATTACK YOU CAN THROW!

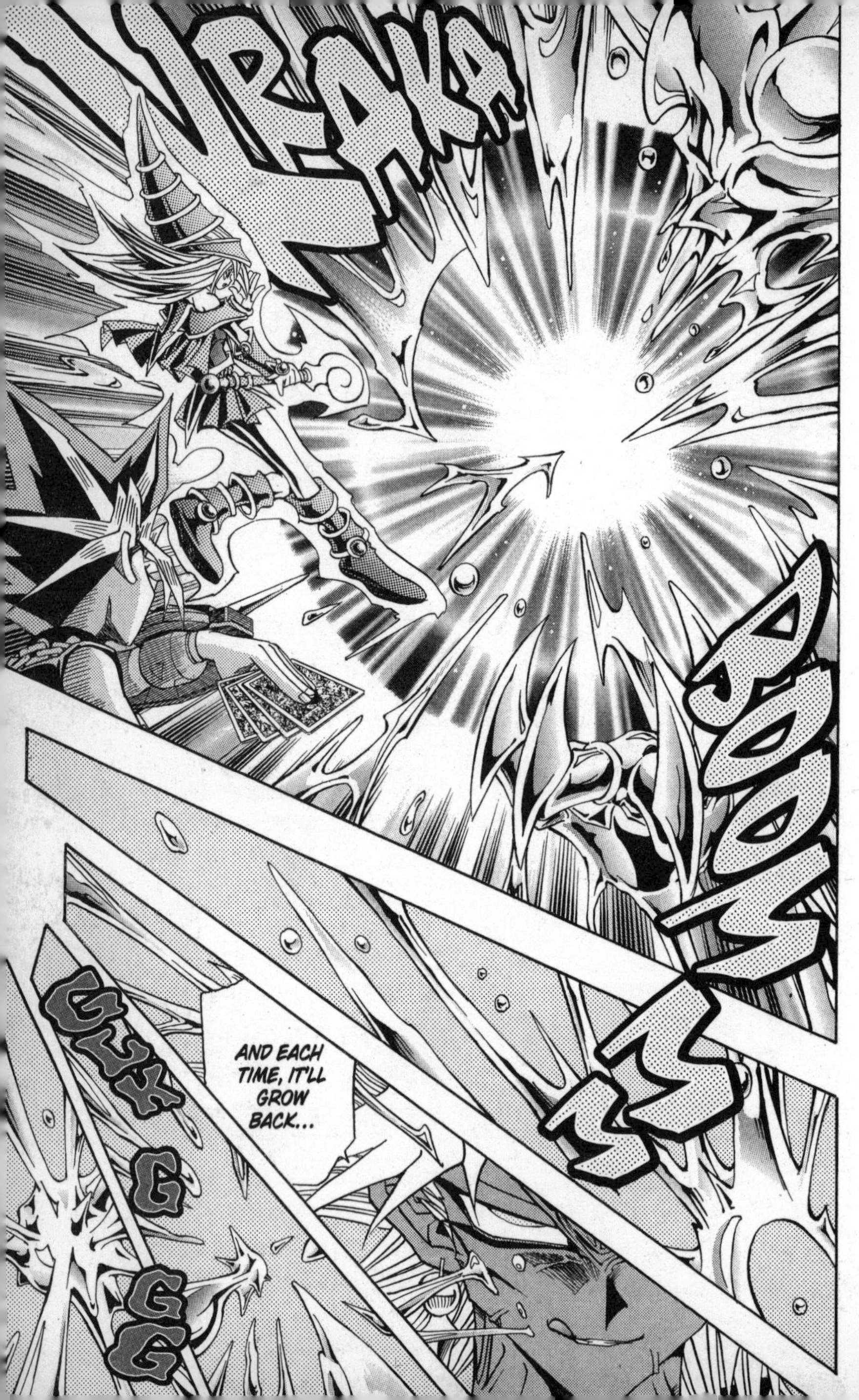
VRAKA
BOOM
AND EACH TIME, IT'LL GROW BACK...
GLK
G
G
G

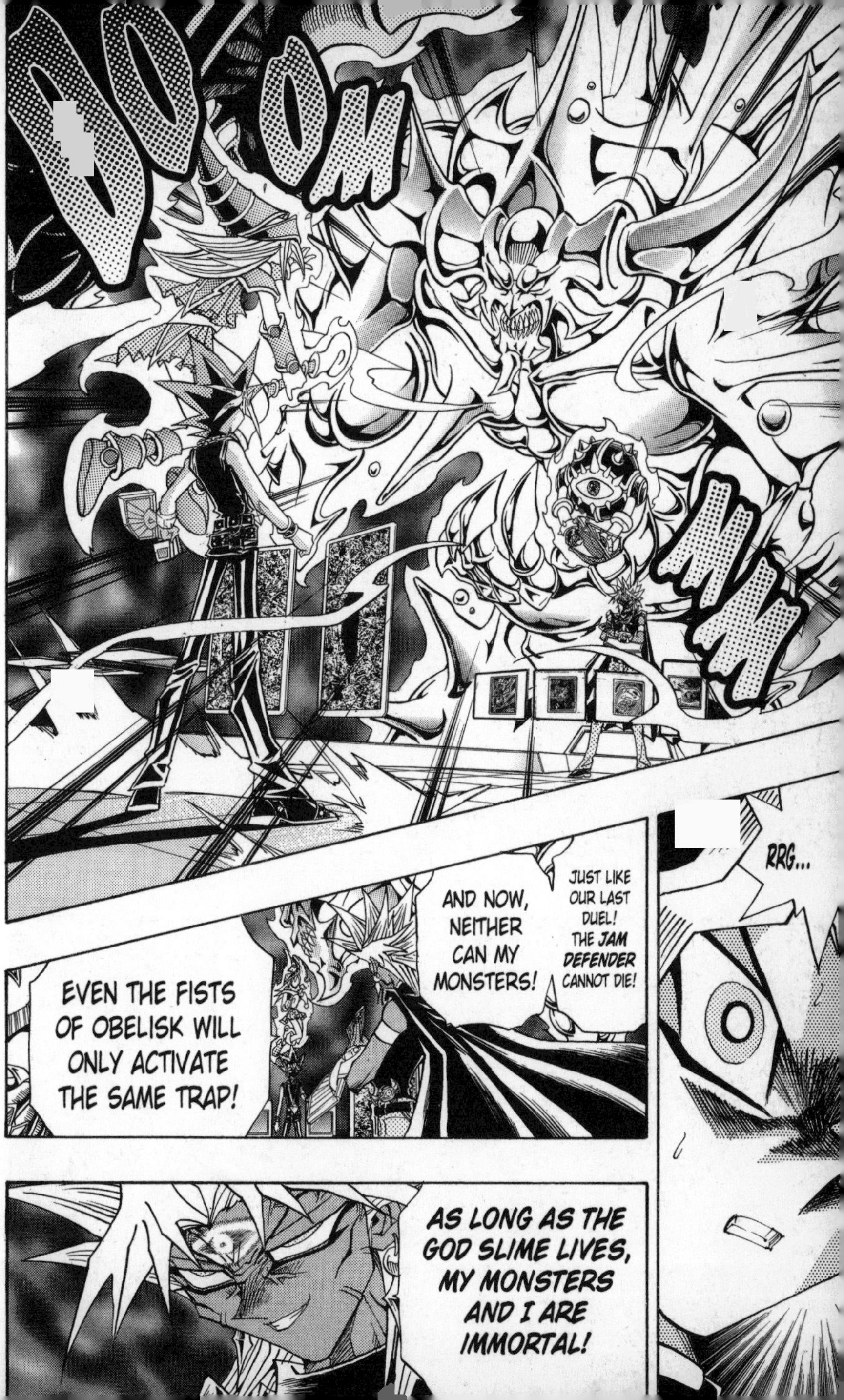
RRG...
JUST LIKE OUR LAST DUEL! THE JAM DEFENDER CANNOT DIE!
AND NOW, NEITHER CAN MY MONSTERS!
EVEN THE FISTS OF OBELISK WILL ONLY ACTIVATE THE SAME TRAP!
AS LONG AS THE GOD SLIME LIVES, MY MONSTERS AND I ARE IMMORTAL!

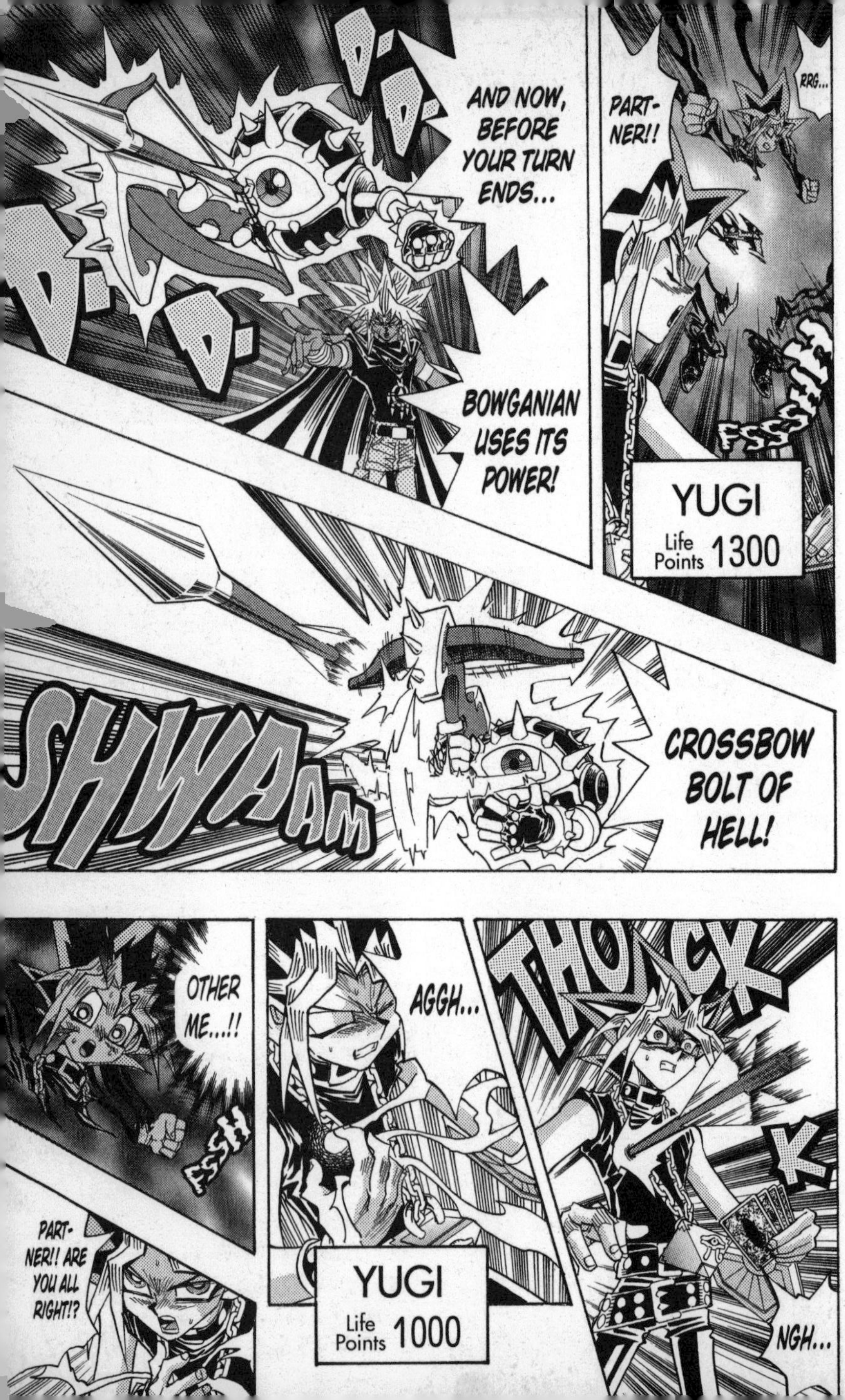
PART-NER!!
RRG...
YUGI
Life Points 1300
AND NOW, BEFORE YOUR TURN ENDS...
BOWGANIAN USES ITS POWER!
SHWAAM
CROSSBOW BOLT OF HELL!
NGH...
AGGH...
YUGI
Life Points 1000
OTHER ME...!!
PART-NER!! ARE YOU ALL RIGHT!?

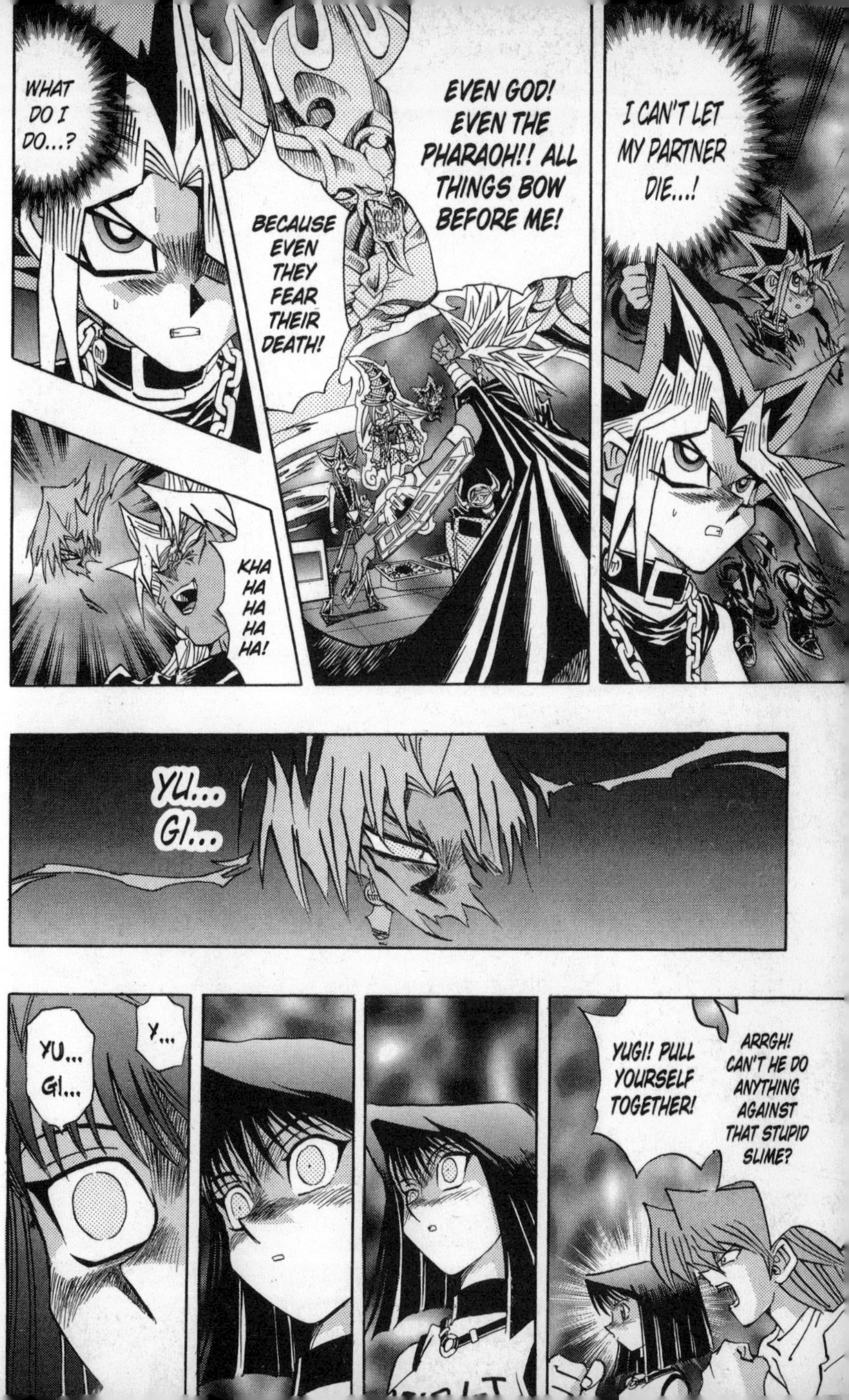
I CAN'T LET MY PARTNER DIE...!
EVEN GOD! EVEN THE PHARAOH!! ALL THINGS BOW BEFORE ME!
BECAUSE EVEN THEY FEAR THEIR DEATH!
WHAT DO I DO...?
KHA HA HA HA HA!
YU... GI...
ARRGH! CAN'T HE DO ANYTHING AGAINST THAT STUPID SLIME?
YUGI! PULL YOURSELF TOGETHER!
Y...
YU... GI...

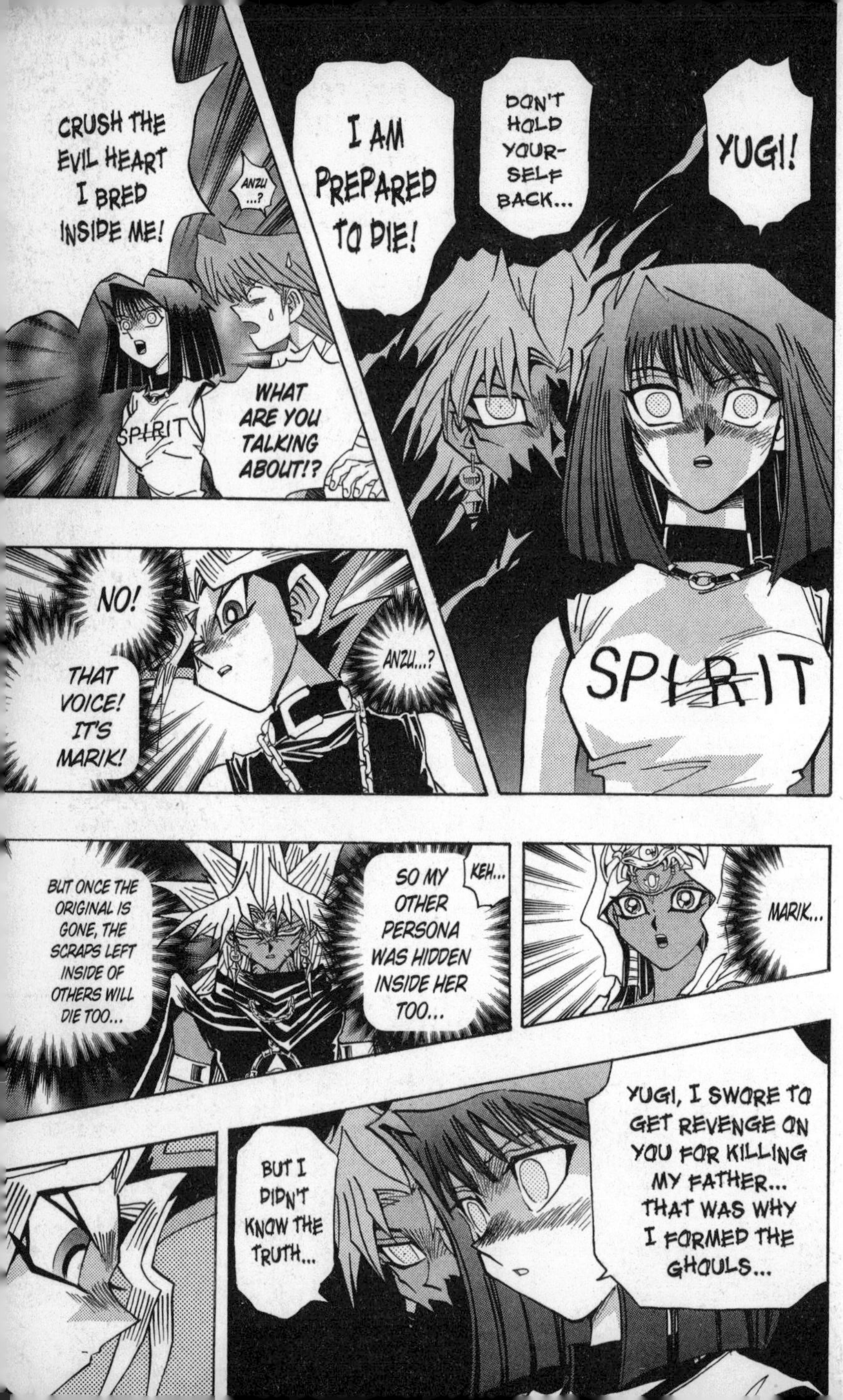
YUGI!!
DON'T HOLD YOURSELF BACK...
I AM PREPARED TO DIE!
CRUSH THE EVIL HEART I BRED INSIDE ME!
ANZU ...?
WHAT ARE YOU TALKING ABOUT!?
SPIRIT
ANZU...?
NO!
THAT VOICE! IT'S MARIK!
MARIK...
KEH...
SO MY OTHER PERSONA WAS HIDDEN INSIDE HER TOO...
BUT ONCE THE ORIGINAL IS GONE, THE SCRAPS LEFT INSIDE OF OTHERS WILL DIE TOO...
YUGI, I SWORE TO GET REVENGE ON YOU FOR KILLING MY FATHER... THAT WAS WHY I FORMED THE GHOULS...
BUT I DIDN'T KNOW THE TRUTH...

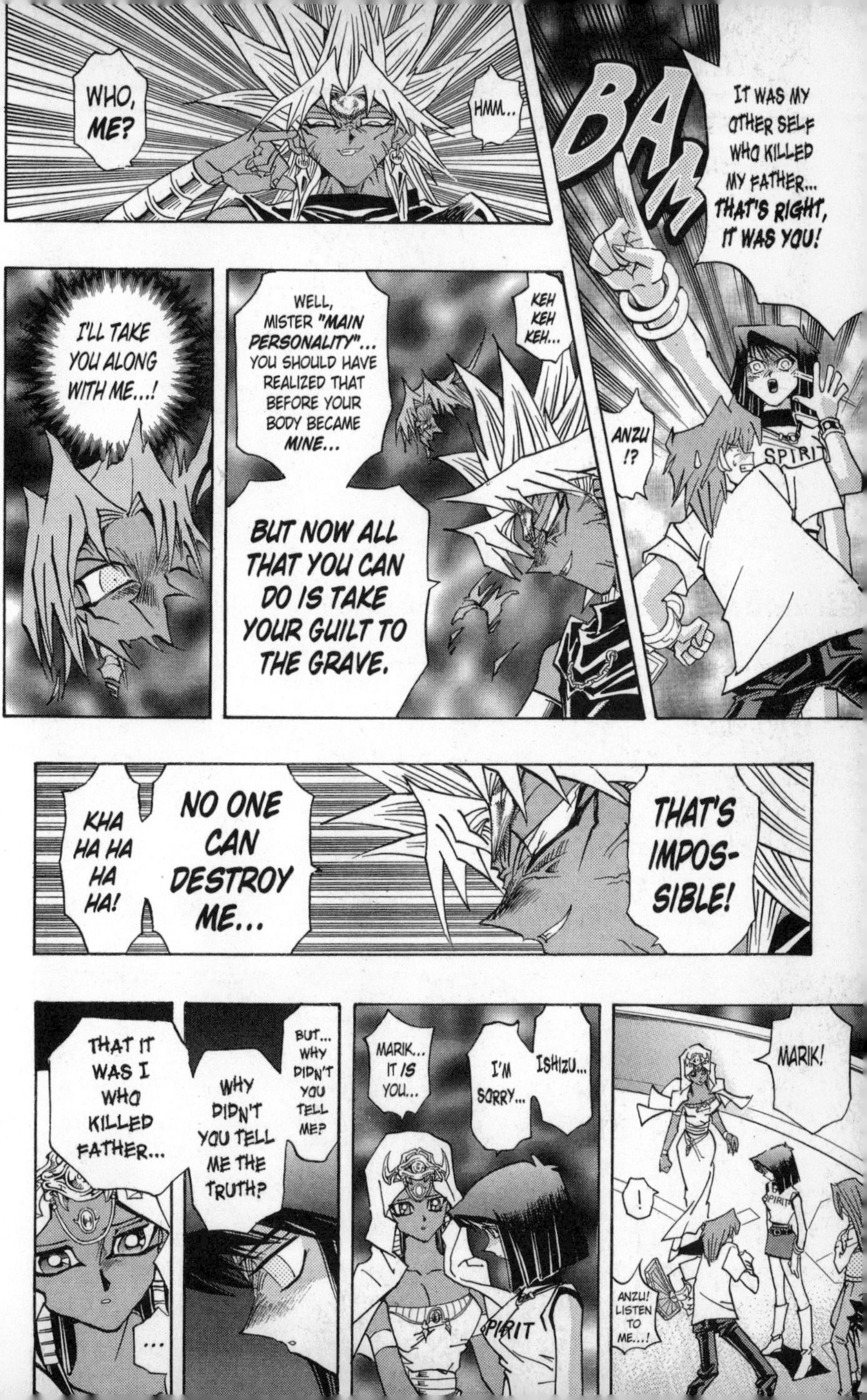
BAM
IT WAS MY OTHER SELF WHO KILLED MY FATHER... THAT'S RIGHT, IT WAS YOU!
SPIRIT
ANZU !?
HMM...
WHO, ME?
KEH KEH KEH...
WELL, MISTER "MAIN PERSONALITY"... YOU SHOULD HAVE REALIZED THAT BEFORE YOUR BODY BECAME MINE...
BUT NOW ALL THAT YOU CAN DO IS TAKE YOUR GUILT TO THE GRAVE.
I'LL TAKE YOU ALONG WITH ME...!
THAT'S IMPOS-SIBLE!
NO ONE CAN DESTROY ME...
KHA HA HA HA HA!
MARIK!
!
SPIRIT
ANZU! LISTEN TO ME...!
ISHIZU...
I'M SORRY...
MARIK... IT IS YOU...
PIRIT
BUT... WHY DIDN'T YOU TELL ME?
WHY DIDN'T YOU TELL ME THE TRUTH?
THAT IT WAS I WHO KILLED FATHER...
...

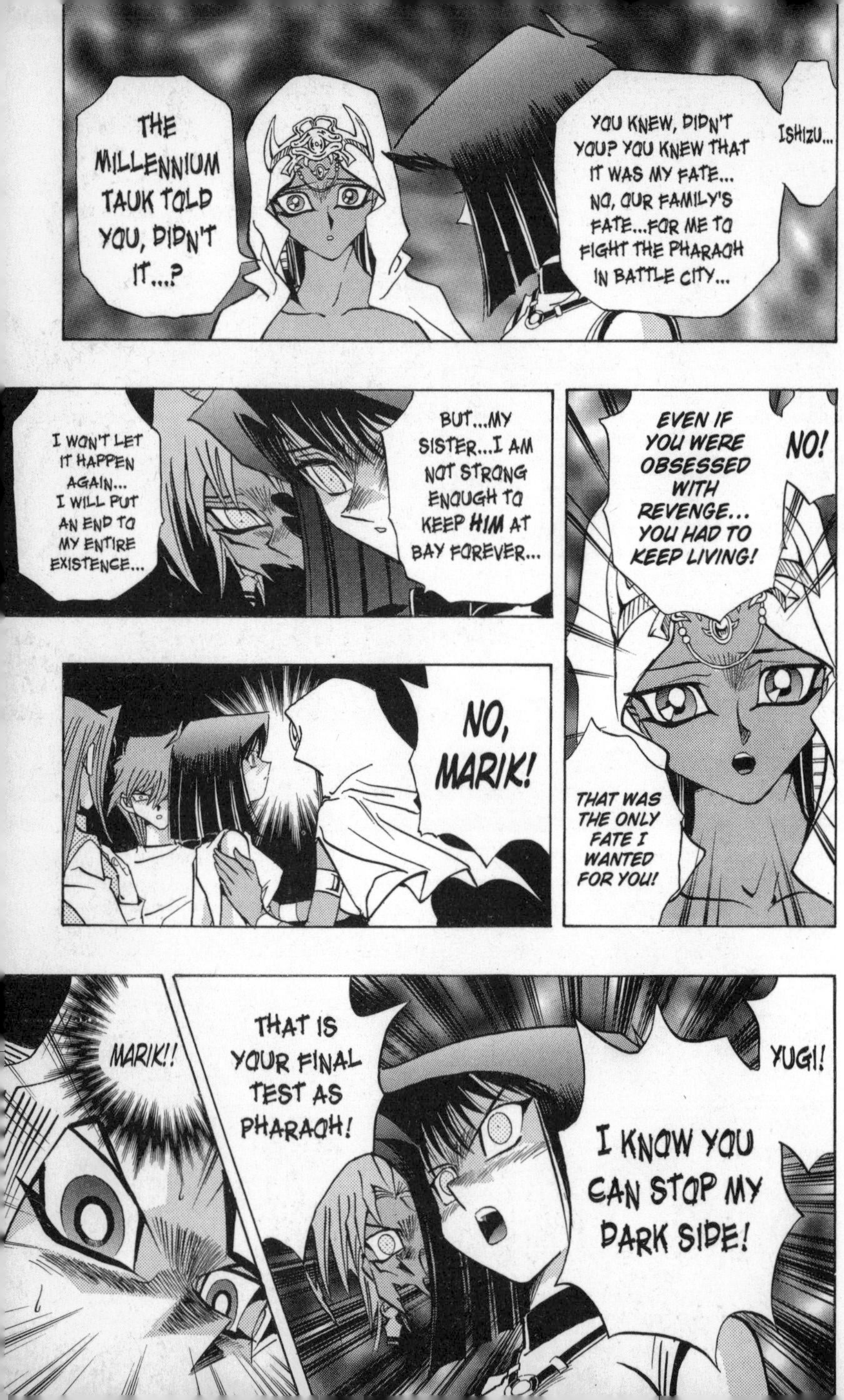
ISHIZU...
YOU KNEW, DIDN'T YOU? YOU KNEW THAT IT WAS MY FATE... NO, OUR FAMILY'S FATE...FOR ME TO FIGHT THE PHARAOH IN BATTLE CITY...
THE MILLENNIUM TAUK TOLD YOU, DIDN'T IT...?
NO!
EVEN IF YOU WERE OBSESSED WITH REVENGE... YOU HAD TO KEEP LIVING!
THAT WAS THE ONLY FATE I WANTED FOR YOU!
BUT...MY SISTER...I AM NOT STRONG ENOUGH TO KEEP HIM AT BAY FOREVER...
I WON'T LET IT HAPPEN AGAIN... I WILL PUT AN END TO MY ENTIRE EXISTENCE...
NO, MARIK!
YUGI!
I KNOW YOU CAN STOP MY DARK SIDE!
THAT IS YOUR FINAL TEST AS PHARAOH!
MARIK!!

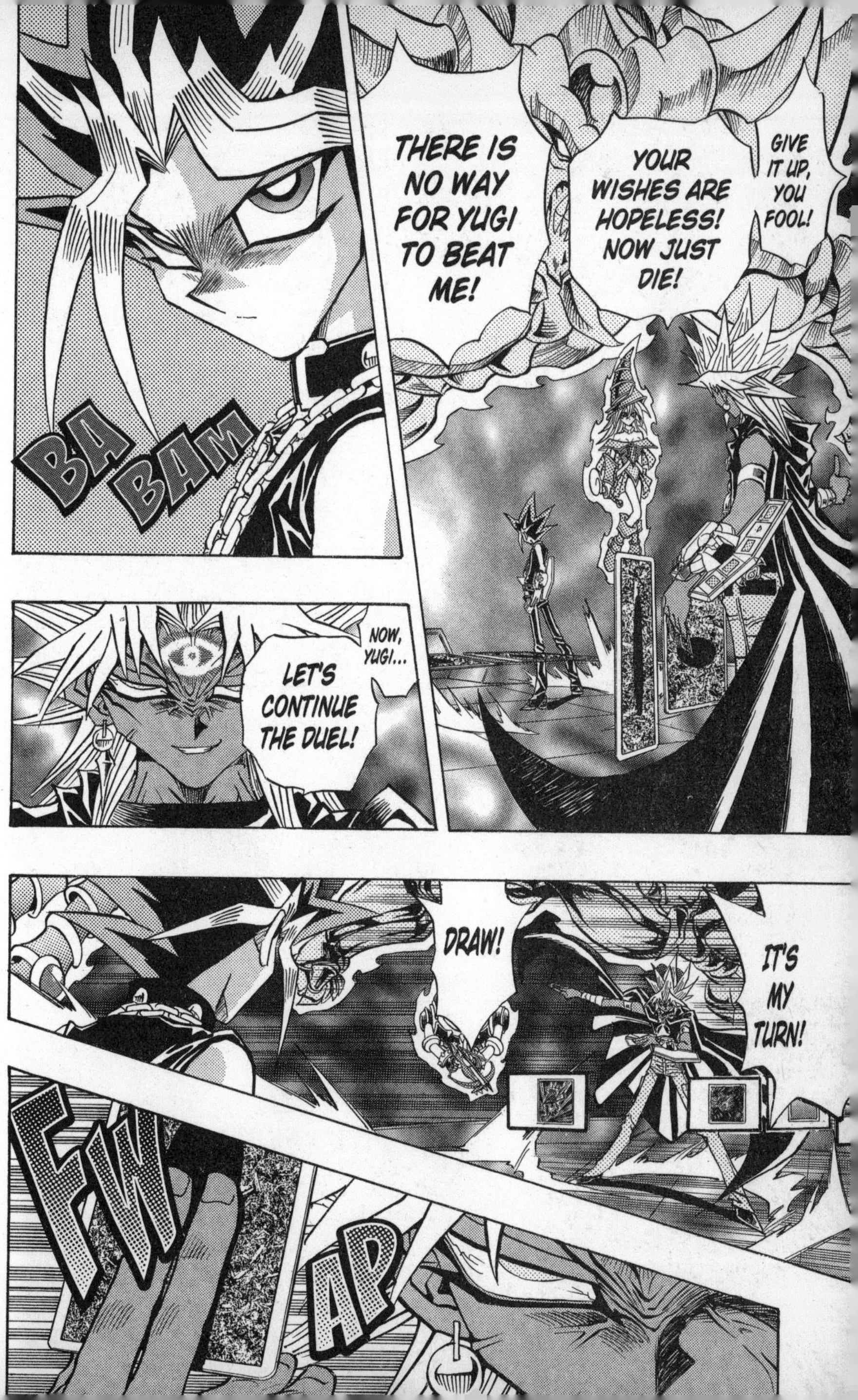
GIVE IT UP, YOU FOOL!
YOUR WISHES ARE HOPELESS! NOW JUST DIE!
THERE IS NO WAY FOR YUGI TO BEAT ME!
BA BAM
NOW, YUGI...
LET'S CONTINUE THE DUEL!
IT'S MY TURN!
DRAW!
FWAP

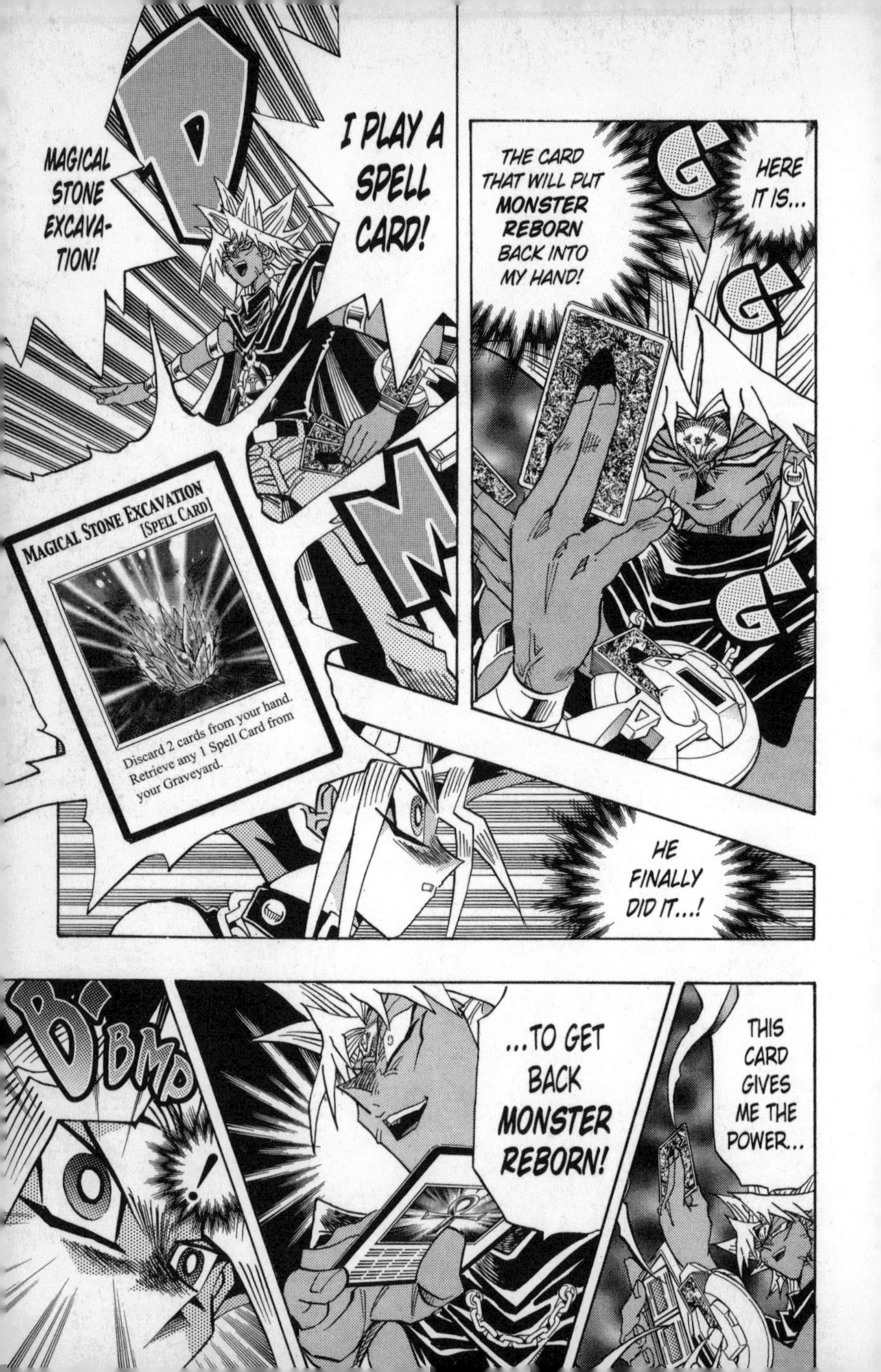
HERE IT IS...
THE CARD THAT WILL PUT MONSTER REBORN BACK INTO MY HAND!
G G G
I PLAY A SPELL CARD!
MAGICAL STONE EXCAVATION!
MAGICAL STONE EXCAVATION
[SPELL CARD]
Discard 2 cards from your hand. Retrieve any 1 Spell Card from your Graveyard.
HE FINALLY DID IT...!
THIS CARD GIVES ME THE POWER...
...TO GET BACK MONSTER REBORN!
BDMP
!

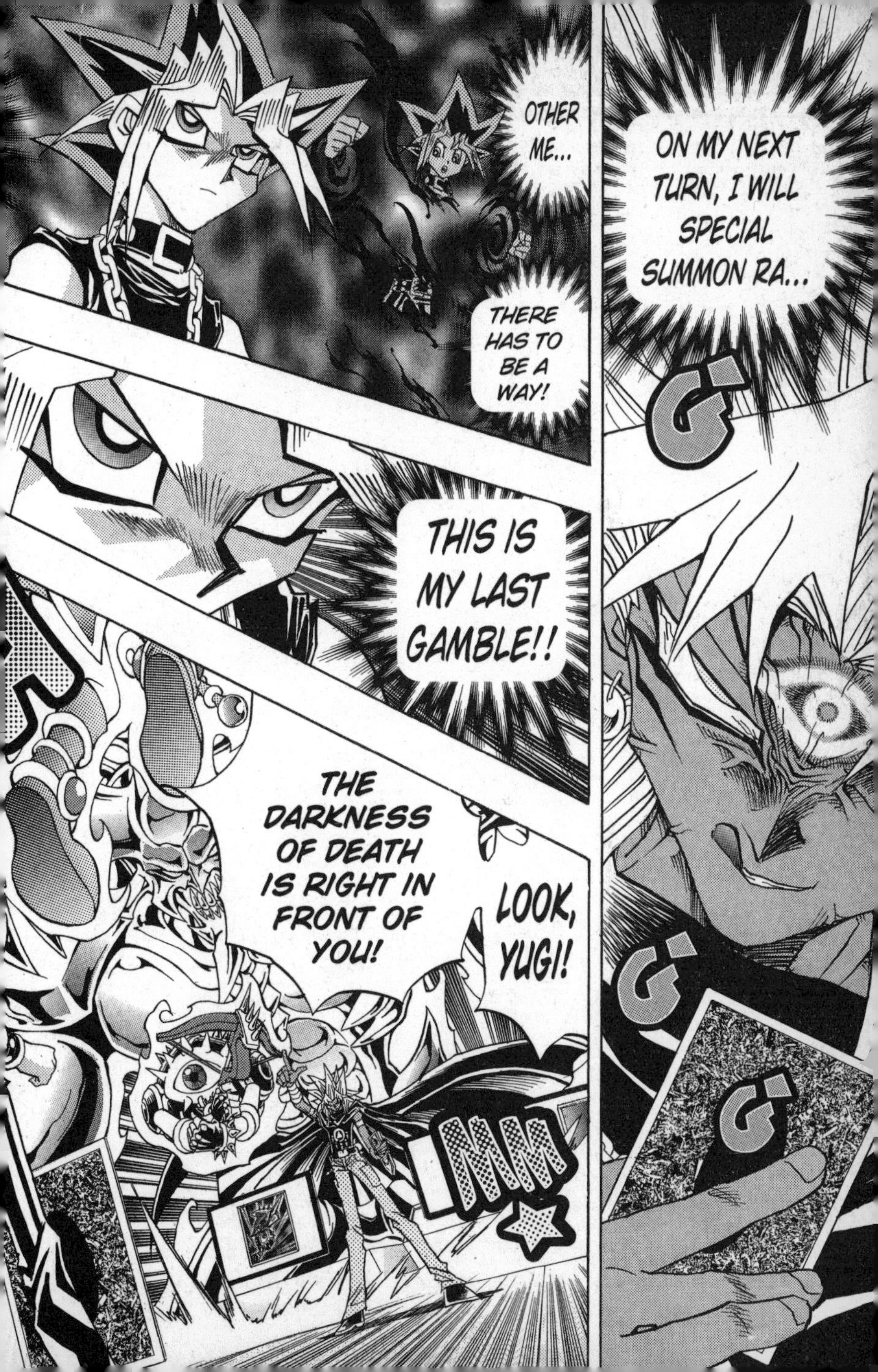
ON MY NEXT TURN, I WILL SPECIAL SUMMON RA...
G
G
G
OTHER ME...
THERE HAS TO BE A WAY!
THIS IS MY LAST GAMBLE!!
LOOK, YUGI!
THE DARKNESS OF DEATH IS RIGHT IN FRONT OF YOU!
MM

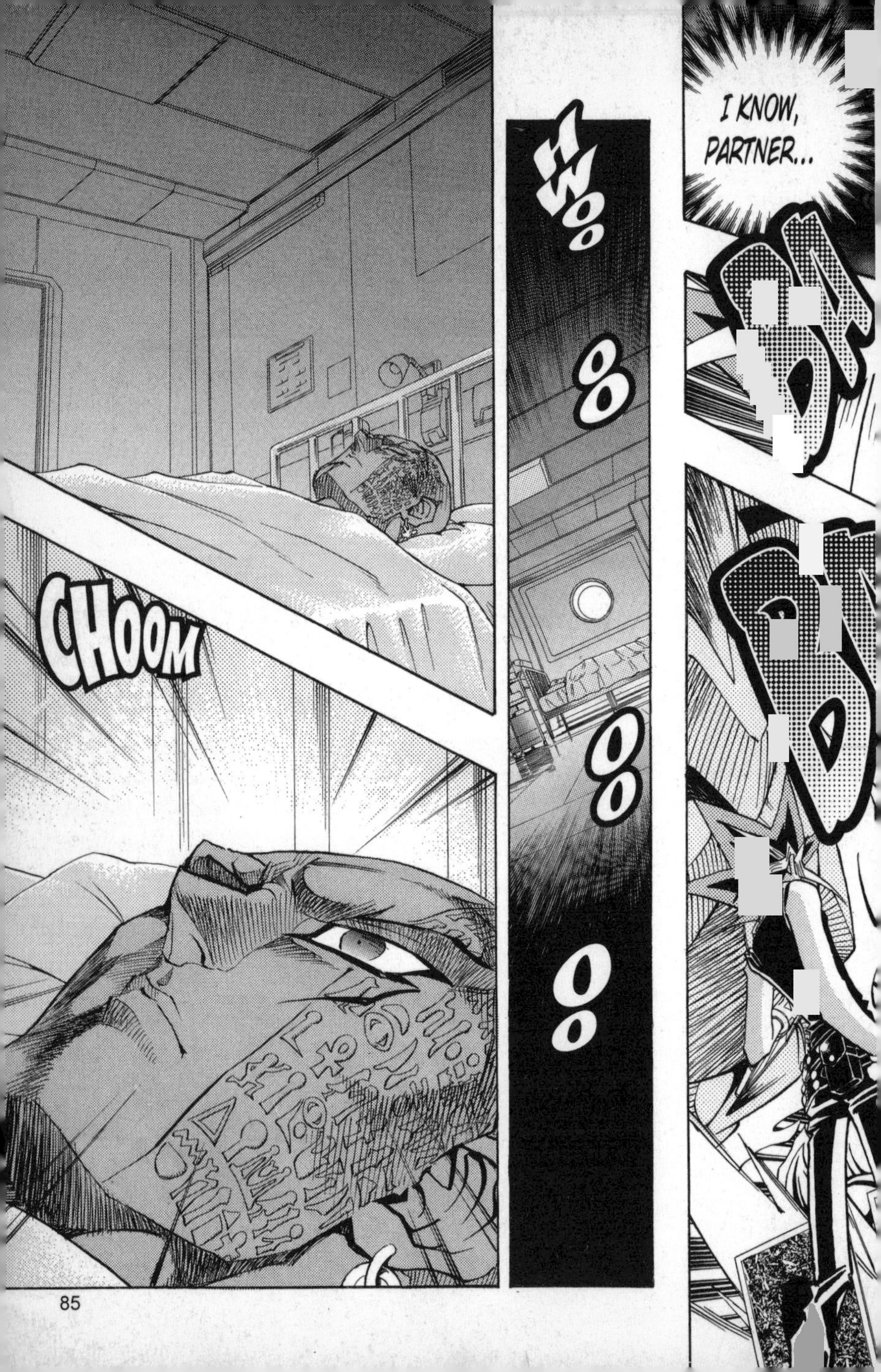
I KNOW, PARTNER...
CHOOM

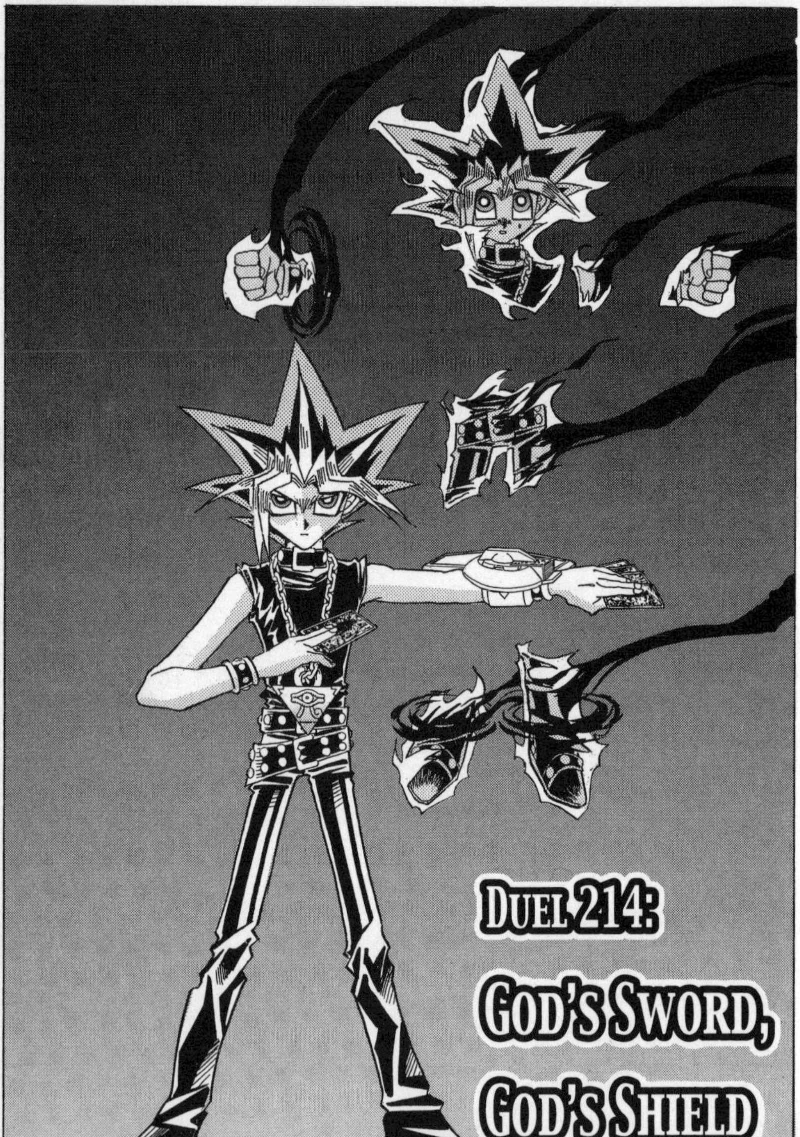
Duel 214:
God's Sword,
God's Shield

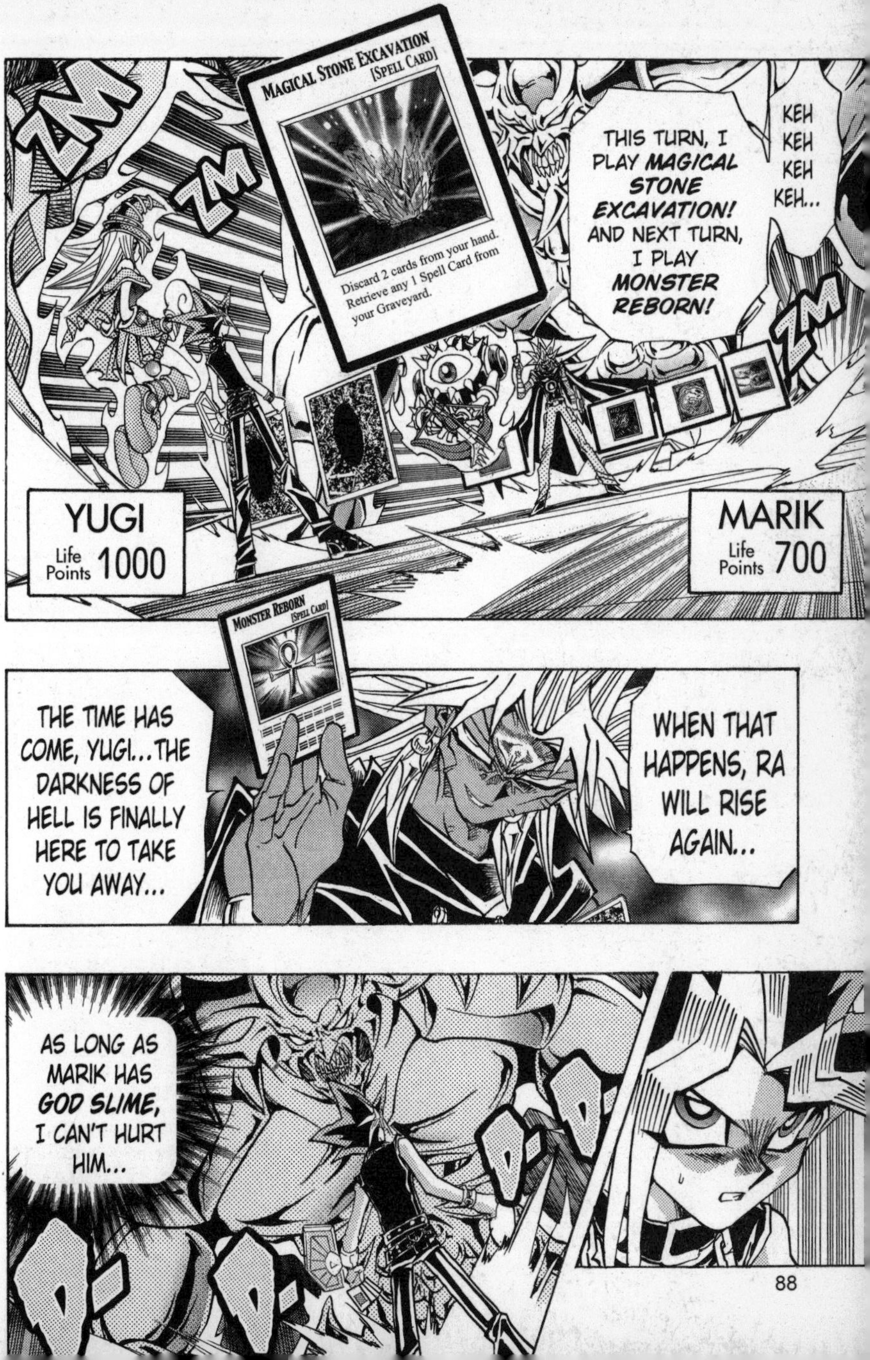
KEH KEH KEH KEH...
THIS TURN, I PLAY MAGICAL STONE EXCAVATION! AND NEXT TURN, I PLAY MONSTER REBORN!
MAGICAL STONE EXCAVATION [SPELL CARD]
Discard 2 cards from your hand. Retrieve any 1 Spell Card from your Graveyard.
ZM
ZM
ZM
MARIK Life Points 700
YUGI Life Points 1000
MONSTER REBORN [SPELL CARD]
WHEN THAT HAPPENS, RA WILL RISE AGAIN...
THE TIME HAS COME, YUGI...THE DARKNESS OF HELL IS FINALLY HERE TO TAKE YOU AWAY...
AS LONG AS MARIK HAS GOD SLIME, I CAN'T HURT HIM...

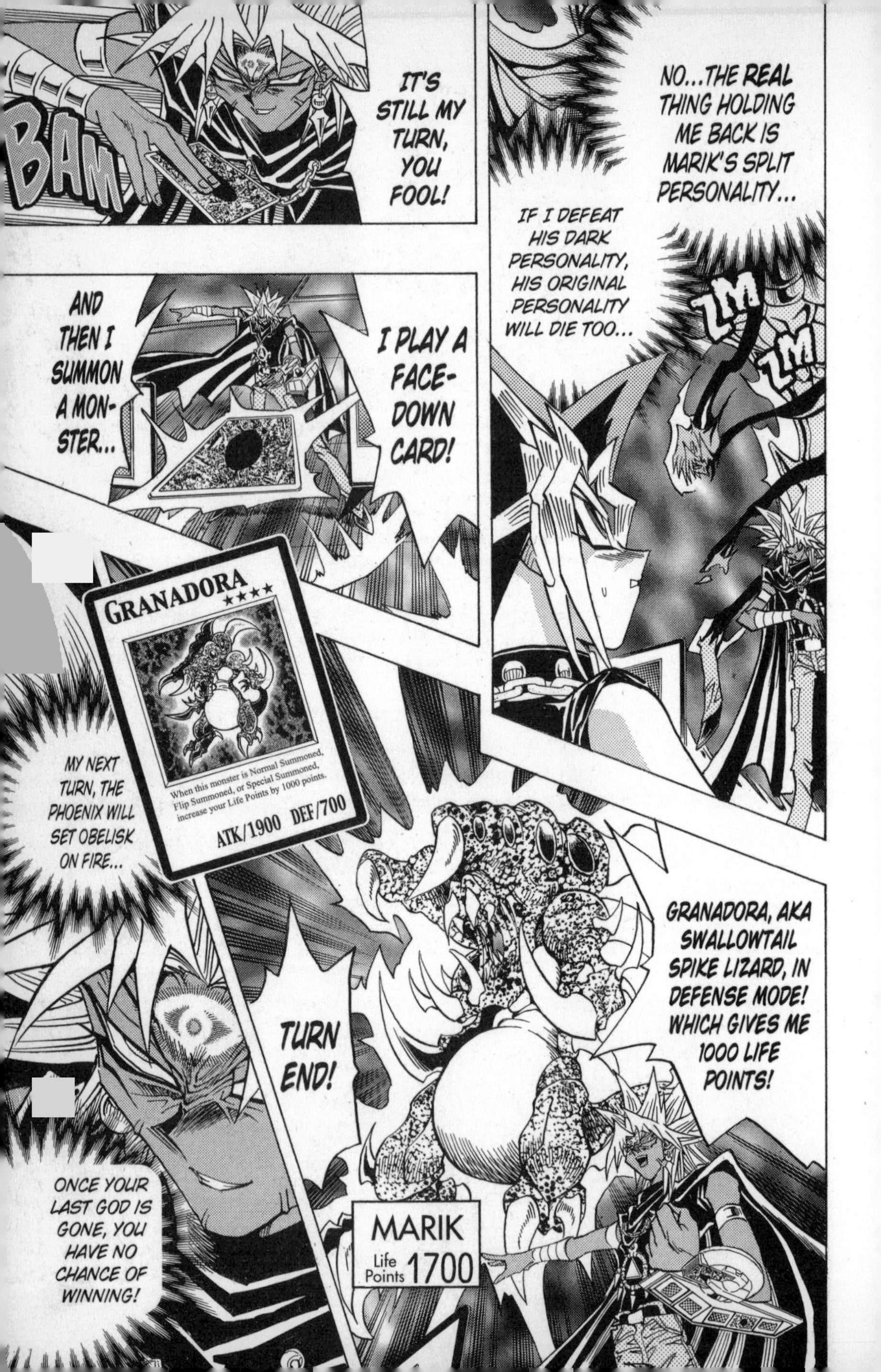
NO...THE REAL THING HOLDING ME BACK IS MARIK'S SPLIT PERSONALITY...
IF I DEFEAT HIS DARK PERSONALITY, HIS ORIGINAL PERSONALITY WILL DIE TOO...
ZM
ZM
IT'S STILL MY TURN, YOU FOOL!
BAM
I PLAY A FACE-DOWN CARD!
AND THEN I SUMMON A MON-STER...
GRANADORA ★★★★
When this monster is Normal Summoned, Flip Summoned, or Special Summoned, increase your Life Points by 1000 points.
ATK/1900 DEF/700
GRANADORA, AKA SWALLOWTAIL SPIKE LIZARD, IN DEFENSE MODE! WHICH GIVES ME 1000 LIFE POINTS!
TURN END!
MARIK
Life Points 1700
MY NEXT TURN, THE PHOENIX WILL SET OBELISK ON FIRE...
ONCE YOUR LAST GOD IS GONE, YOU HAVE NO CHANCE OF WINNING!

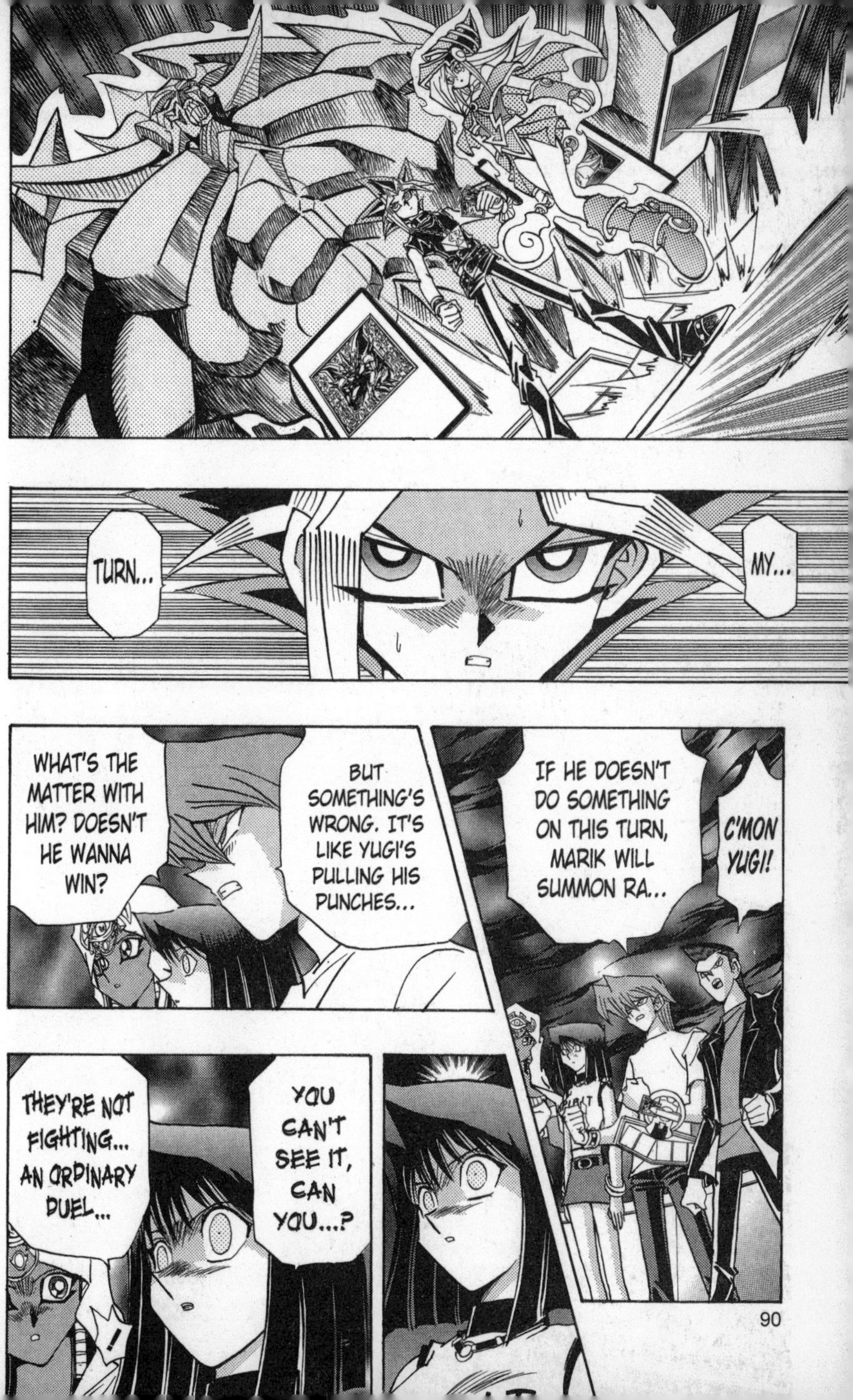
MY...
TURN...
C'MON YUGI!
IF HE DOESN'T DO SOMETHING ON THIS TURN, MARIK WILL SUMMON RA...
BUT SOMETHING'S WRONG. IT'S LIKE YUGI'S PULLING HIS PUNCHES...
WHAT'S THE MATTER WITH HIM? DOESN'T HE WANNA WIN?
YOU CAN'T SEE IT, CAN YOU...?
THEY'RE NOT FIGHTING... AN ORDINARY DUEL...
!

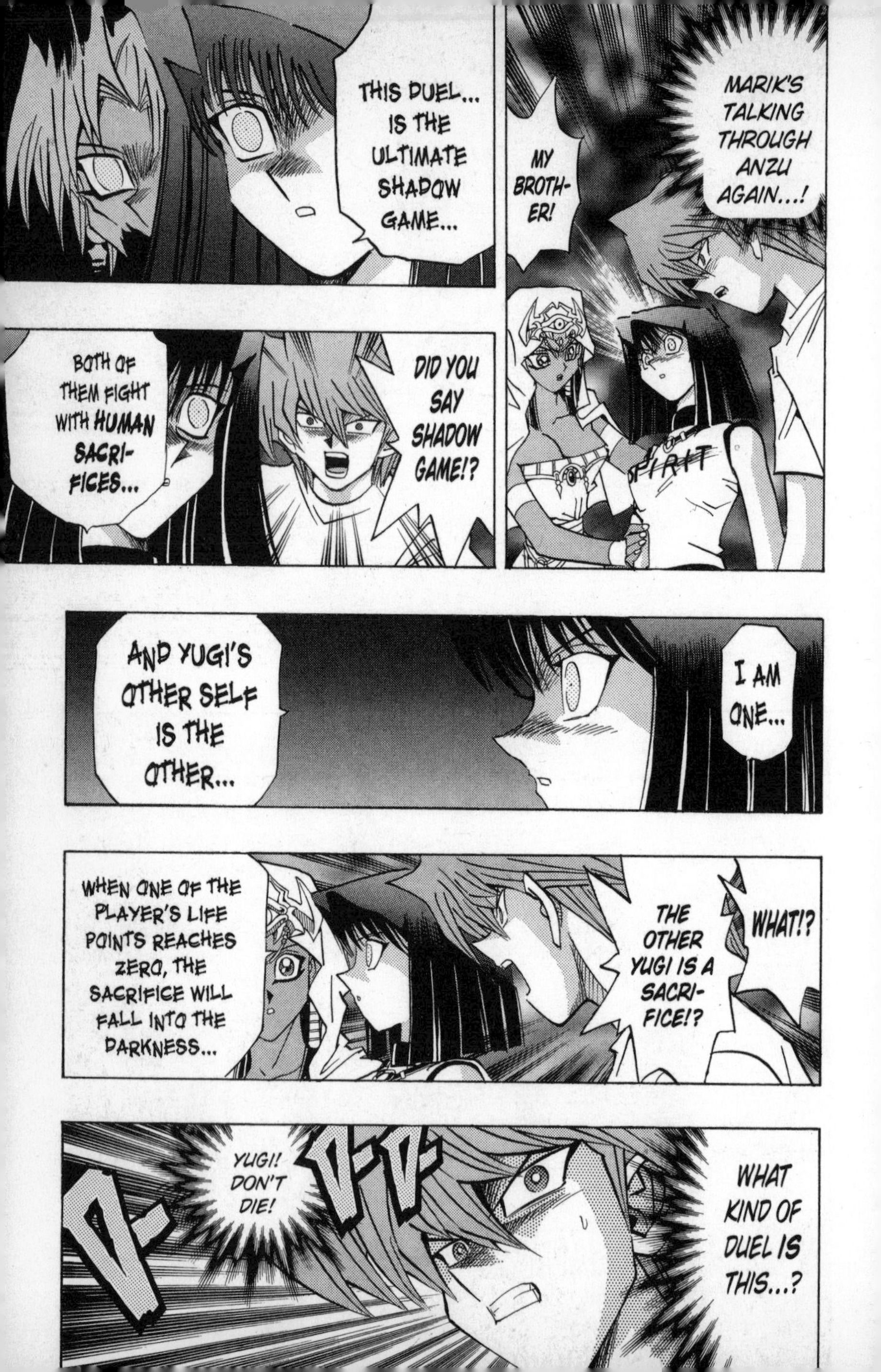
MARIK'S TALKING THROUGH ANZU AGAIN...!
MY BROTHER!
THIS DUEL... IS THE ULTIMATE SHADOW GAME...
DID YOU SAY SHADOW GAME!?
BOTH OF THEM FIGHT WITH HUMAN SACRIFICES...
I AM ONE...
AND YUGI'S OTHER SELF IS THE OTHER...
WHAT!?
THE OTHER YUGI IS A SACRIFICE!?
WHEN ONE OF THE PLAYER'S LIFE POINTS REACHES ZERO, THE SACRIFICE WILL FALL INTO THE DARKNESS...
WHAT KIND OF DUEL IS THIS...?
YUGI! DON'T DIE!

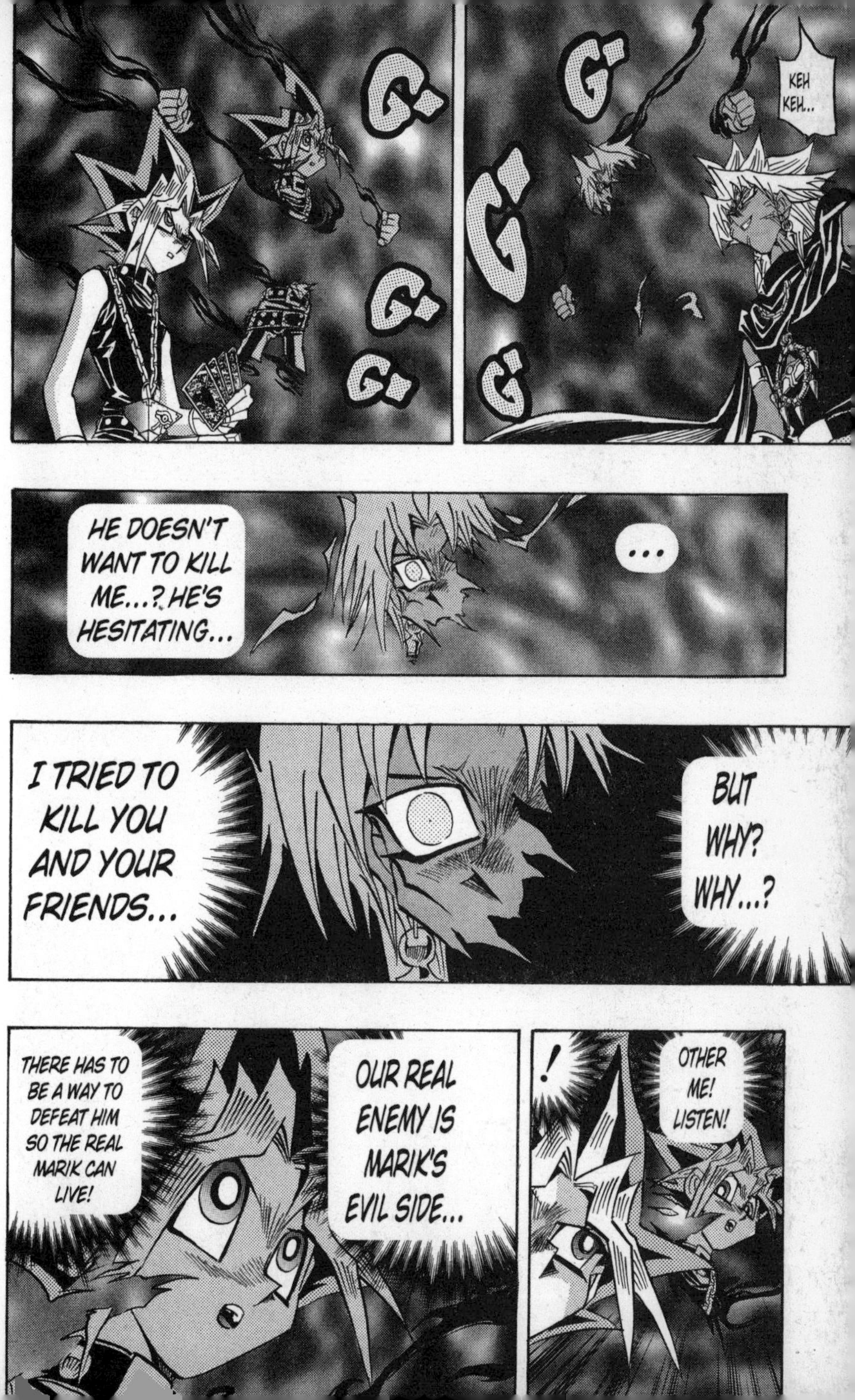
KEH KEH...
G
G
G
G
G
G
...
HE DOESN'T WANT TO KILL ME...? HE'S HESITATING...
I TRIED TO KILL YOU AND YOUR FRIENDS...
BUT WHY? WHY...?
OTHER ME! LISTEN!
!
OUR REAL ENEMY IS MARIK'S EVIL SIDE...
THERE HAS TO BE A WAY TO DEFEAT HIM SO THE REAL MARIK CAN LIVE!

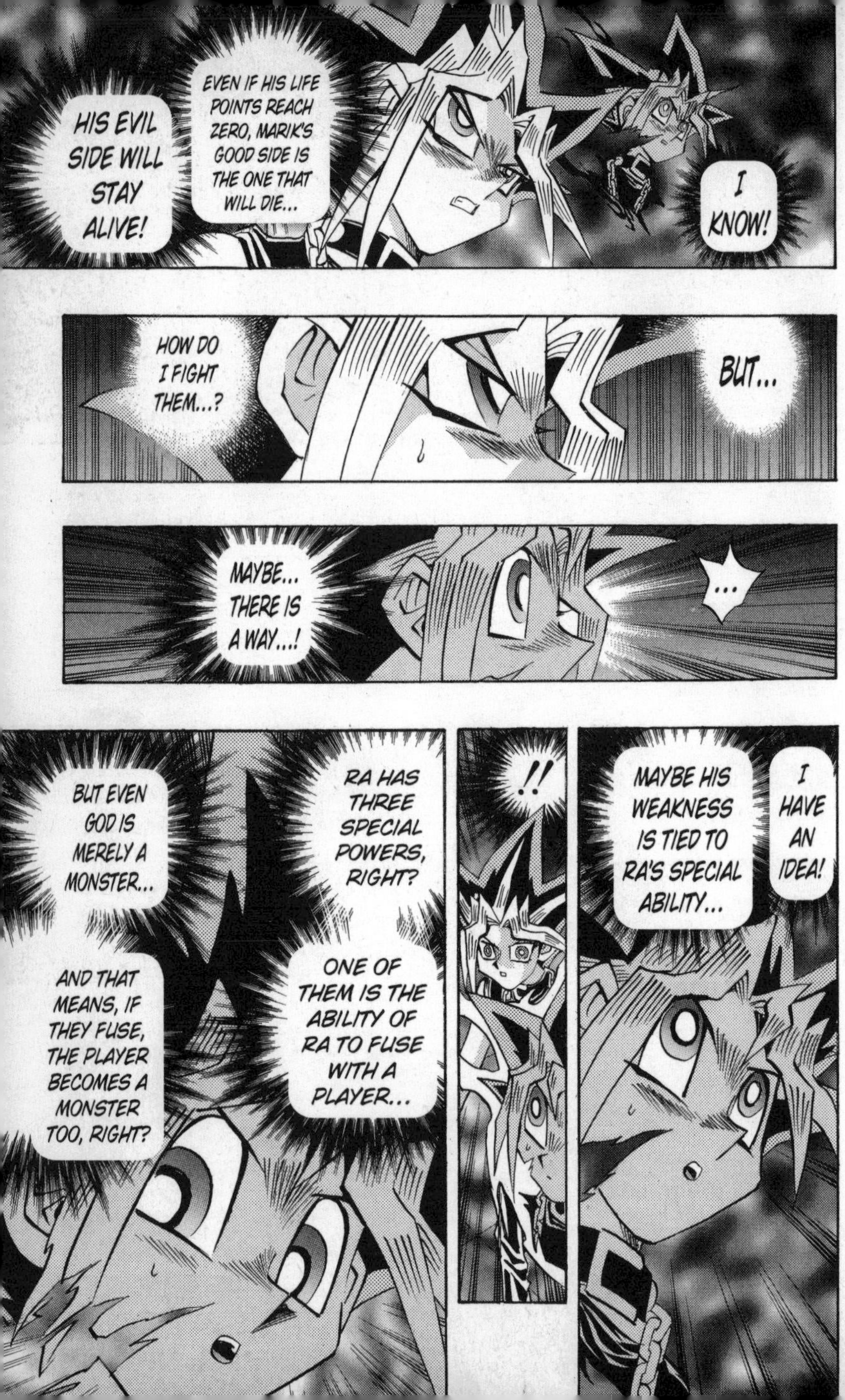
I KNOW!
EVEN IF HIS LIFE POINTS REACH ZERO, MARIK'S GOOD SIDE IS THE ONE THAT WILL DIE...
HIS EVIL SIDE WILL STAY ALIVE!
BUT...
HOW DO I FIGHT THEM...?
...
MAYBE... THERE IS A WAY...!
I HAVE AN IDEA!
MAYBE HIS WEAKNESS IS TIED TO RA'S SPECIAL ABILITY...
!!
RA HAS THREE SPECIAL POWERS, RIGHT?
BUT EVEN GOD IS MERELY A MONSTER...
ONE OF THEM IS THE ABILITY OF RA TO FUSE WITH A PLAYER...
AND THAT MEANS, IF THEY FUSE, THE PLAYER BECOMES A MONSTER TOO, RIGHT?

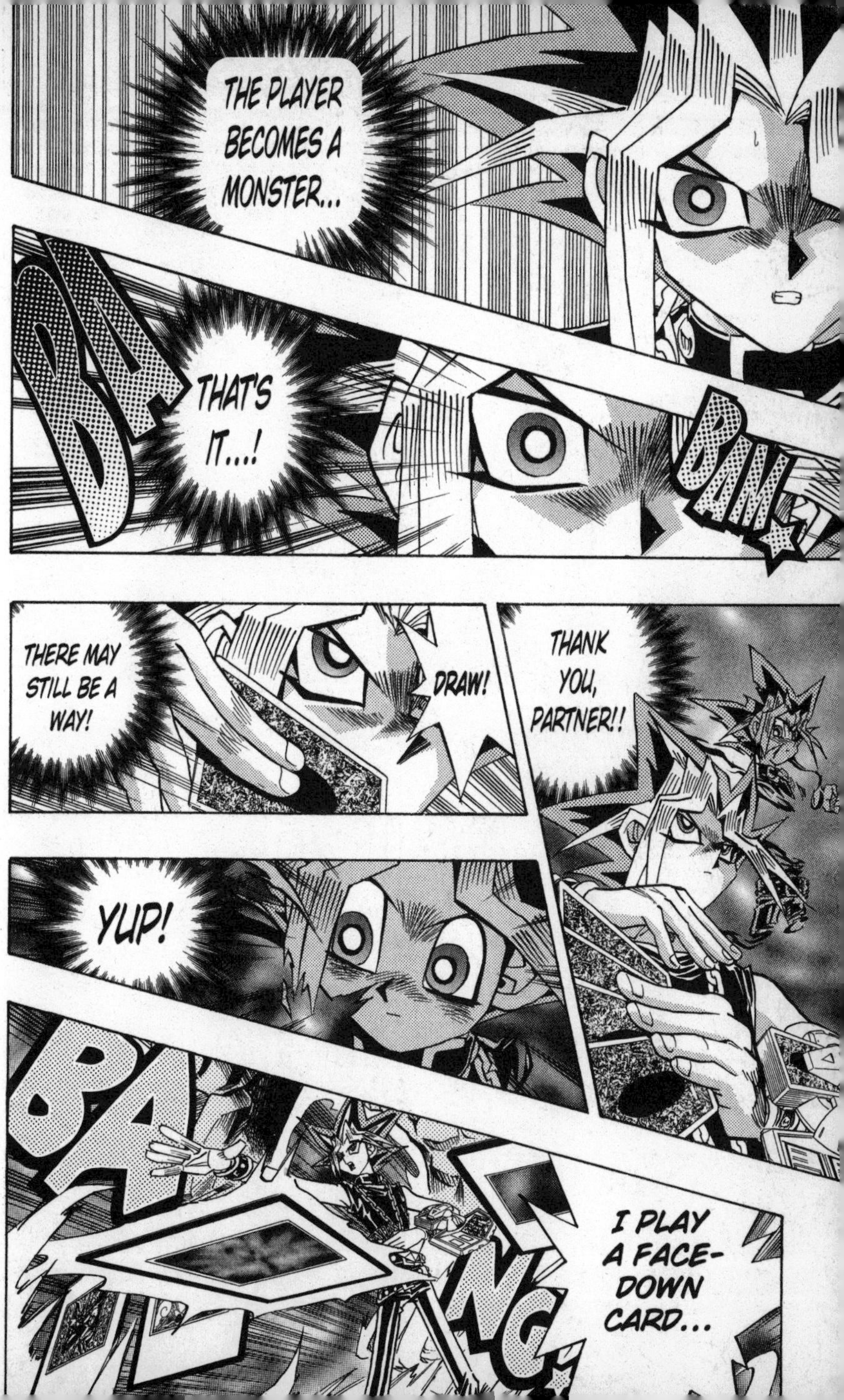
THE PLAYER BECOMES A MONSTER...
BAM
THAT'S IT...!
THANK YOU, PARTNER!!
DRAW!
THERE MAY STILL BE A WAY!
YUP!
I PLAY A FACE-DOWN CARD...

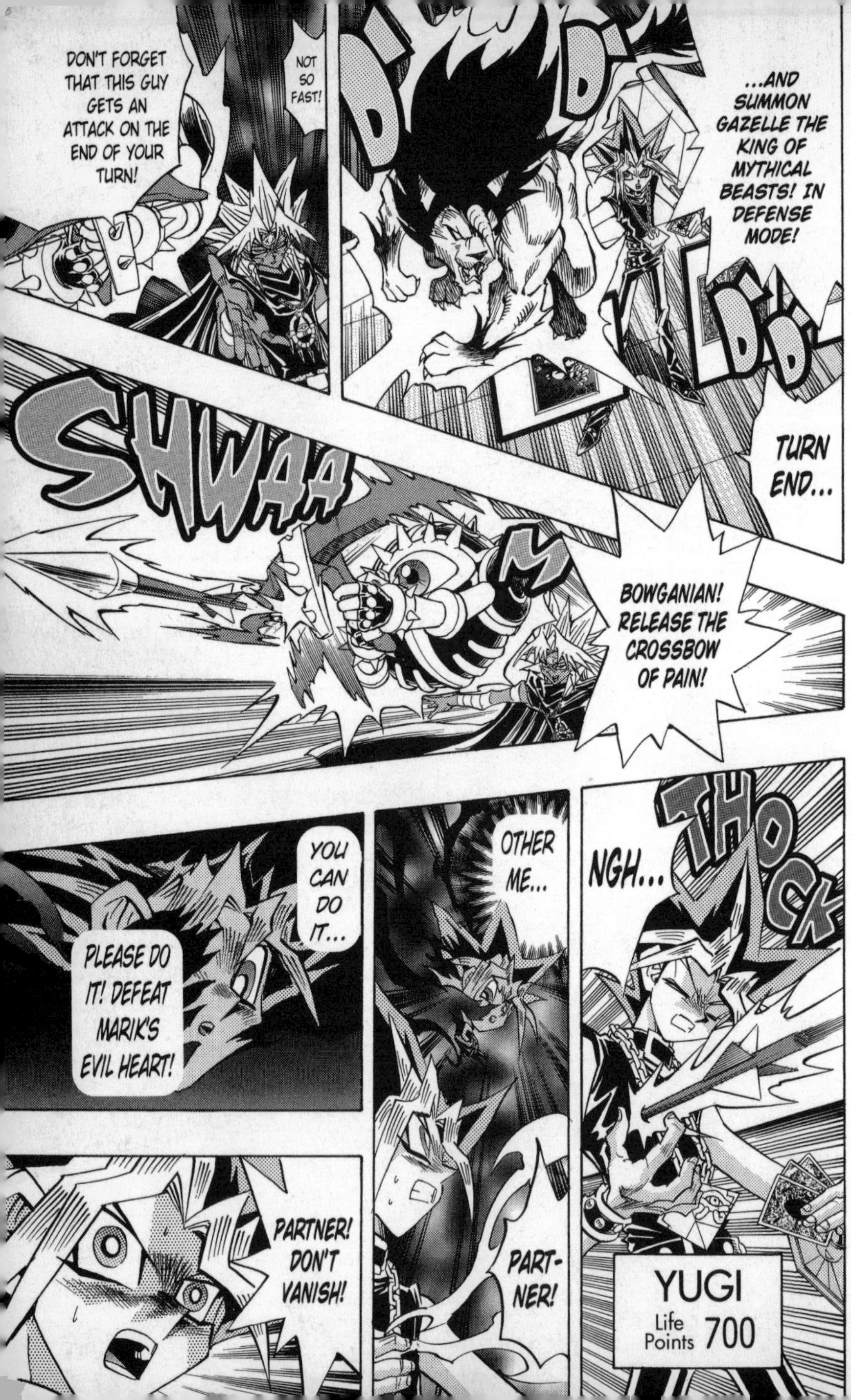
...AND SUMMON GAZELLE THE KING OF MYTHICAL BEASTS! IN DEFENSE MODE!
DOD
DOD
TURN END...
NOT SO FAST!
DON'T FORGET THAT THIS GUY GETS AN ATTACK ON THE END OF YOUR TURN!
SHWAA
BOWGANIAN! RELEASE THE CROSSBOW OF PAIN!
THOCK
NGH...
YUGI
Life Points 700
OTHER ME...
YOU CAN DO IT...
PLEASE DO IT! DEFEAT MARIK'S EVIL HEART!
PART-NER!
PARTNER! DON'T VANISH!

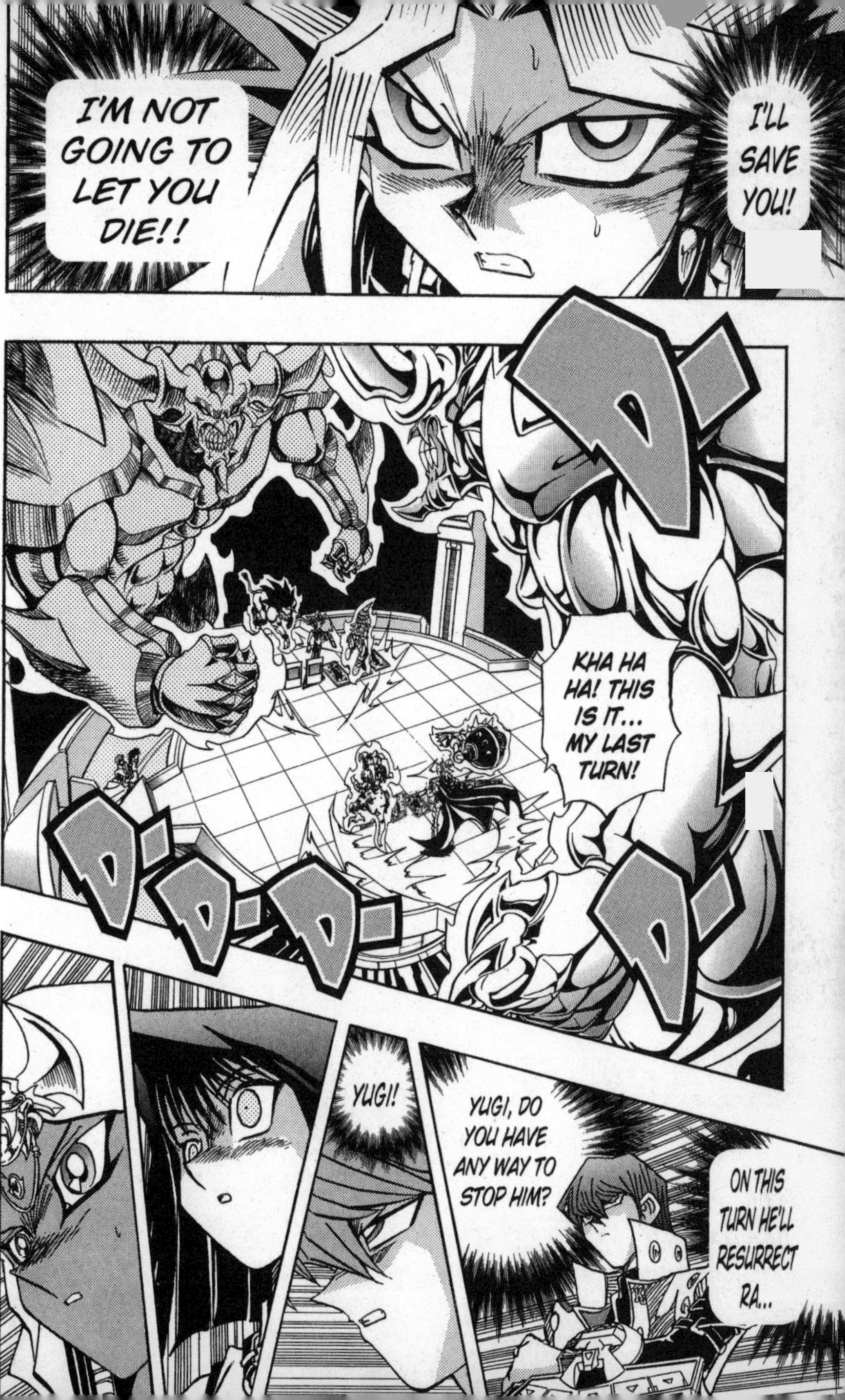
I'LL SAVE YOU!
I'M NOT GOING TO LET YOU DIE!!
KHA HA HA! THIS IS IT... MY LAST TURN!
YUGI, DO YOU HAVE ANY WAY TO STOP HIM?
ON THIS TURN HE'LL RESURRECT RA...
YUGI!

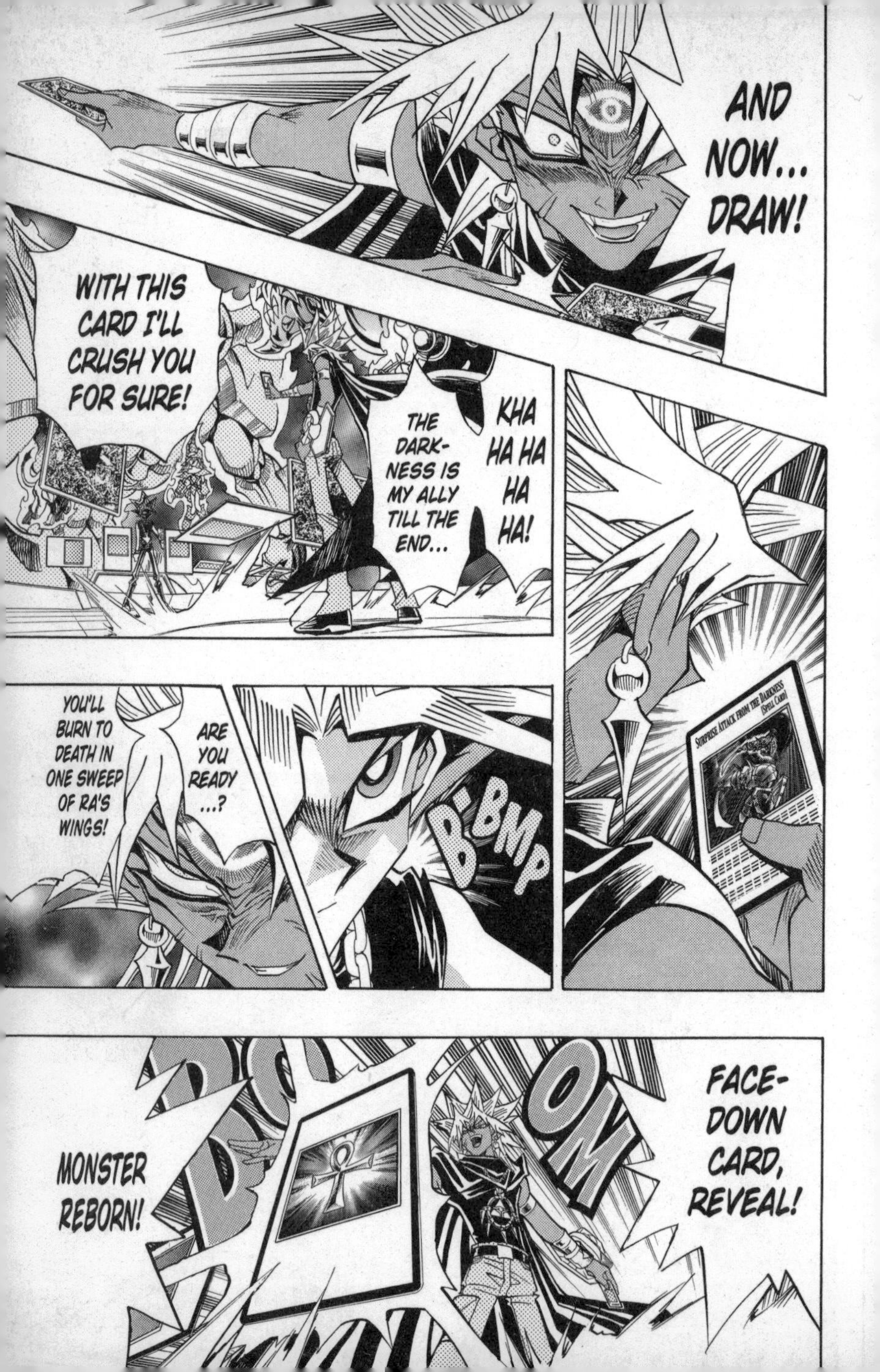
AND NOW... DRAW!
SURPRISE ATTACK FROM THE DARKNESS
[SPELL CARD]
WITH THIS CARD I'LL CRUSH YOU FOR SURE!
THE DARKNESS IS MY ALLY TILL THE END...
KHA HA HA HA HA!
B-BMP
ARE YOU READY ...?
YOU'LL BURN TO DEATH IN ONE SWEEP OF RA'S WINGS!
FACE-DOWN CARD, REVEAL!
MONSTER REBORN!

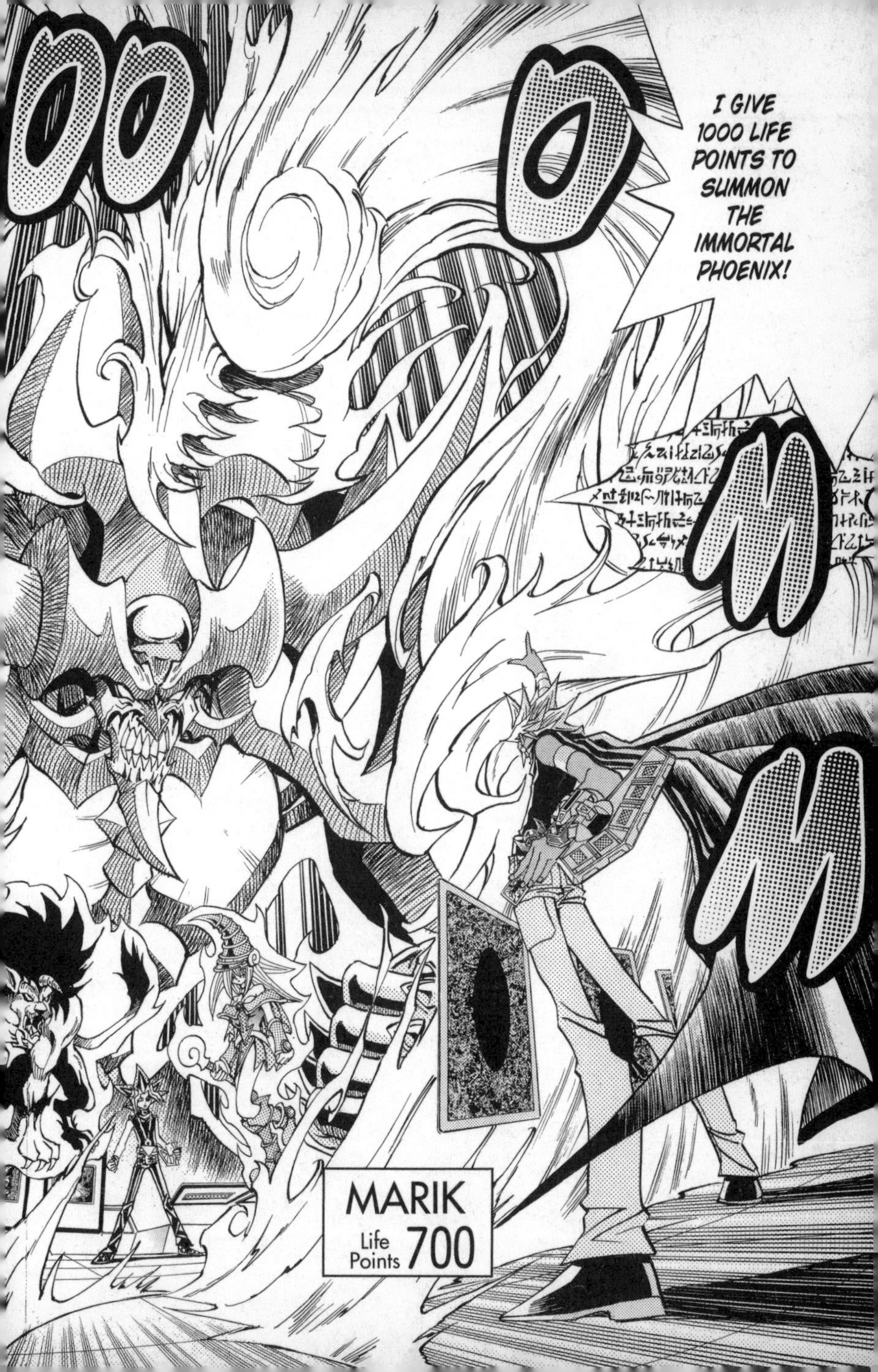
I GIVE 1000 LIFE POINTS TO SUMMON THE IMMORTAL PHOENIX!
OOOMM
MARIK
Life Points 700

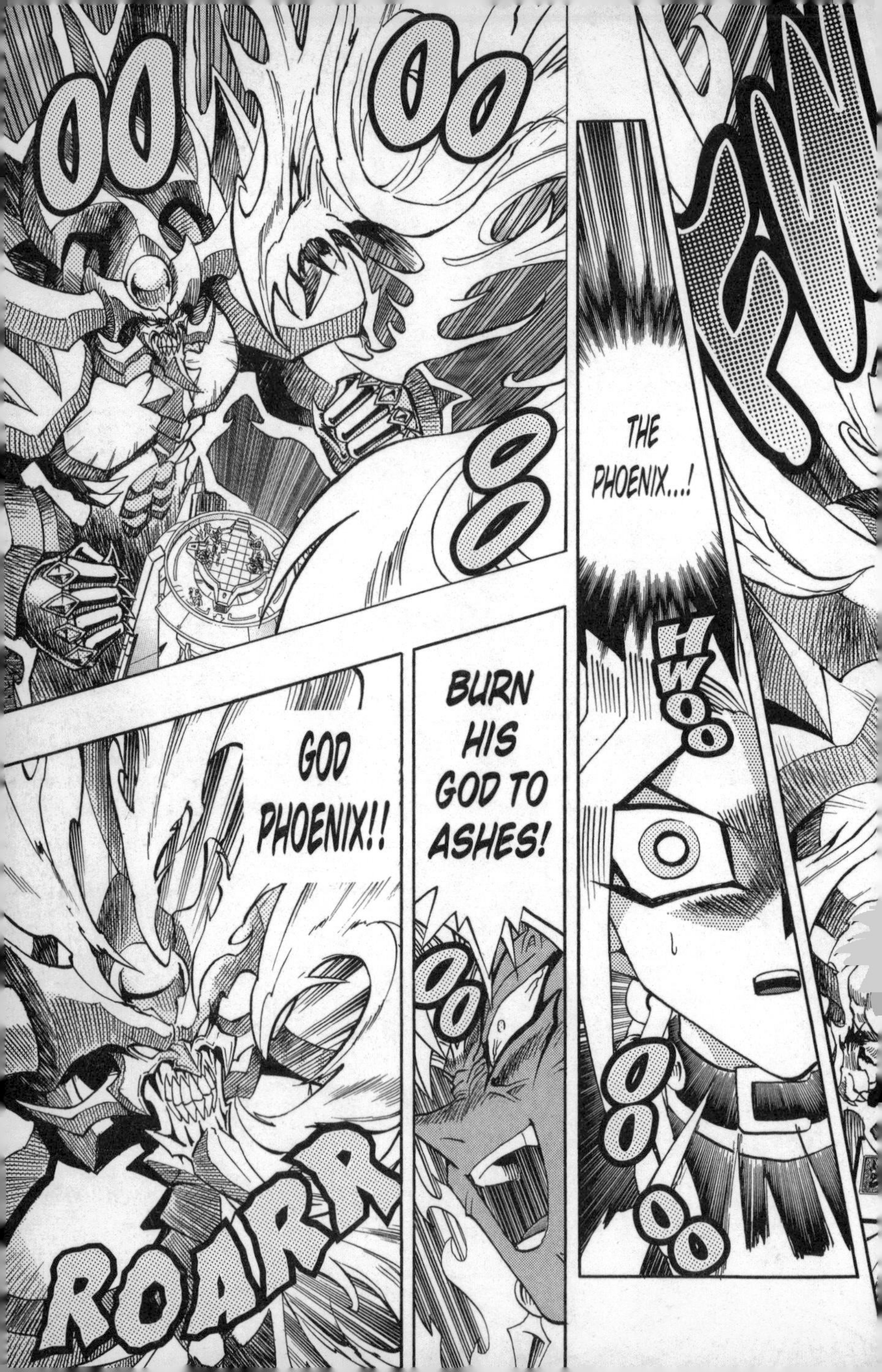
THE PHOENIX...!
BURN HIS GOD TO ASHES!
GOD PHOENIX!!
ROARR

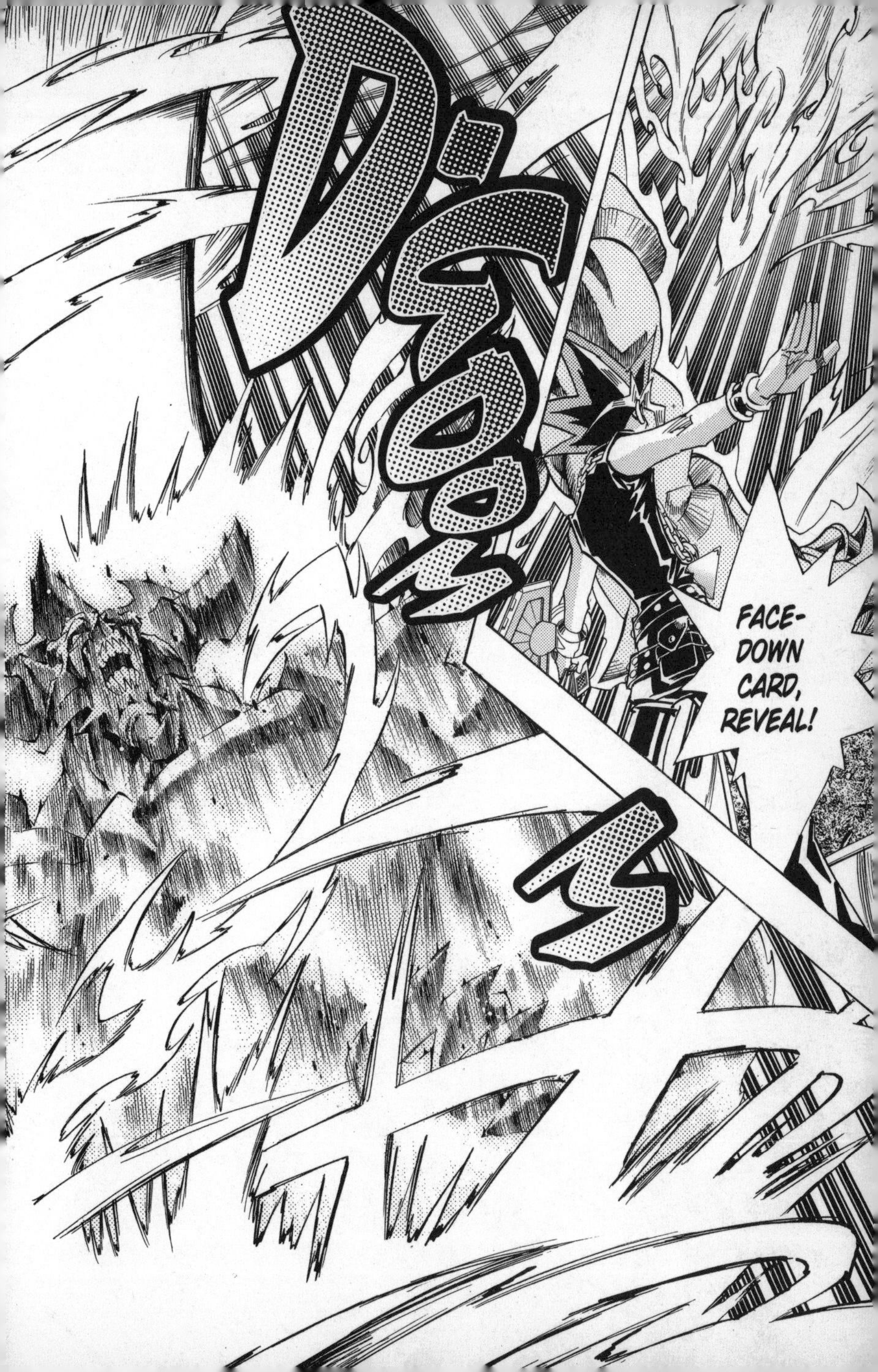
FACE-DOWN CARD, REVEAL!

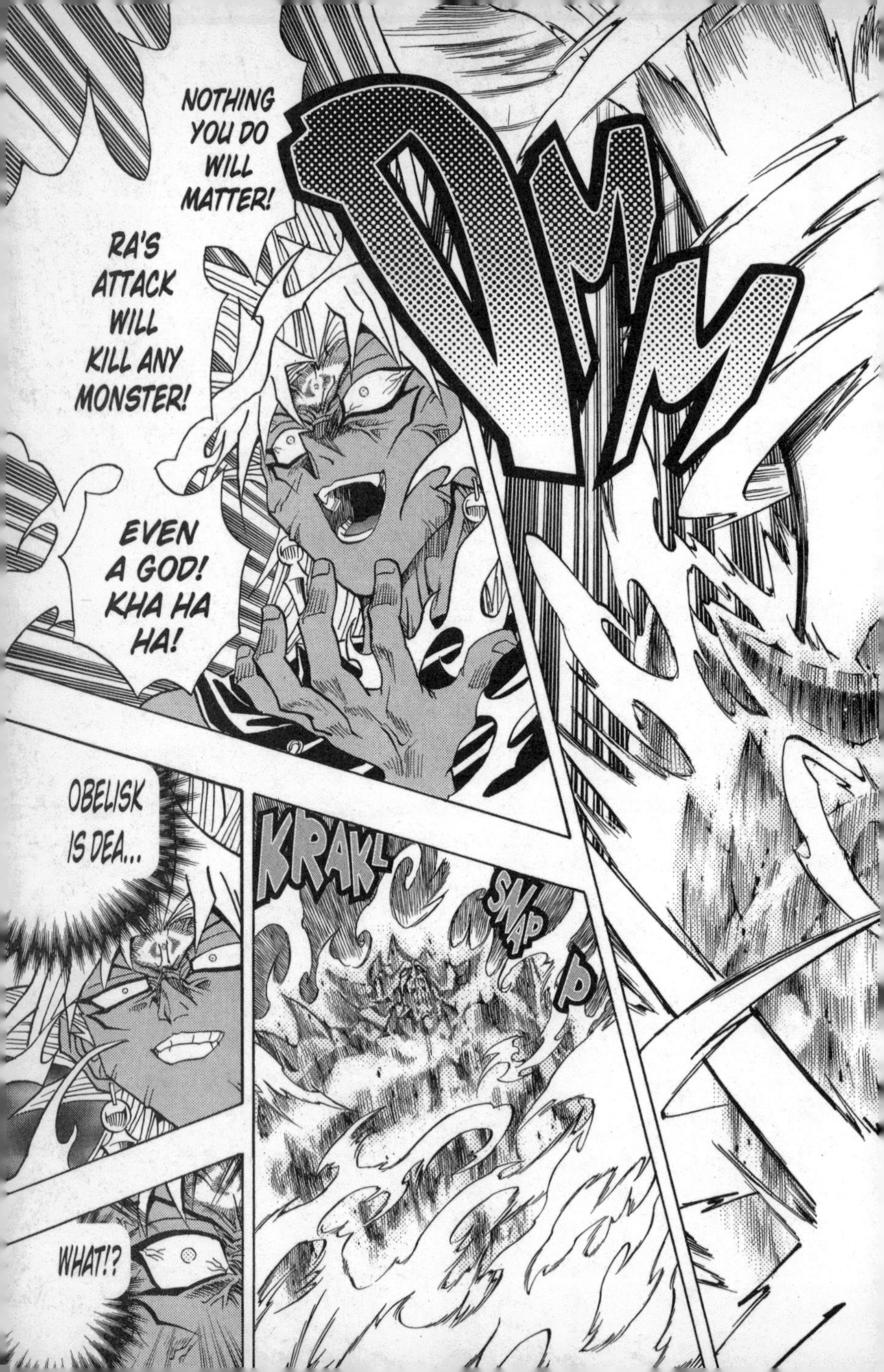
NOTHING YOU DO WILL MATTER!
RA'S ATTACK WILL KILL ANY MONSTER!
EVEN A GOD! KHA HA HA!
KRAKL
SNAP
P
OBELISK IS DEA...
WHAT!?

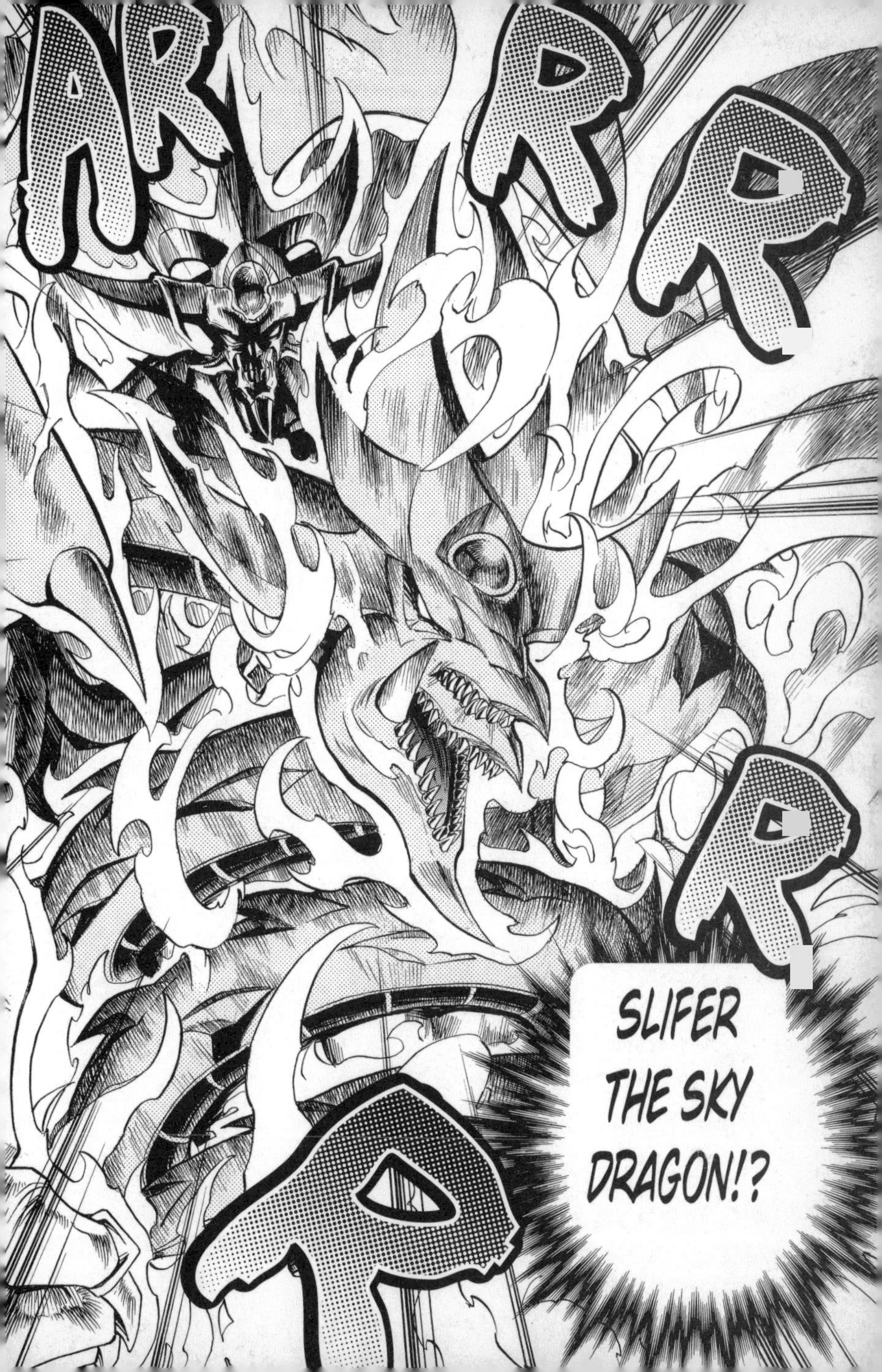
ARRRRR
SLIFER THE SKY DRAGON!?

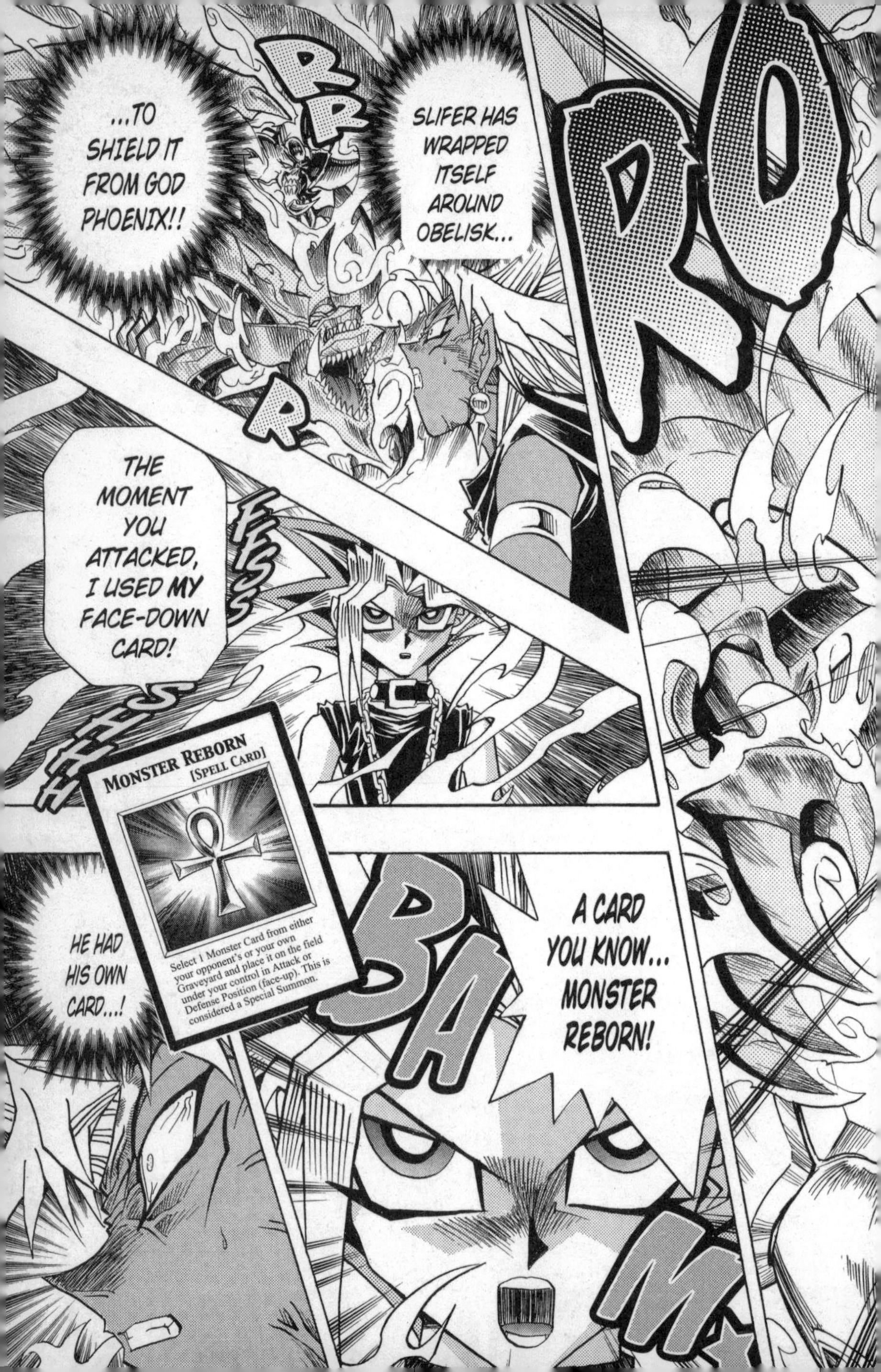
DO
SLIFER HAS WRAPPED ITSELF AROUND OBELISK...
RR
...TO SHIELD IT FROM GOD PHOENIX!!
R
THE MOMENT YOU ATTACKED, I USED MY FACE-DOWN CARD!
FFSSS
SHHH
MONSTER REBORN
[SPELL CARD]
Select 1 Monster Card from either your opponent's or your own Graveyard and place it on the field under your control in Attack or Defense Position (face-up). This is considered a Special Summon.
A CARD YOU KNOW... MONSTER REBORN!
BA
M
HE HAD HIS OWN CARD...!

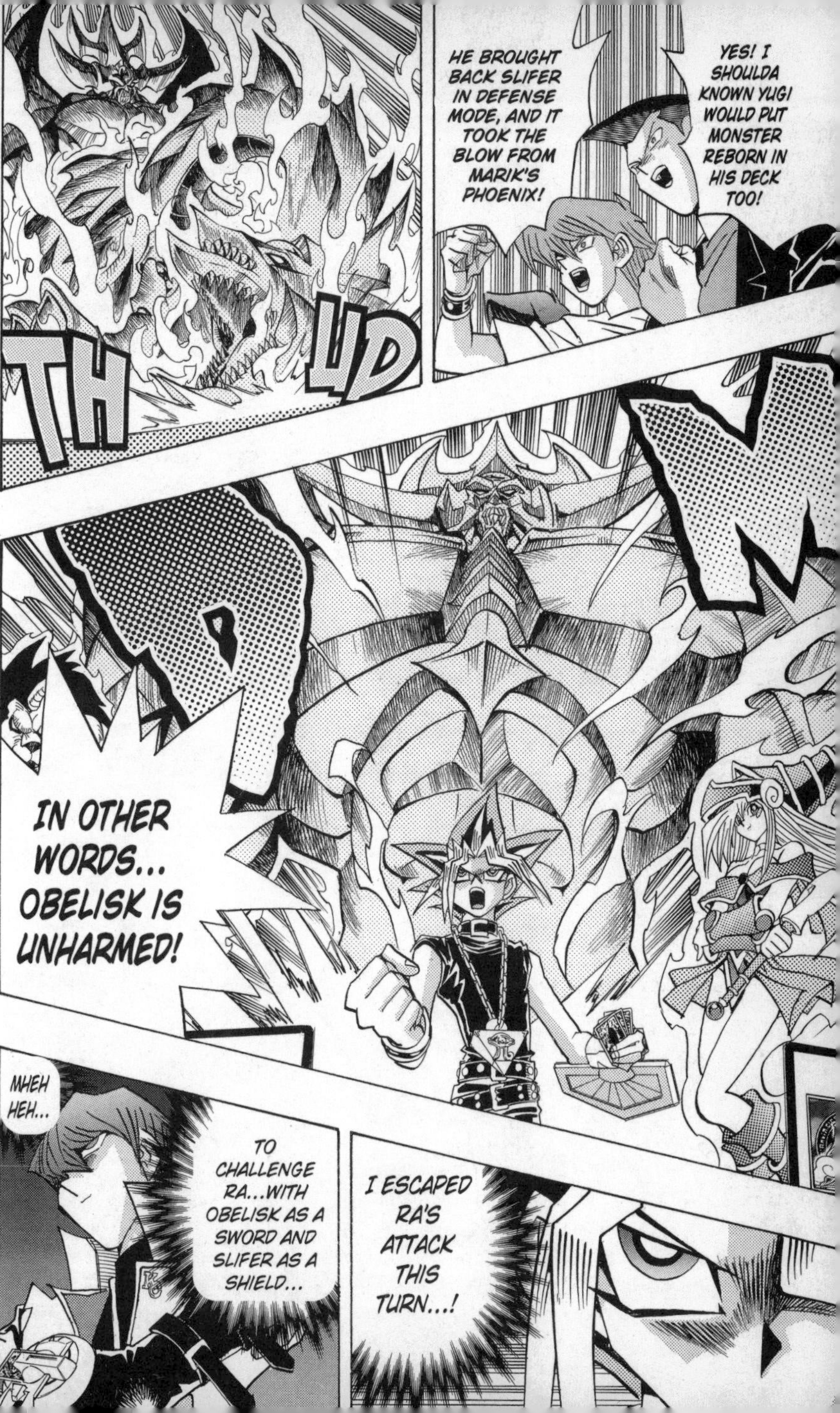
YES! I SHOULDA KNOWN YUGI WOULD PUT MONSTER REBORN IN HIS DECK TOO!
HE BROUGHT BACK SLIFER IN DEFENSE MODE, AND IT TOOK THE BLOW FROM MARIK'S PHOENIX!
THUD
IN OTHER WORDS... OBELISK IS UNHARMED!
I ESCAPED RA'S ATTACK THIS TURN...!
MHEH HEH...
TO CHALLENGE RA...WITH OBELISK AS A SWORD AND SLIFER AS A SHIELD...

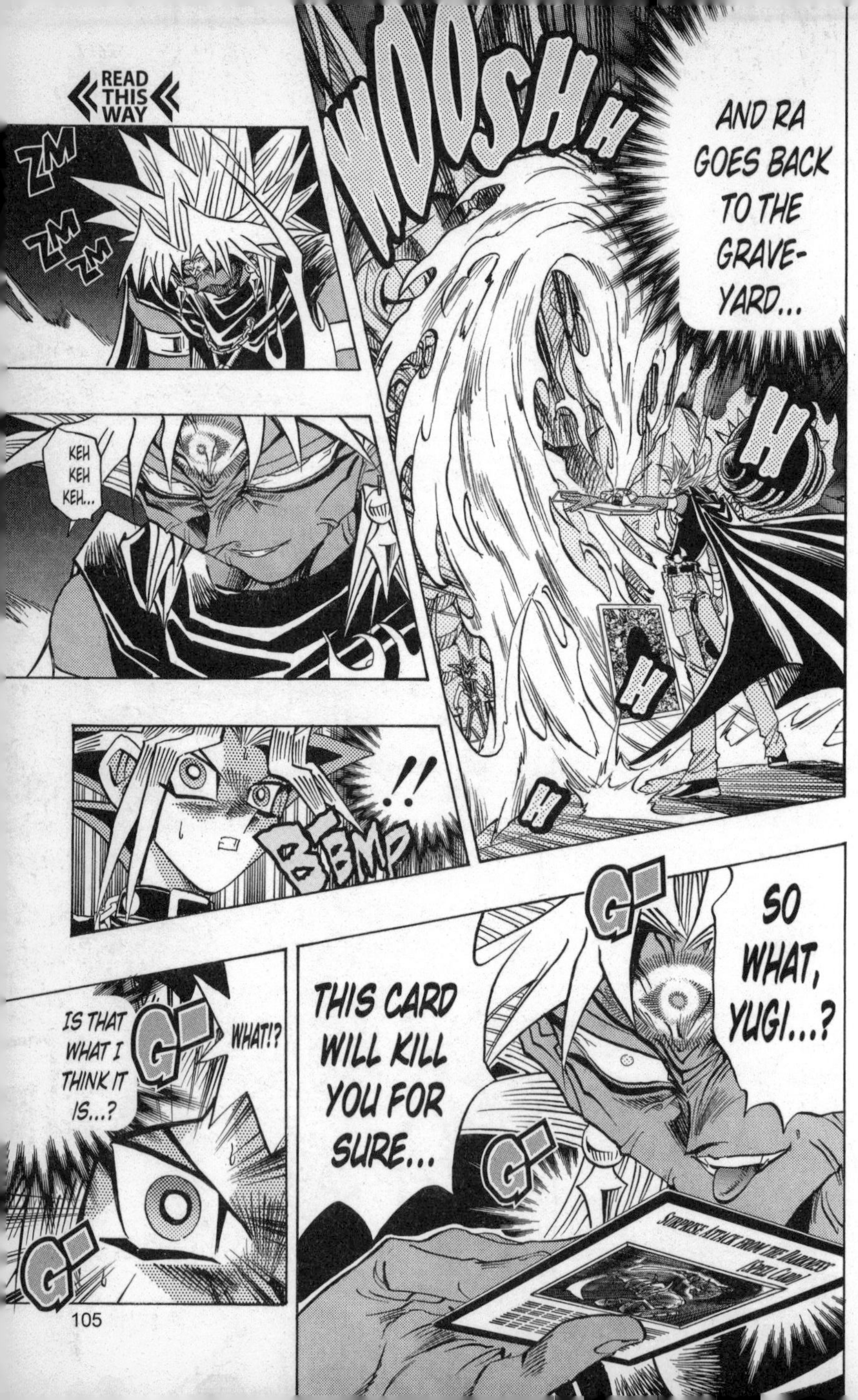
READ THIS WAY
WOOSHHH
AND RA GOES BACK TO THE GRAVE-YARD...
H
H
H
ZM ZM ZM
KEH KEH KEH...
!!
BMP
G
SO WHAT, YUGI...?
THIS CARD WILL KILL YOU FOR SURE...
G
SURPRISE ATTACK FROM THE DARKNESS
SPELL CARD
G
WHAT!?
IS THAT WHAT I THINK IT IS...?
G

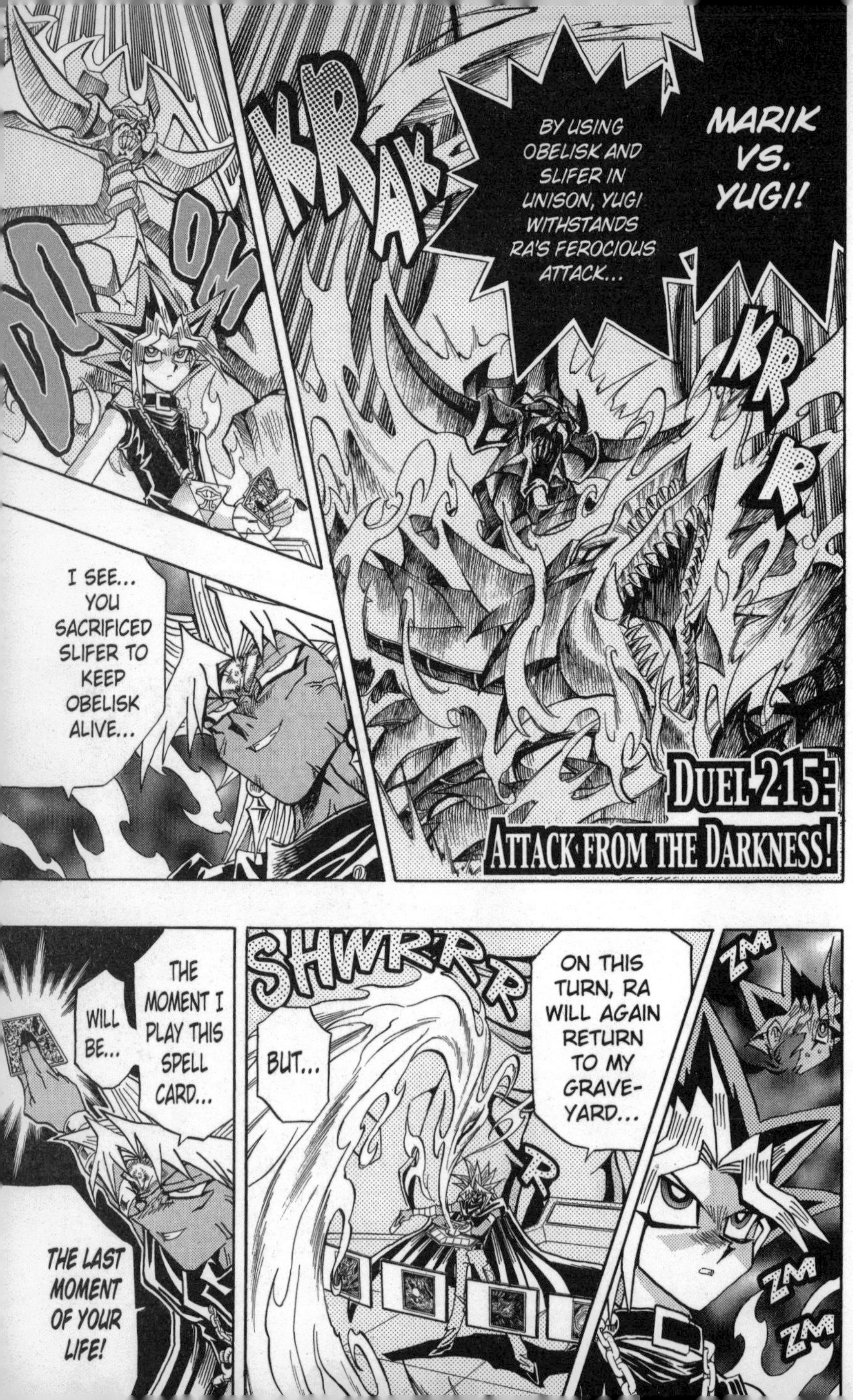
MARIK VS. YUGI!
BY USING OBELISK AND SLIFER IN UNISON, YUGI WITHSTANDS RA'S FEROCIOUS ATTACK...
KRAK
KR R
DUEL 215:
ATTACK FROM THE DARKNESS!
DOOOM
I SEE... YOU SACRIFICED SLIFER TO KEEP OBELISK ALIVE...
ZM
ZM
ZM
SHWRRRR
ON THIS TURN, RA WILL AGAIN RETURN TO MY GRAVEYARD...
BUT...
THE MOMENT I PLAY THIS SPELL CARD...
WILL BE...
THE LAST MOMENT OF YOUR LIFE!

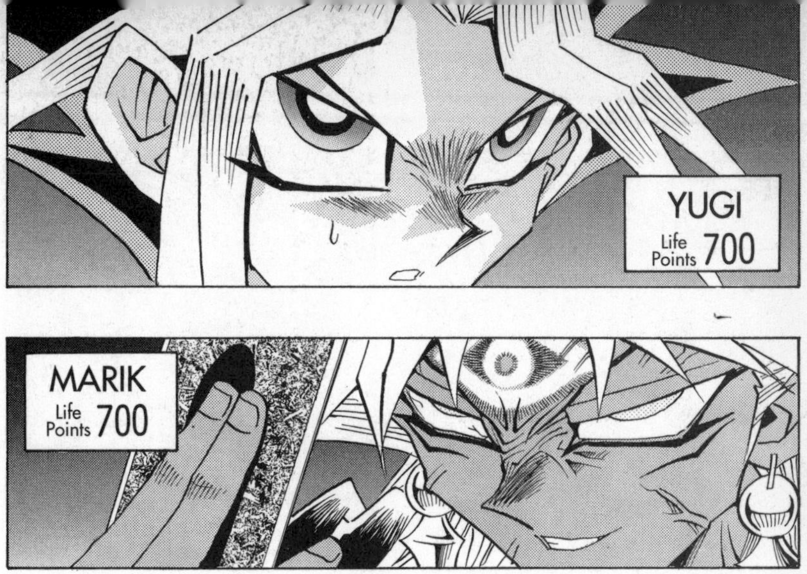
YUGI
Life Points 700
MARIK
Life Points 700

# Duel 215: Attack from the Darkness!

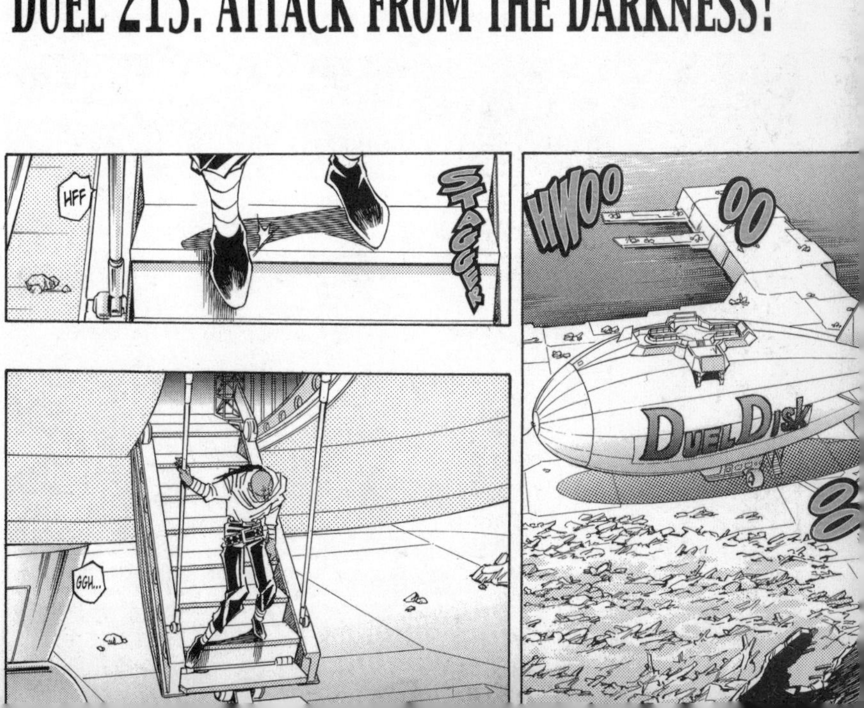
HWOOOOO
STAGGER
HFF
GGH...

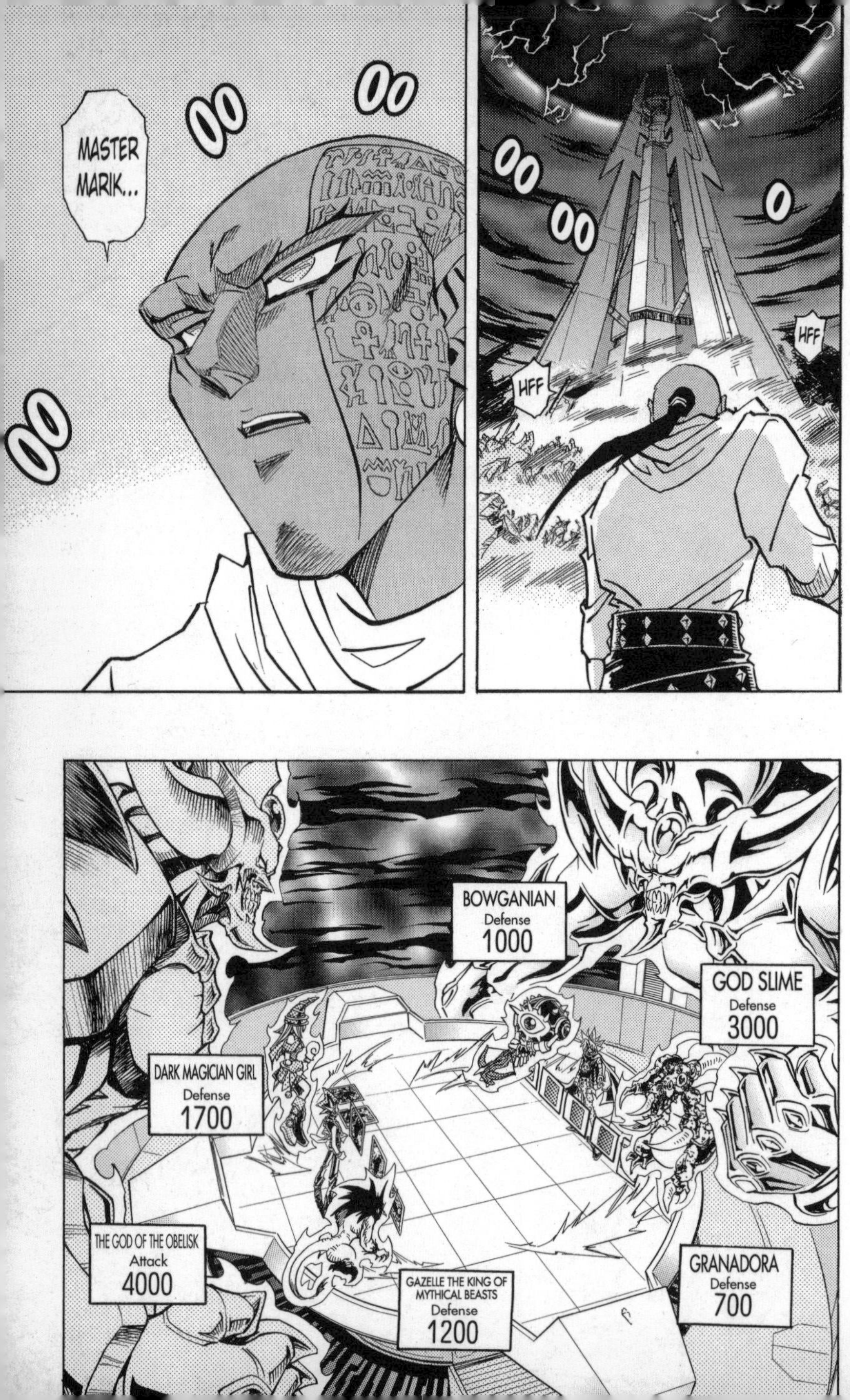
OO
OO
OO
O
HFF
HFF
OO
OO
MASTER MARIK...
OO
BOWGANIAN
Defense
1000
GOD SLIME
Defense
3000
DARK MAGICIAN GIRL
Defense
1700
GRANADORA
Defense
700
GAZELLE THE KING OF MYTHICAL BEASTS
Defense
1200
THE GOD OF THE OBELISK
Attack
4000

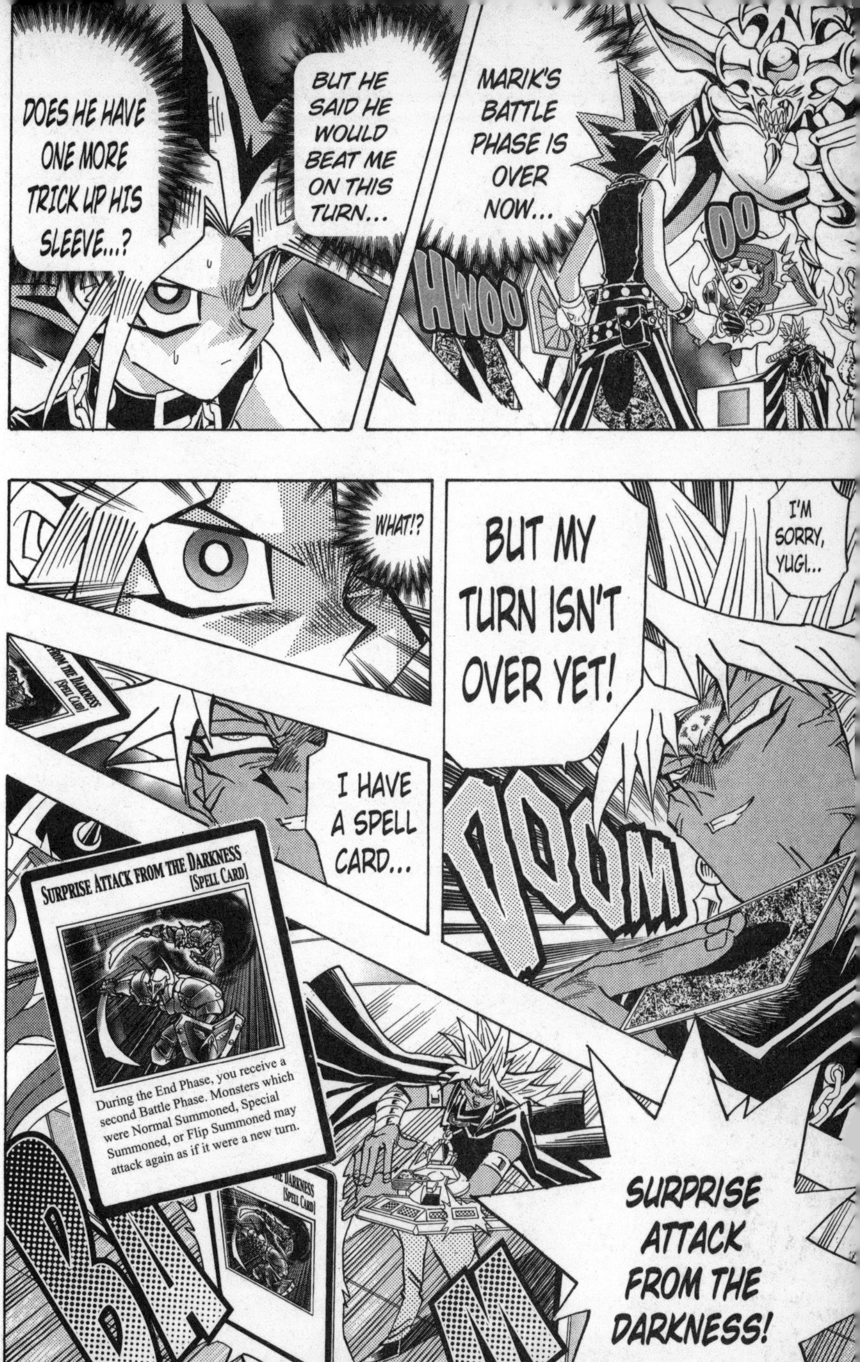
MARIK'S BATTLE PHASE IS OVER NOW...
OO
HWOO
BUT HE SAID HE WOULD BEAT ME ON THIS TURN...
DOES HE HAVE ONE MORE TRICK UP HIS SLEEVE...?
I'M SORRY, YUGI...
BUT MY TURN ISN'T OVER YET!
I HAVE A SPELL CARD...
DOOM
WHAT!?
SURPRISE ATTACK FROM THE DARKNESS
[SPELL CARD]
During the End Phase, you receive a second Battle Phase. Monsters which were Normal Summoned, Special Summoned, or Flip Summoned may attack again as if it were a new turn.
SURPRISE ATTACK FROM THE DARKNESS!

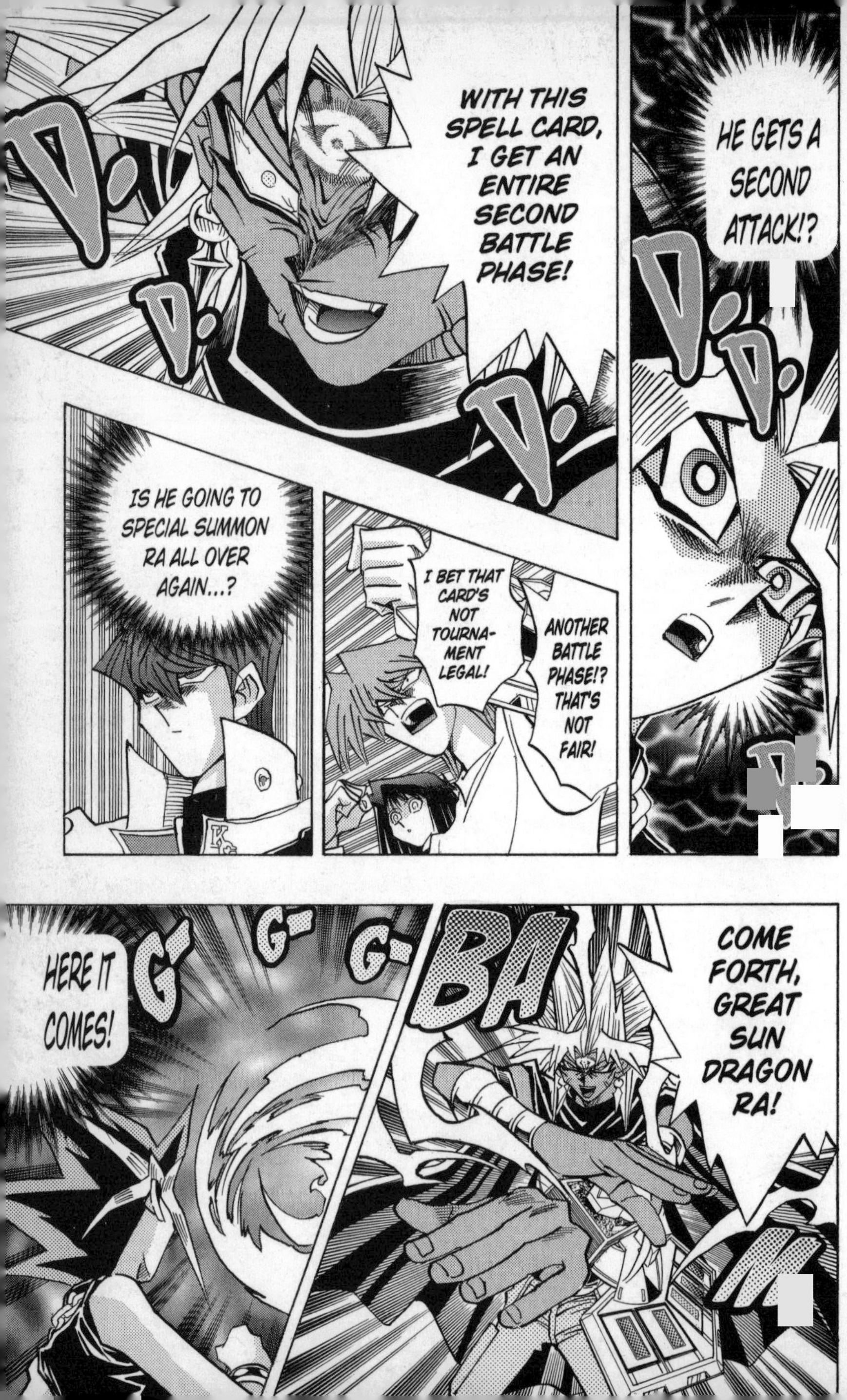
HE GETS A SECOND ATTACK!?
D. D. D.
WITH THIS SPELL CARD, I GET AN ENTIRE SECOND BATTLE PHASE!
D. D. D.
ANOTHER BATTLE PHASE!? THAT'S NOT FAIR!
I BET THAT CARD'S NOT TOURNAMENT LEGAL!
IS HE GOING TO SPECIAL SUMMON RA ALL OVER AGAIN...?
COME FORTH, GREAT SUN DRAGON RA!
BA
G- G- G-
HERE IT COMES!

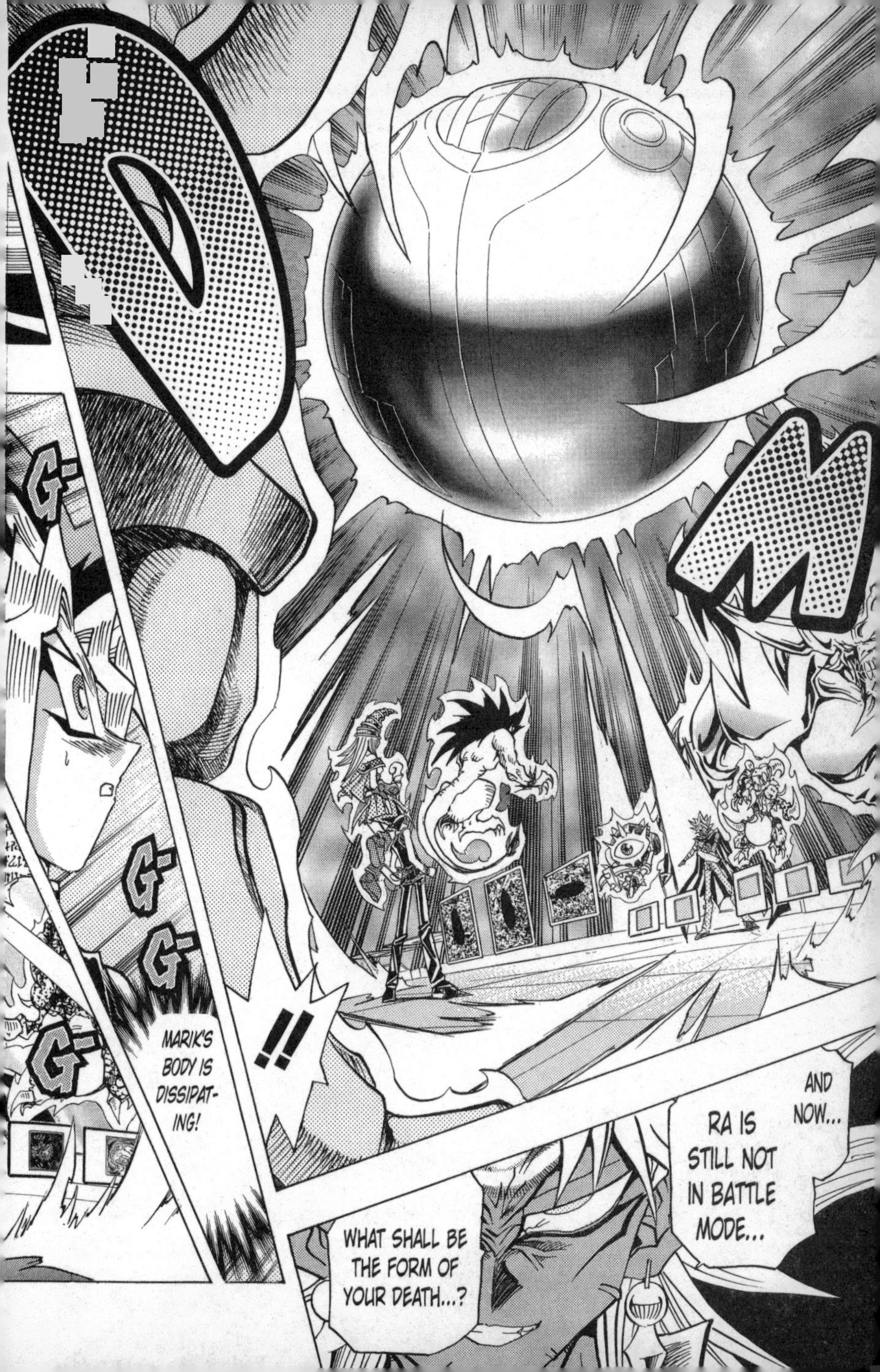
M
!!
AND NOW...
RA IS STILL NOT IN BATTLE MODE...
WHAT SHALL BE THE FORM OF YOUR DEATH...?
G-
G-
G-
G-
MARIK'S BODY IS DISSIPATING!

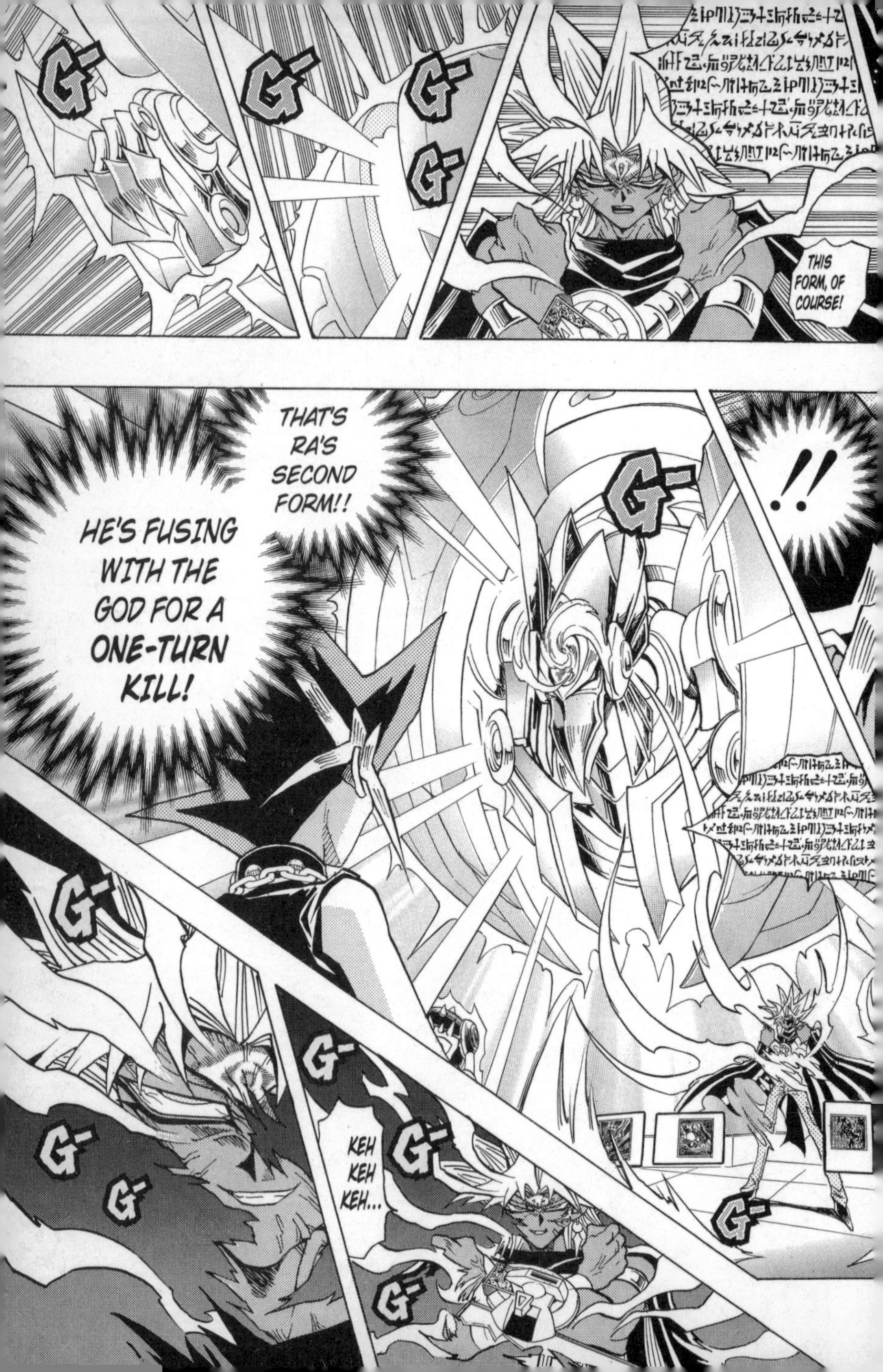
THIS FORM, OF COURSE!
G-
G-
G-
G-
!!
G-
THAT'S RA'S SECOND FORM!!
HE'S FUSING WITH THE GOD FOR A ONE-TURN KILL!
G-
G-
G-
KEH KEH KEH...
G-
G-
G-
G-

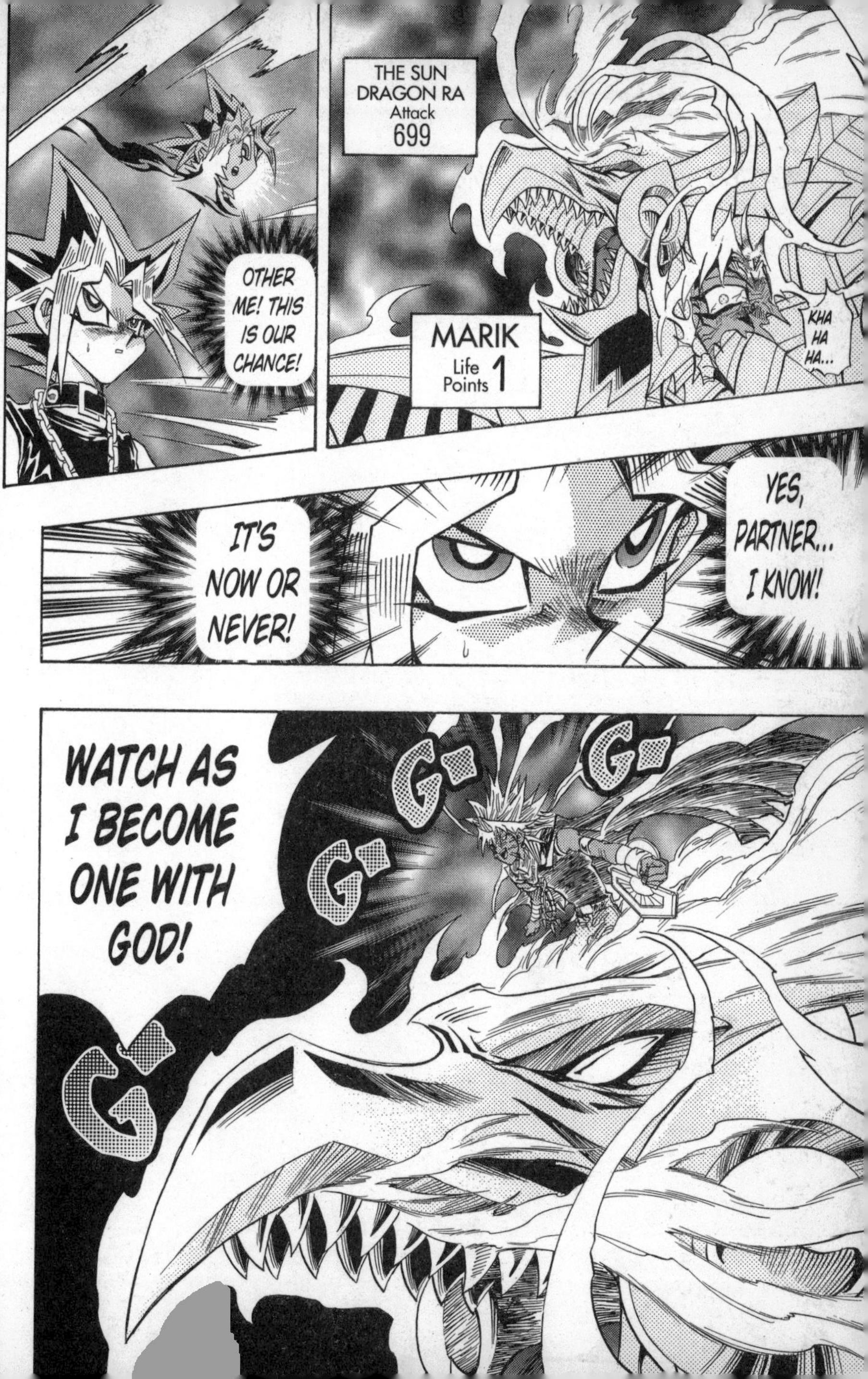
THE SUN DRAGON RA Attack 699
KHA HA HA...
MARIK Life Points 1
OTHER ME! THIS IS OUR CHANCE!
YES, PARTNER... I KNOW!
IT'S NOW OR NEVER!
G-
G-
G-
WATCH AS I BECOME ONE WITH GOD!
G-
G-

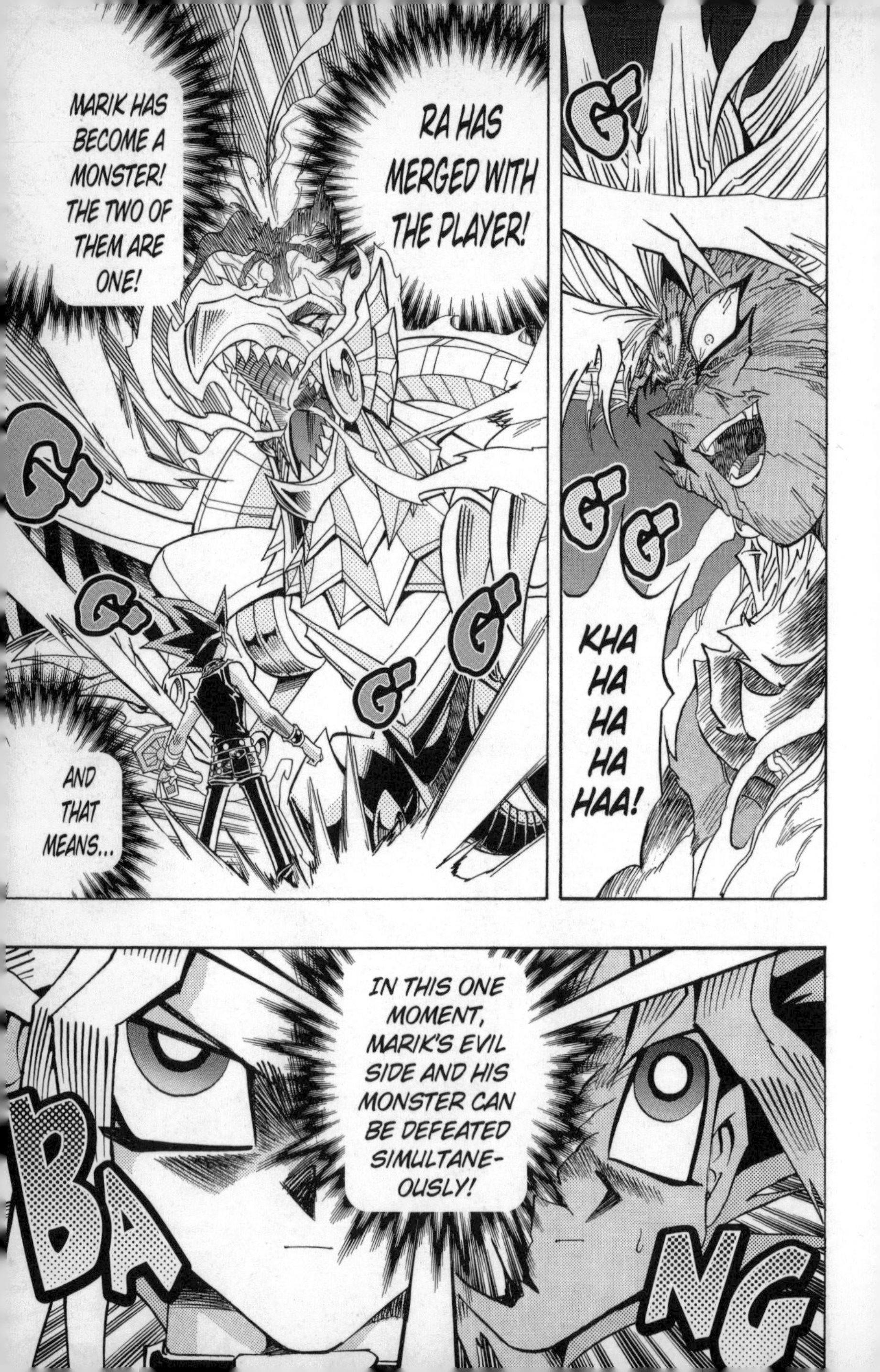
G
G
G
KHA HA HA HA HAA!
RA HAS MERGED WITH THE PLAYER!
MARIK HAS BECOME A MONSTER! THE TWO OF THEM ARE ONE!
G
G
G
G
AND THAT MEANS...
IN THIS ONE MOMENT, MARIK'S EVIL SIDE AND HIS MONSTER CAN BE DEFEATED SIMULTANE-OUSLY!
BANG

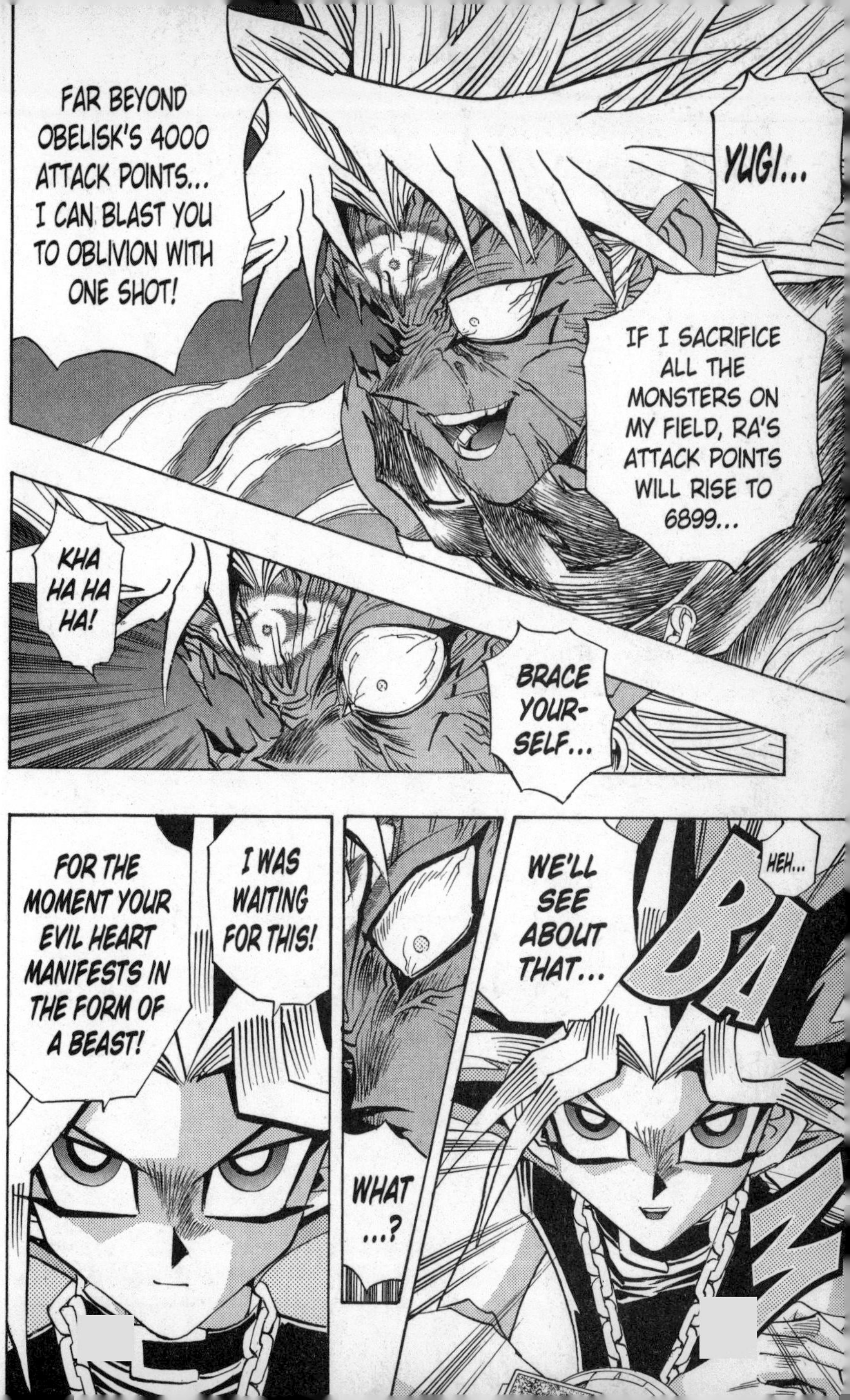
YUGI...
IF I SACRIFICE ALL THE MONSTERS ON MY FIELD, RA'S ATTACK POINTS WILL RISE TO 6899...
FAR BEYOND OBELISK'S 4000 ATTACK POINTS... I CAN BLAST YOU TO OBLIVION WITH ONE SHOT!
BRACE YOURSELF...
KHA HA HA HA!
HEH...
BA
WE'LL SEE ABOUT THAT...
WHAT ...?
I WAS WAITING FOR THIS!
FOR THE MOMENT YOUR EVIL HEART MANIFESTS IN THE FORM OF A BEAST!

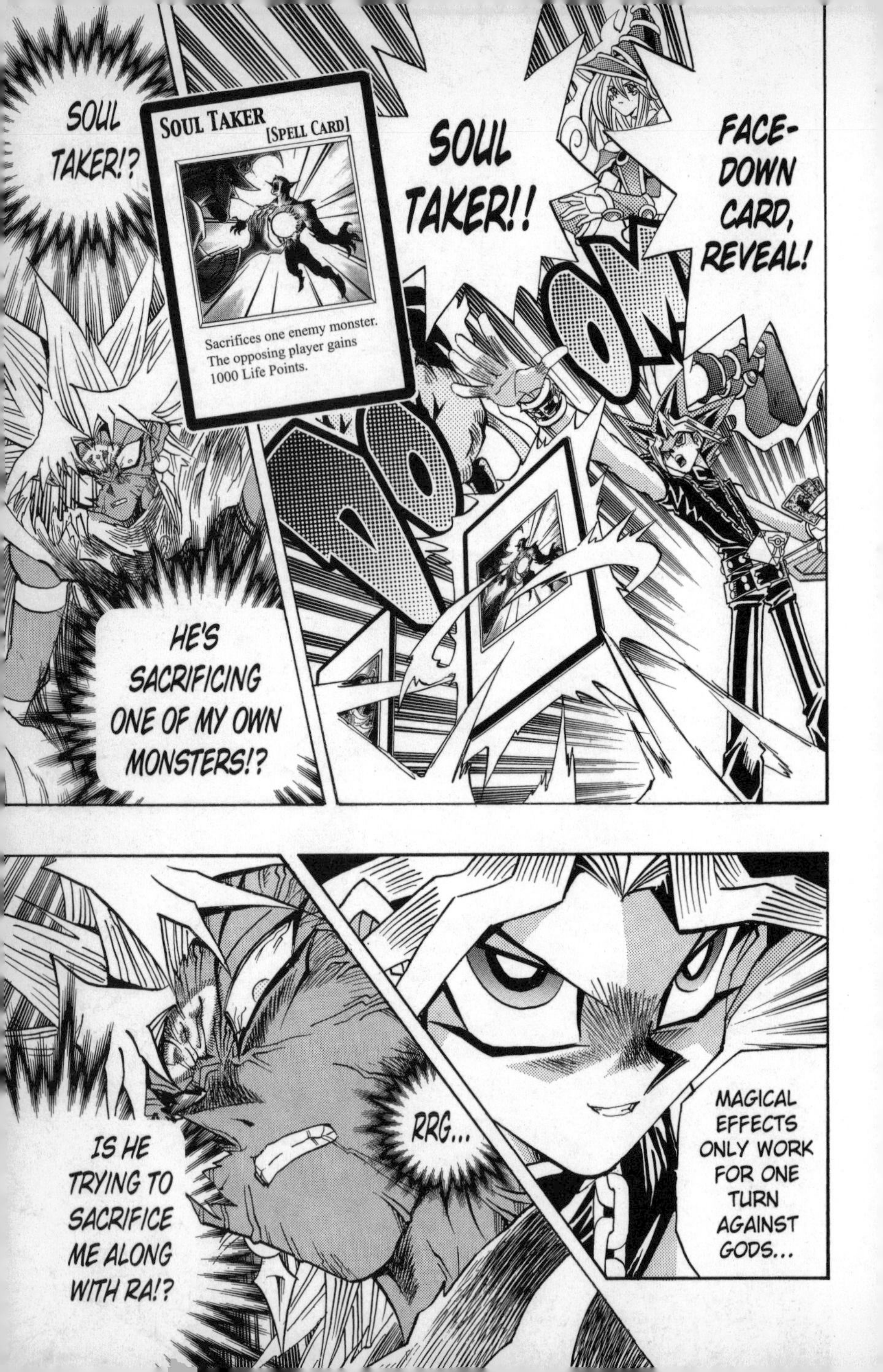
FACE-DOWN CARD, REVEAL!
SOUL TAKER!!
DOOOM
SOUL TAKER
[SPELL CARD]
Sacrifices one enemy monster. The opposing player gains 1000 Life Points.
SOUL TAKER!?
HE'S SACRIFICING ONE OF MY OWN MONSTERS!?
MAGICAL EFFECTS ONLY WORK FOR ONE TURN AGAINST GODS...
RRG...
IS HE TRYING TO SACRIFICE ME ALONG WITH RA!?

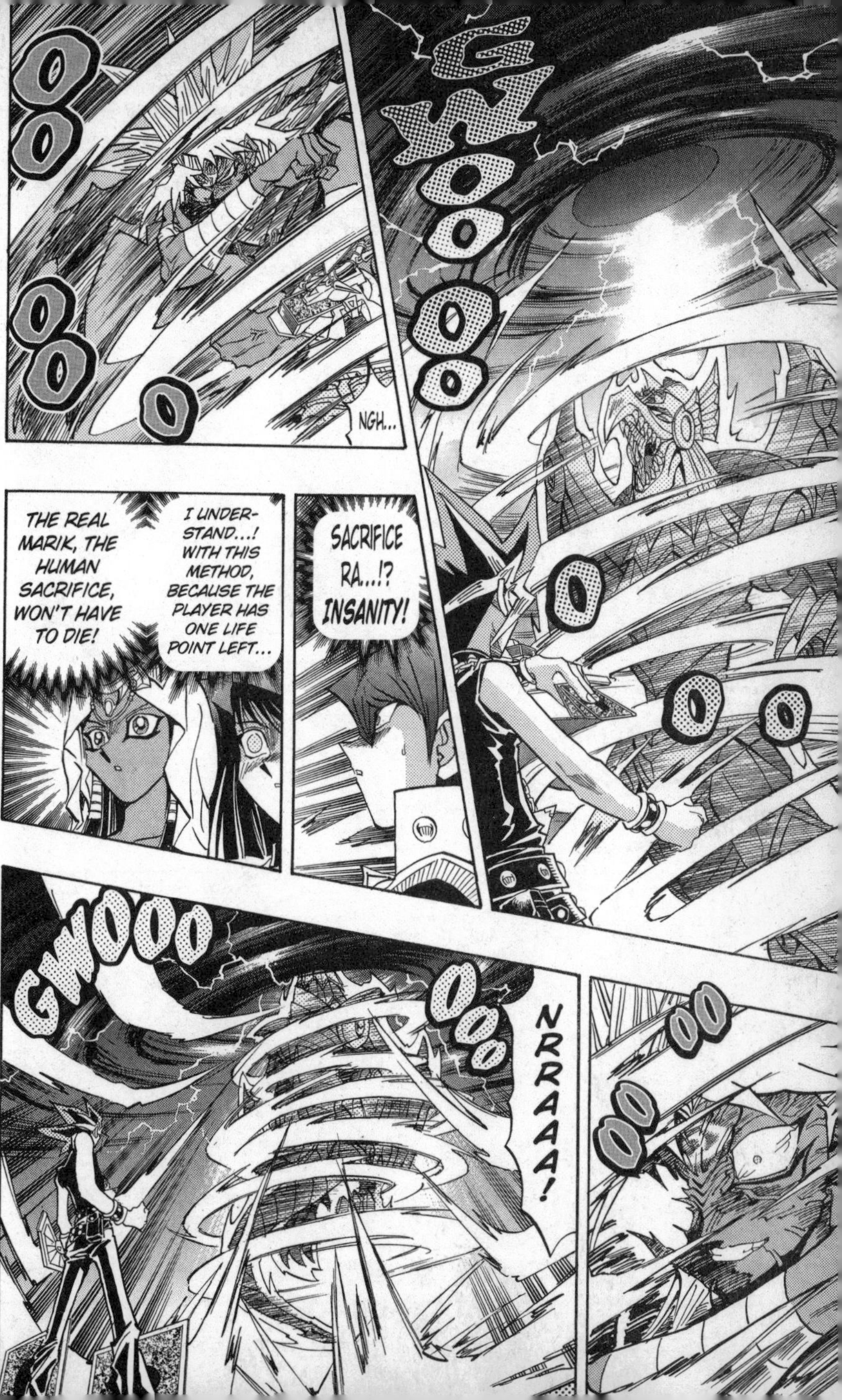
GWOOOOOOO
OOO
OOOOO
NGH...
SACRIFICE RA...!? INSANITY!
I UNDER-STAND...! WITH THIS METHOD, BECAUSE THE PLAYER HAS ONE LIFE POINT LEFT...
THE REAL MARIK, THE HUMAN SACRIFICE, WON'T HAVE TO DIE!
OOOO
GWOOOOOO
NRRAAAA!

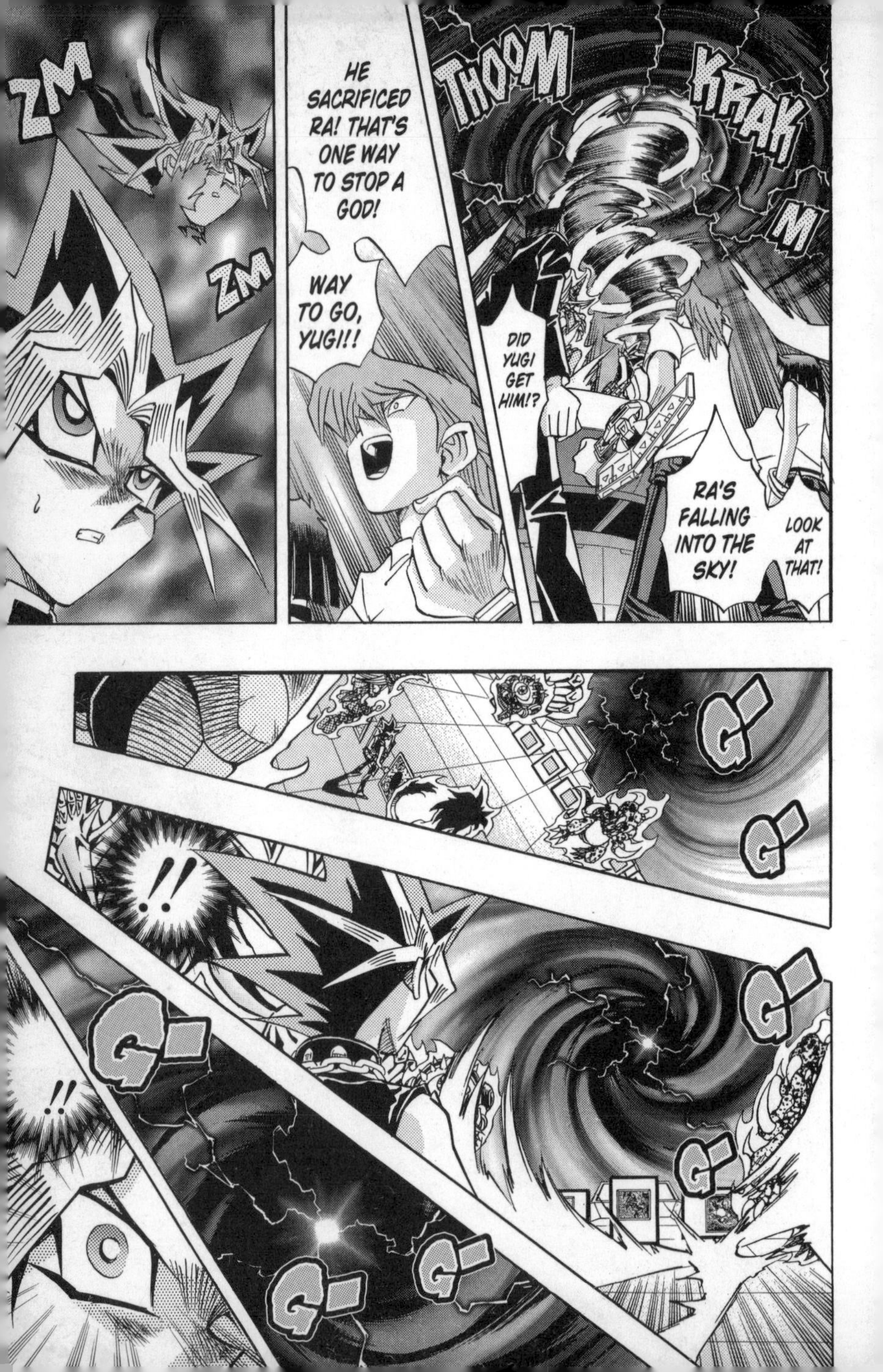
KRAK
M
THOOM
DID YUGI GET HIM!?
LOOK AT THAT!
RA'S FALLING INTO THE SKY!
HE SACRIFICED RA! THAT'S ONE WAY TO STOP A GOD!
WAY TO GO, YUGI!!
ZM
ZM
G
G
!!
G
G
G
G
G
!!

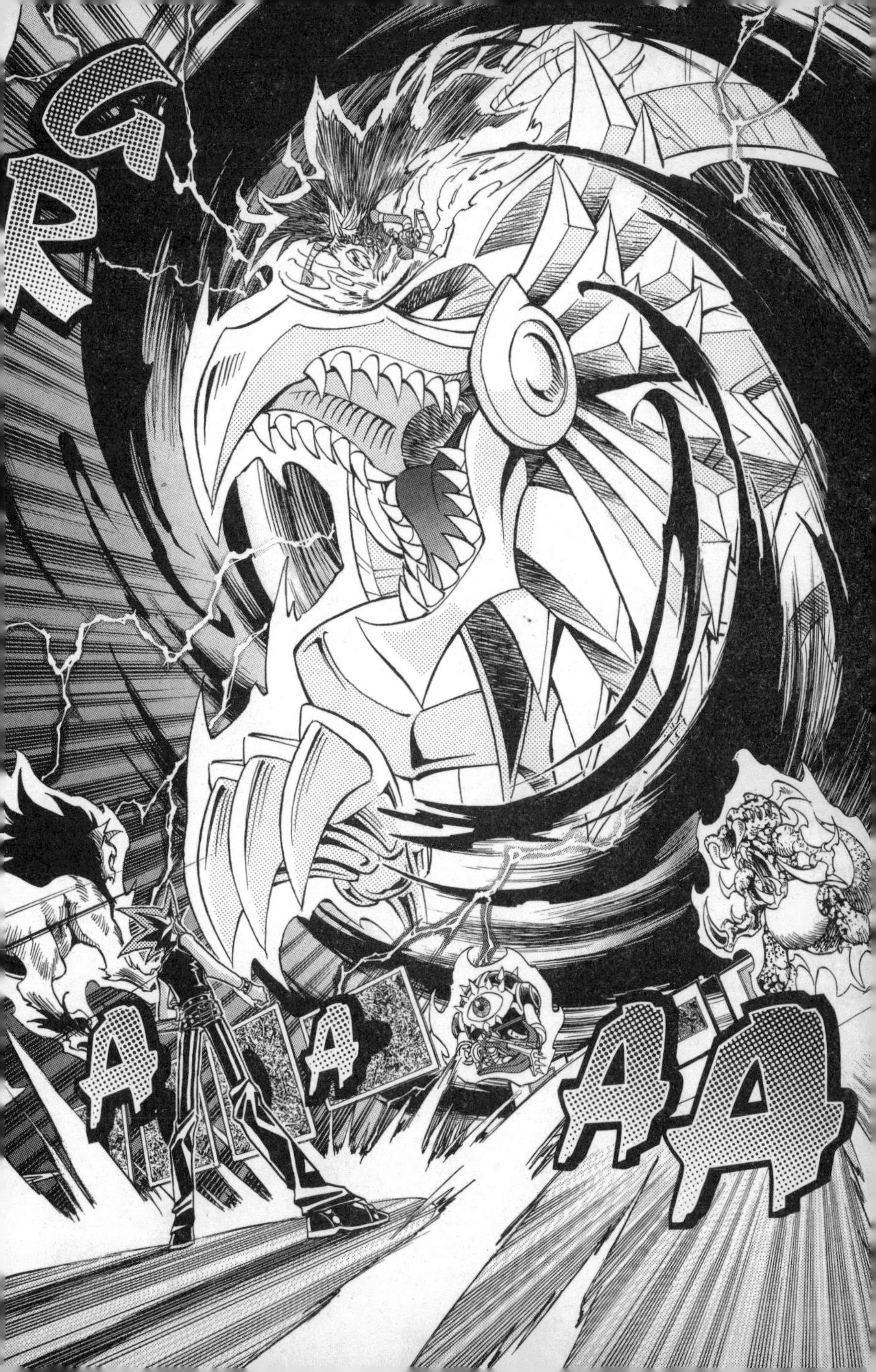
GRAAAA

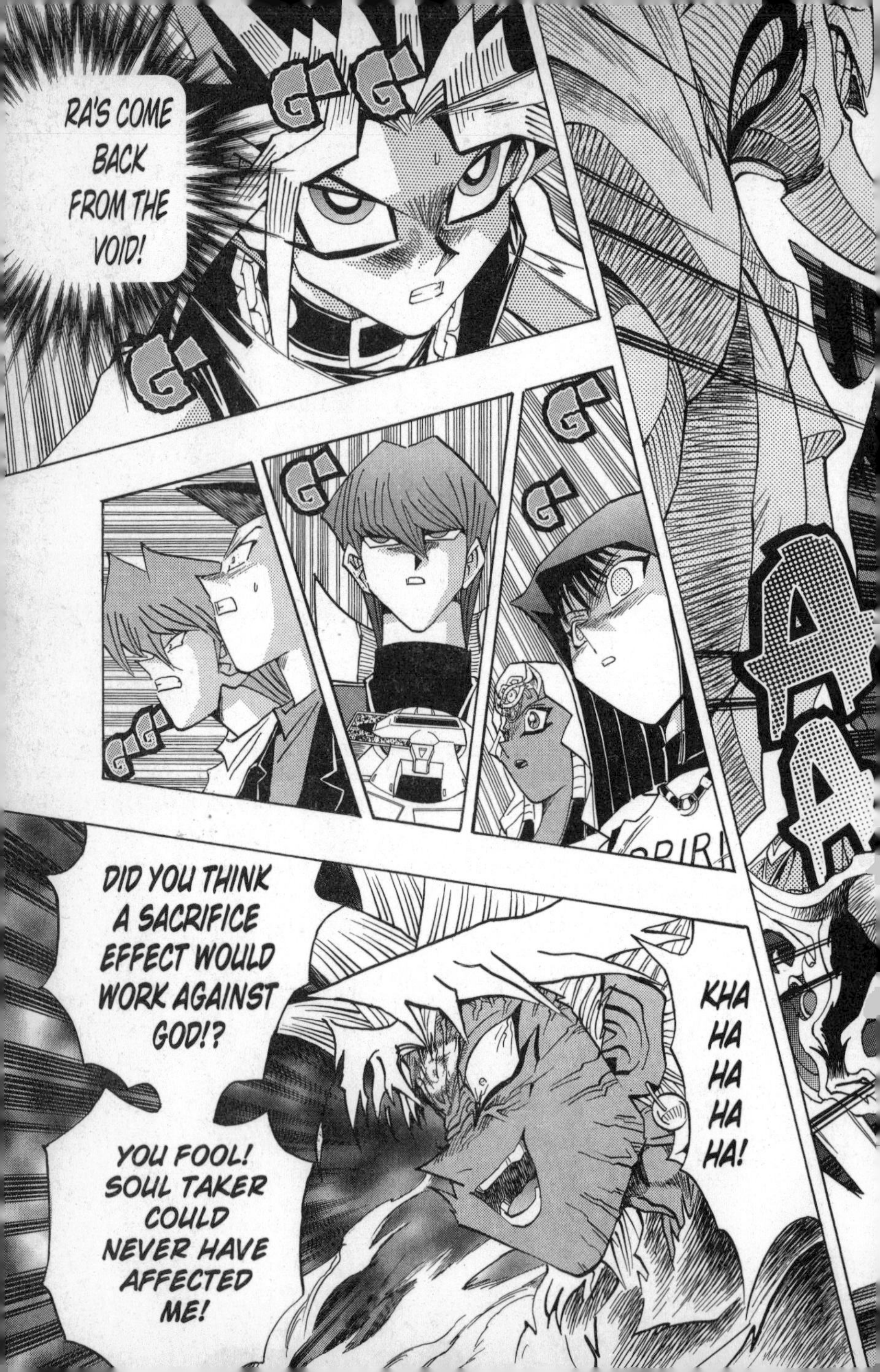
RA'S COME BACK FROM THE VOID!
DID YOU THINK A SACRIFICE EFFECT WOULD WORK AGAINST GOD!?
KHA HA HA HA HA!
YOU FOOL! SOUL TAKER COULD NEVER HAVE AFFECTED ME!

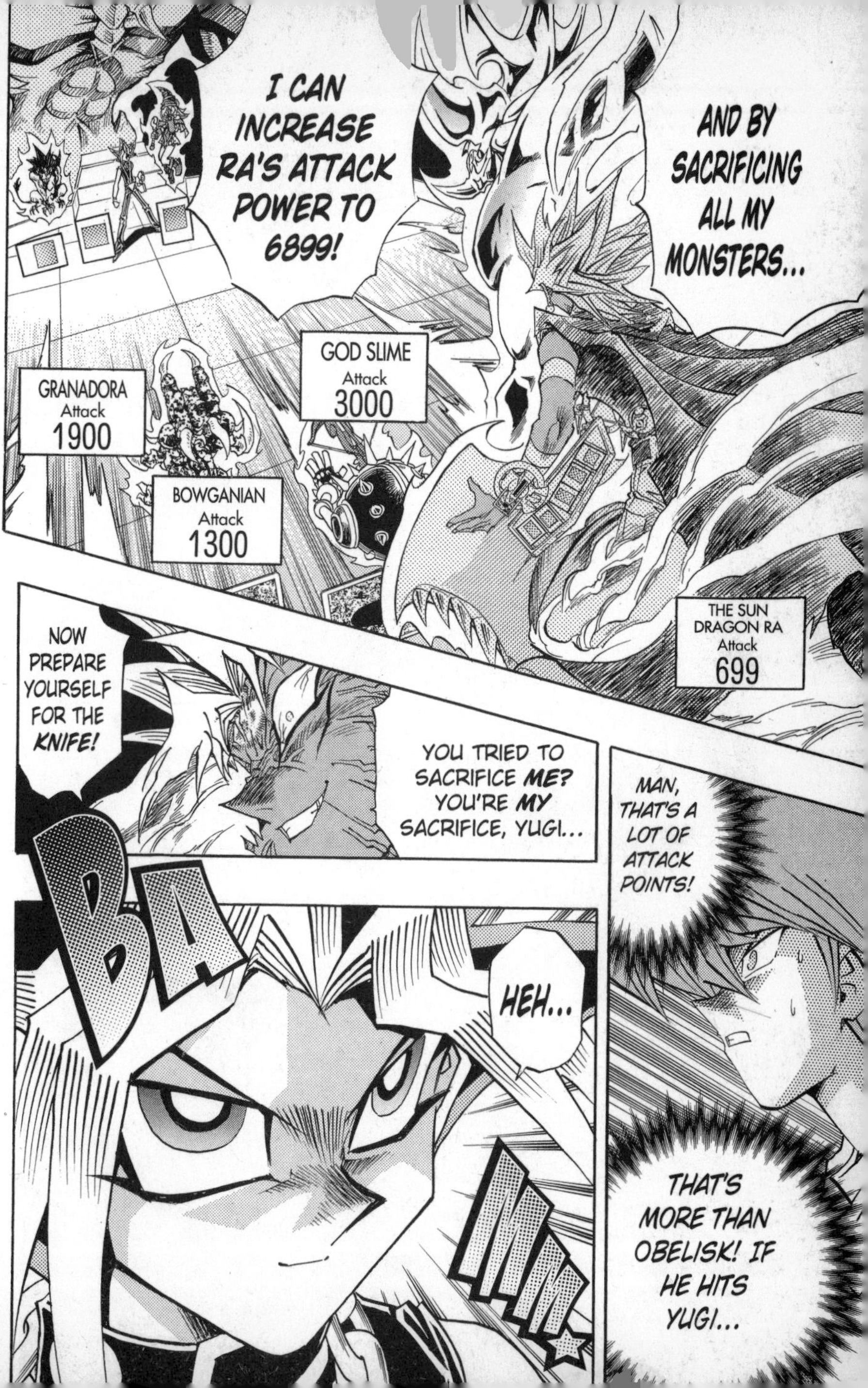
AND BY SACRIFICING ALL MY MONSTERS...
I CAN INCREASE RA'S ATTACK POWER TO 6899!
GOD SLIME Attack 3000
GRANADORA Attack 1900
BOWGANIAN Attack 1300
THE SUN DRAGON RA Attack 699
NOW PREPARE YOURSELF FOR THE *KNIFE!*
YOU TRIED TO SACRIFICE *ME?* YOU'RE *MY* SACRIFICE, YUGI...
MAN, THAT'S A LOT OF ATTACK POINTS!
THAT'S MORE THAN OBELISK! IF HE HITS YUGI...
BA
HEH...
MMM

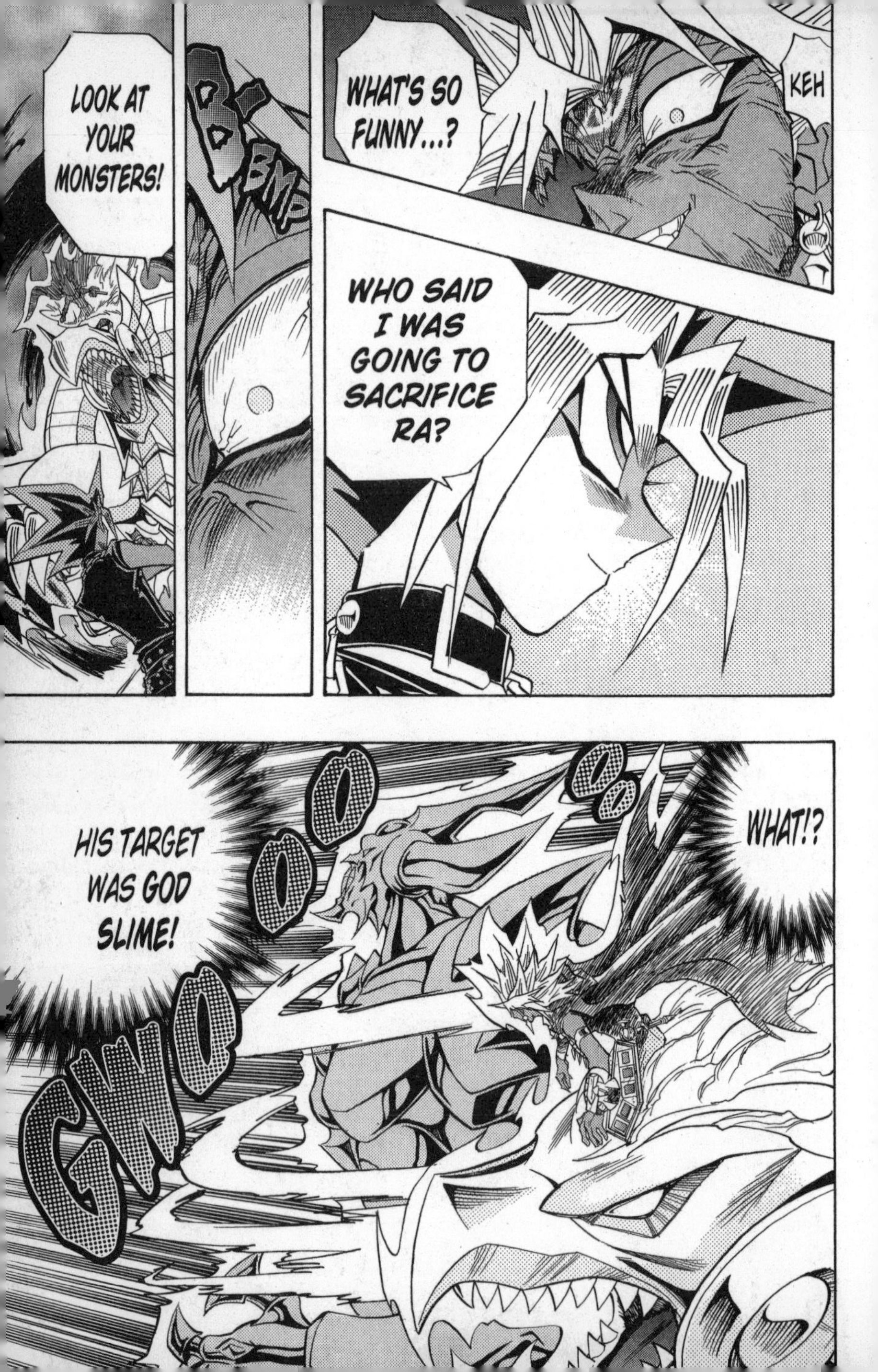
KEH
WHAT'S SO FUNNY...?
WHO SAID I WAS GOING TO SACRIFICE RA?
LOOK AT YOUR MONSTERS!
WHAT!?
HIS TARGET WAS GOD SLIME!
GWOOOO

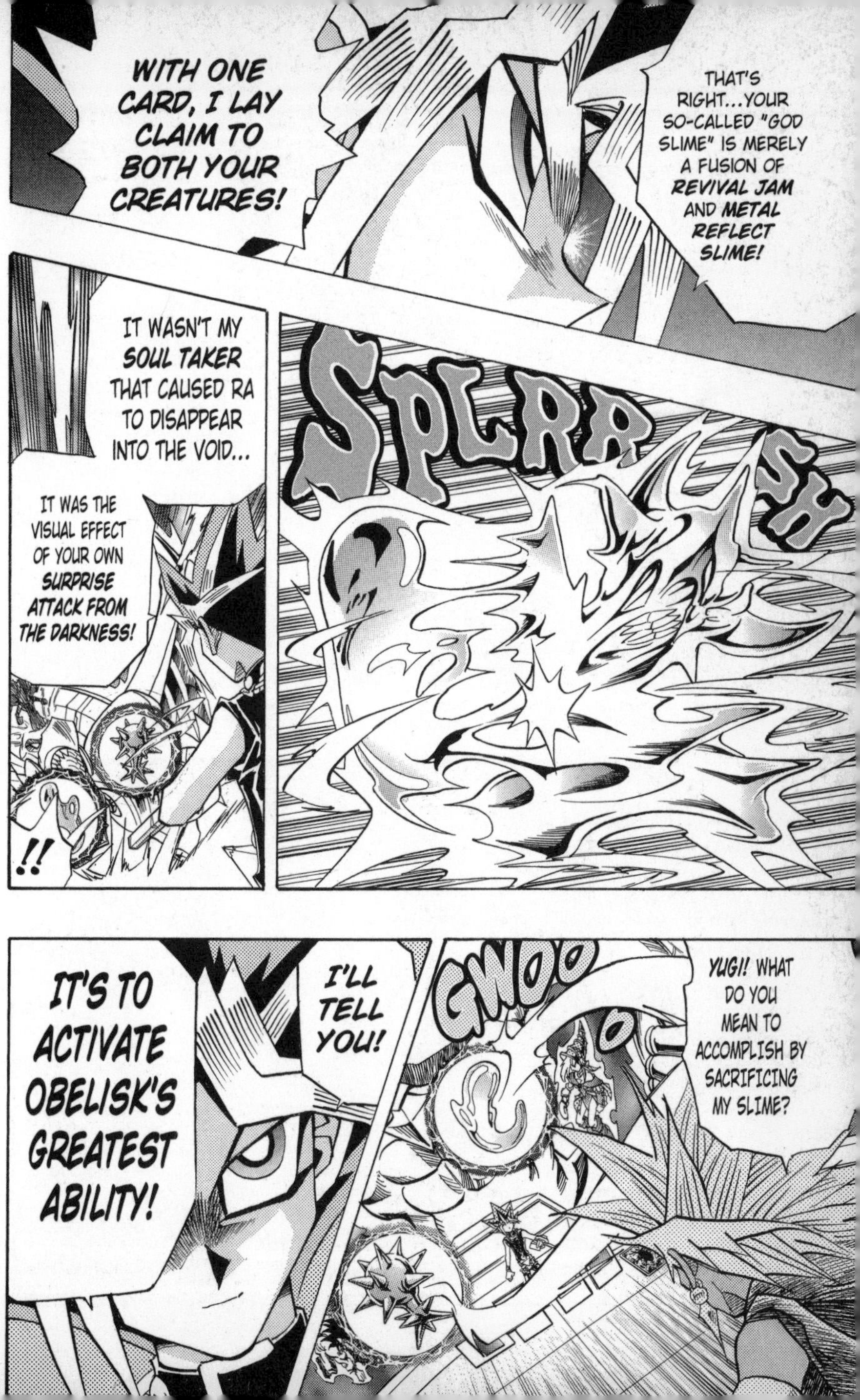
THAT'S RIGHT...YOUR SO-CALLED "GOD SLIME" IS MERELY A FUSION OF REVIVAL JAM AND METAL REFLECT SLIME!
WITH ONE CARD, I LAY CLAIM TO BOTH YOUR CREATURES!
SPLRRSH
IT WASN'T MY SOUL TAKER THAT CAUSED RA TO DISAPPEAR INTO THE VOID...
IT WAS THE VISUAL EFFECT OF YOUR OWN SURPRISE ATTACK FROM THE DARKNESS!
!!
YUGI!! WHAT DO YOU MEAN TO ACCOMPLISH BY SACRIFICING MY SLIME?
GWOO
I'LL TELL YOU!
IT'S TO ACTIVATE OBELISK'S GREATEST ABILITY!

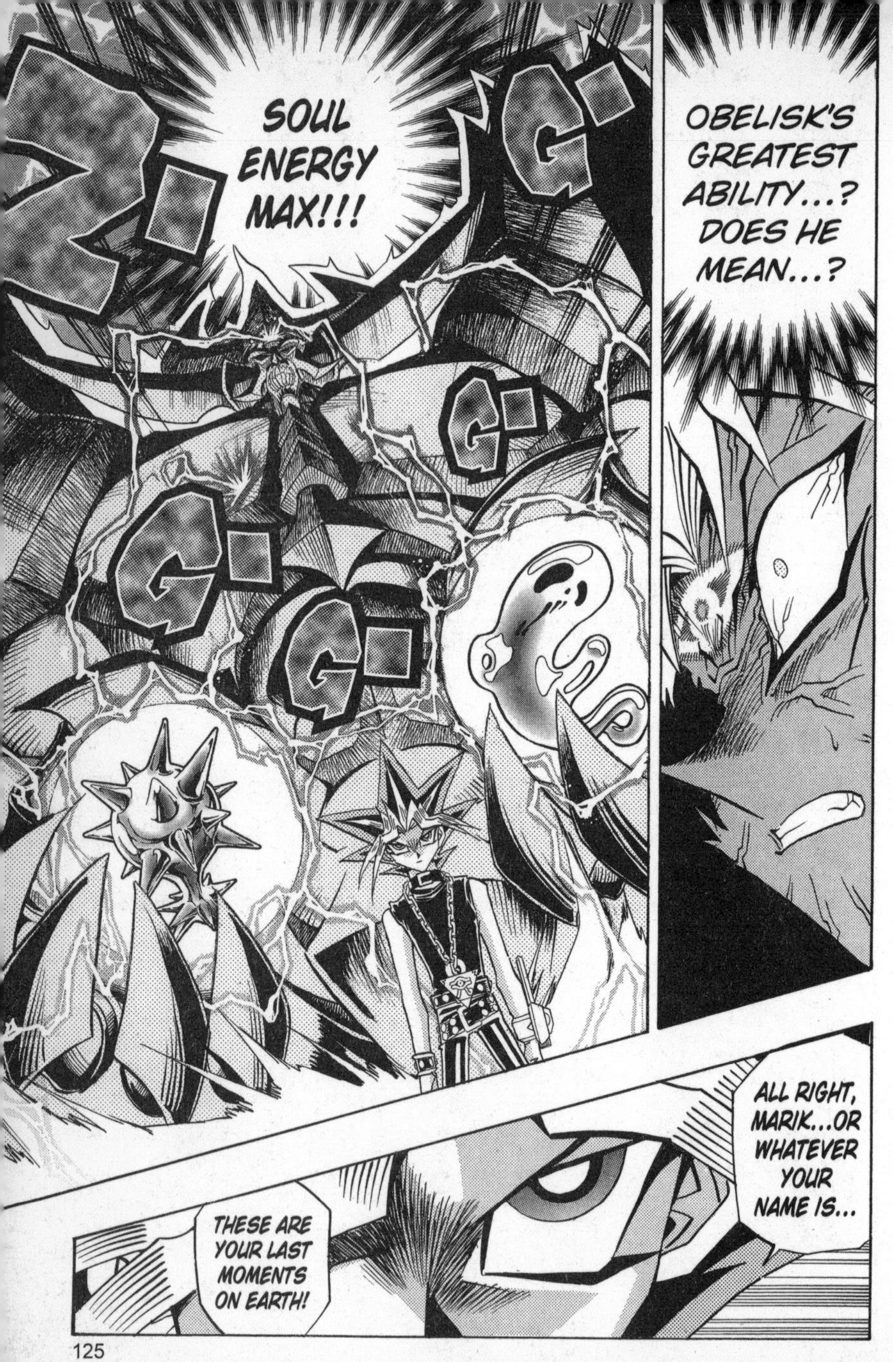
OBELISK'S GREATEST ABILITY...? DOES HE MEAN...?
Z
G
SOUL ENERGY MAX!!!
G
G
G
ALL RIGHT, MARIK...OR WHATEVER YOUR NAME IS...
THESE ARE YOUR LAST MOMENTS ON EARTH!

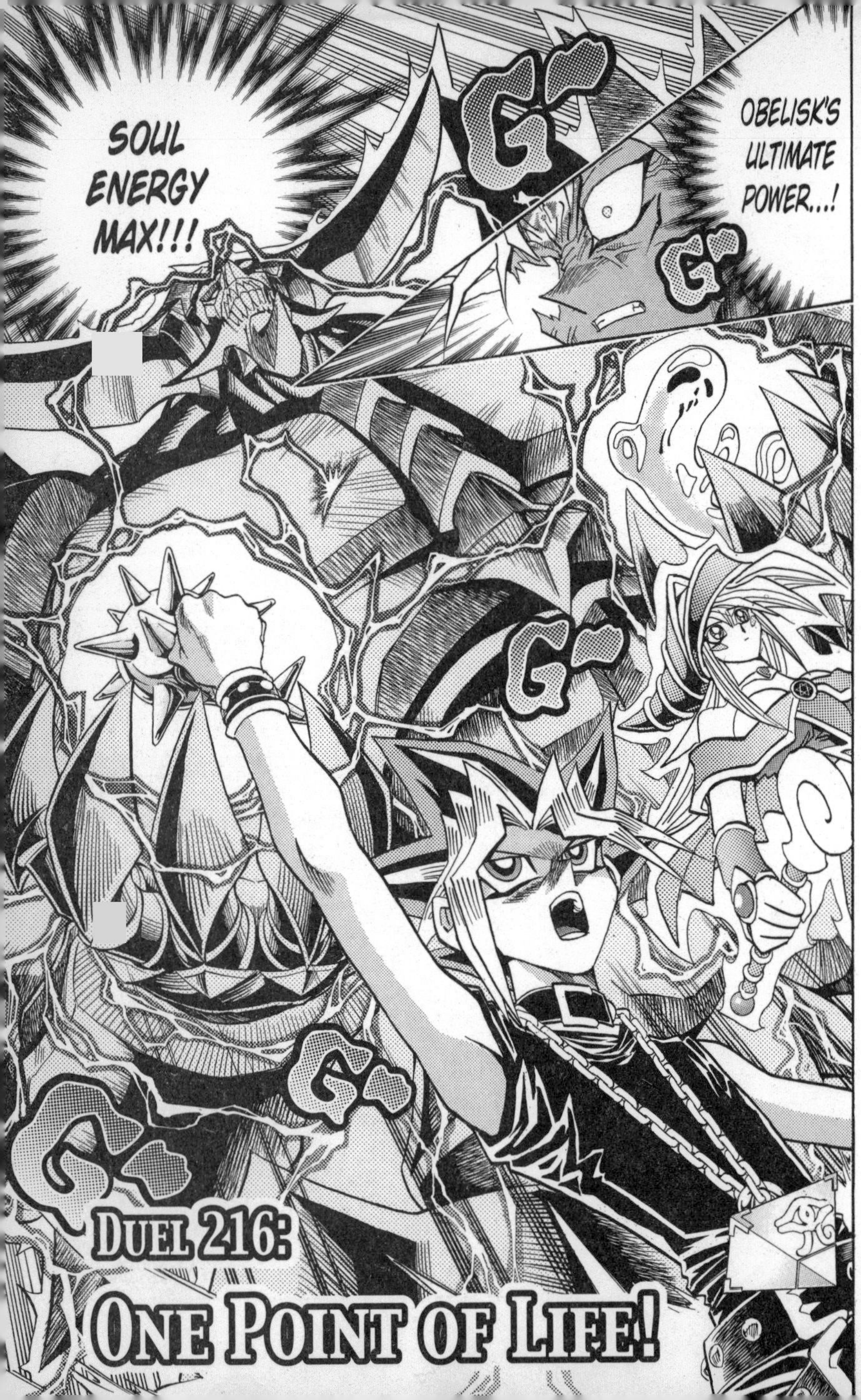
OBELISK'S ULTIMATE POWER...!
G
G
SOUL ENERGY MAX!!!
G
G
G
DUEL 216:
ONE POINT OF LIFE!

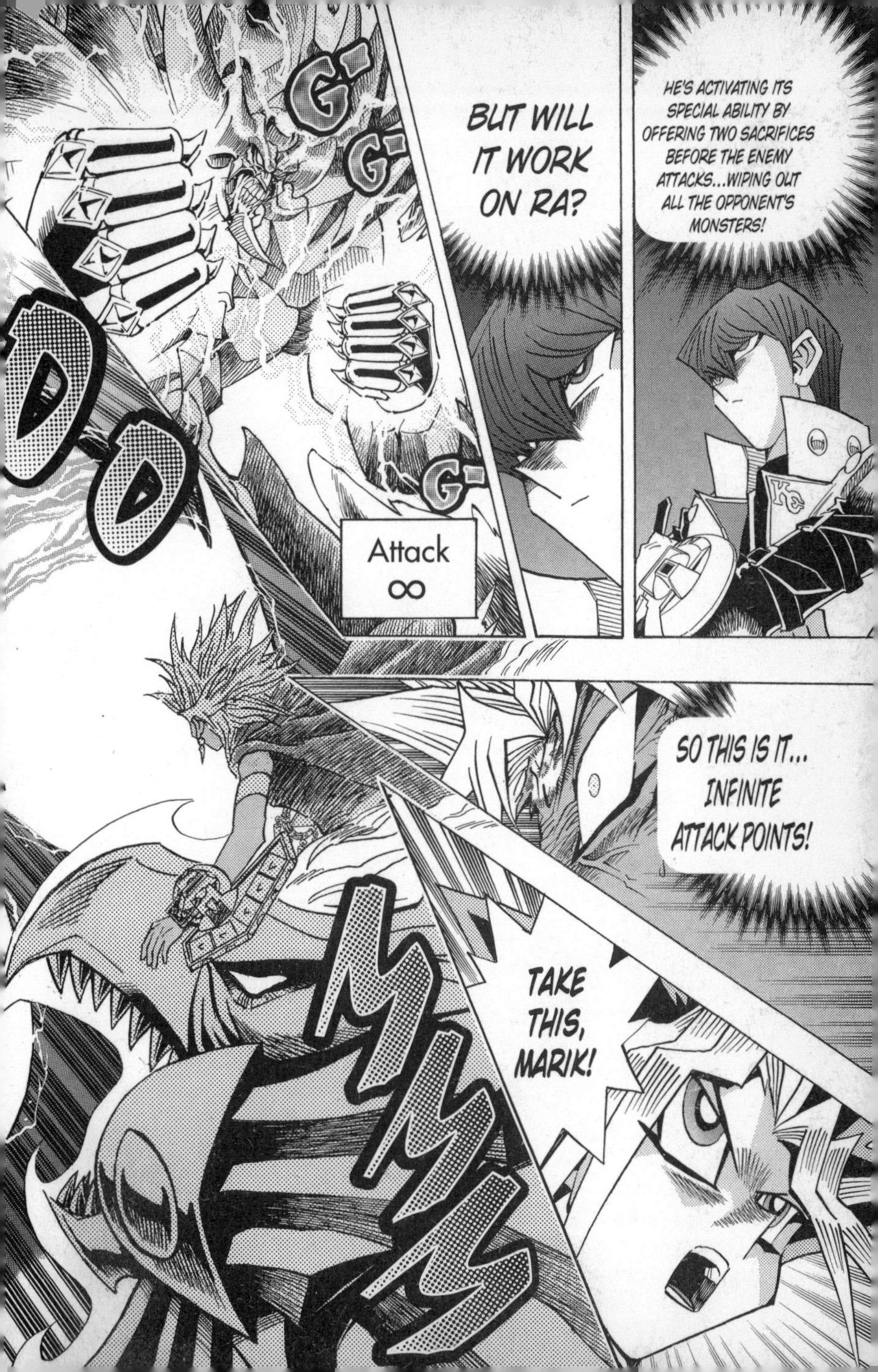
HE'S ACTIVATING ITS SPECIAL ABILITY BY OFFERING TWO SACRIFICES BEFORE THE ENEMY ATTACKS...WIPING OUT ALL THE OPPONENT'S MONSTERS!
BUT WILL IT WORK ON RA?
G-
G-
G-
D
D
Attack ∞
SO THIS IS IT... INFINITE ATTACK POINTS!
TAKE THIS, MARIK!

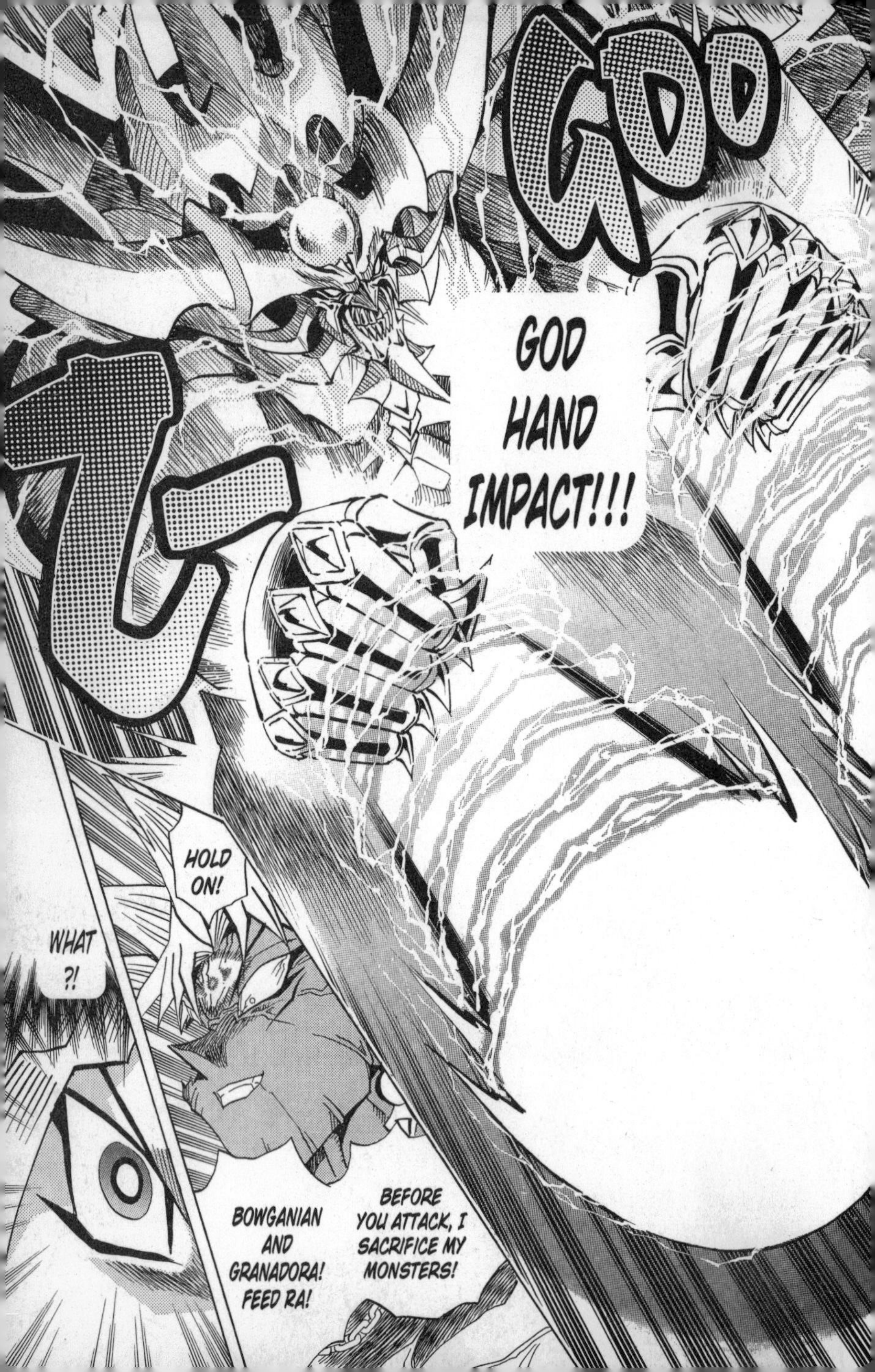
GOD HAND IMPACT!!!
HOLD ON!
WHAT?!
BEFORE YOU ATTACK, I SACRIFICE MY MONSTERS!
BOWGANIAN AND GRANADORA! FEED RA!

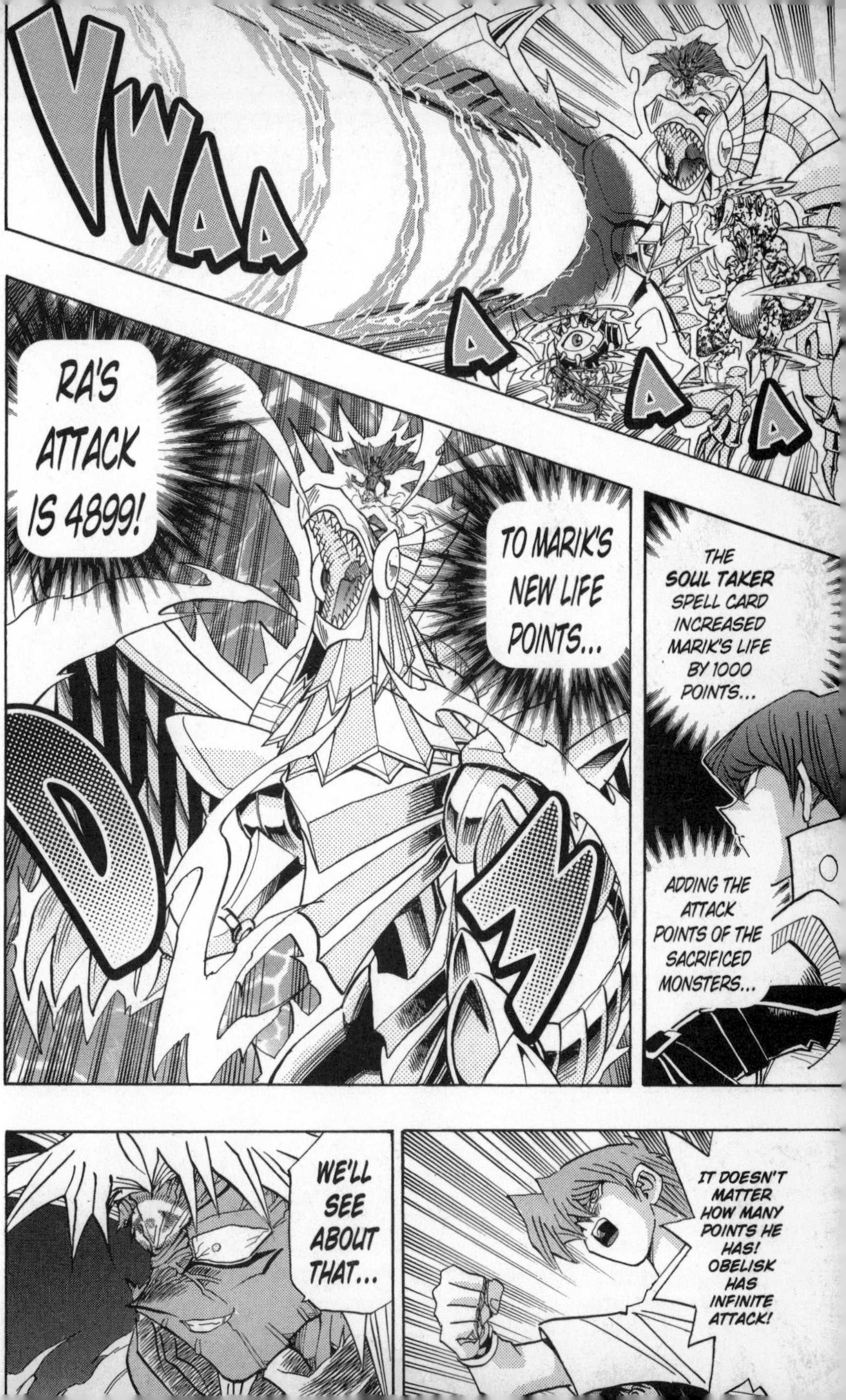
VWAAAAAA
THE SOUL TAKER SPELL CARD INCREASED MARIK'S LIFE BY 1000 POINTS...
ADDING THE ATTACK POINTS OF THE SACRIFICED MONSTERS...
TO MARIK'S NEW LIFE POINTS...
RA'S ATTACK IS 4899!
IT DOESN'T MATTER HOW MANY POINTS HE HAS! OBELISK HAS INFINITE ATTACK!
WE'LL SEE ABOUT THAT...

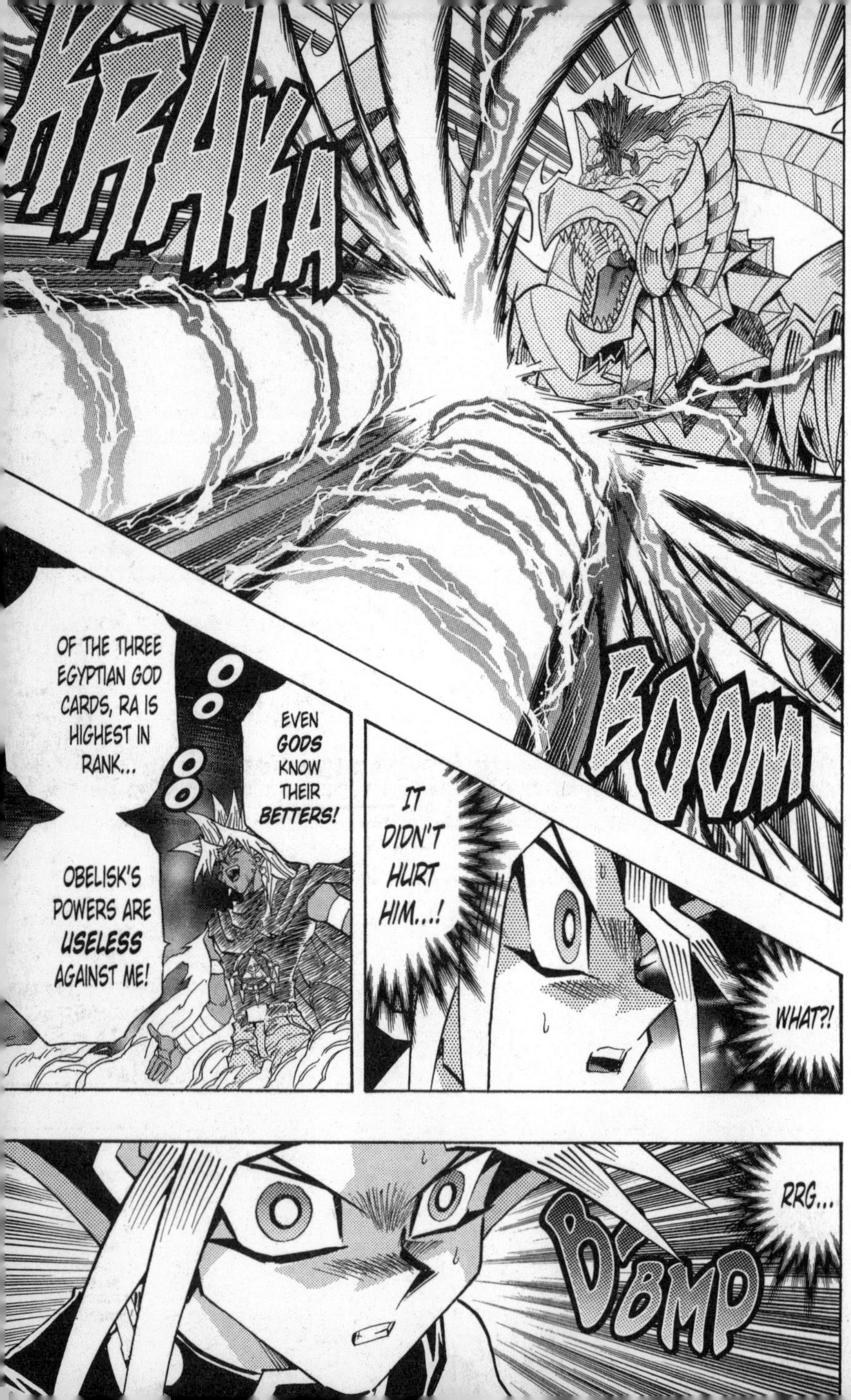
KRAKA
BOOM
IT DIDN'T HURT HIM...!
WHAT?!
OF THE THREE EGYPTIAN GOD CARDS, RA IS HIGHEST IN RANK...
EVEN GODS KNOW THEIR BETTERS!
OBELISK'S POWERS ARE USELESS AGAINST ME!
RRG...
B'BMP

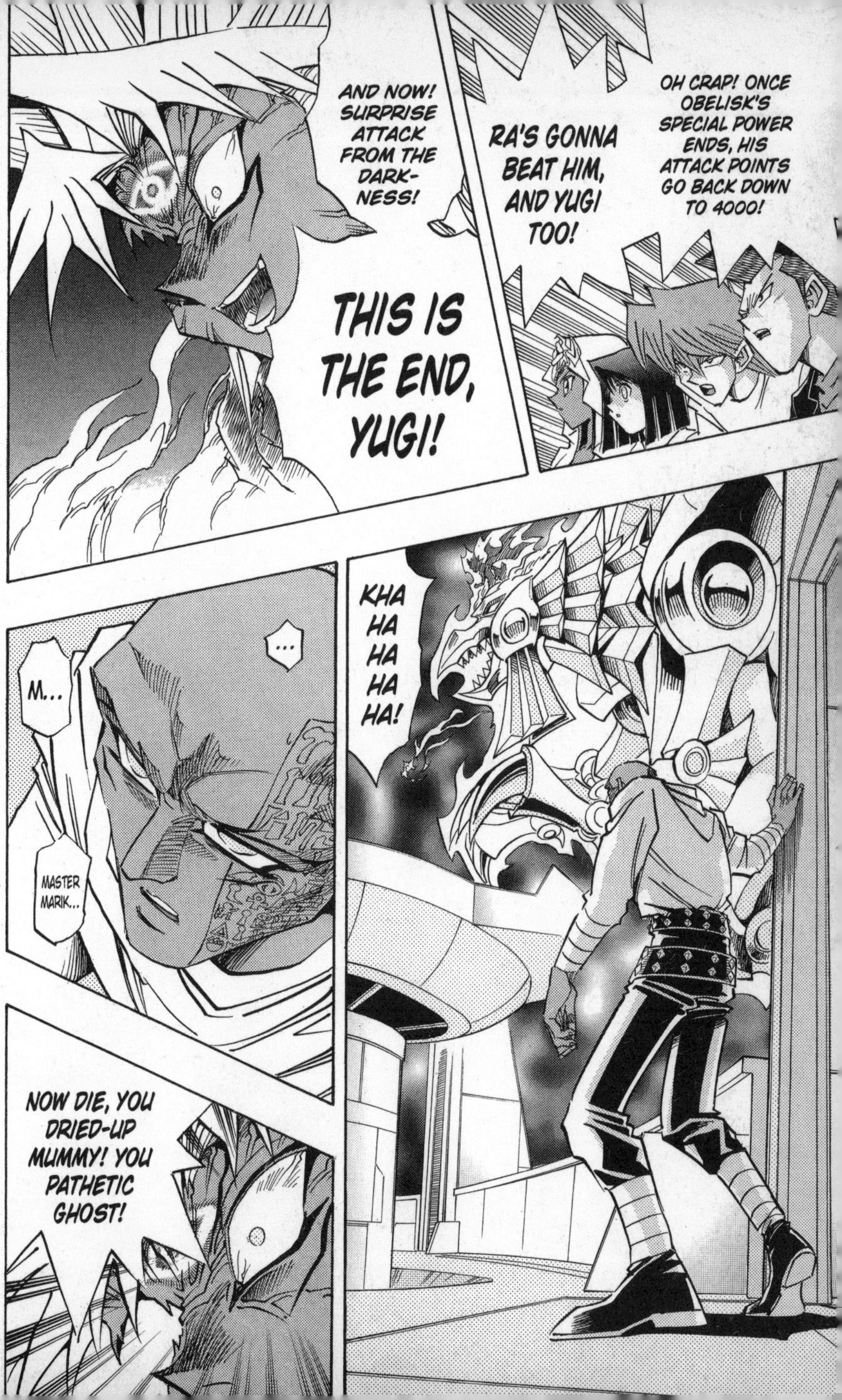
OH CRAP! ONCE OBELISK'S SPECIAL POWER ENDS, HIS ATTACK POINTS GO BACK DOWN TO 4000!
RA'S GONNA BEAT HIM, AND YUGI TOO!
AND NOW! SURPRISE ATTACK FROM THE DARK-NESS!
THIS IS THE END, YUGI!
KHA HA HA HA HA!
...
M...
MASTER MARIK...
NOW DIE, YOU DRIED-UP MUMMY! YOU PATHETIC GHOST!

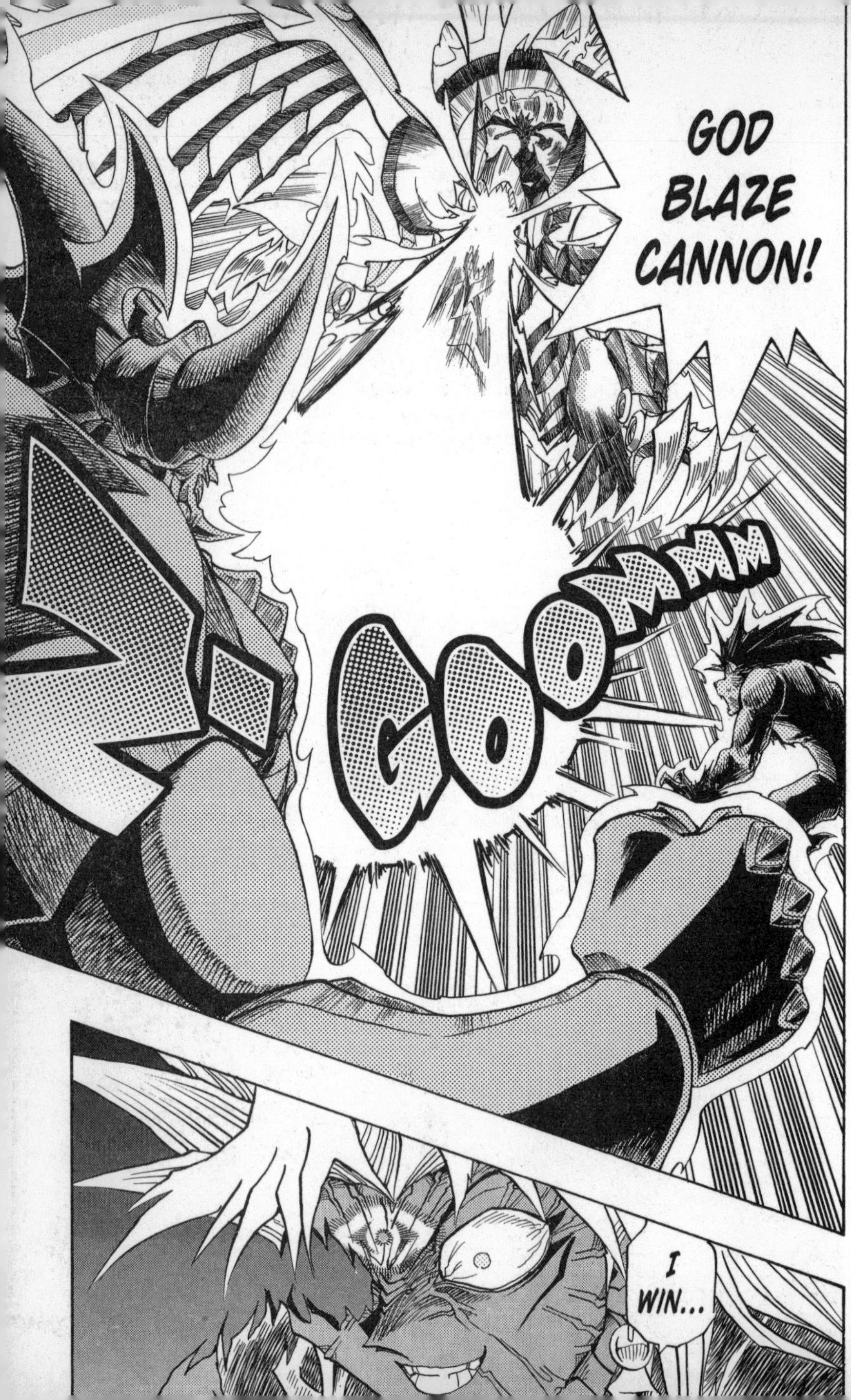
GOD BLAZE CANNON!
GOOMMMM
I WIN...

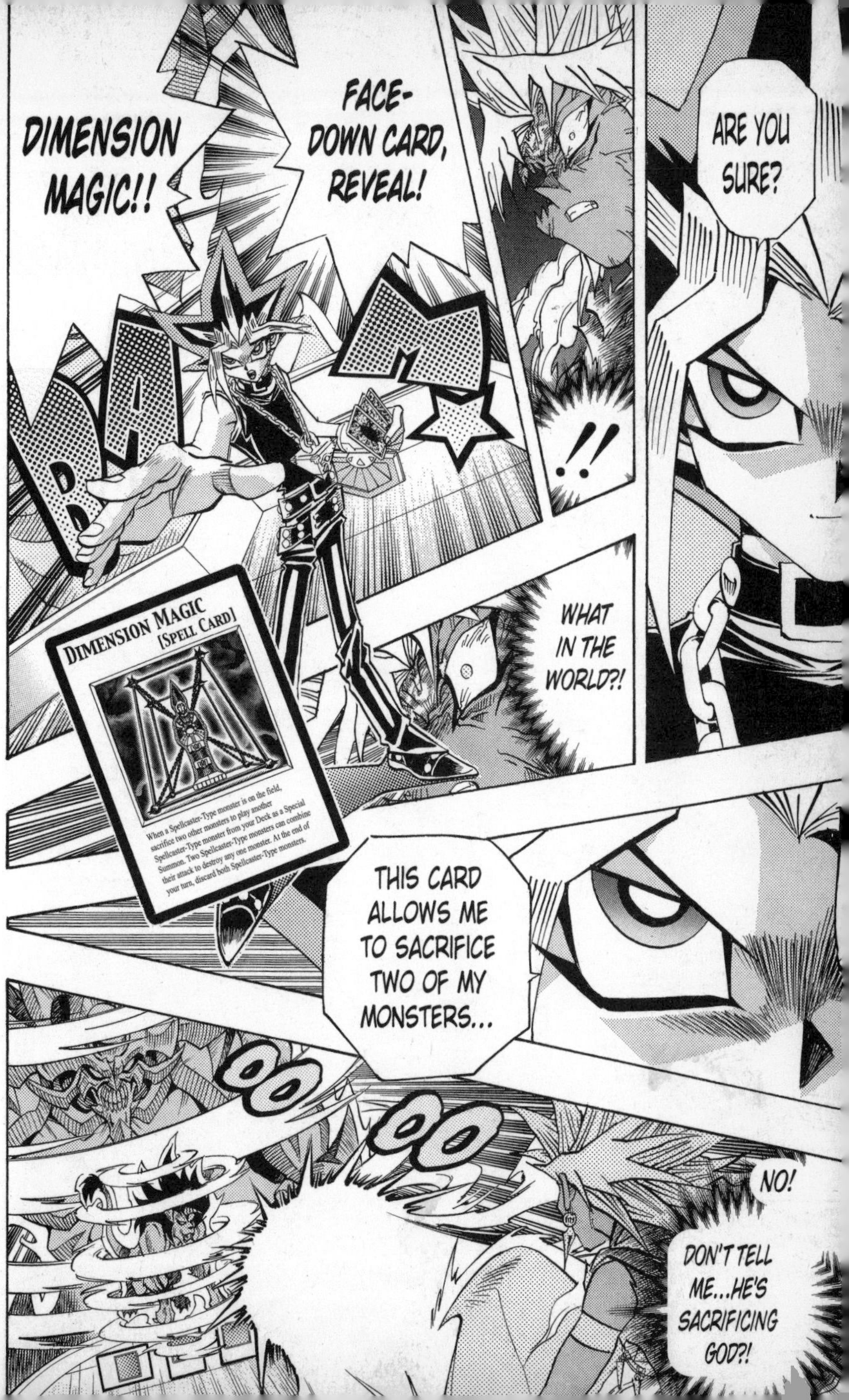
ARE YOU SURE?
!!
WHAT IN THE WORLD?!
FACE-DOWN CARD, REVEAL!
DIMENSION MAGIC!!
DIMENSION MAGIC [SPELL CARD]
When a Spellcaster-Type monster is on the field, sacrifice two other monsters to play another Spellcaster-Type monster from your Deck as a Special Summon. Two Spellcaster-Type monsters can combine their attack to destroy any one monster. At the end of your turn, discard both Spellcaster-Type monsters.
THIS CARD ALLOWS ME TO SACRIFICE TWO OF MY MONSTERS...
NO!
DON'T TELL ME...HE'S SACRIFICING GOD?!

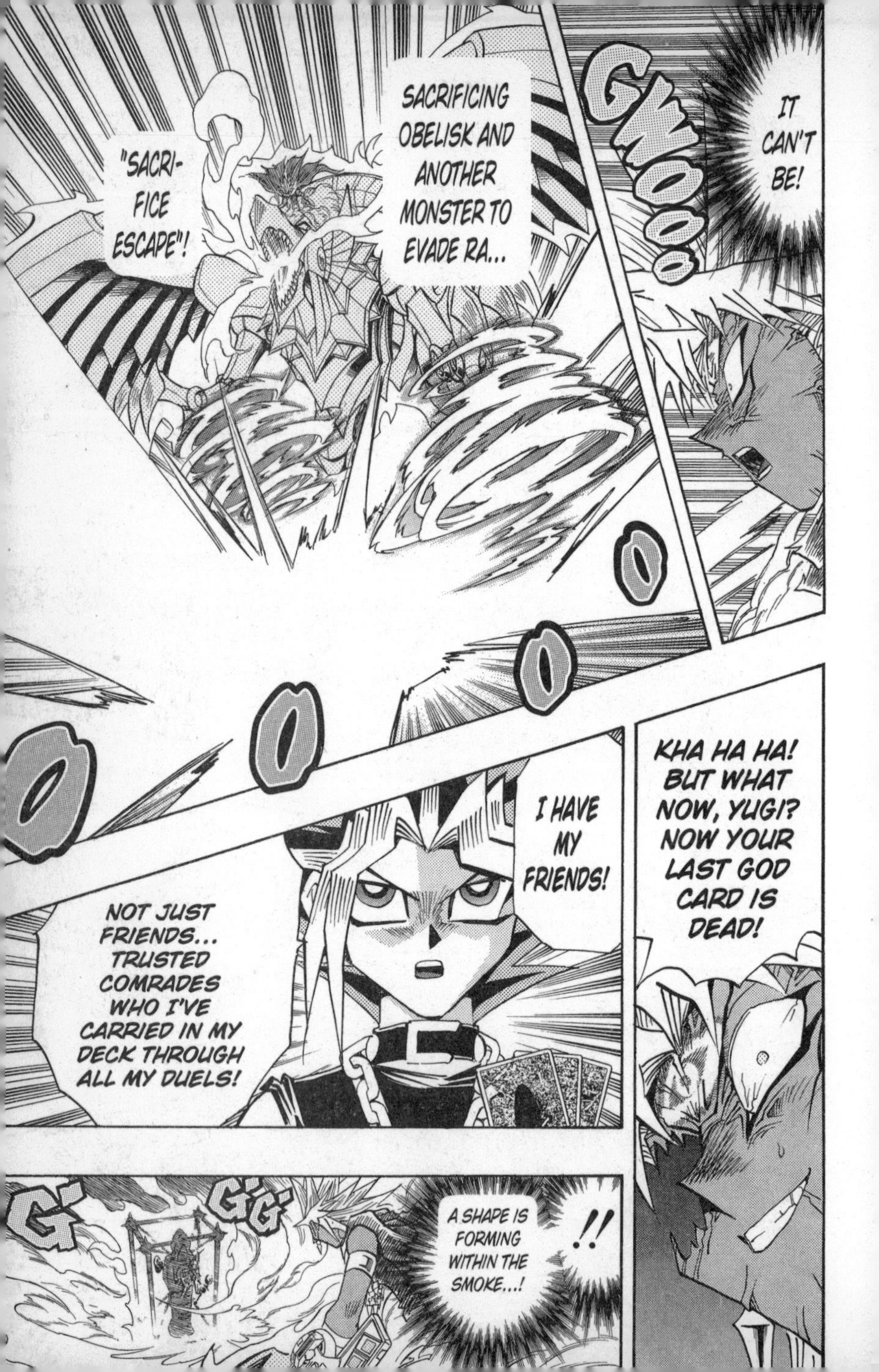
GWOOOO
IT CAN'T BE!
SACRIFICING OBELISK AND ANOTHER MONSTER TO EVADE RA...
"SACRI-FICE ESCAPE"!
OOOO
KHA HA HA! BUT WHAT NOW, YUGI? NOW YOUR LAST GOD CARD IS DEAD!
I HAVE MY FRIENDS!
NOT JUST FRIENDS... TRUSTED COMRADES WHO I'VE CARRIED IN MY DECK THROUGH ALL MY DUELS!
!!
A SHAPE IS FORMING WITHIN THE SMOKE...!
G'G'
G'

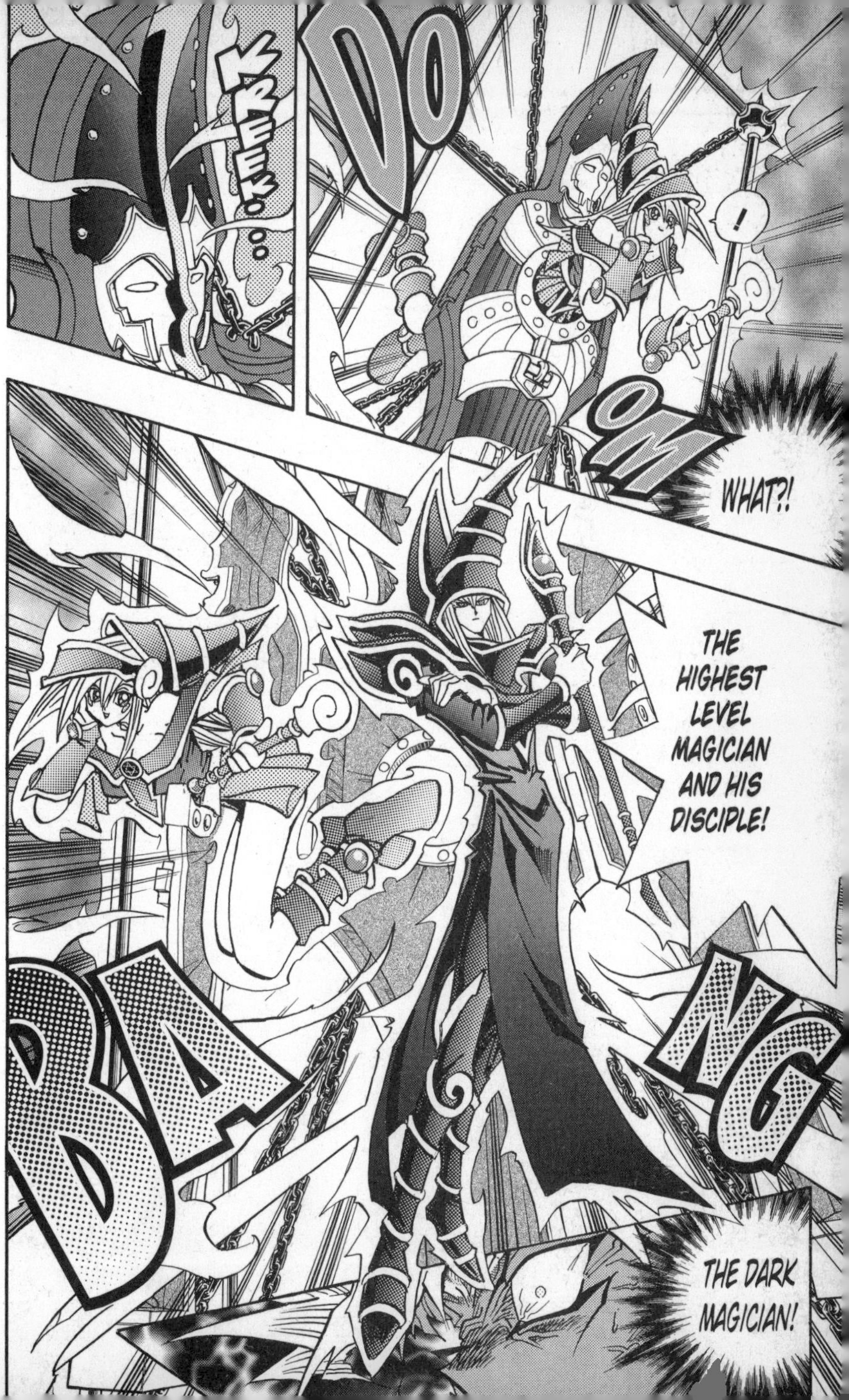
DOOM
!
KREEK...
WHAT?!
THE HIGHEST LEVEL MAGICIAN AND HIS DISCIPLE!
BANG
THE DARK MAGICIAN!

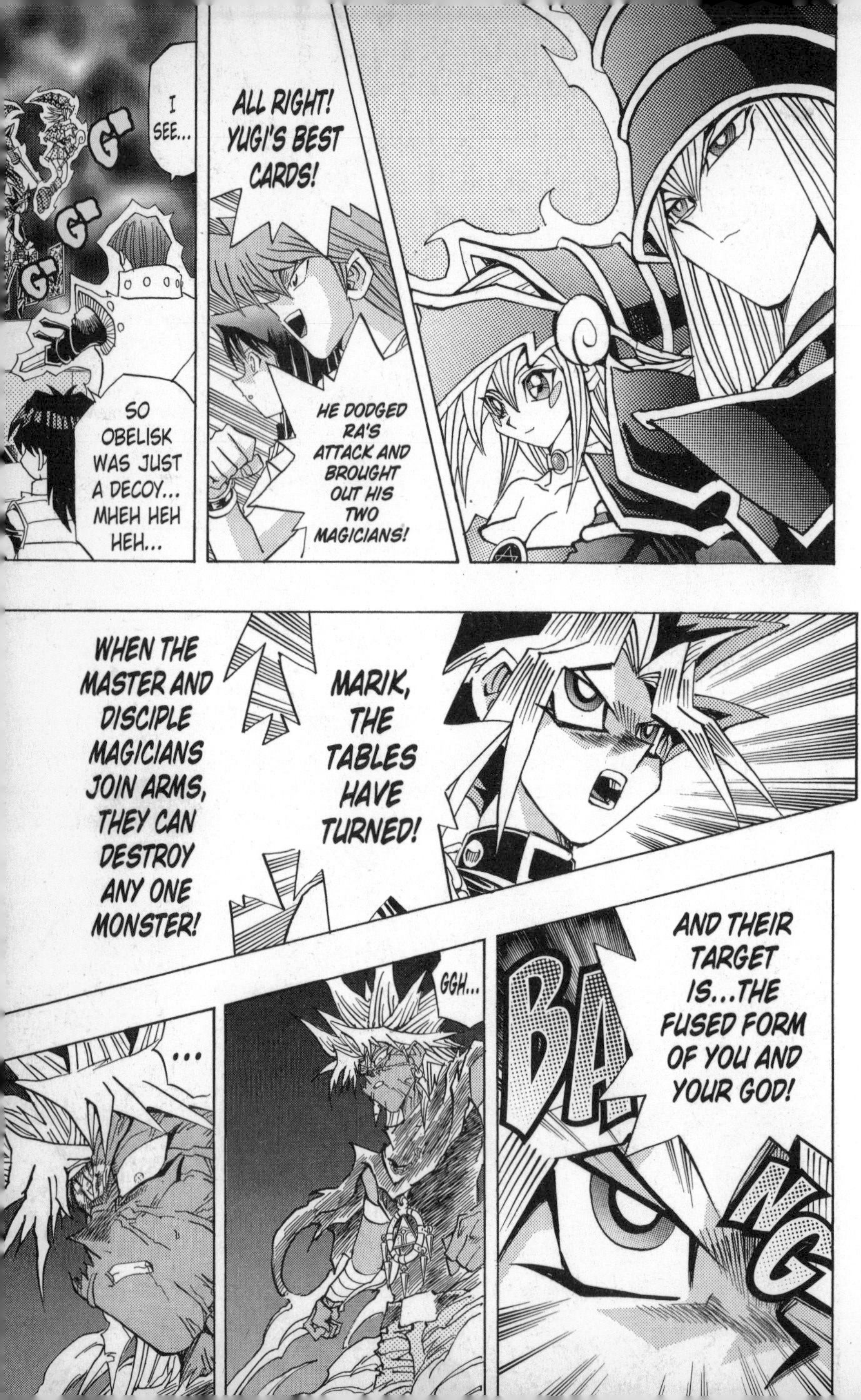
ALL RIGHT! YUGI'S BEST CARDS!
HE DODGED RA'S ATTACK AND BROUGHT OUT HIS TWO MAGICIANS!
I SEE...
G G G
SO OBELISK WAS JUST A DECOY... MHEH HEH HEH...
MARIK, THE TABLES HAVE TURNED!
WHEN THE MASTER AND DISCIPLE MAGICIANS JOIN ARMS, THEY CAN DESTROY ANY ONE MONSTER!
AND THEIR TARGET IS...THE FUSED FORM OF YOU AND YOUR GOD!
BA NG
GGH...
...

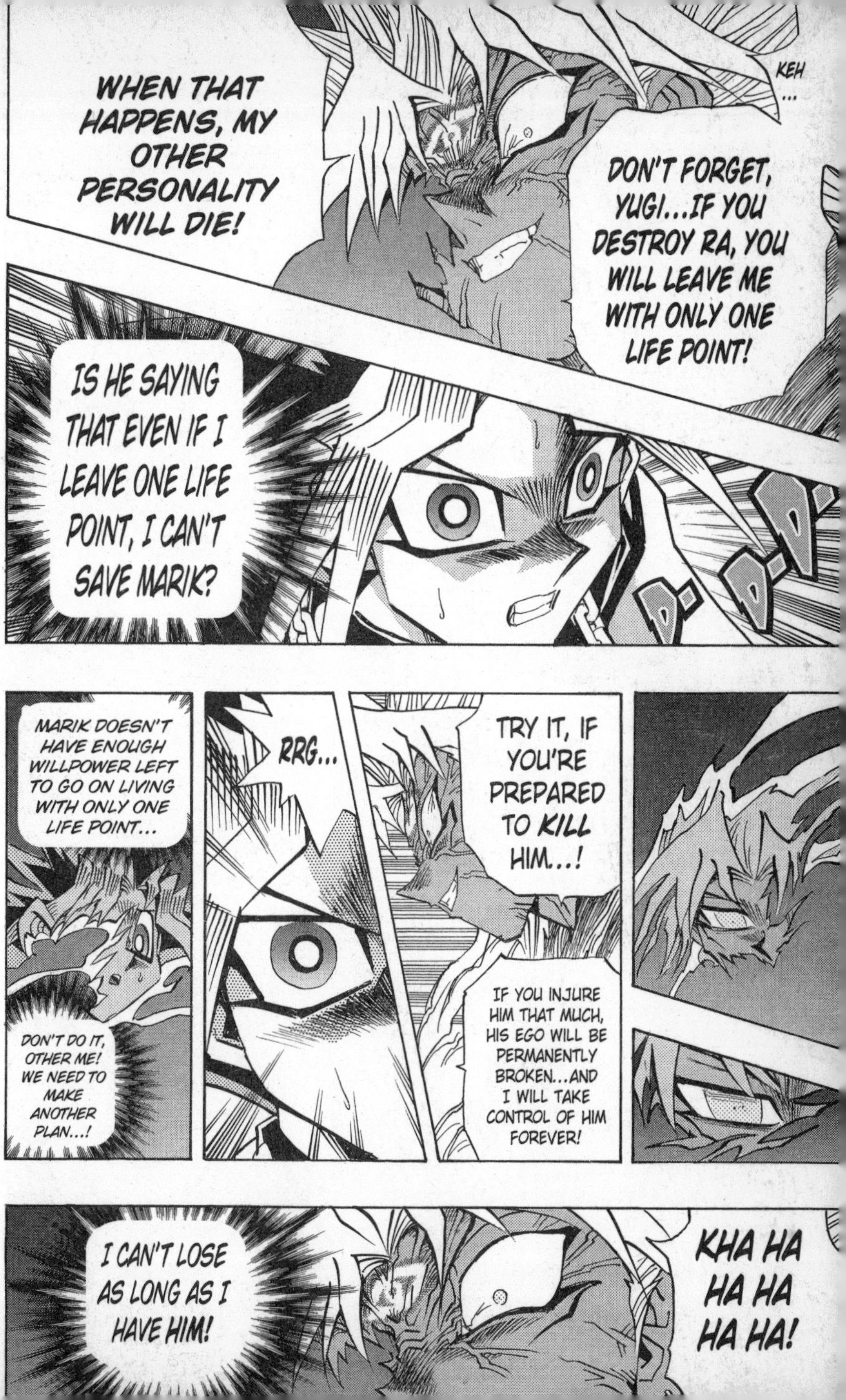
KEH...
DON'T FORGET, YUGI...IF YOU DESTROY RA, YOU WILL LEAVE ME WITH ONLY ONE LIFE POINT!
WHEN THAT HAPPENS, MY OTHER PERSONALITY WILL DIE!
IS HE SAYING THAT EVEN IF I LEAVE ONE LIFE POINT, I CAN'T SAVE MARIK?
TRY IT, IF YOU'RE PREPARED TO KILL HIM...!
IF YOU INJURE HIM THAT MUCH, HIS EGO WILL BE PERMANENTLY BROKEN...AND I WILL TAKE CONTROL OF HIM FOREVER!
RRG...
MARIK DOESN'T HAVE ENOUGH WILLPOWER LEFT TO GO ON LIVING WITH ONLY ONE LIFE POINT...
DON'T DO IT, OTHER ME! WE NEED TO MAKE ANOTHER PLAN...!
KHA HA HA HA HA HA!
I CAN'T LOSE AS LONG AS I HAVE HIM!

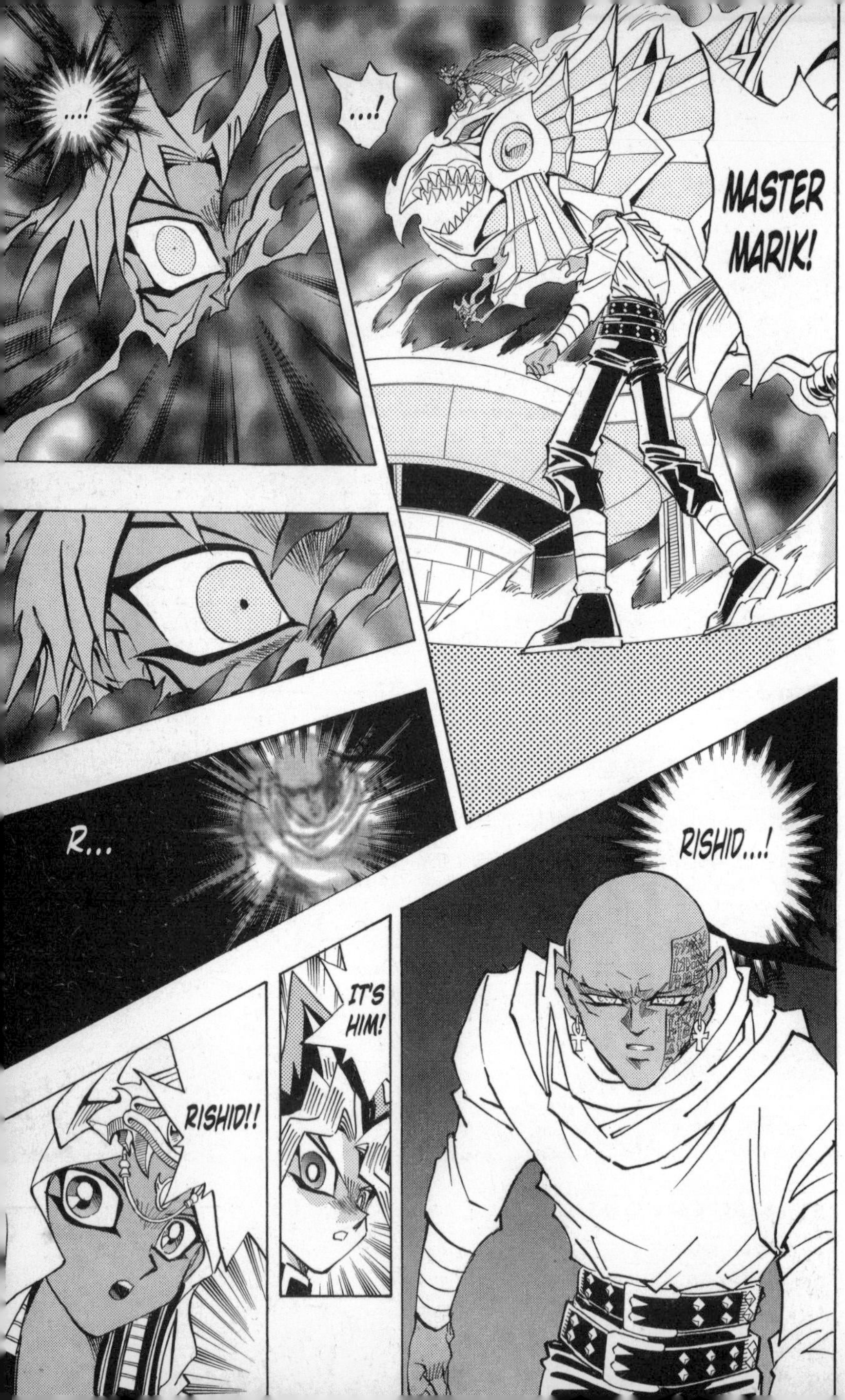
...!
MASTER MARIK!
...!
R...
RISHID...!
IT'S HIM!
RISHID!!

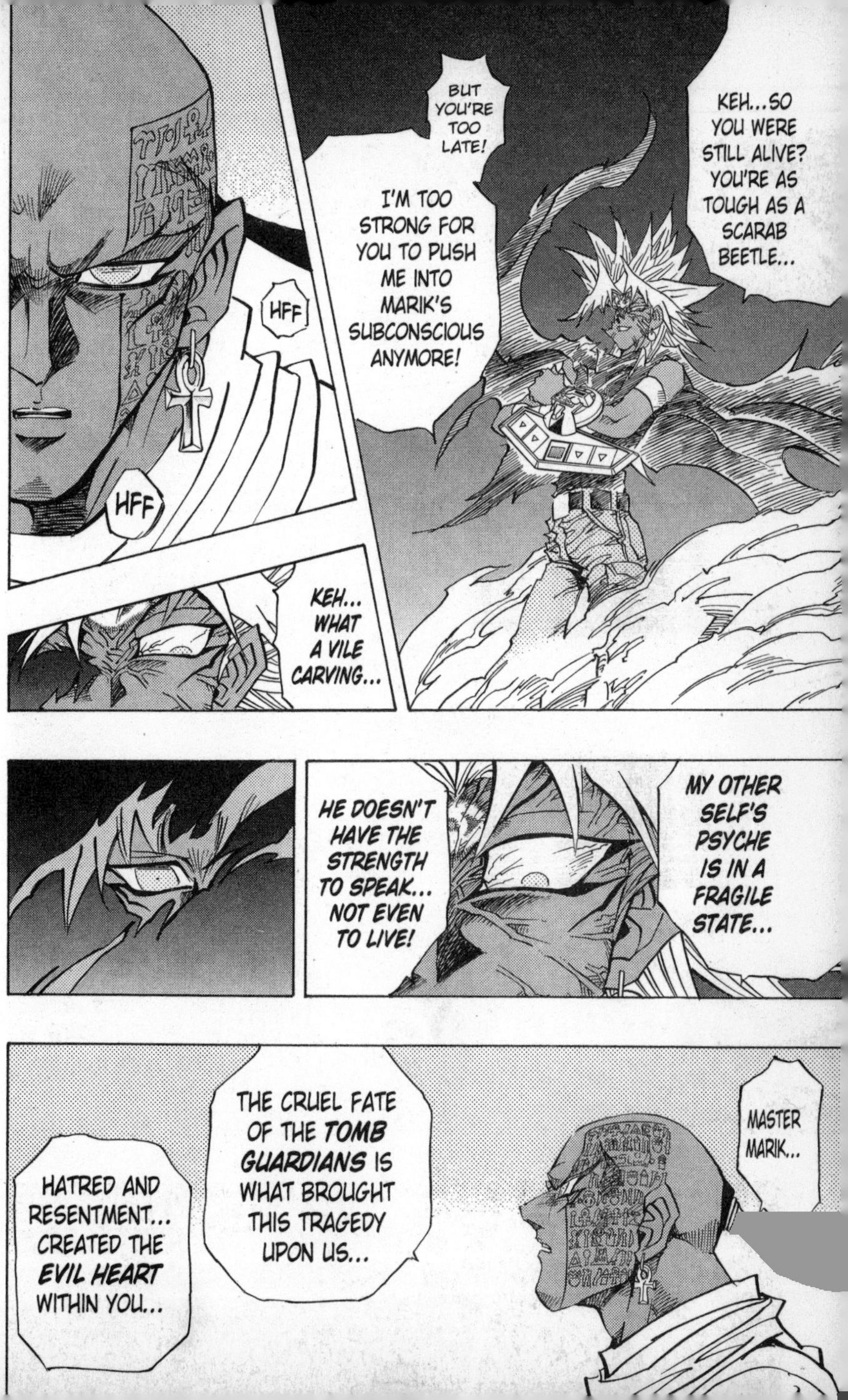
KEH...SO YOU WERE STILL ALIVE? YOU'RE AS TOUGH AS A SCARAB BEETLE...
BUT YOU'RE TOO LATE!
I'M TOO STRONG FOR YOU TO PUSH ME INTO MARIK'S SUBCONSCIOUS ANYMORE!
HFF
HFF
KEH... WHAT A VILE CARVING...
MY OTHER SELF'S PSYCHE IS IN A FRAGILE STATE...
HE DOESN'T HAVE THE STRENGTH TO SPEAK... NOT EVEN TO LIVE!
MASTER MARIK...
THE CRUEL FATE OF THE *TOMB GUARDIANS* IS WHAT BROUGHT THIS TRAGEDY UPON US...
HATRED AND RESENTMENT... CREATED THE *EVIL HEART* WITHIN YOU...

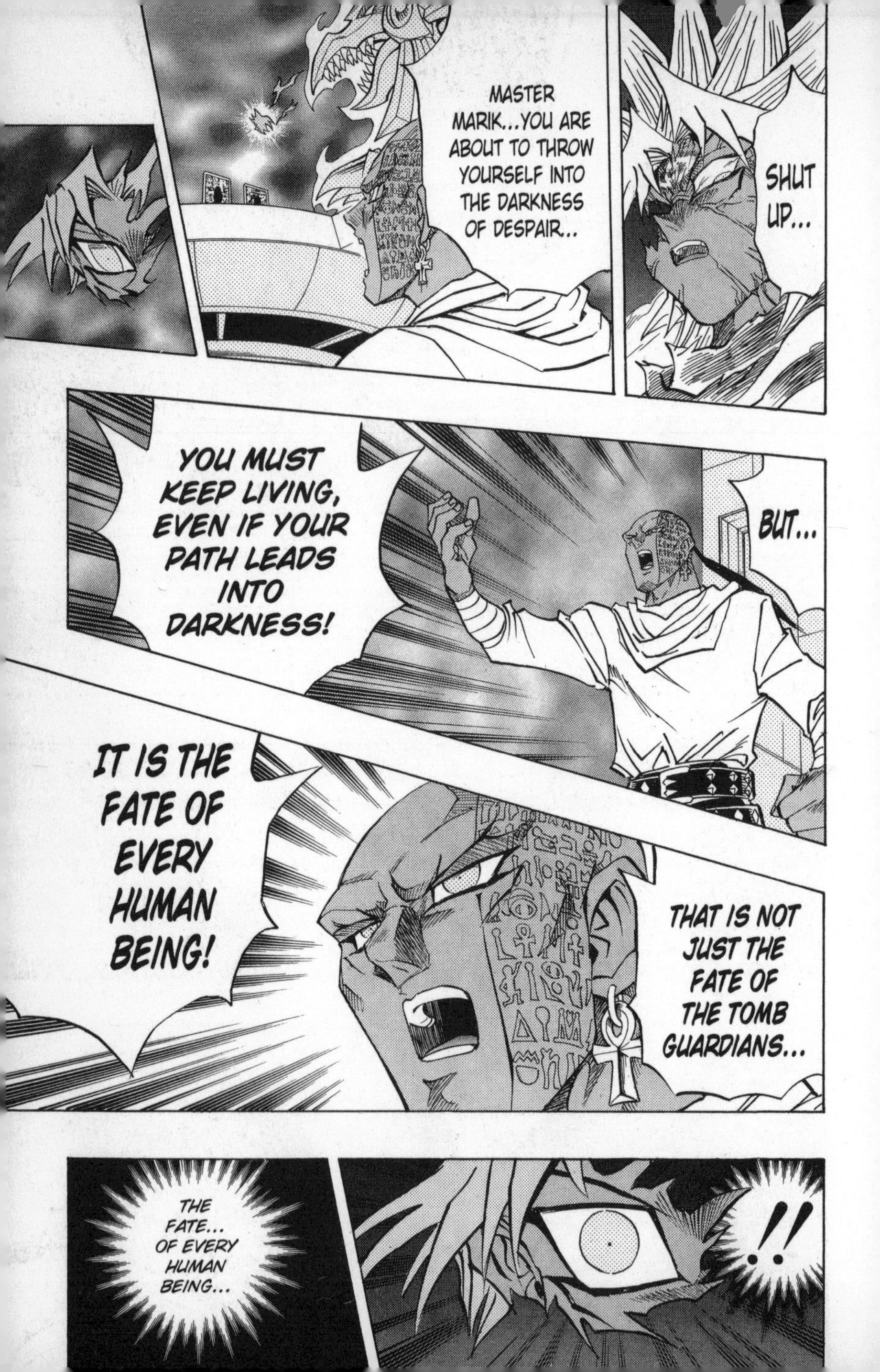
SHUT UP...
MASTER MARIK...YOU ARE ABOUT TO THROW YOURSELF INTO THE DARKNESS OF DESPAIR...
BUT...
YOU MUST KEEP LIVING, EVEN IF YOUR PATH LEADS INTO DARKNESS!
THAT IS NOT JUST THE FATE OF THE TOMB GUARDIANS...
IT IS THE FATE OF EVERY HUMAN BEING!
!!
THE FATE... OF EVERY HUMAN BEING...

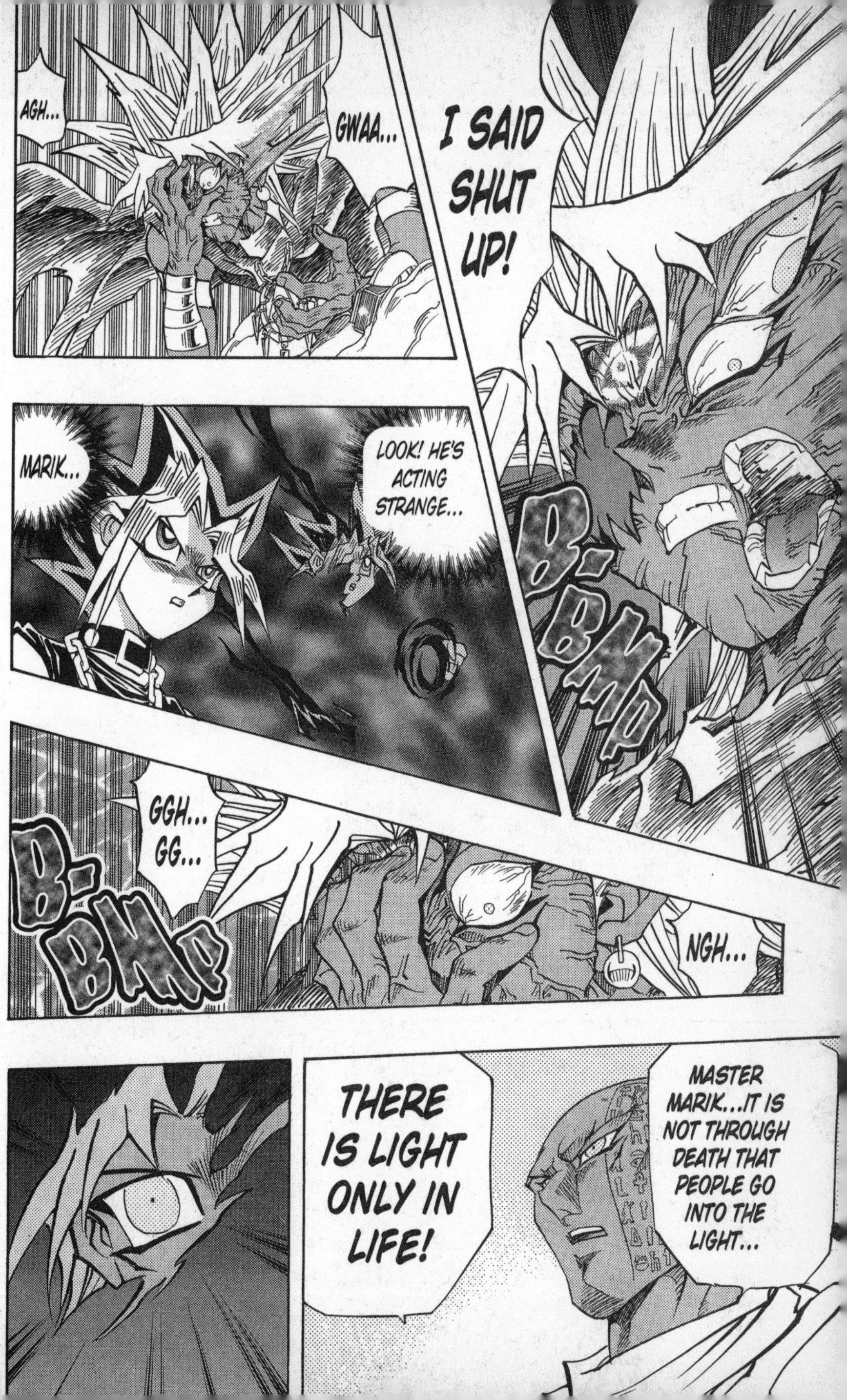
I SAID SHUT UP!
B-BMP
GWAA...
AGH...
LOOK! HE'S ACTING STRANGE...
MARIK...
NGH...
GGH... GG...
B-BMP
MASTER MARIK...IT IS NOT THROUGH DEATH THAT PEOPLE GO INTO THE LIGHT...
THERE IS LIGHT ONLY IN LIFE!

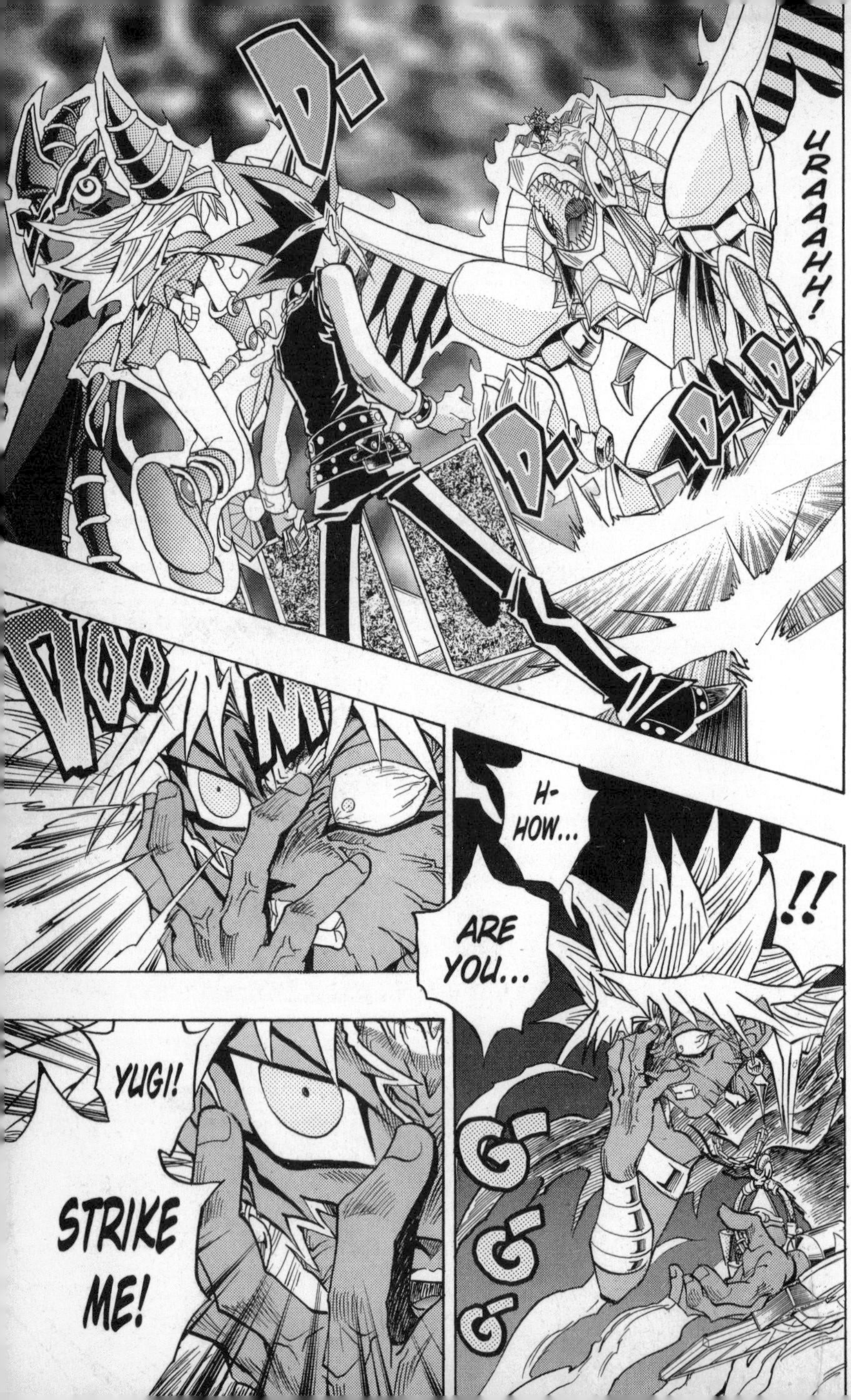
URAAAAHH!
D!
D! D! D!
DOOM
H- HOW...
ARE YOU...
!!
G G G
YUGI!
STRIKE ME!

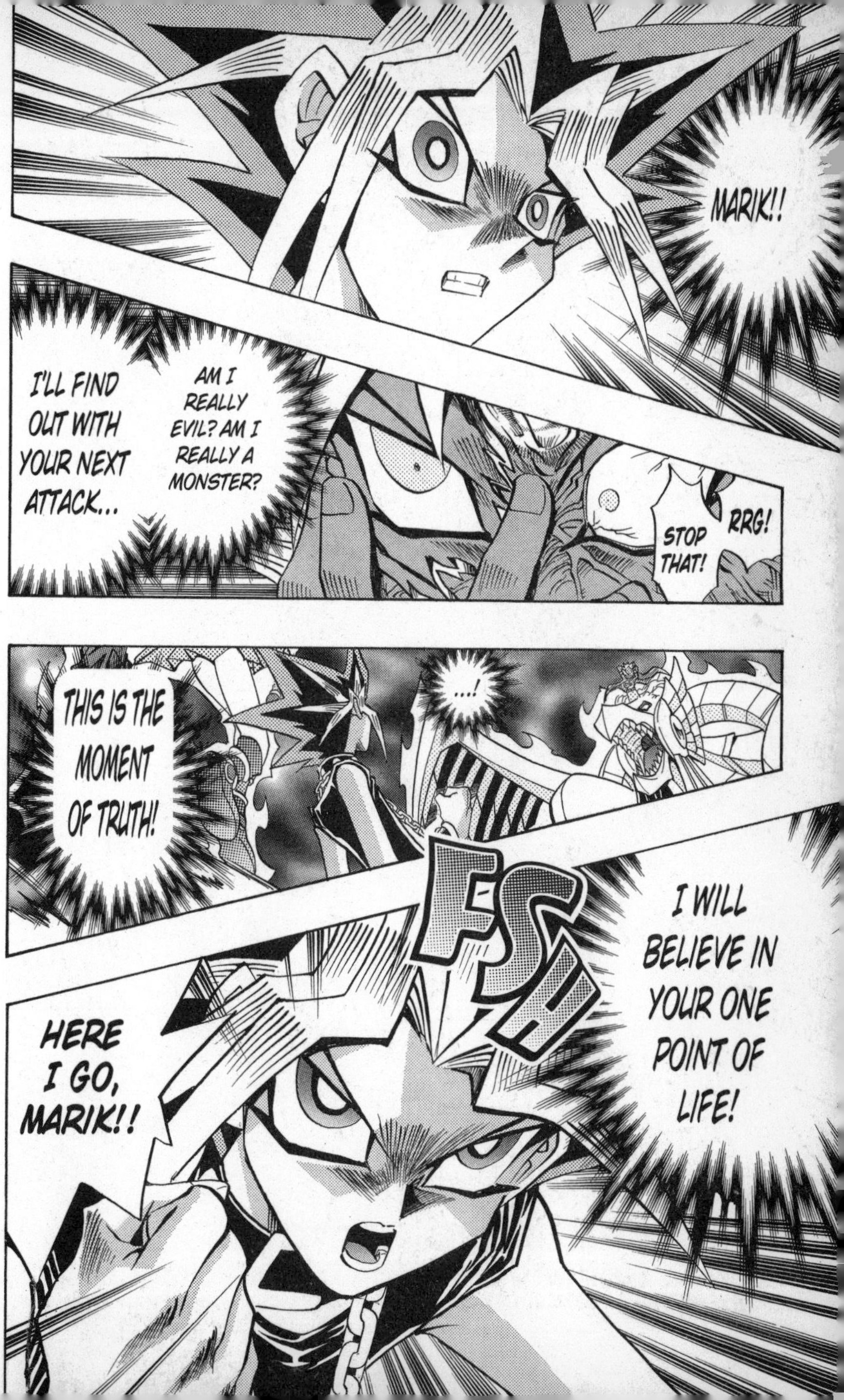
MARIK!!
RRG!
STOP THAT!
AM I REALLY EVIL? AM I REALLY A MONSTER?
I'LL FIND OUT WITH YOUR NEXT ATTACK...
...!
THIS IS THE MOMENT OF TRUTH!
FSH
I WILL BELIEVE IN YOUR ONE POINT OF LIFE!
HERE I GO, MARIK!!

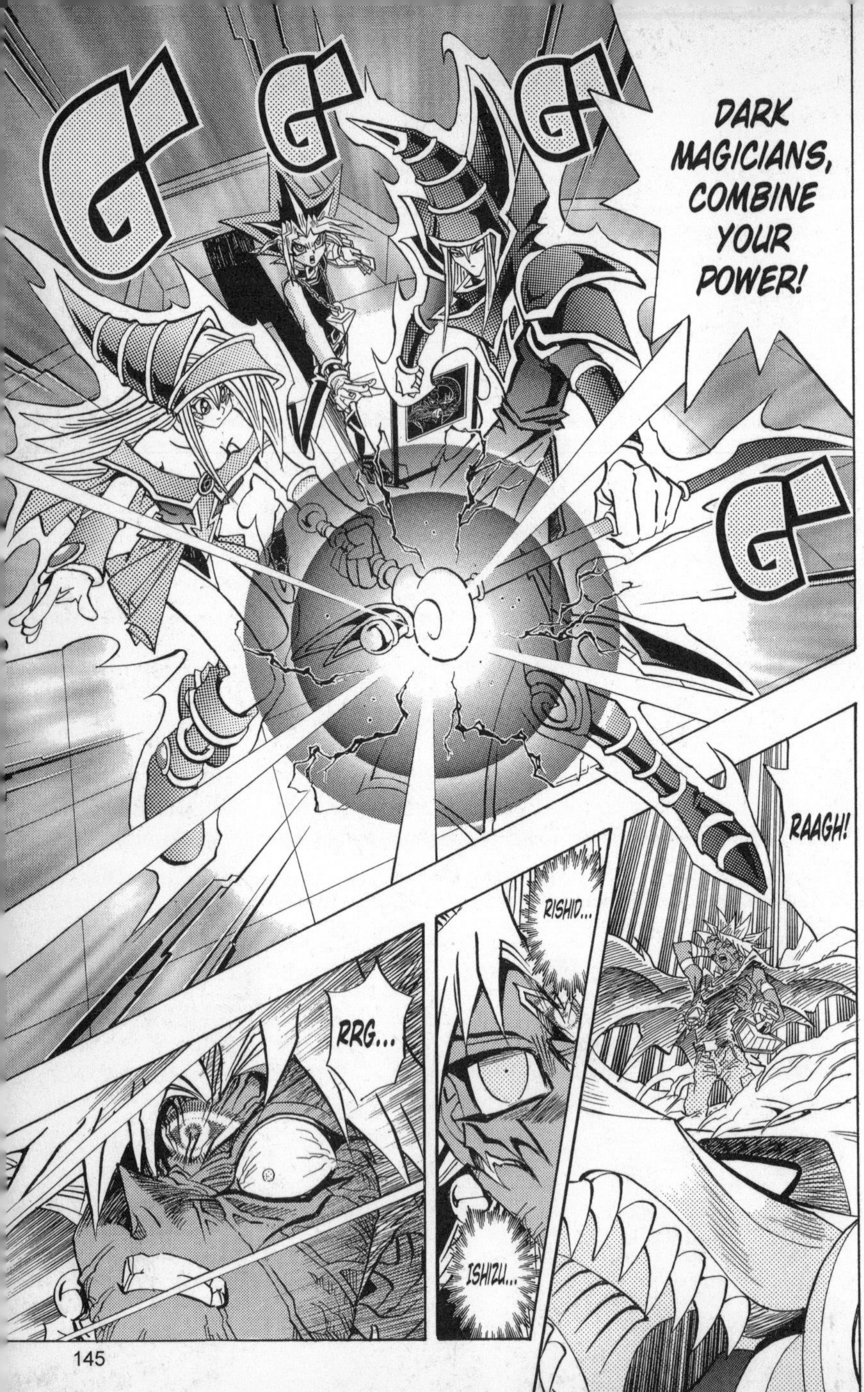
G G G
DARK MAGICIANS, COMBINE YOUR POWER!
G
RAAGH!
RISHID...
ISHIZU...
RRG...

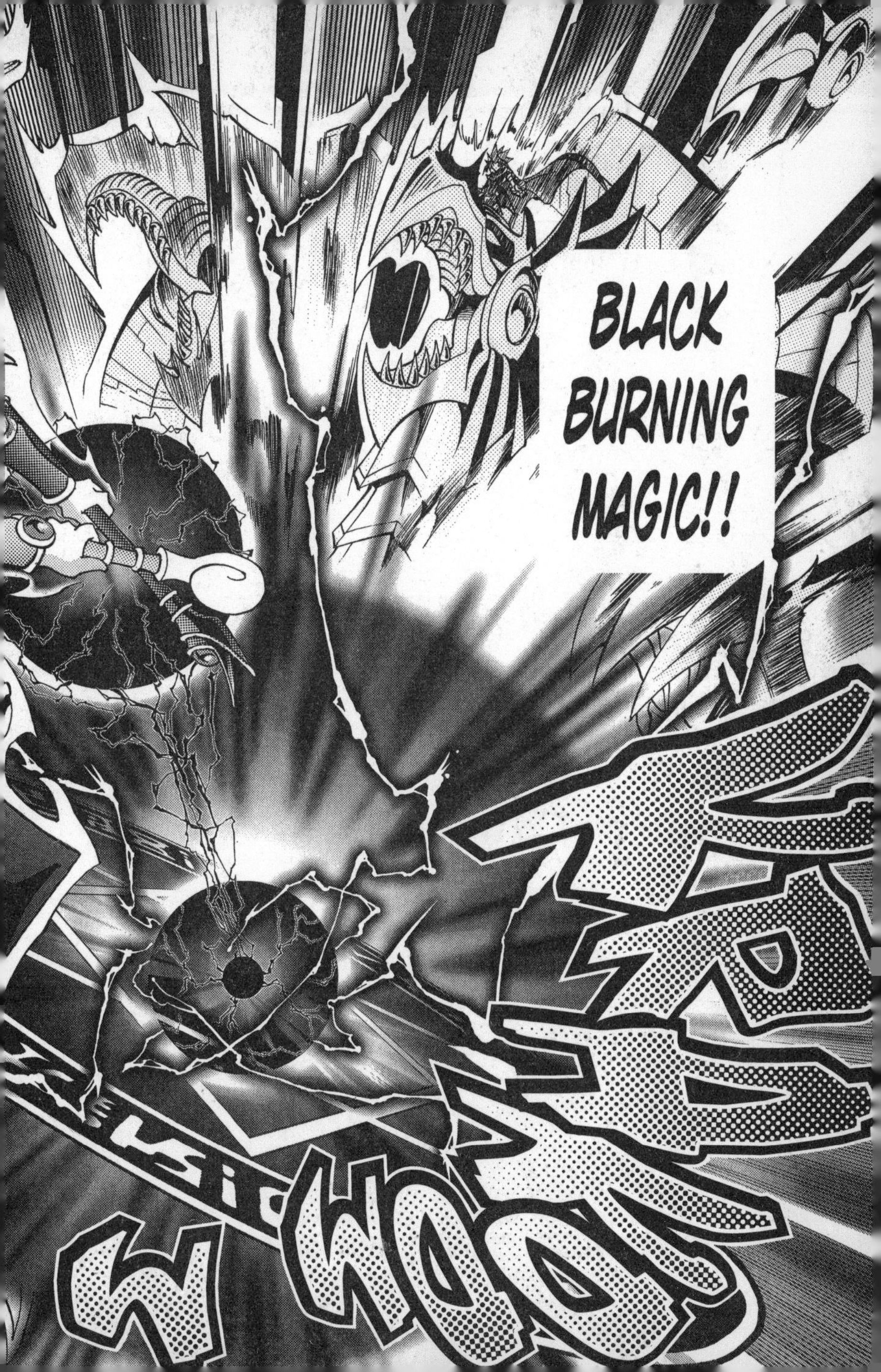
BLACK BURNING MAGIC!!

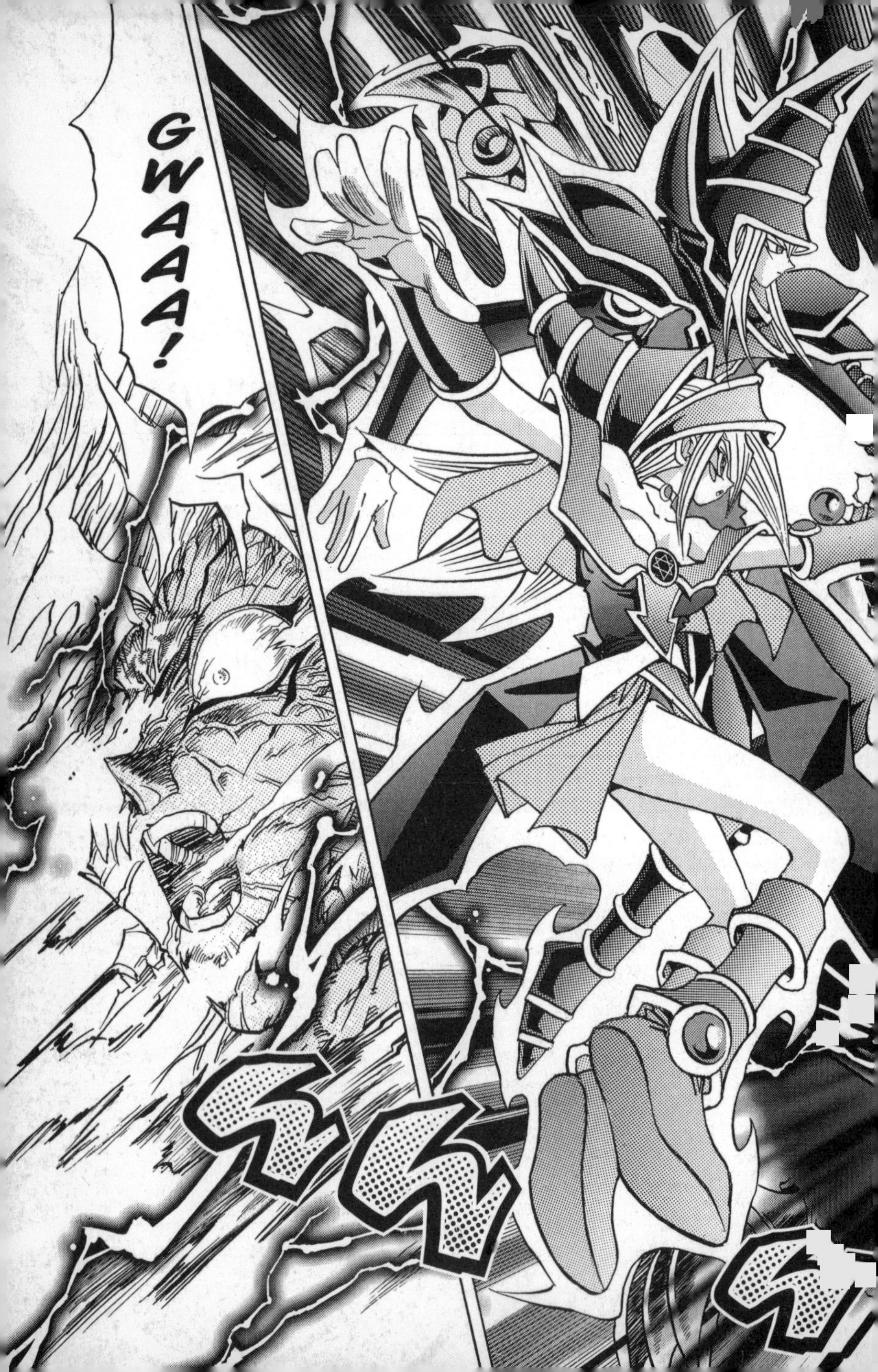
GWAAAA!

# DUEL 217: THAN CURSE THE DARKNESS

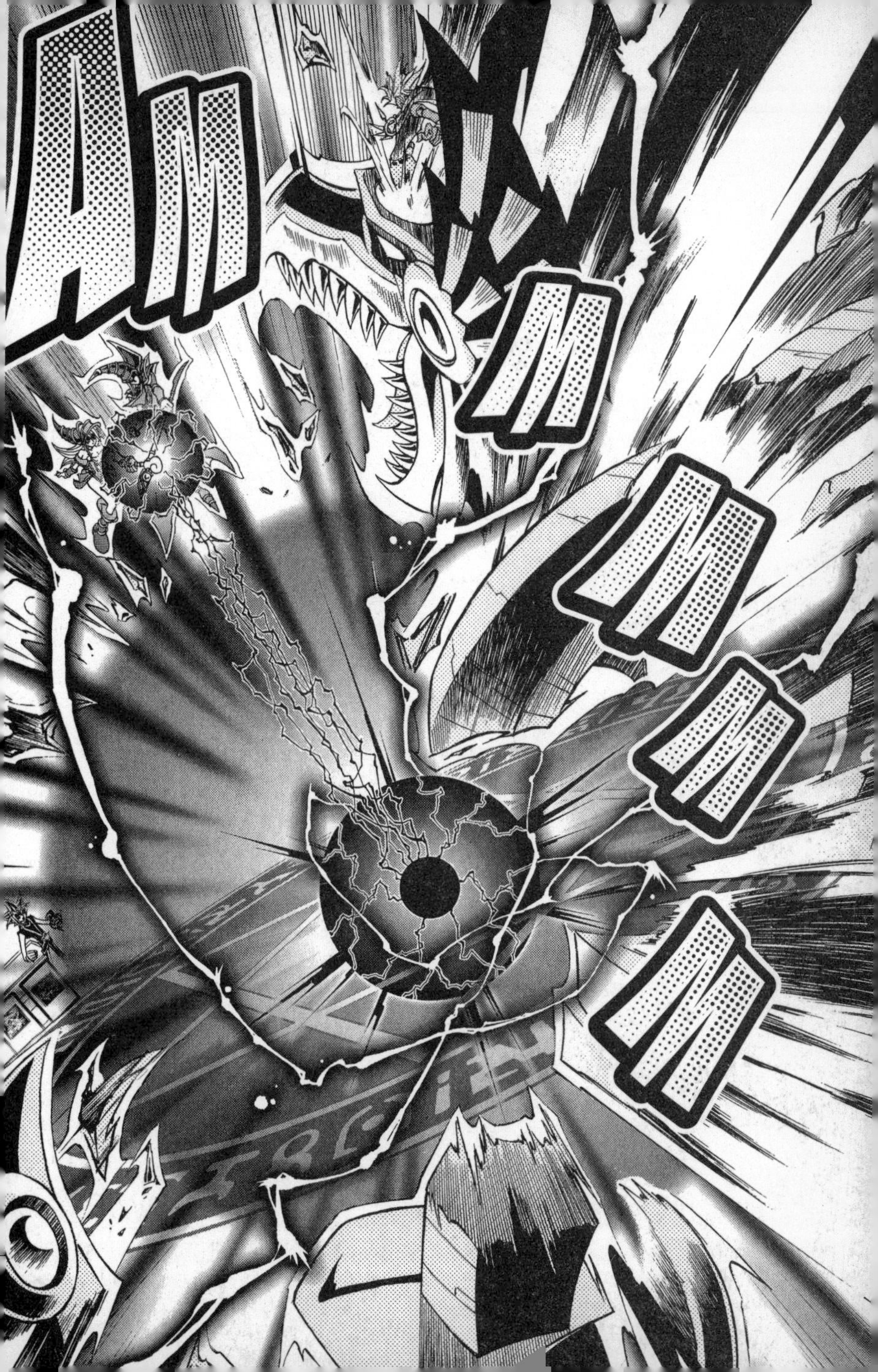
AMMMMM

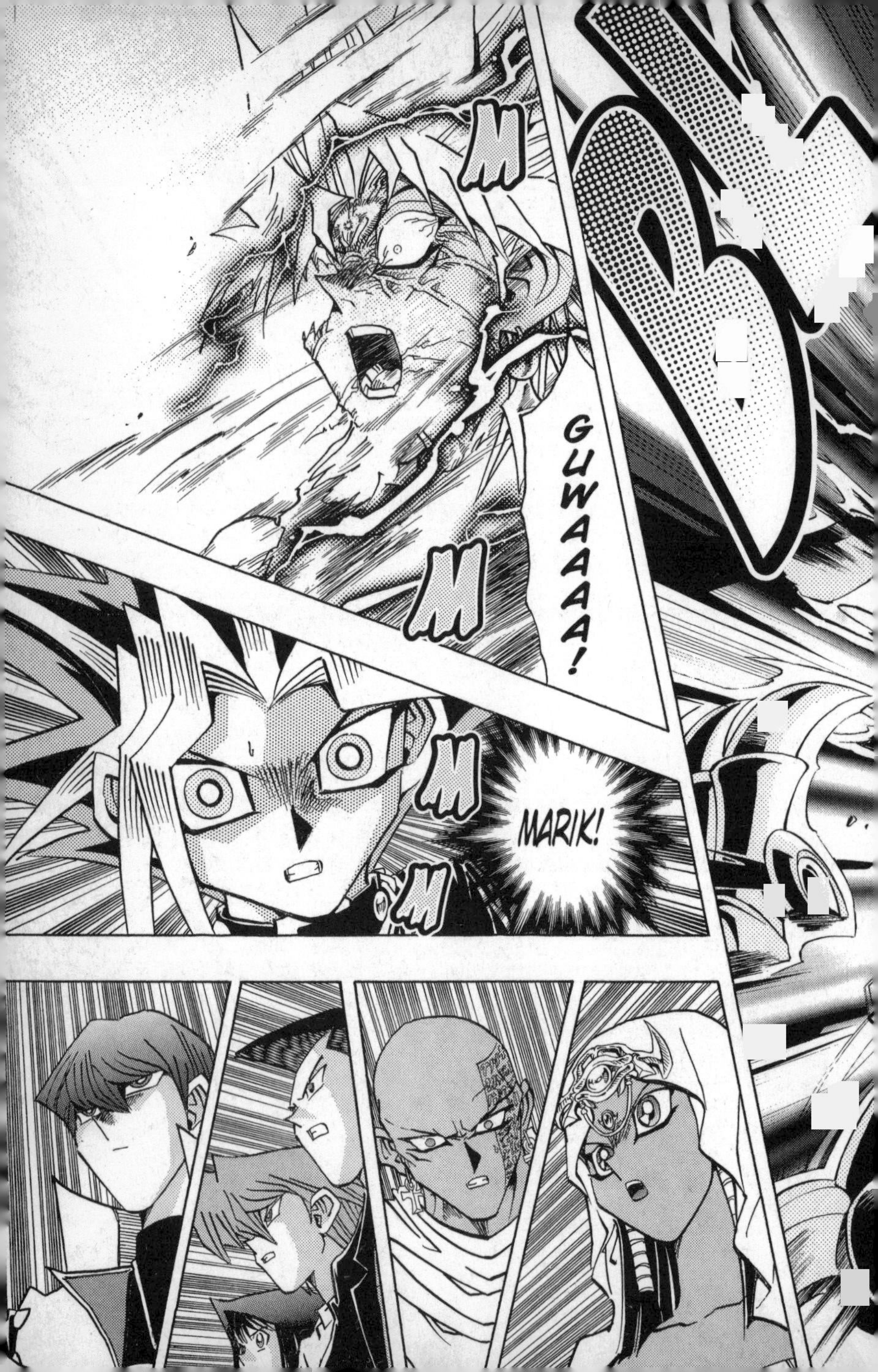
GUWAAAAA!
MMMM
MARIK!

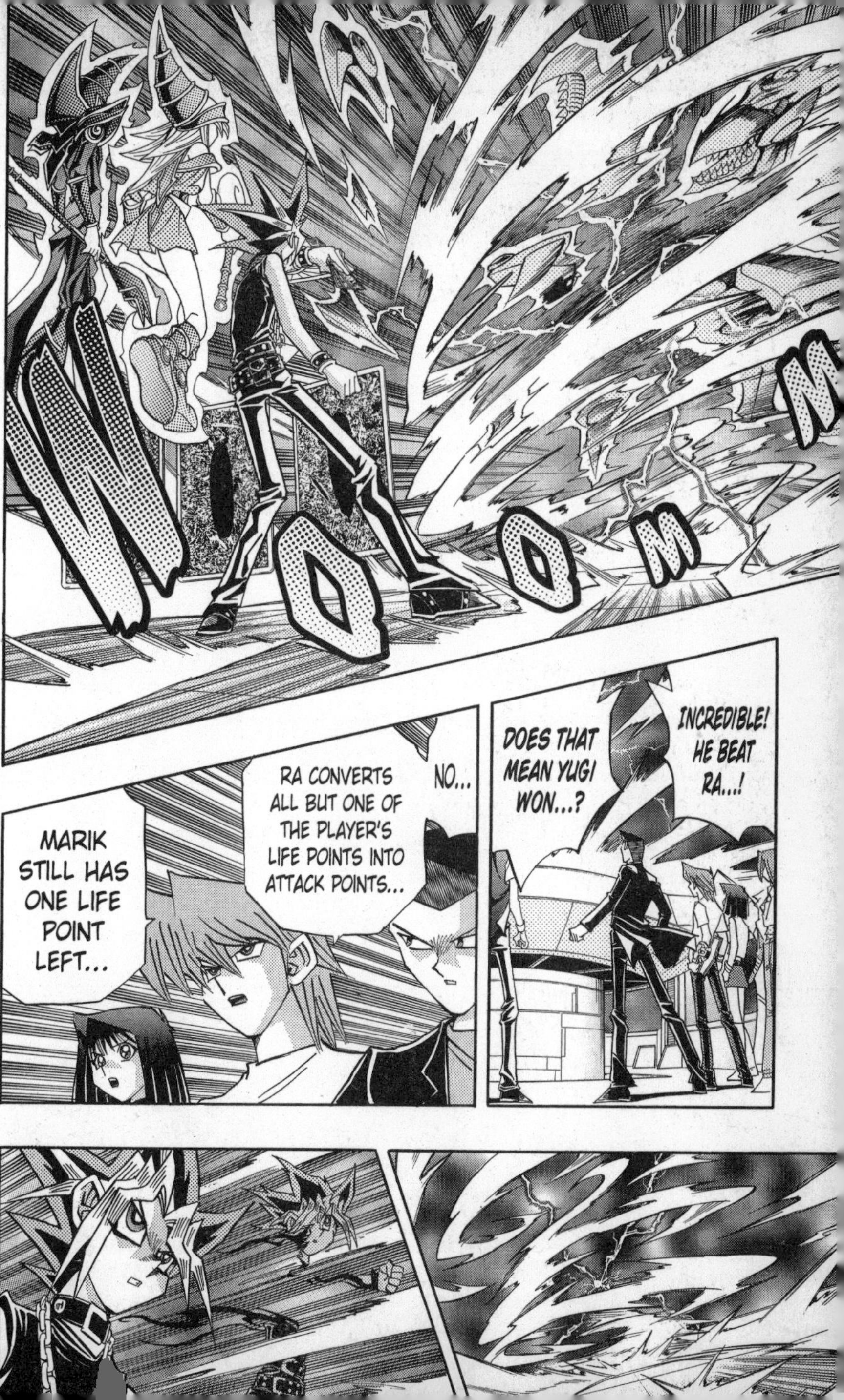
WOOMMM
INCREDIBLE! HE BEAT RA...!
DOES THAT MEAN YUGI WON...?
NO...
RA CONVERTS ALL BUT ONE OF THE PLAYER'S LIFE POINTS INTO ATTACK POINTS...
MARIK STILL HAS ONE LIFE POINT LEFT...

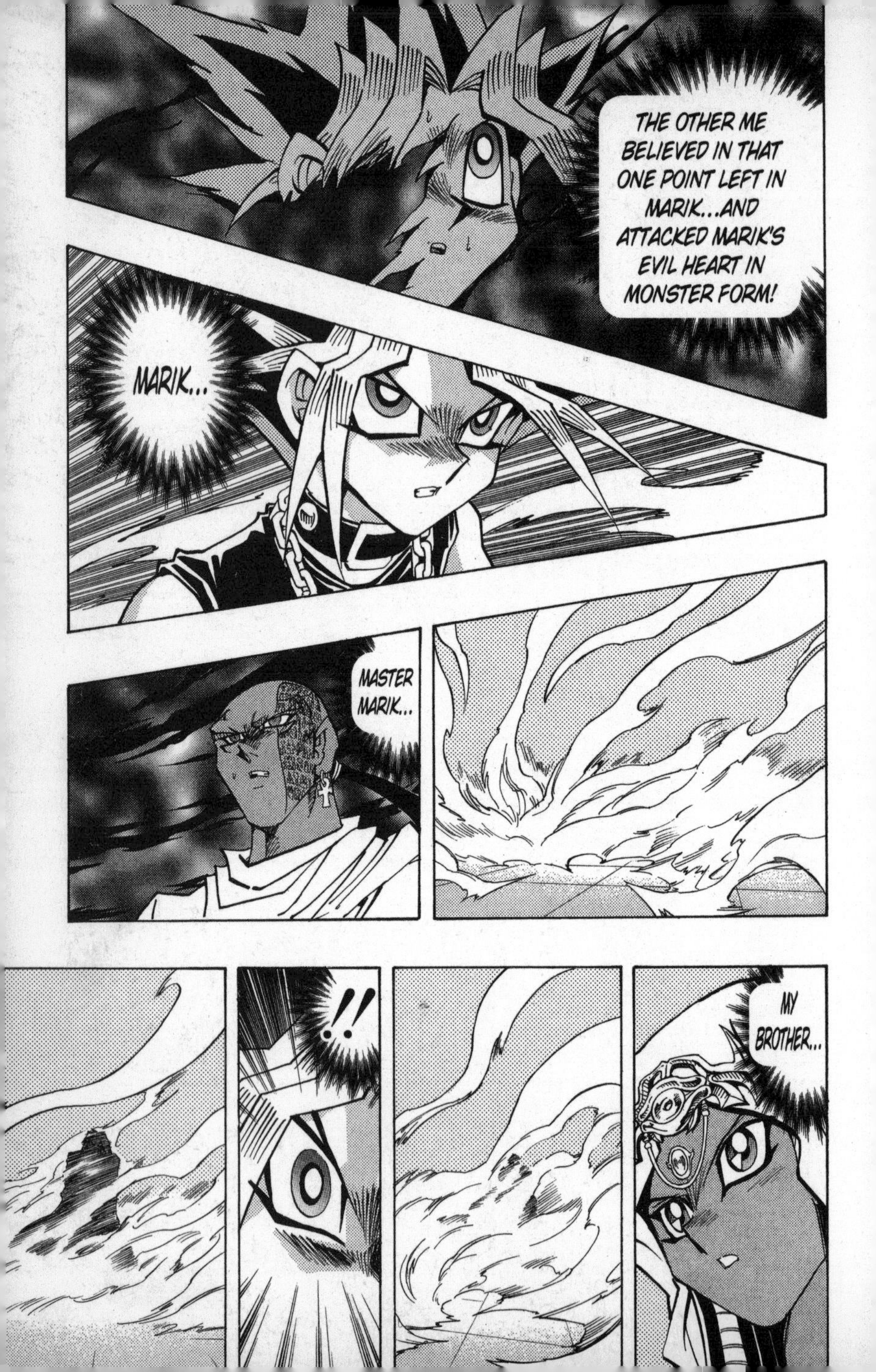
THE OTHER ME BELIEVED IN THAT ONE POINT LEFT IN MARIK...AND ATTACKED MARIK'S EVIL HEART IN MONSTER FORM!
MARIK...
MASTER MARIK...
MY BROTHER...
!!

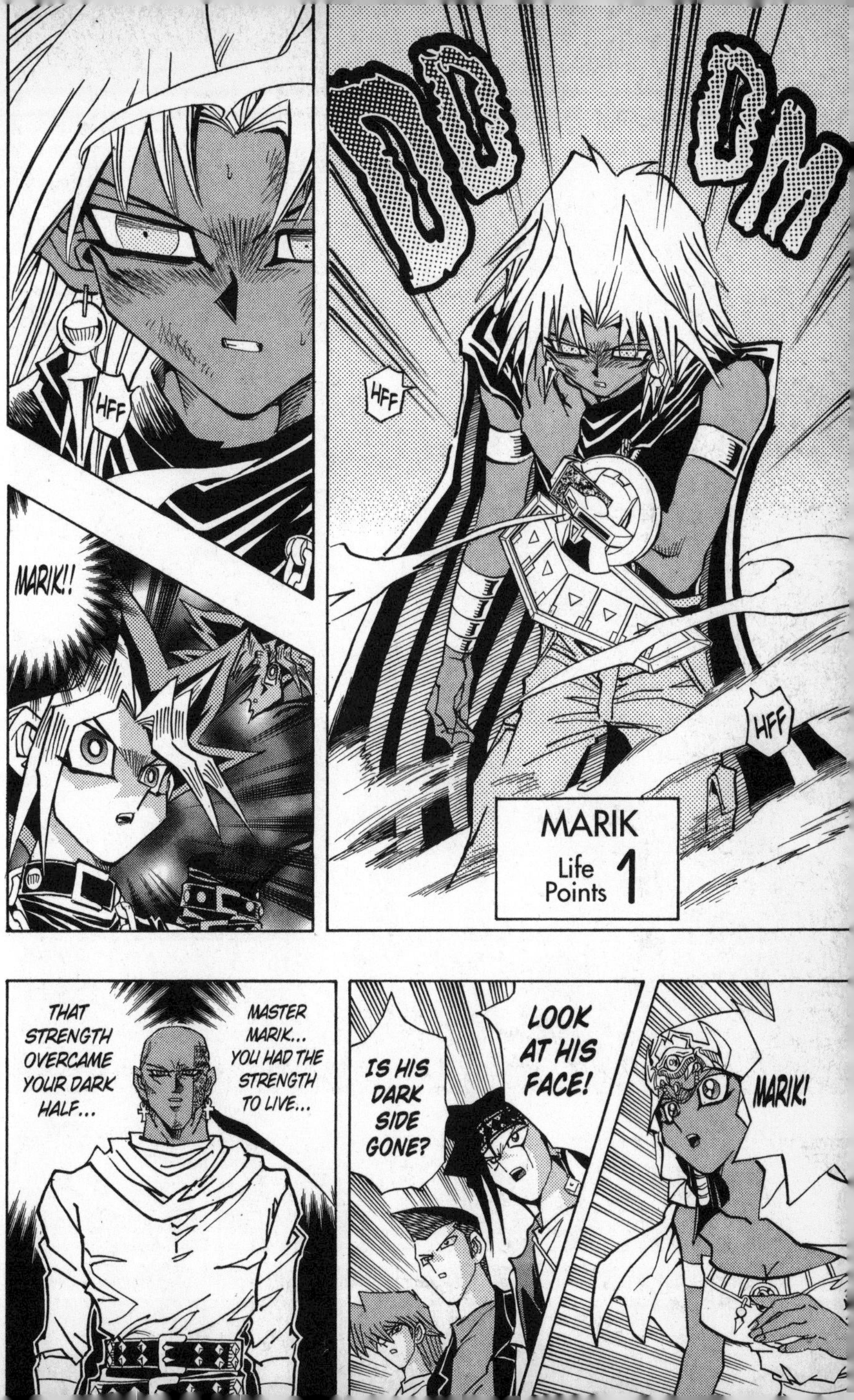
HFF
HFF
MARIK
Life Points 1
HFF
MARIK!!
MARIK!
LOOK AT HIS FACE!
IS HIS DARK SIDE GONE?
MASTER MARIK... YOU HAD THE STRENGTH TO LIVE...
THAT STRENGTH OVERCAME YOUR DARK HALF...

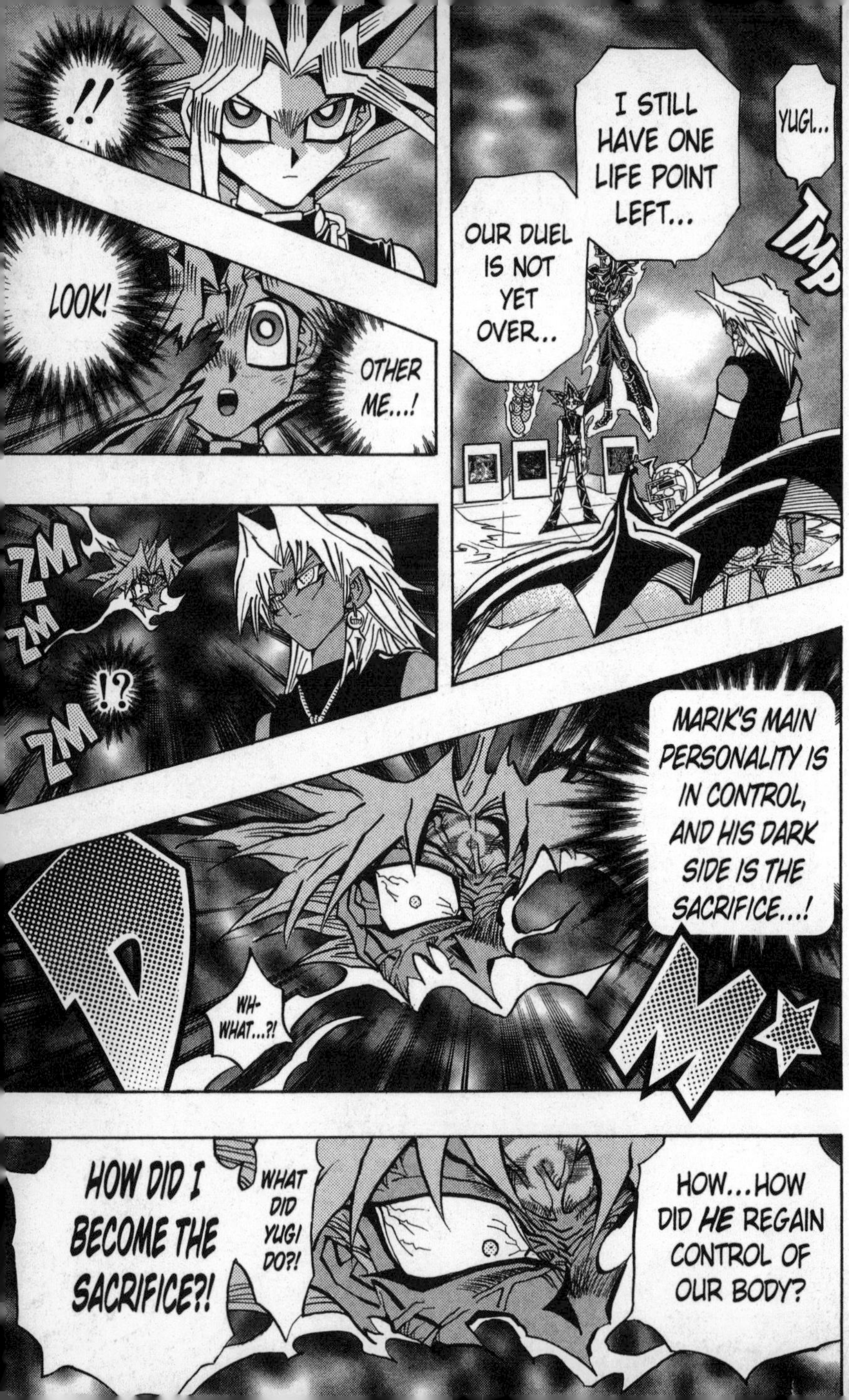
YUGI...
TMP
I STILL HAVE ONE LIFE POINT LEFT...
OUR DUEL IS NOT YET OVER...
!!
LOOK!
OTHER ME...!
ZM
ZM
!?
ZM
MARIK'S MAIN PERSONALITY IS IN CONTROL, AND HIS DARK SIDE IS THE SACRIFICE...!
DOM
WH- WHAT...?!
HOW...HOW DID HE REGAIN CONTROL OF OUR BODY?
WHAT DID YUGI DO?!
HOW DID I BECOME THE SACRIFICE?!

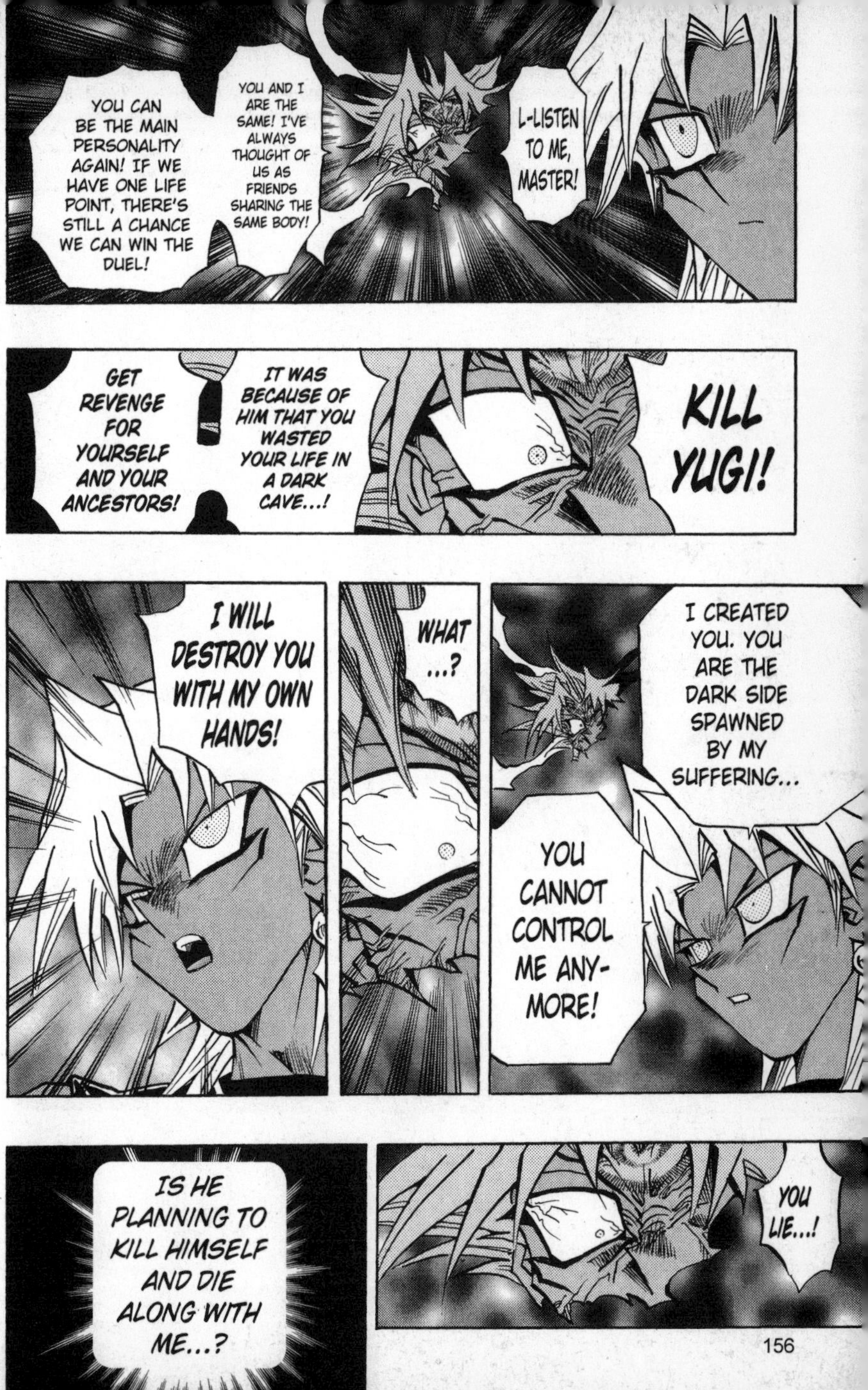
L-LISTEN TO ME, MASTER!
YOU AND I ARE THE SAME! I'VE ALWAYS THOUGHT OF US AS FRIENDS SHARING THE SAME BODY!
YOU CAN BE THE MAIN PERSONALITY AGAIN! IF WE HAVE ONE LIFE POINT, THERE'S STILL A CHANCE WE CAN WIN THE DUEL!
KILL YUGI!
IT WAS BECAUSE OF HIM THAT YOU WASTED YOUR LIFE IN A DARK CAVE...!
GET REVENGE FOR YOURSELF AND YOUR ANCESTORS!
I CREATED YOU. YOU ARE THE DARK SIDE SPAWNED BY MY SUFFERING...
YOU CANNOT CONTROL ME ANY-MORE!
WHAT ...?
I WILL DESTROY YOU WITH MY OWN HANDS!
YOU LIE...!
IS HE PLANNING TO KILL HIMSELF AND DIE ALONG WITH ME...?

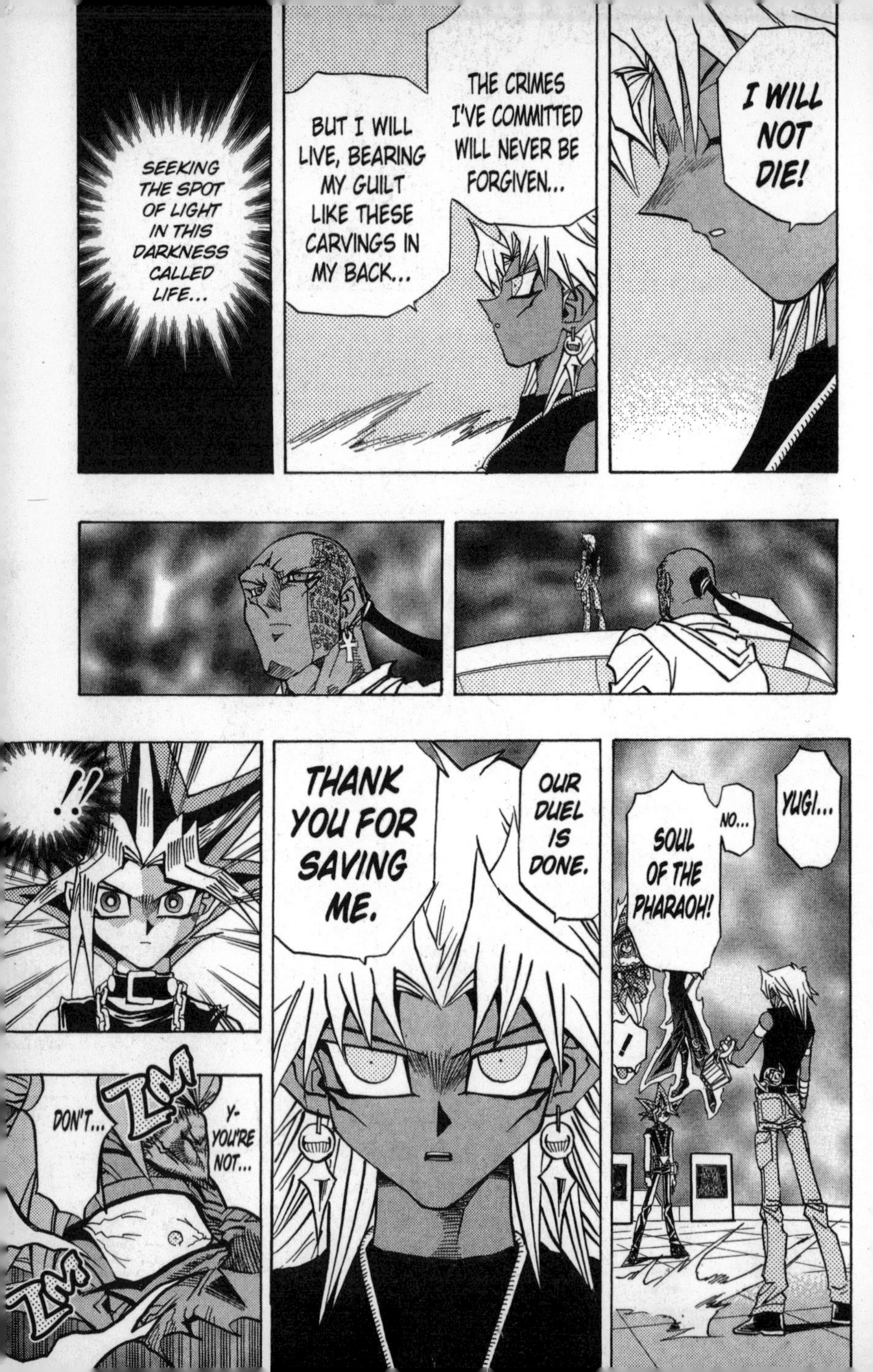
I WILL NOT DIE!
THE CRIMES I'VE COMMITTED WILL NEVER BE FORGIVEN...
BUT I WILL LIVE, BEARING MY GUILT LIKE THESE CARVINGS IN MY BACK...
SEEKING THE SPOT OF LIGHT IN THIS DARKNESS CALLED LIFE...
YUGI...
NO...
SOUL OF THE PHARAOH!
!
OUR DUEL IS DONE.
THANK YOU FOR SAVING ME.
!!
Y-YOU'RE NOT...
ZM
DON'T...
ZM

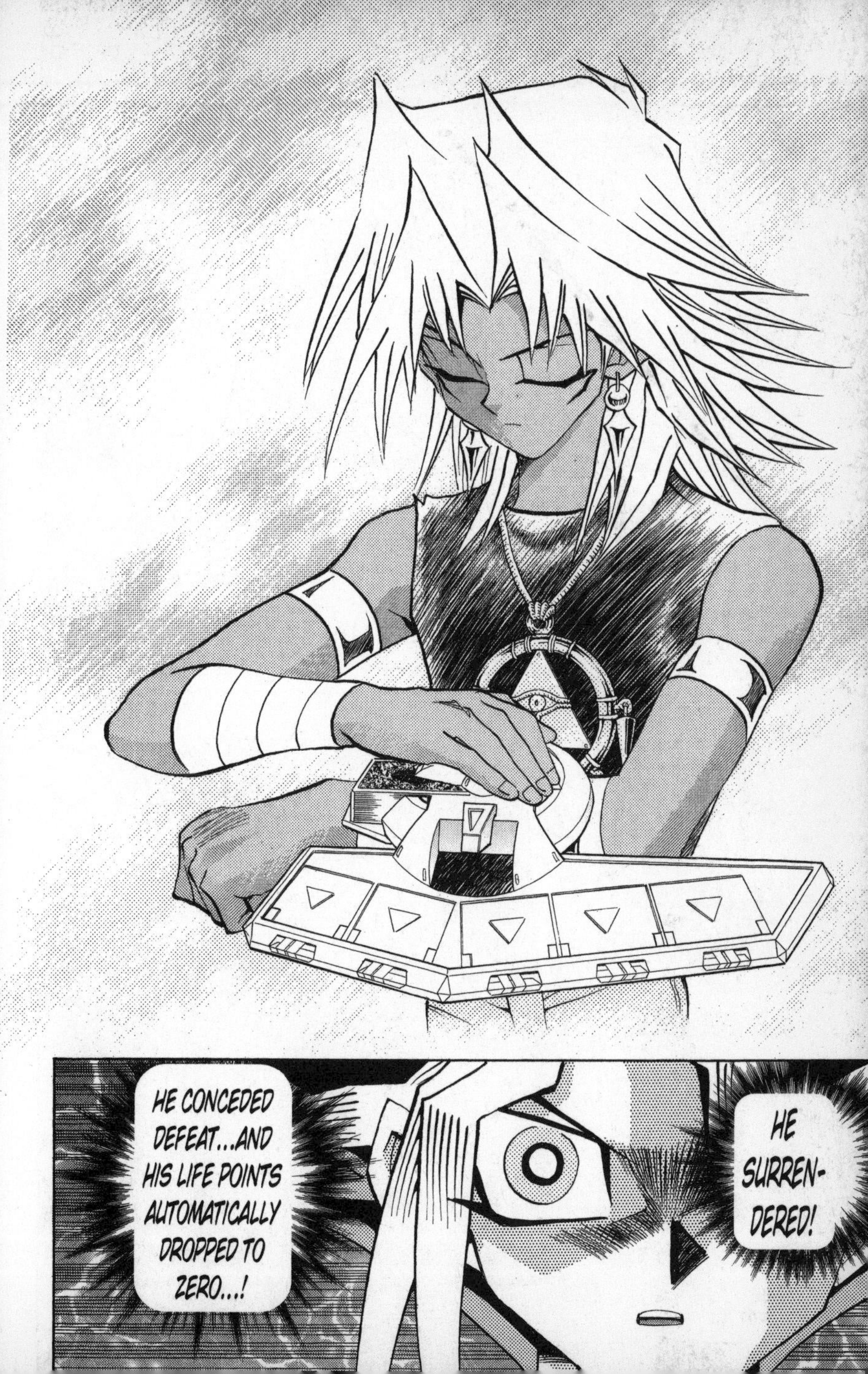
HE SURREN-DERED!
HE CONCEDED DEFEAT...AND HIS LIFE POINTS AUTOMATICALLY DROPPED TO ZERO...!

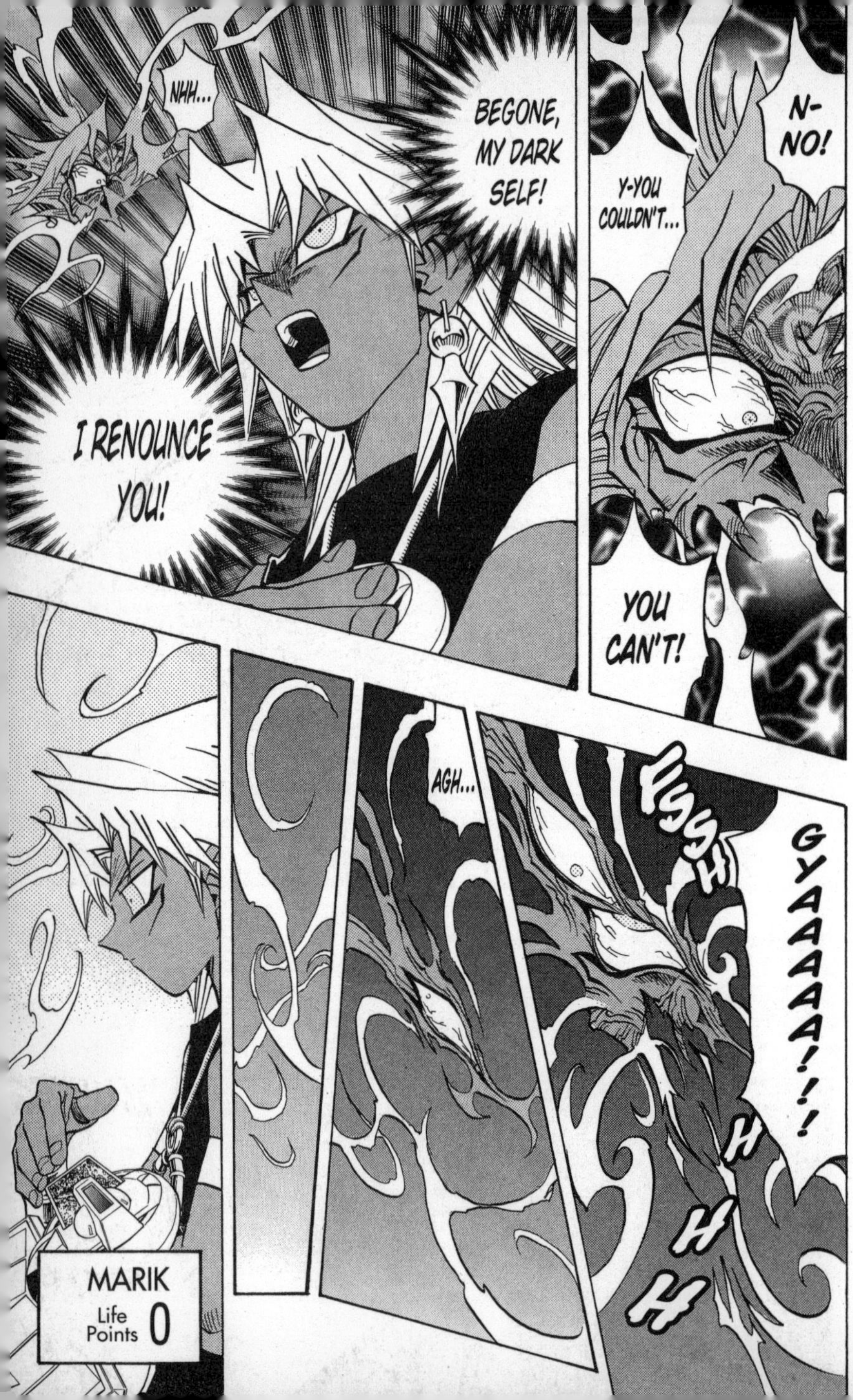
N-NO!
Y-YOU COULDN'T...
YOU CAN'T!
BEGONE, MY DARK SELF!
NHH...
I RENOUNCE YOU!
GYAAAAAA!!!
FSSHHHHH
AGH...
MARIK
Life Points 0

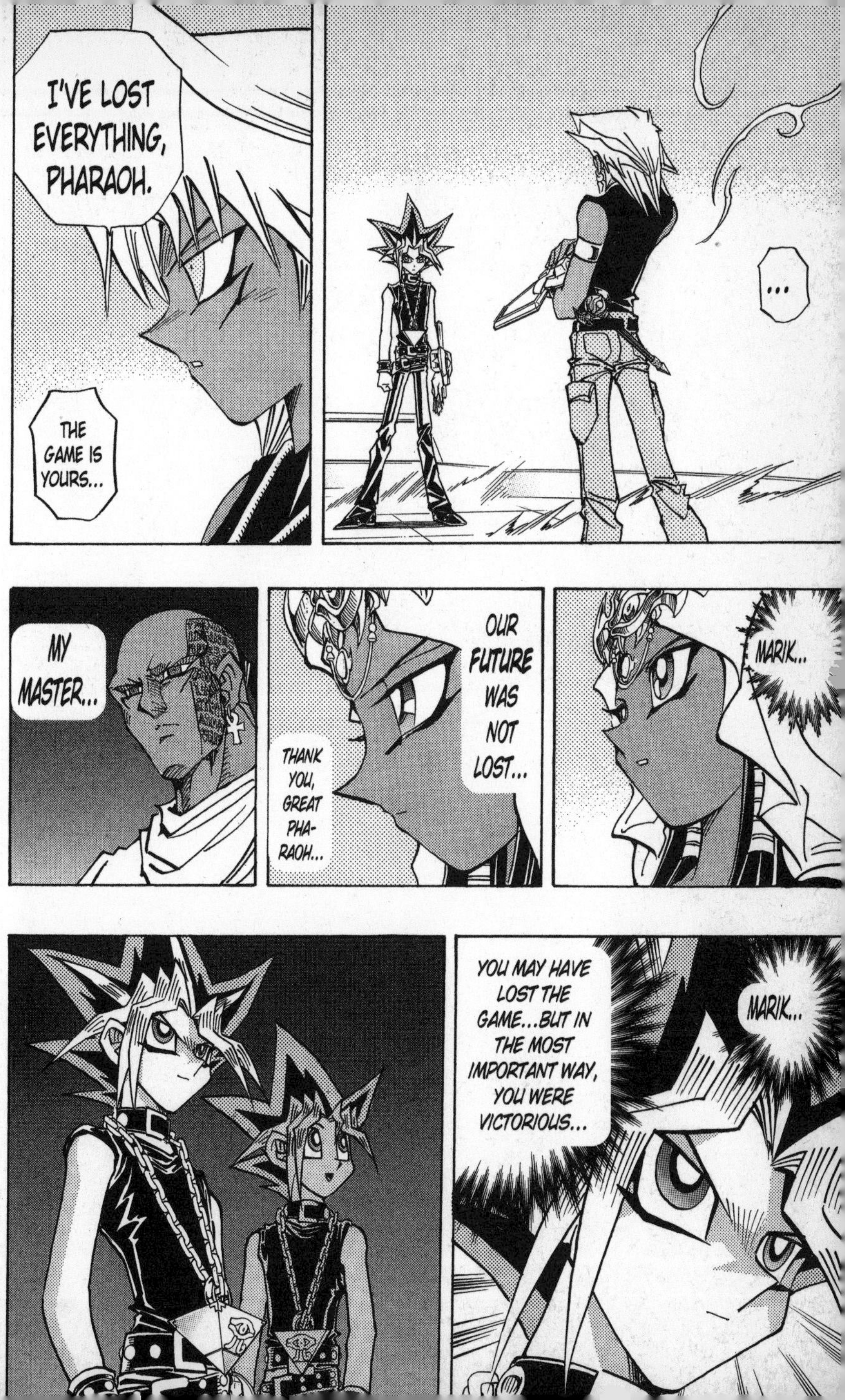
...
I'VE LOST EVERYTHING, PHARAOH.
THE GAME IS YOURS...
MARIK...
OUR FUTURE WAS NOT LOST...
THANK YOU, GREAT PHA-RAOH...
MY MASTER...
MARIK...
YOU MAY HAVE LOST THE GAME...BUT IN THE MOST IMPORTANT WAY, YOU WERE VICTORIOUS...

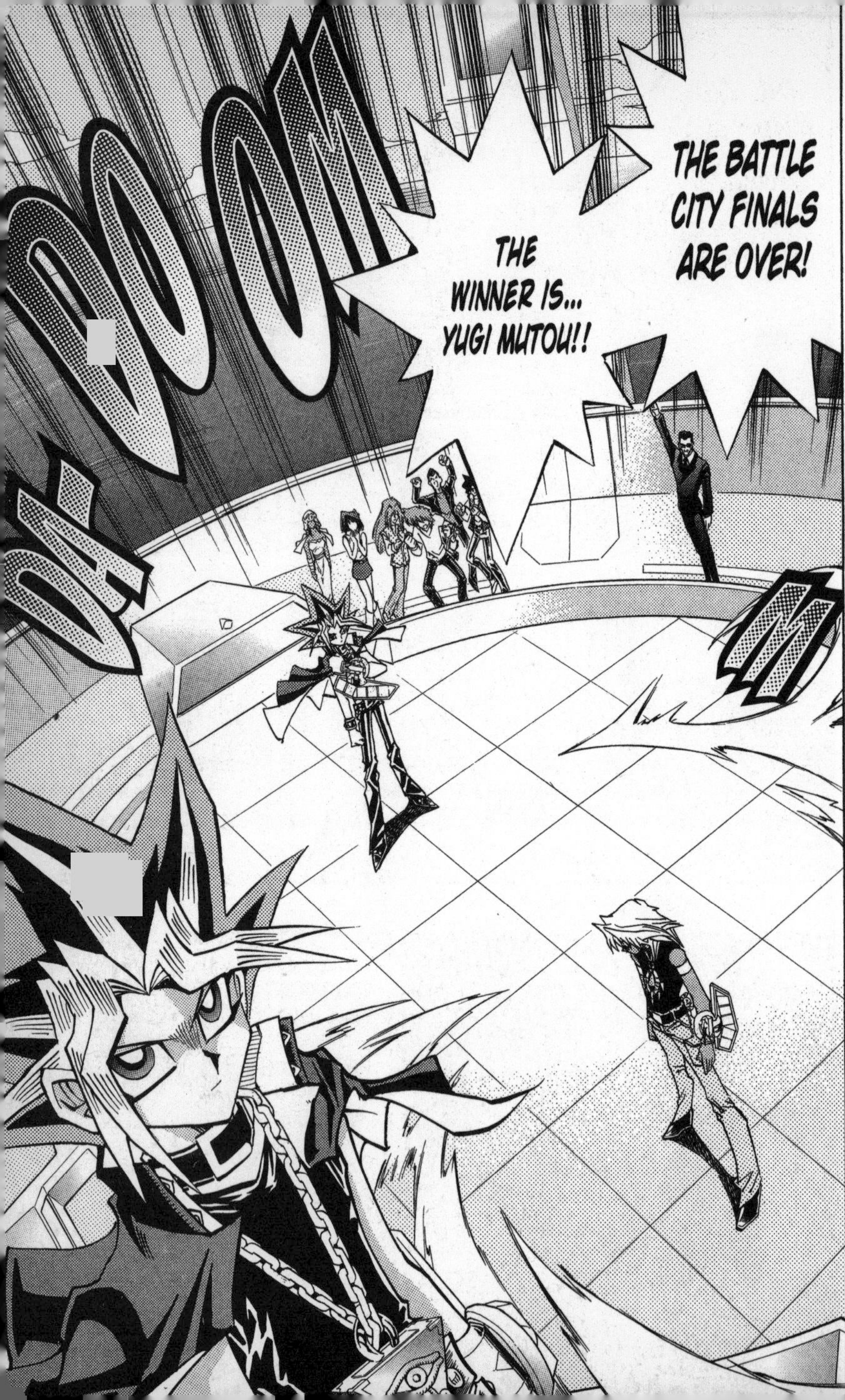
THE BATTLE CITY FINALS ARE OVER!
THE WINNER IS... YUGI MUTOU!!
DA-DOOM

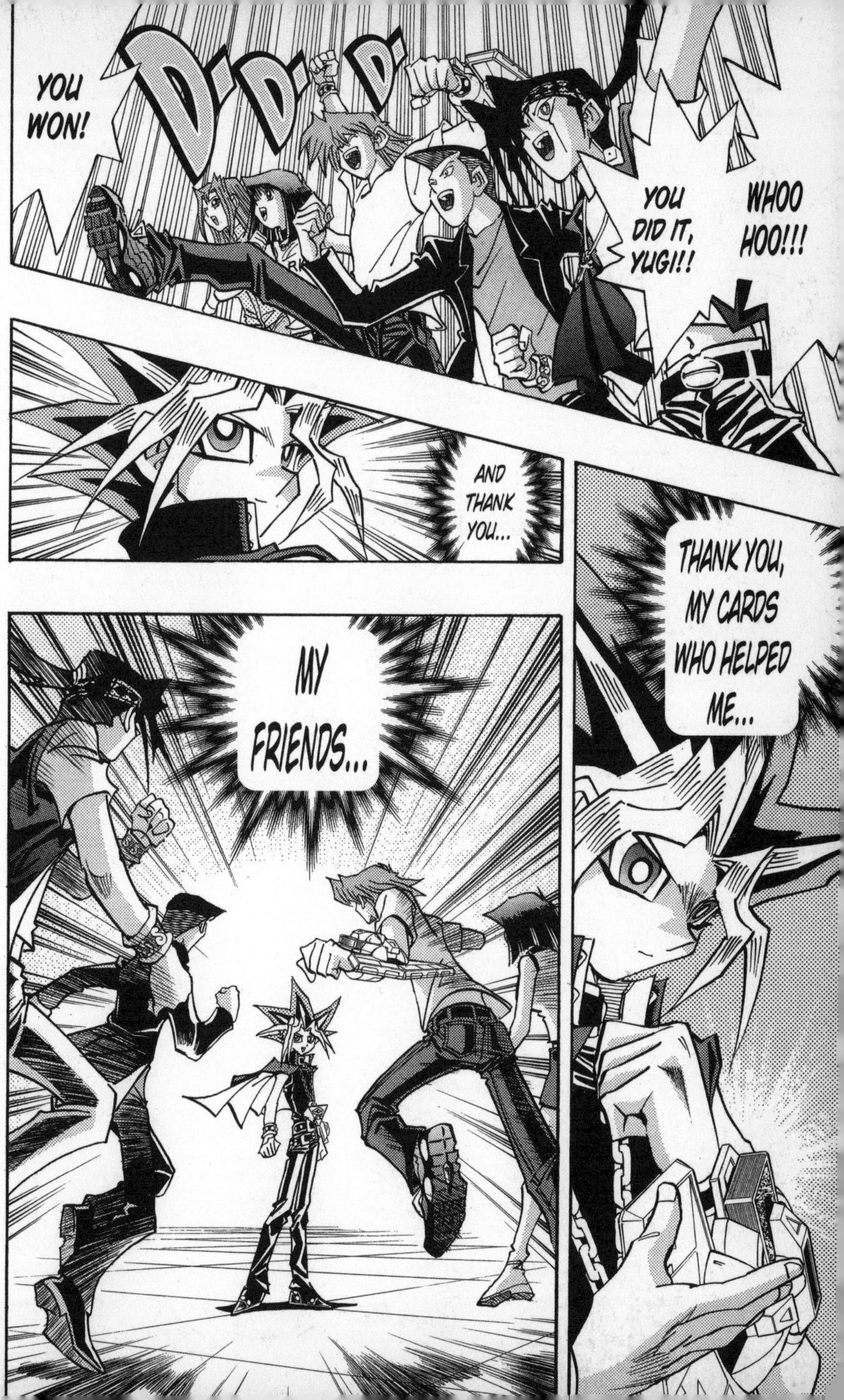
WHOO HOO!!!
YOU DID IT, YUGI!!
D-D-D
YOU WON!
THANK YOU, MY CARDS WHO HELPED ME...
AND THANK YOU...
MY FRIENDS...

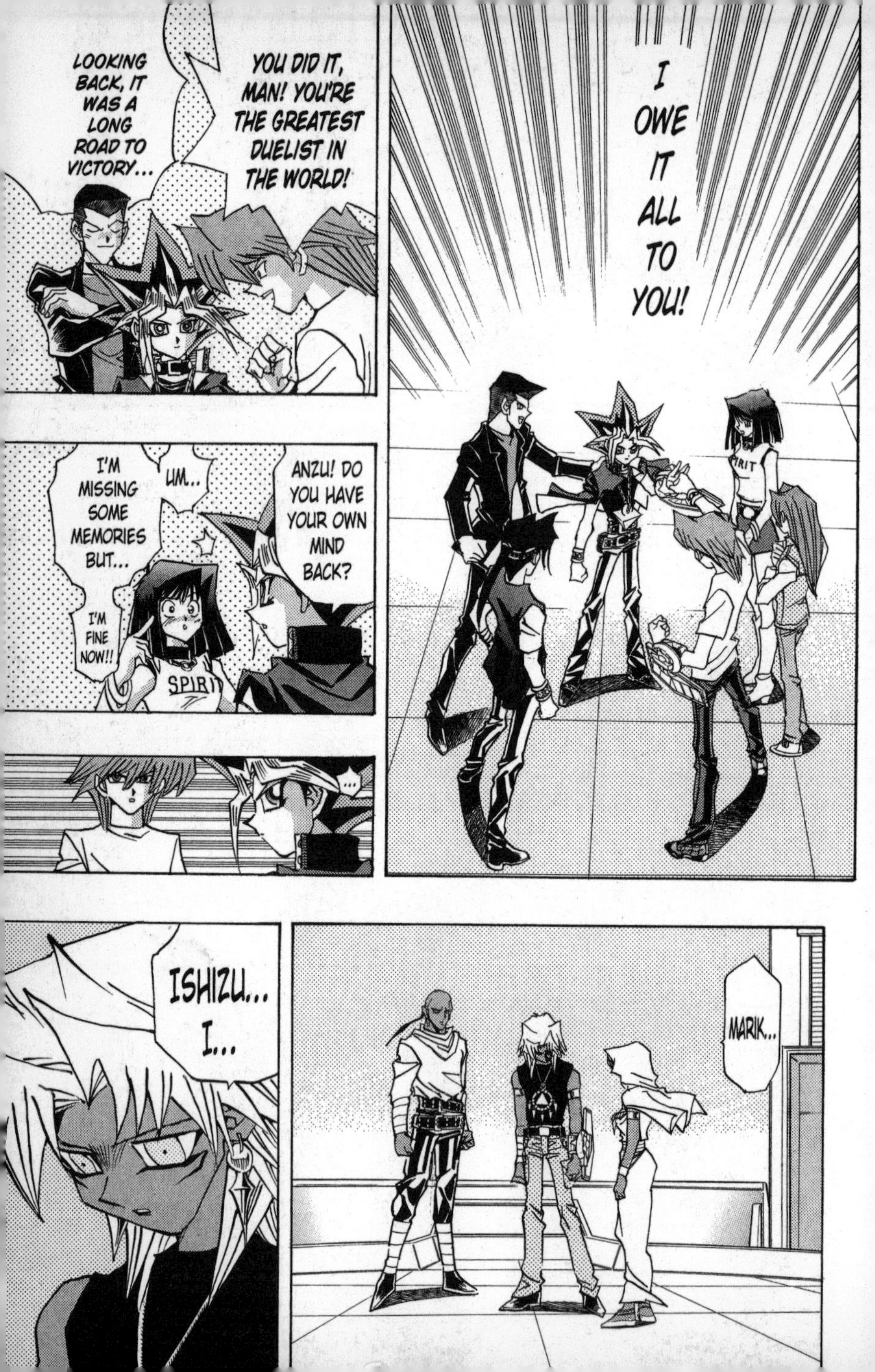
I OWE IT ALL TO YOU!
YOU DID IT, MAN! YOU'RE THE GREATEST DUELIST IN THE WORLD!
LOOKING BACK, IT WAS A LONG ROAD TO VICTORY...
ANZU! DO YOU HAVE YOUR OWN MIND BACK?
UM...
I'M MISSING SOME MEMORIES BUT...
I'M FINE NOW!!
...
MARIK...
ISHIZU... I...

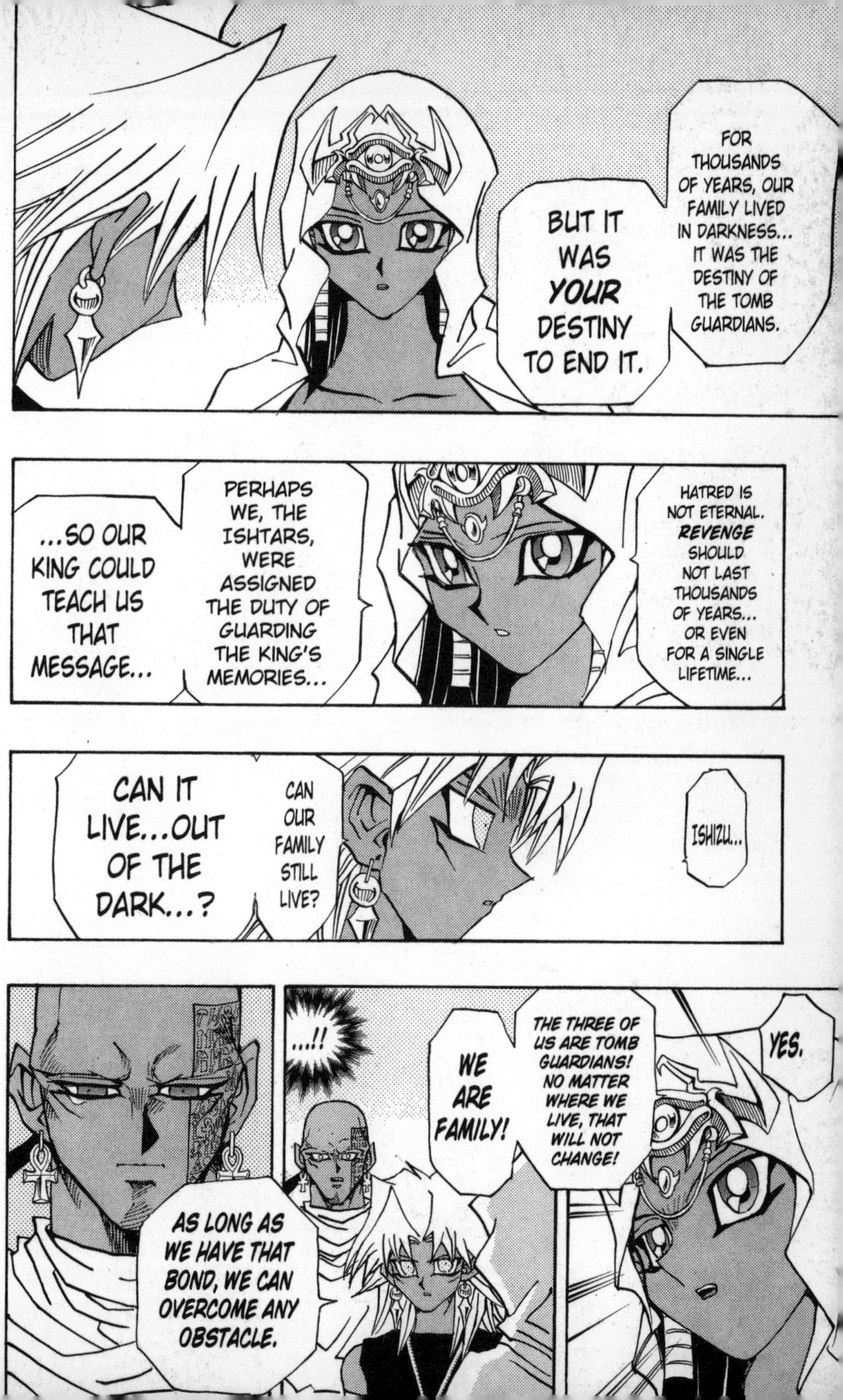
FOR THOUSANDS OF YEARS, OUR FAMILY LIVED IN DARKNESS... IT WAS THE DESTINY OF THE TOMB GUARDIANS.
BUT IT WAS YOUR DESTINY TO END IT.
HATRED IS NOT ETERNAL. REVENGE SHOULD NOT LAST THOUSANDS OF YEARS... OR EVEN FOR A SINGLE LIFETIME...
PERHAPS WE, THE ISHTARS, WERE ASSIGNED THE DUTY OF GUARDING THE KING'S MEMORIES...
...SO OUR KING COULD TEACH US THAT MESSAGE...
ISHIZU...
CAN OUR FAMILY STILL LIVE?
CAN IT LIVE...OUT OF THE DARK...?
YES.
THE THREE OF US ARE TOMB GUARDIANS! NO MATTER WHERE WE LIVE, THAT WILL NOT CHANGE!
WE ARE FAMILY!
...!!
AS LONG AS WE HAVE THAT BOND, WE CAN OVERCOME ANY OBSTACLE.

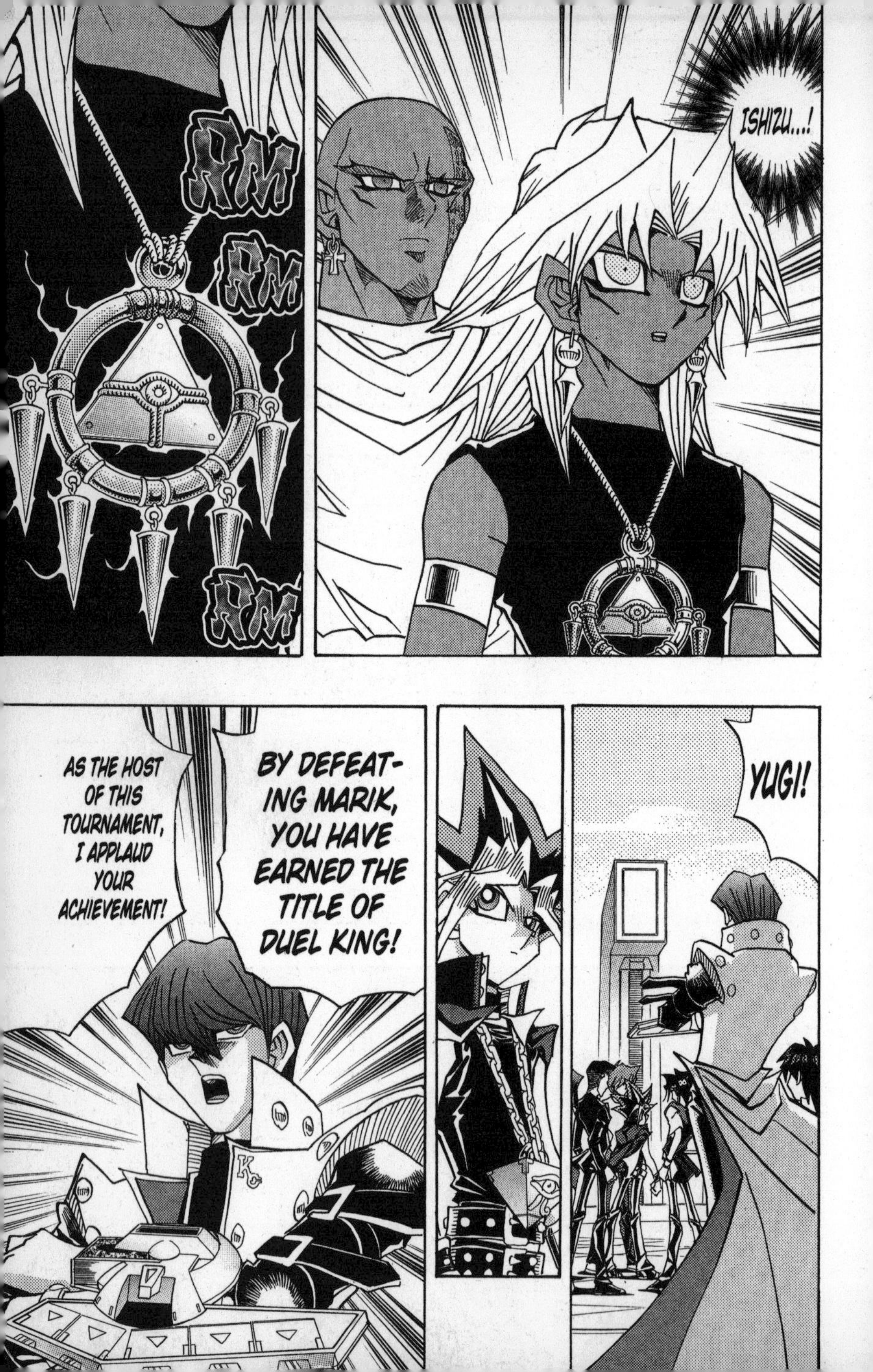
ISHIZU...!
RM
RM
RM
YUGI!
BY DEFEAT-ING MARIK, YOU HAVE EARNED THE TITLE OF DUEL KING!
AS THE HOST OF THIS TOURNAMENT, I APPLAUD YOUR ACHIEVEMENT!

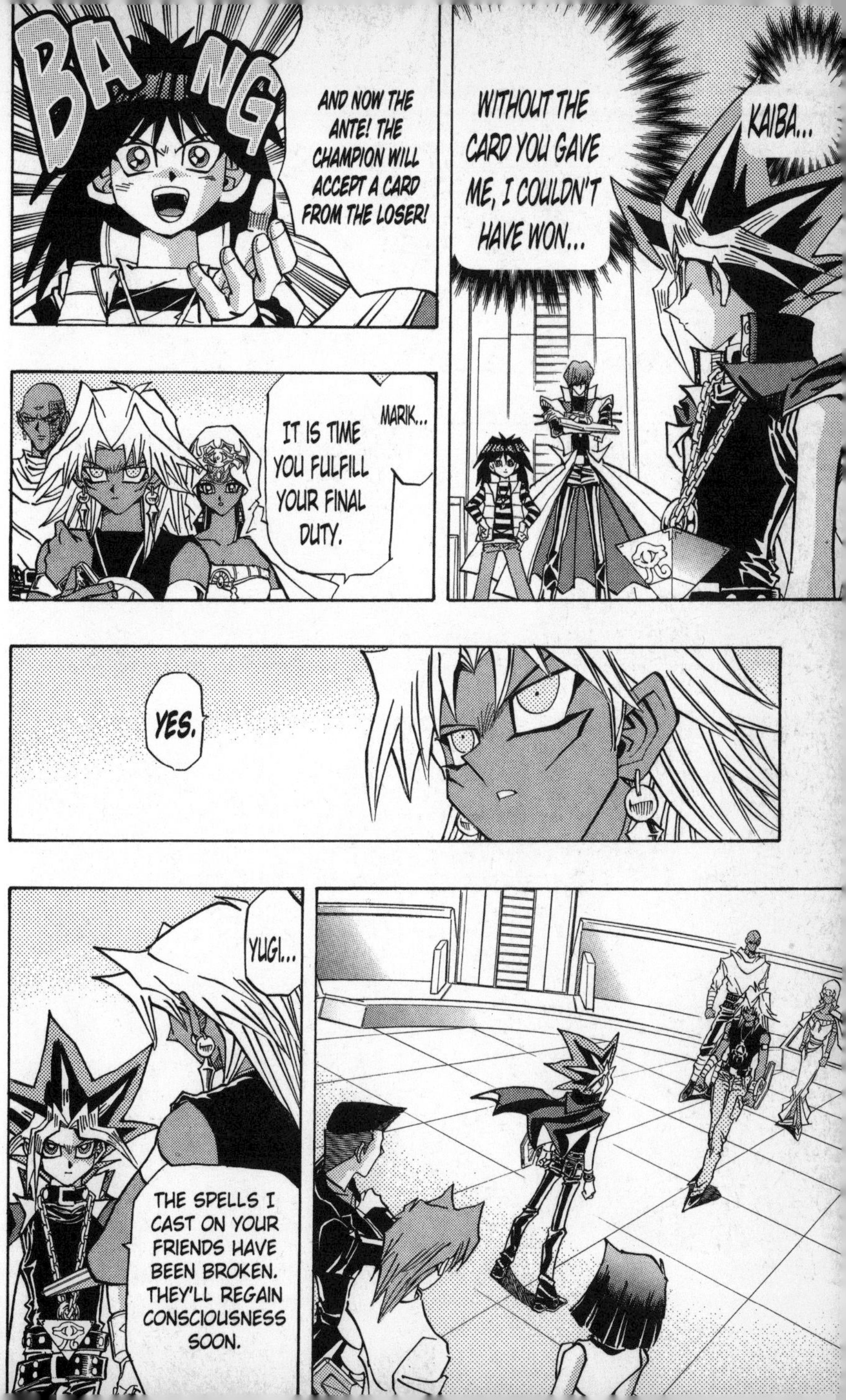
KAIBA...
WITHOUT THE CARD YOU GAVE ME, I COULDN'T HAVE WON...
BANG
AND NOW THE ANTE! THE CHAMPION WILL ACCEPT A CARD FROM THE LOSER!
MARIK...
IT IS TIME YOU FULFILL YOUR FINAL DUTY.
YES.
YUGI...
THE SPELLS I CAST ON YOUR FRIENDS HAVE BEEN BROKEN. THEY'LL REGAIN CONSCIOUSNESS SOON.

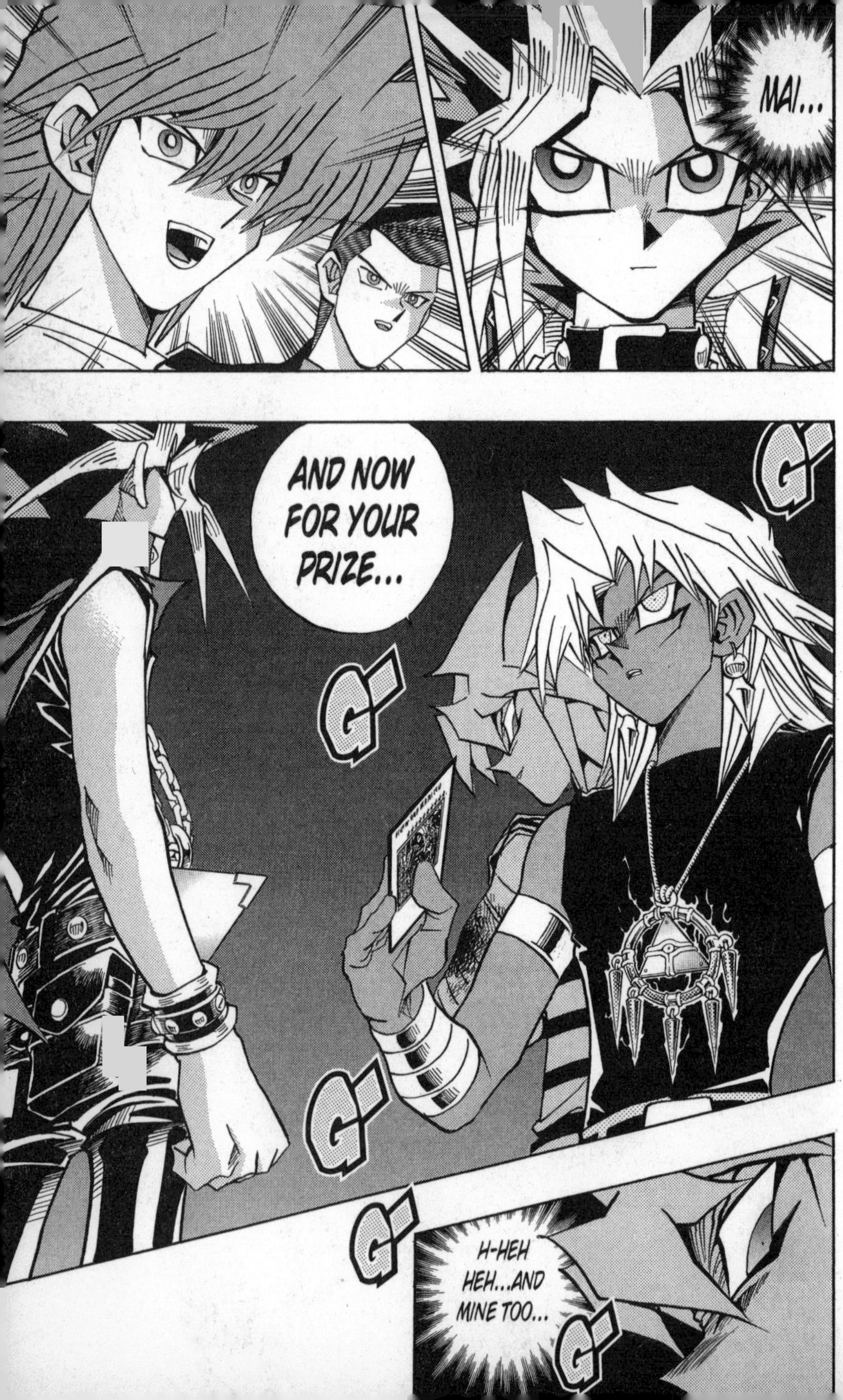
MAI...
AND NOW FOR YOUR PRIZE...
G
G
G
G
H-HEH HEH...AND MINE TOO...
G

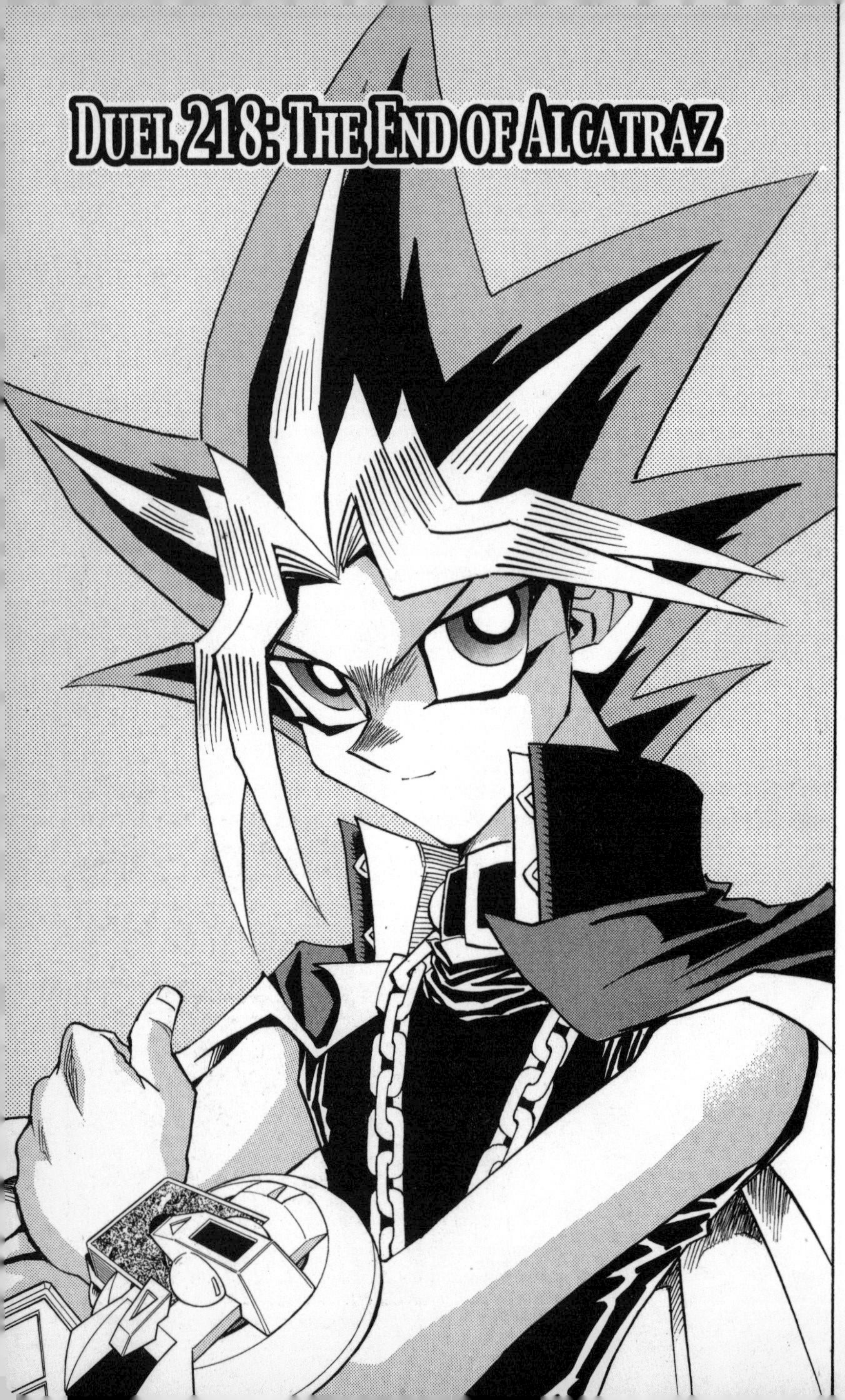
Duel 218: The End of Alcatraz

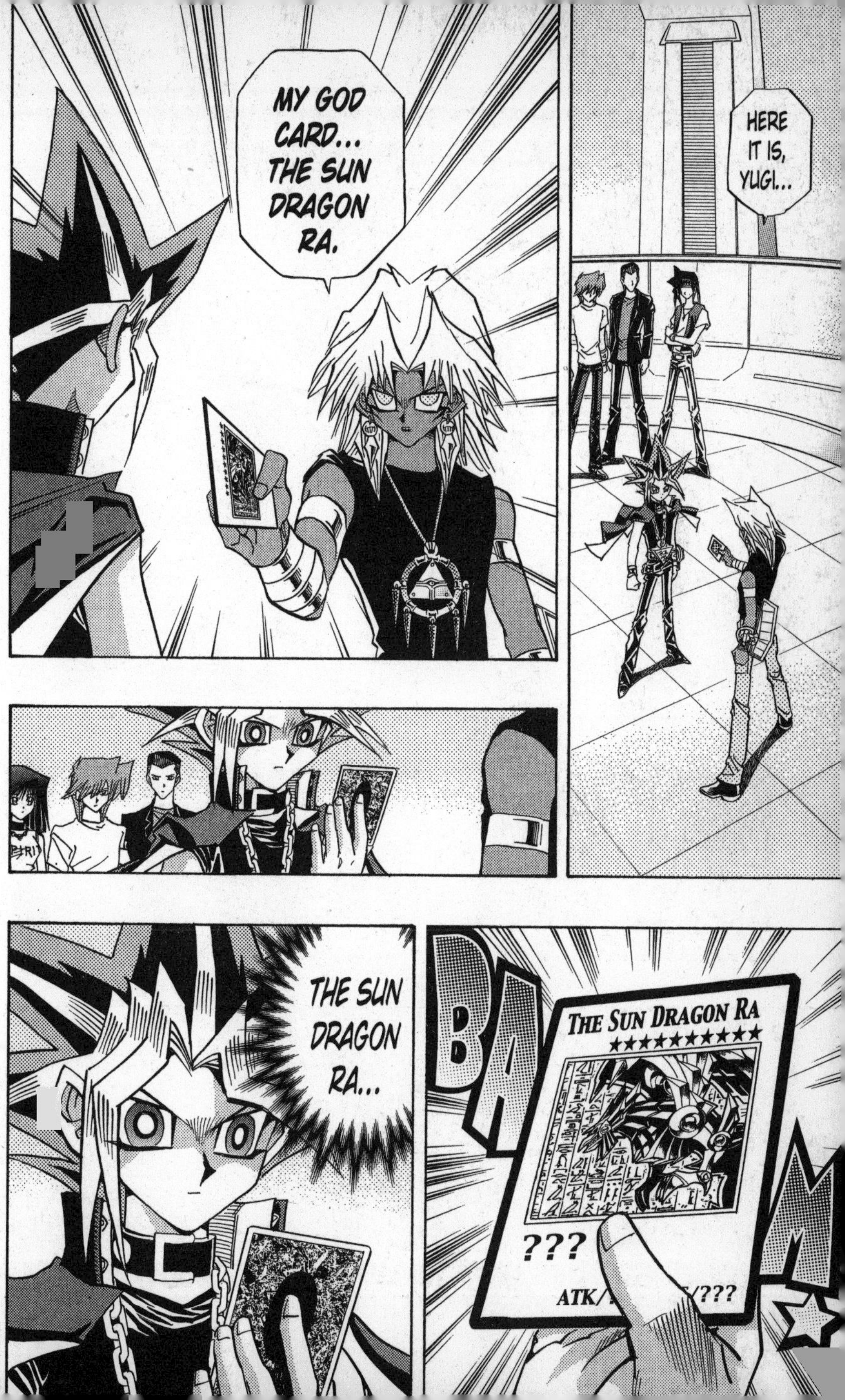
HERE IT IS, YUGI...
MY GOD CARD... THE SUN DRAGON RA.
BAM
THE SUN DRAGON RA
???
THE SUN DRAGON RA...

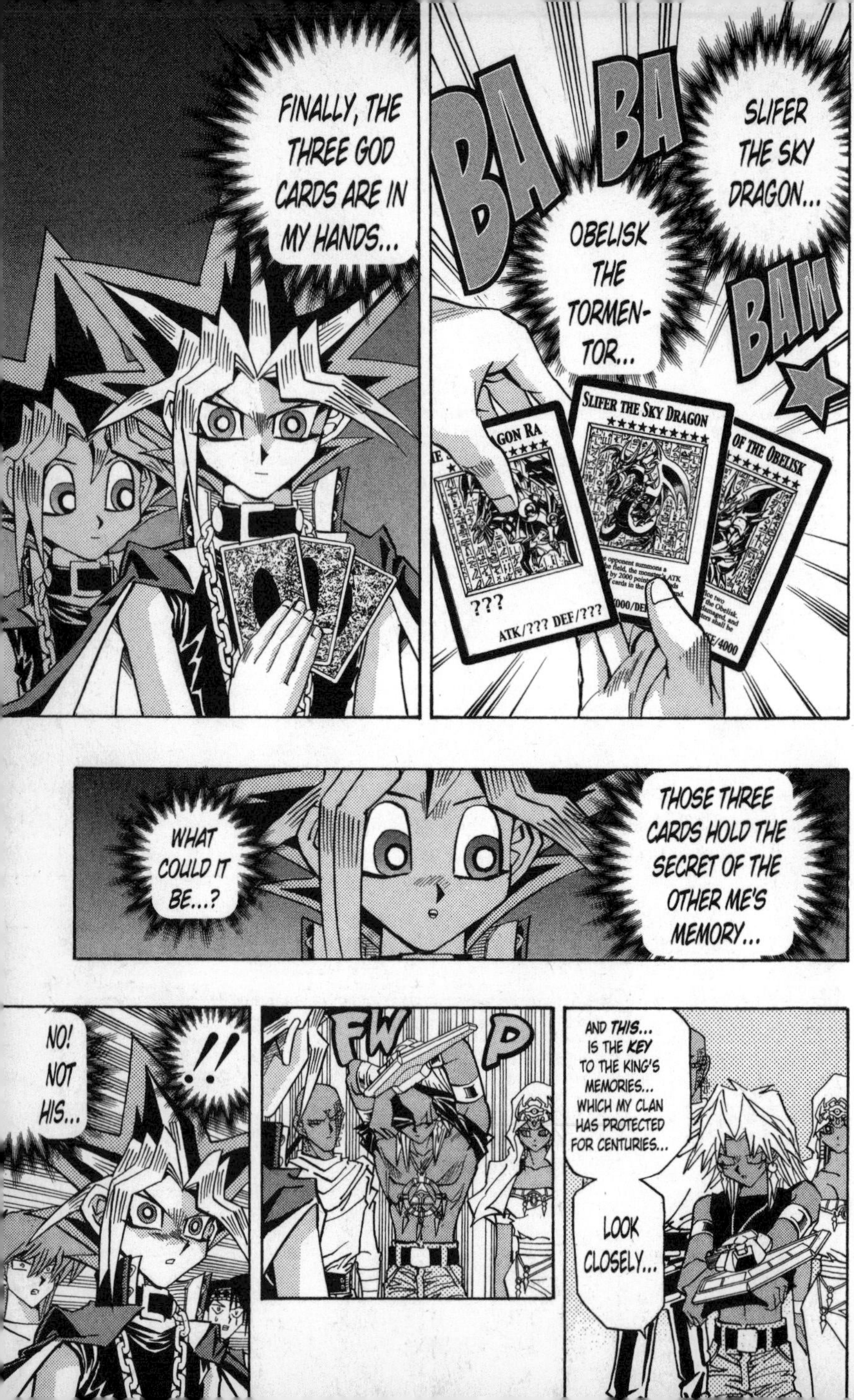
SLIFER THE SKY DRAGON...
BA BA
OBELISK THE TORMEN-TOR...
BAM
SLIFER THE SKY DRAGON
???
ATK/??? DEF/???
FINALLY, THE THREE GOD CARDS ARE IN MY HANDS...
THOSE THREE CARDS HOLD THE SECRET OF THE OTHER ME'S MEMORY...
WHAT COULD IT BE...?
AND THIS... IS THE KEY TO THE KING'S MEMORIES... WHICH MY CLAN HAS PROTECTED FOR CENTURIES...
LOOK CLOSELY...
FWP
!!
NO! NOT HIS...

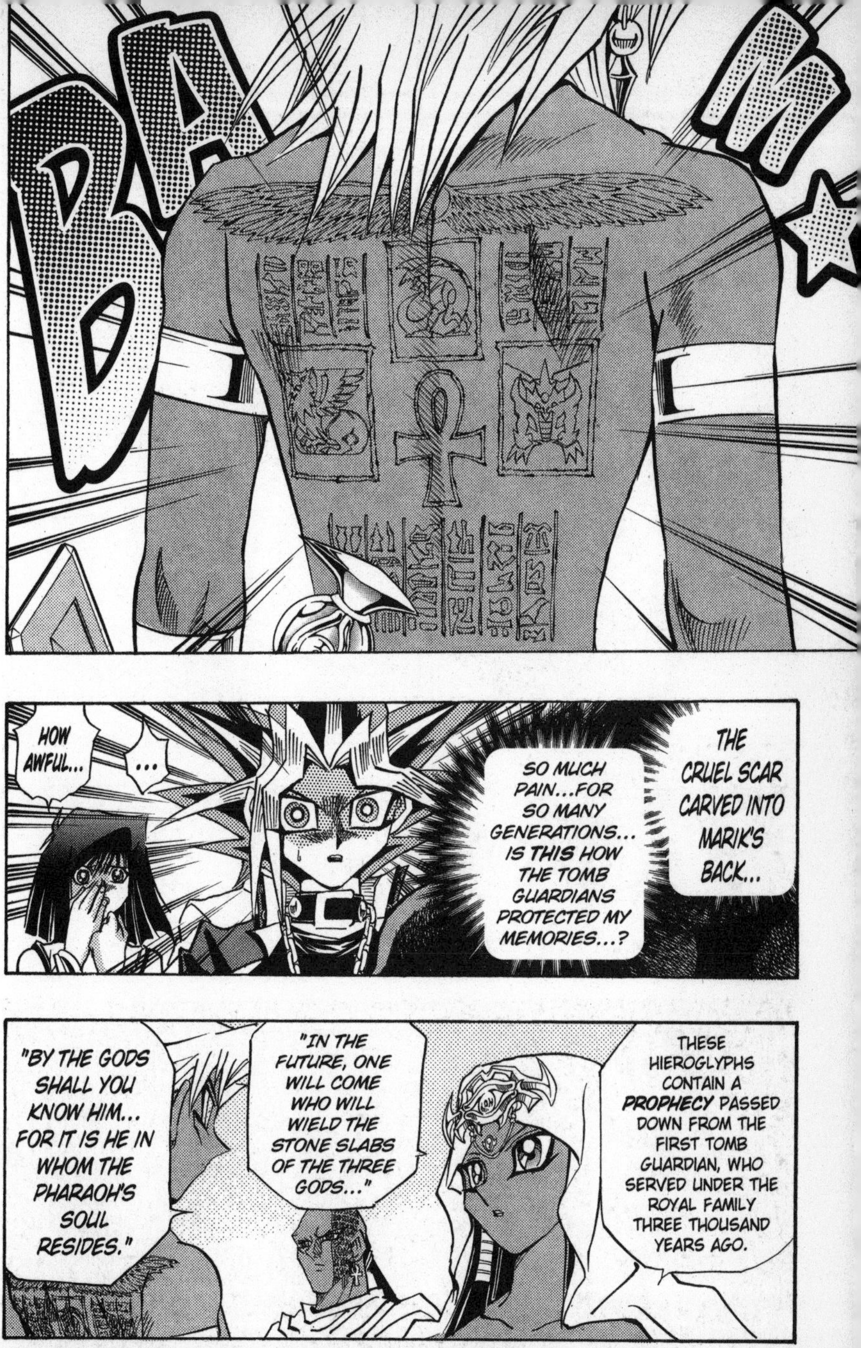
DAM
THE CRUEL SCAR CARVED INTO MARIK'S BACK...
SO MUCH PAIN...FOR SO MANY GENERATIONS... IS THIS HOW THE TOMB GUARDIANS PROTECTED MY MEMORIES...?
...
HOW AWFUL...
THESE HIEROGLYPHS CONTAIN A PROPHECY PASSED DOWN FROM THE FIRST TOMB GUARDIAN, WHO SERVED UNDER THE ROYAL FAMILY THREE THOUSAND YEARS AGO.
"IN THE FUTURE, ONE WILL COME WHO WILL WIELD THE STONE SLABS OF THE THREE GODS..."
"BY THE GODS SHALL YOU KNOW HIM... FOR IT IS HE IN WHOM THE PHARAOH'S SOUL RESIDES."

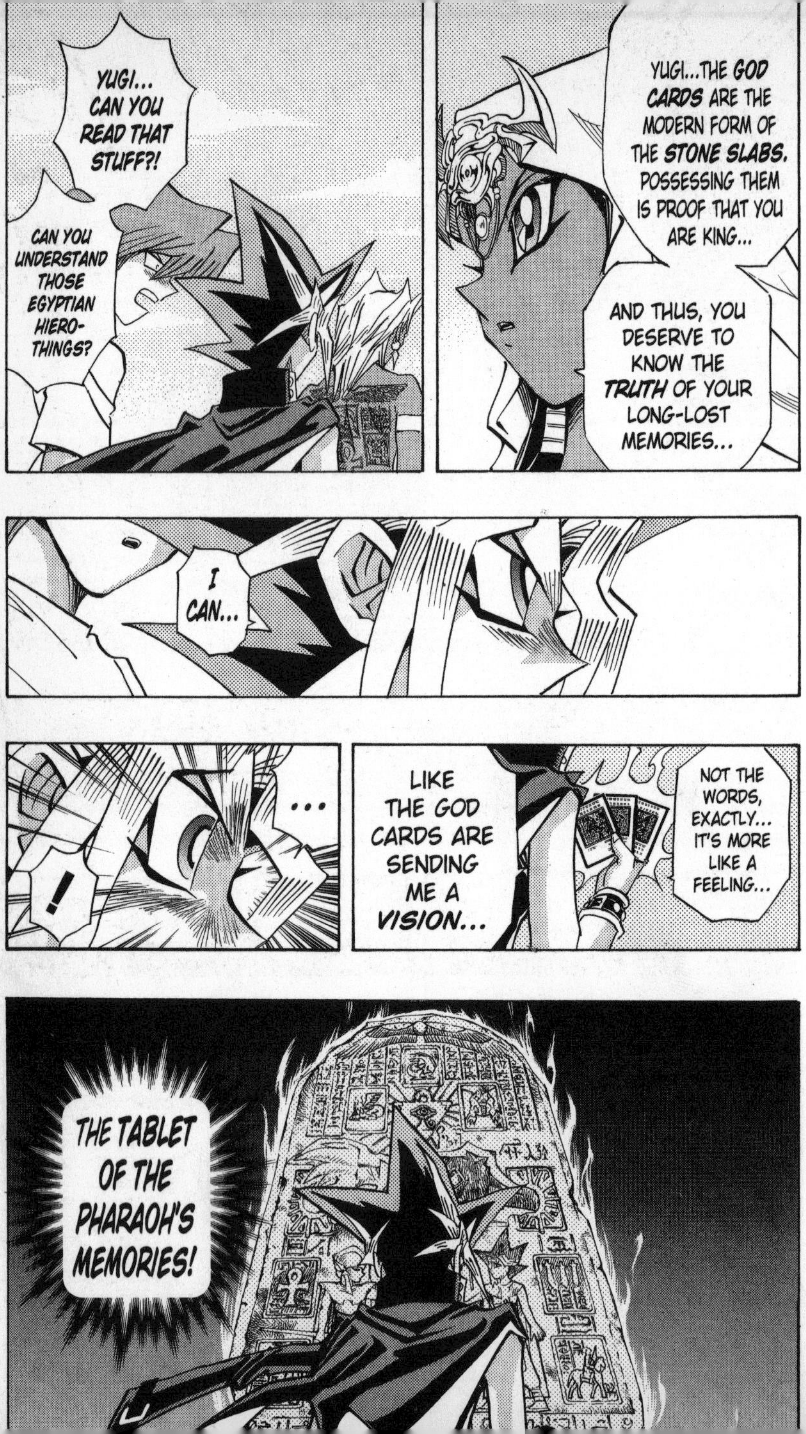
YUGI...THE GOD CARDS ARE THE MODERN FORM OF THE STONE SLABS. POSSESSING THEM IS PROOF THAT YOU ARE KING...
AND THUS, YOU DESERVE TO KNOW THE TRUTH OF YOUR LONG-LOST MEMORIES...
YUGI... CAN YOU READ THAT STUFF?!
CAN YOU UNDERSTAND THOSE EGYPTIAN HIERO-THINGS?
I CAN...
NOT THE WORDS, EXACTLY... IT'S MORE LIKE A FEELING...
LIKE THE GOD CARDS ARE SENDING ME A VISION...
...
!
THE TABLET OF THE PHARAOH'S MEMORIES!

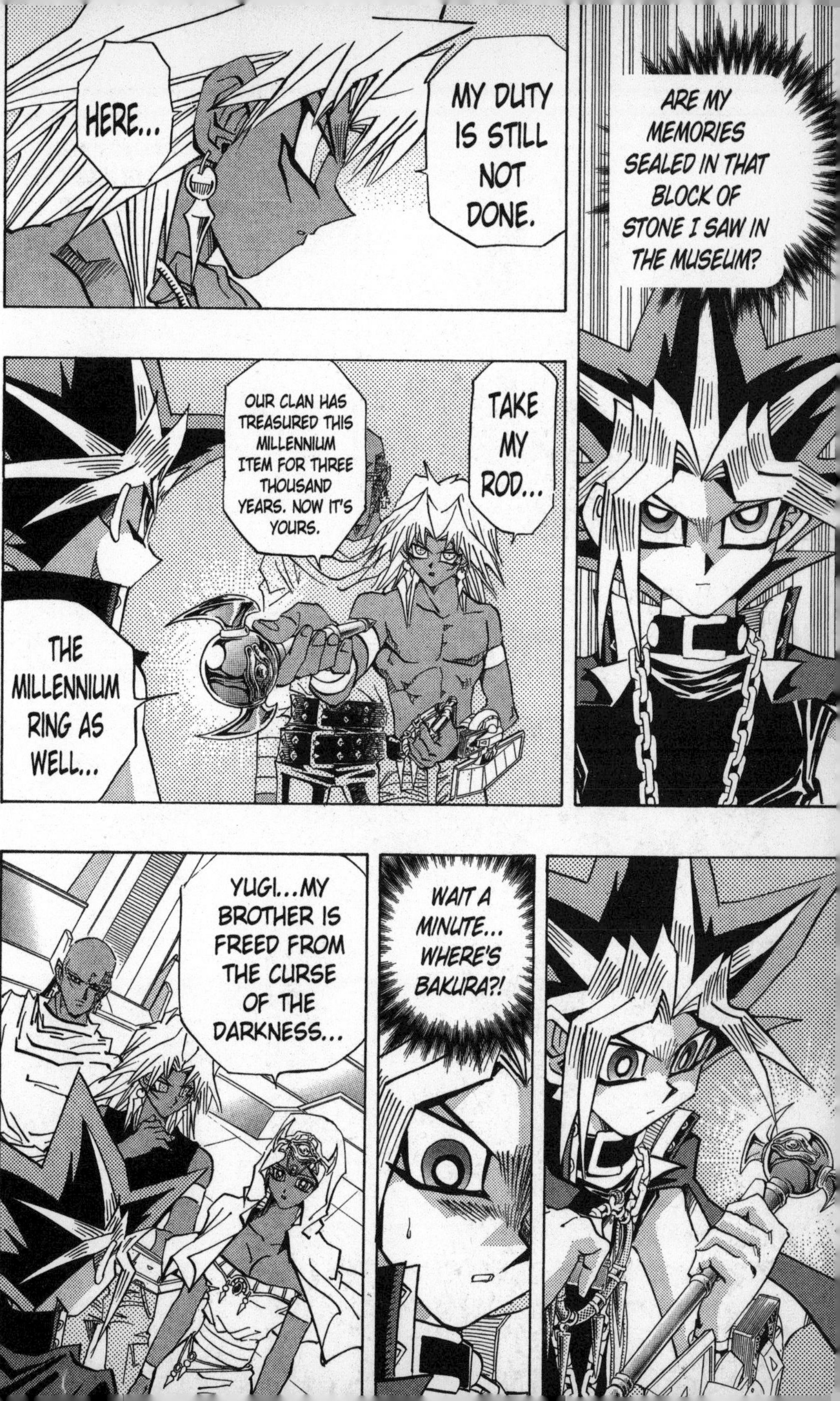
ARE MY MEMORIES SEALED IN THAT BLOCK OF STONE I SAW IN THE MUSEUM?
MY DUTY IS STILL NOT DONE.
HERE...
TAKE MY ROD...
OUR CLAN HAS TREASURED THIS MILLENNIUM ITEM FOR THREE THOUSAND YEARS. NOW IT'S YOURS.
THE MILLENNIUM RING AS WELL...
WAIT A MINUTE... WHERE'S BAKURA?!
YUGI...MY BROTHER IS FREED FROM THE CURSE OF THE DARKNESS...

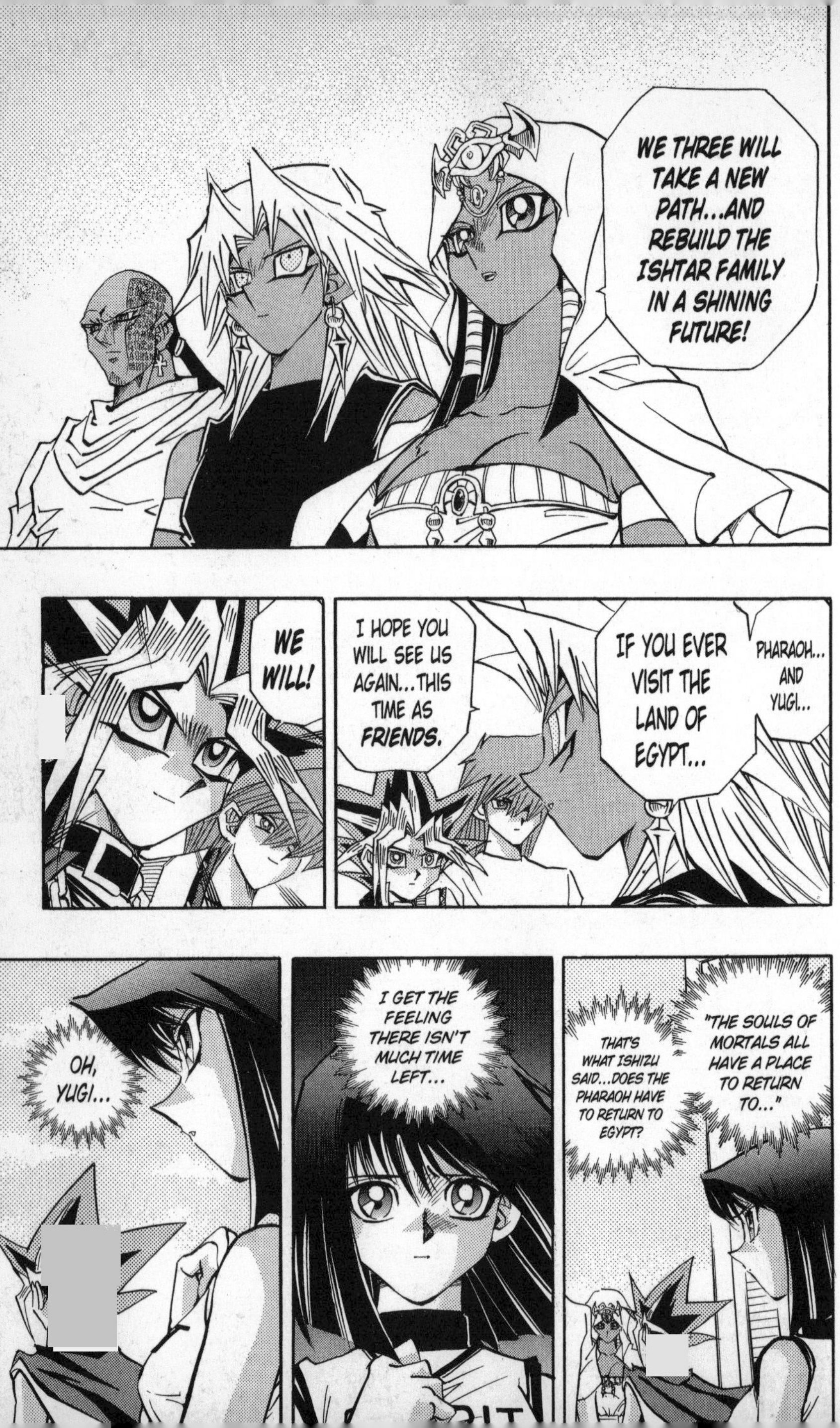
WE THREE WILL TAKE A NEW PATH...AND REBUILD THE ISHTAR FAMILY IN A SHINING FUTURE!
PHARAOH... AND YUGI...
IF YOU EVER VISIT THE LAND OF EGYPT...
I HOPE YOU WILL SEE US AGAIN...THIS TIME AS FRIENDS.
WE WILL!
"THE SOULS OF MORTALS ALL HAVE A PLACE TO RETURN TO..."
THAT'S WHAT ISHIZU SAID...DOES THE PHARAOH HAVE TO RETURN TO EGYPT?
I GET THE FEELING THERE ISN'T MUCH TIME LEFT...
OH, YUGI...

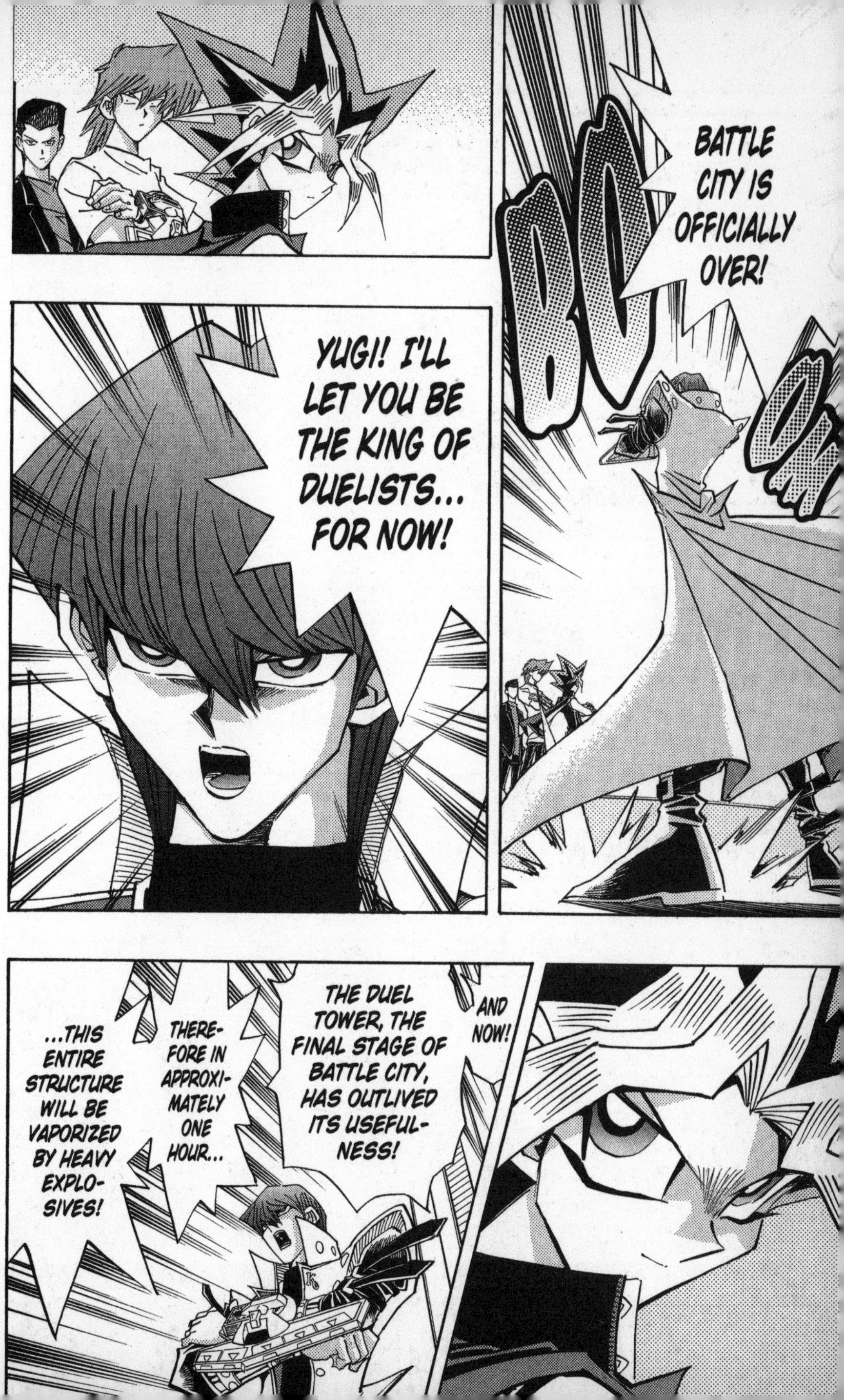

BATTLE CITY IS OFFICIALLY OVER!
YUGI! I'LL LET YOU BE THE KING OF DUELISTS... FOR NOW!
AND NOW!
THE DUEL TOWER, THE FINAL STAGE OF BATTLE CITY, HAS OUTLIVED ITS USEFULNESS!
THEREFORE IN APPROXIMATELY ONE HOUR...
...THIS ENTIRE STRUCTURE WILL BE VAPORIZED BY HEAVY EXPLOSIVES!

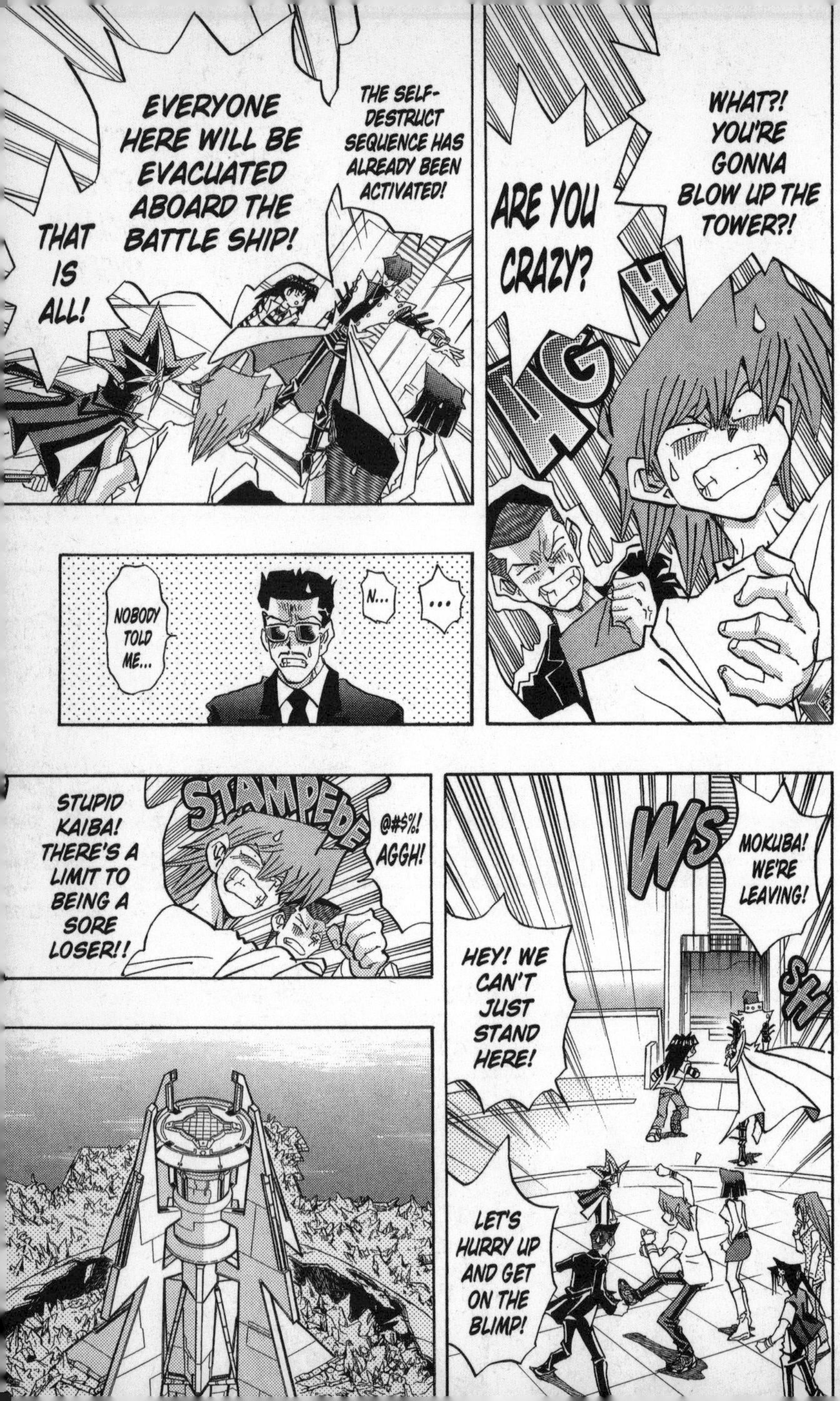
WHAT?! YOU'RE GONNA BLOW UP THE TOWER?!
ARE YOU CRAZY?
THE SELF-DESTRUCT SEQUENCE HAS ALREADY BEEN ACTIVATED!
EVERYONE HERE WILL BE EVACUATED ABOARD THE BATTLE SHIP!
THAT IS ALL!
N...
...
NOBODY TOLD ME...
MOKUBA! WE'RE LEAVING!
WS
SH
HEY! WE CAN'T JUST STAND HERE!
LET'S HURRY UP AND GET ON THE BLIMP!
@#$%! AGGH!
STAMPEDE
STUPID KAIBA! THERE'S A LIMIT TO BEING A SORE LOSER!!

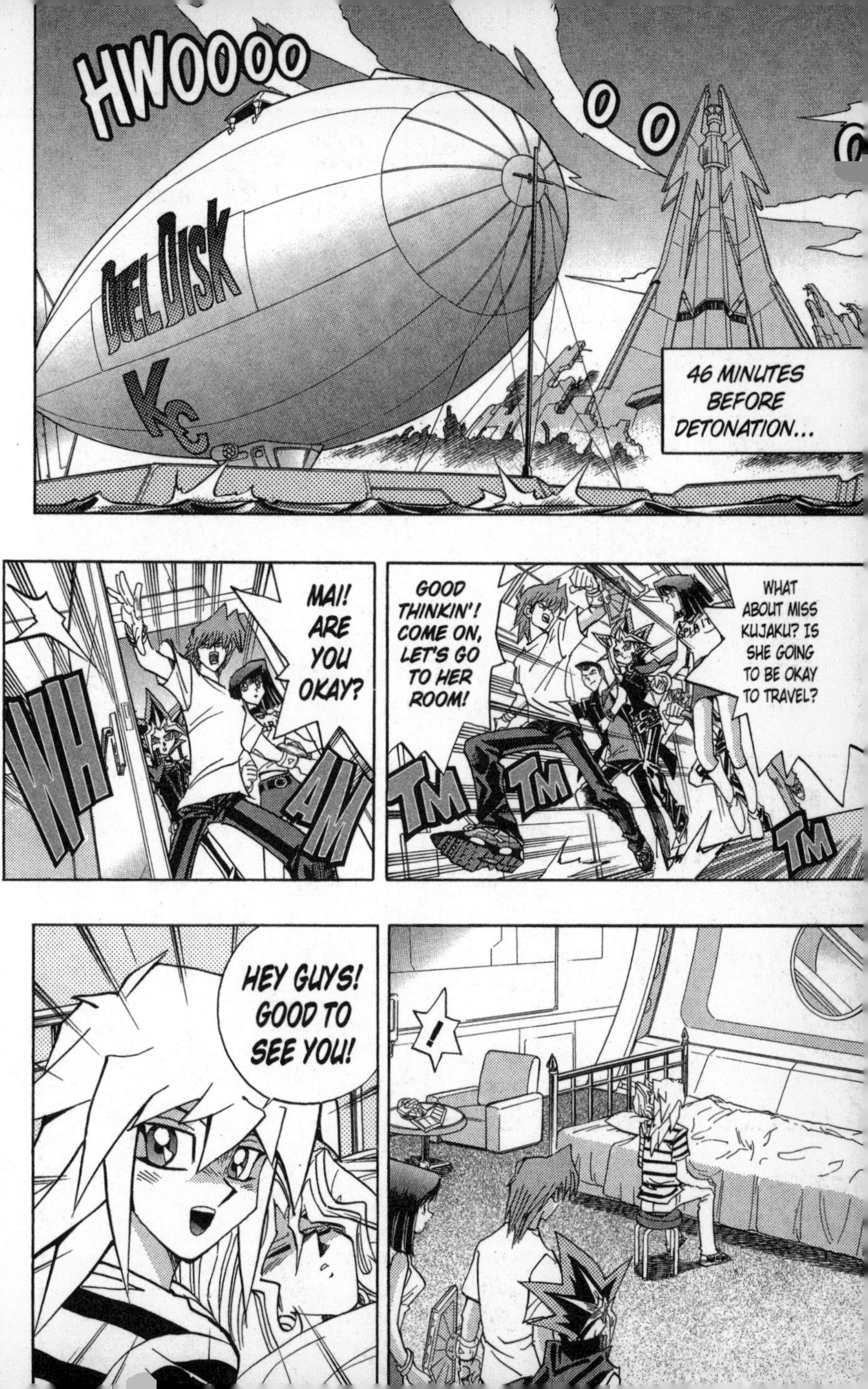
HWOOOO
OOO
46 MINUTES BEFORE DETONATION...
WHAT ABOUT MISS KUJAKU? IS SHE GOING TO BE OKAY TO TRAVEL?
GOOD THINKIN'! COME ON, LET'S GO TO HER ROOM!
TM TM TM
MAI! ARE YOU OKAY?
WHAM
!
HEY GUYS! GOOD TO SEE YOU!

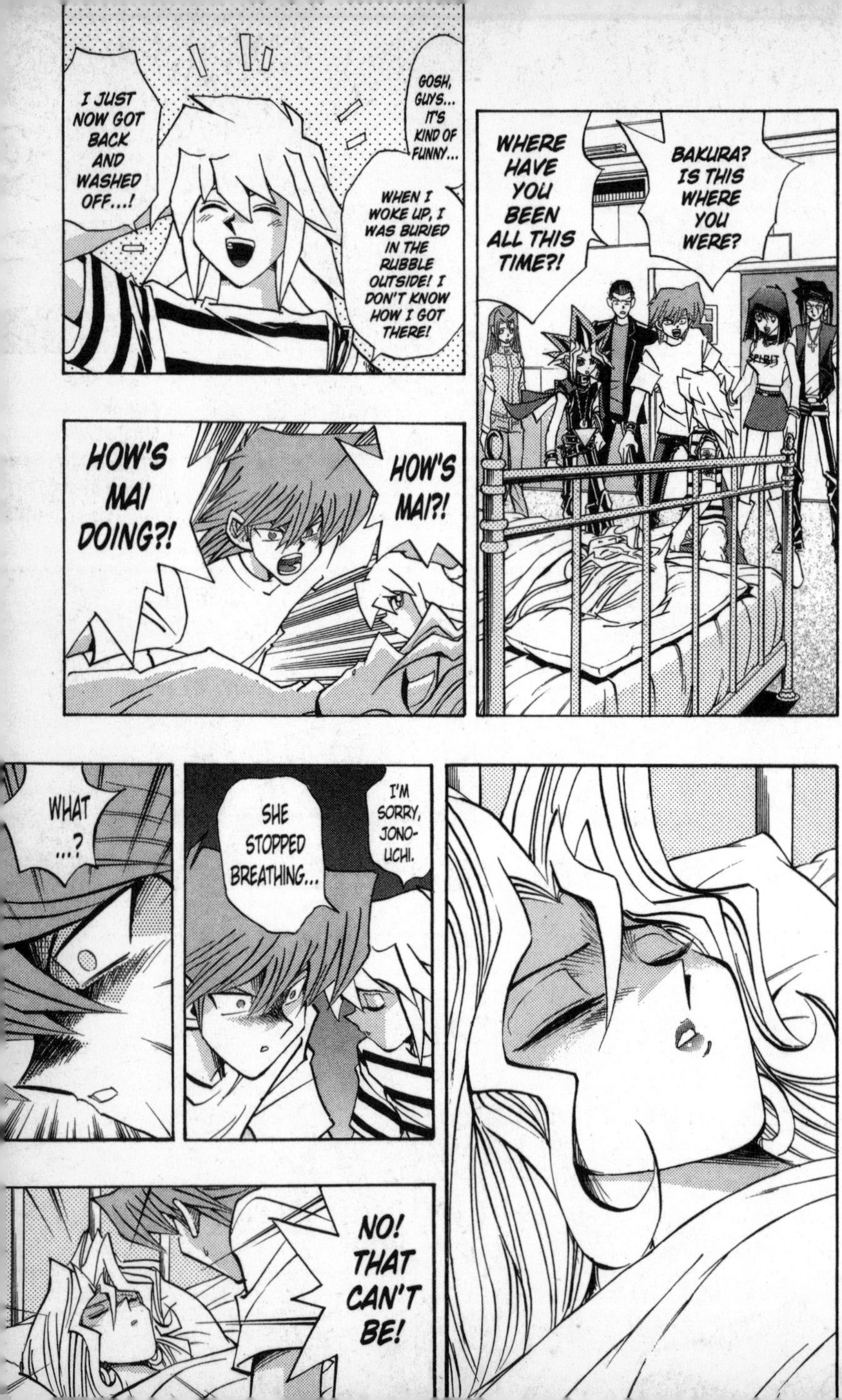
BAKURA? IS THIS WHERE YOU WERE?
WHERE HAVE YOU BEEN ALL THIS TIME?!
GOSH, GUYS... IT'S KIND OF FUNNY...
WHEN I WOKE UP, I WAS BURIED IN THE RUBBLE OUTSIDE! I DON'T KNOW HOW I GOT THERE!
I JUST NOW GOT BACK AND WASHED OFF...!
HOW'S MAI?!
HOW'S MAI DOING?!
I'M SORRY, JONO-UCHI.
SHE STOPPED BREATHING...
WHAT ...?
NO! THAT CAN'T BE!

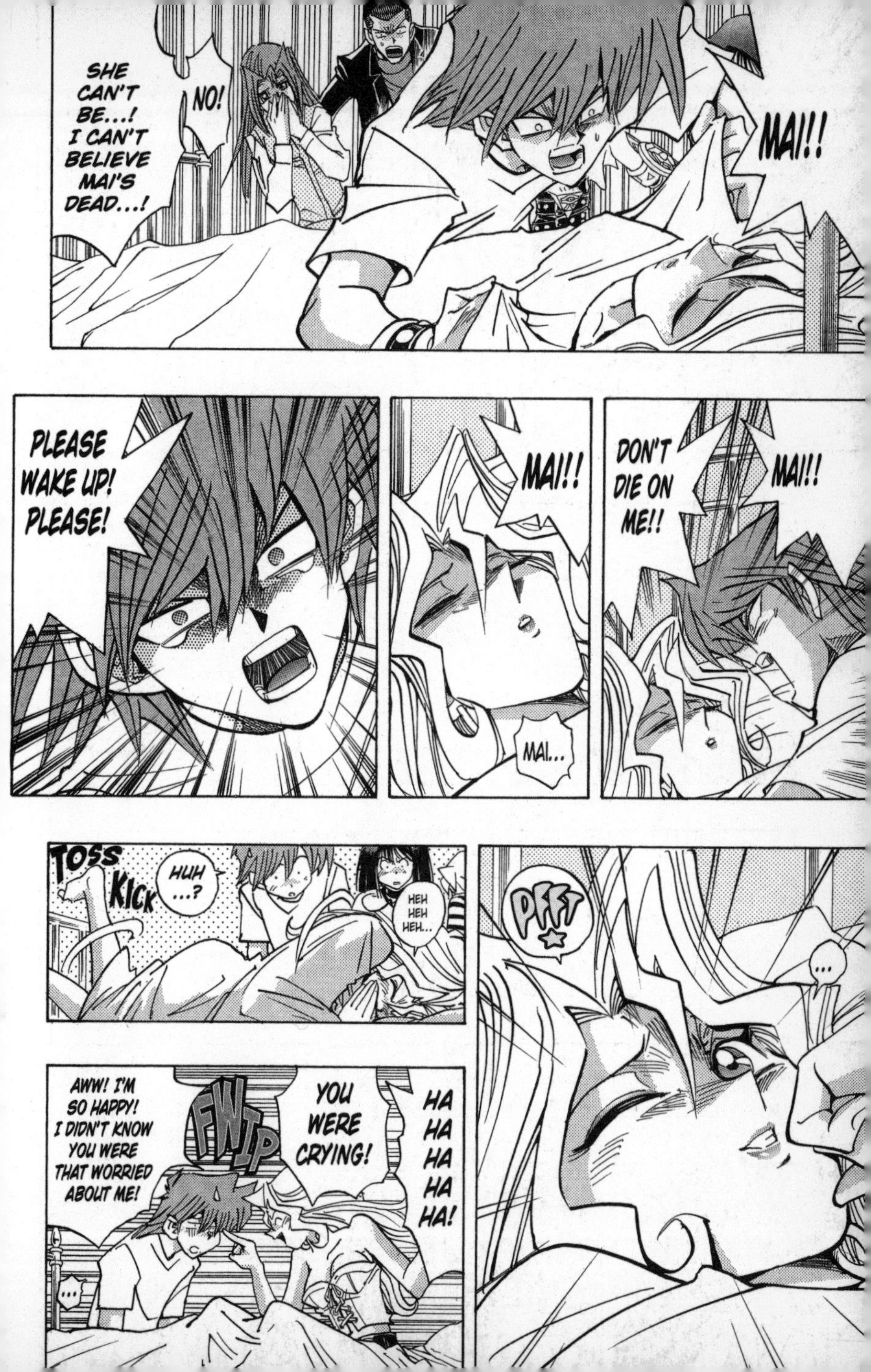
MAI!!
NO!
SHE CAN'T BE...! I CAN'T BELIEVE MAI'S DEAD...!
MAI!!
DON'T DIE ON ME!!
MAI!!
MAI...
PLEASE WAKE UP! PLEASE!
PFFT
...
HEH HEH HEH...
HUH ...?
TOSS
KICK
HA HA HA HA HA HA!
YOU WERE CRYING!
FWIP
AWW! I'M SO HAPPY! I DIDN'T KNOW YOU WERE THAT WORRIED ABOUT ME!
...

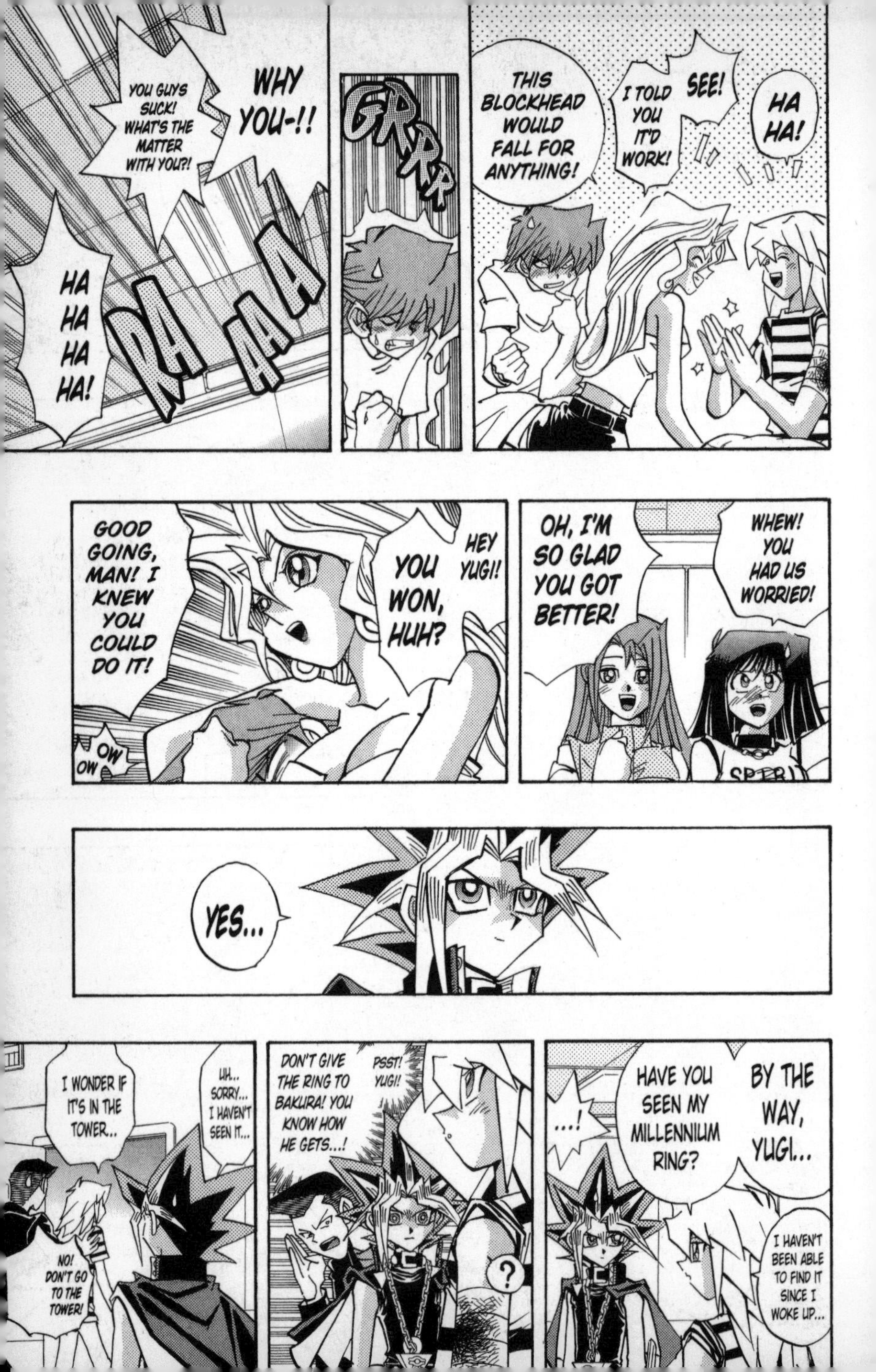
HA HA!
SEE!
I TOLD YOU IT'D WORK!
THIS BLOCKHEAD WOULD FALL FOR ANYTHING!
GRRR
WHY YOU-!!
YOU GUYS SUCK! WHAT'S THE MATTER WITH YOU?!
HA HA HA HA!
WHEW! YOU HAD US WORRIED!
OH, I'M SO GLAD YOU GOT BETTER!
HEY YUGI!
YOU WON, HUH?
GOOD GOING, MAN! I KNEW YOU COULD DO IT!
OW OW
YES...
BY THE WAY, YUGI...
HAVE YOU SEEN MY MILLENNIUM RING?
...!
I HAVEN'T BEEN ABLE TO FIND IT SINCE I WOKE UP...
PSST! YUGI!
DON'T GIVE THE RING TO BAKURA! YOU KNOW HOW HE GETS...!
?
UH... SORRY... I HAVEN'T SEEN IT...
I WONDER IF IT'S IN THE TOWER...
NO! DON'T GO TO THE TOWER!

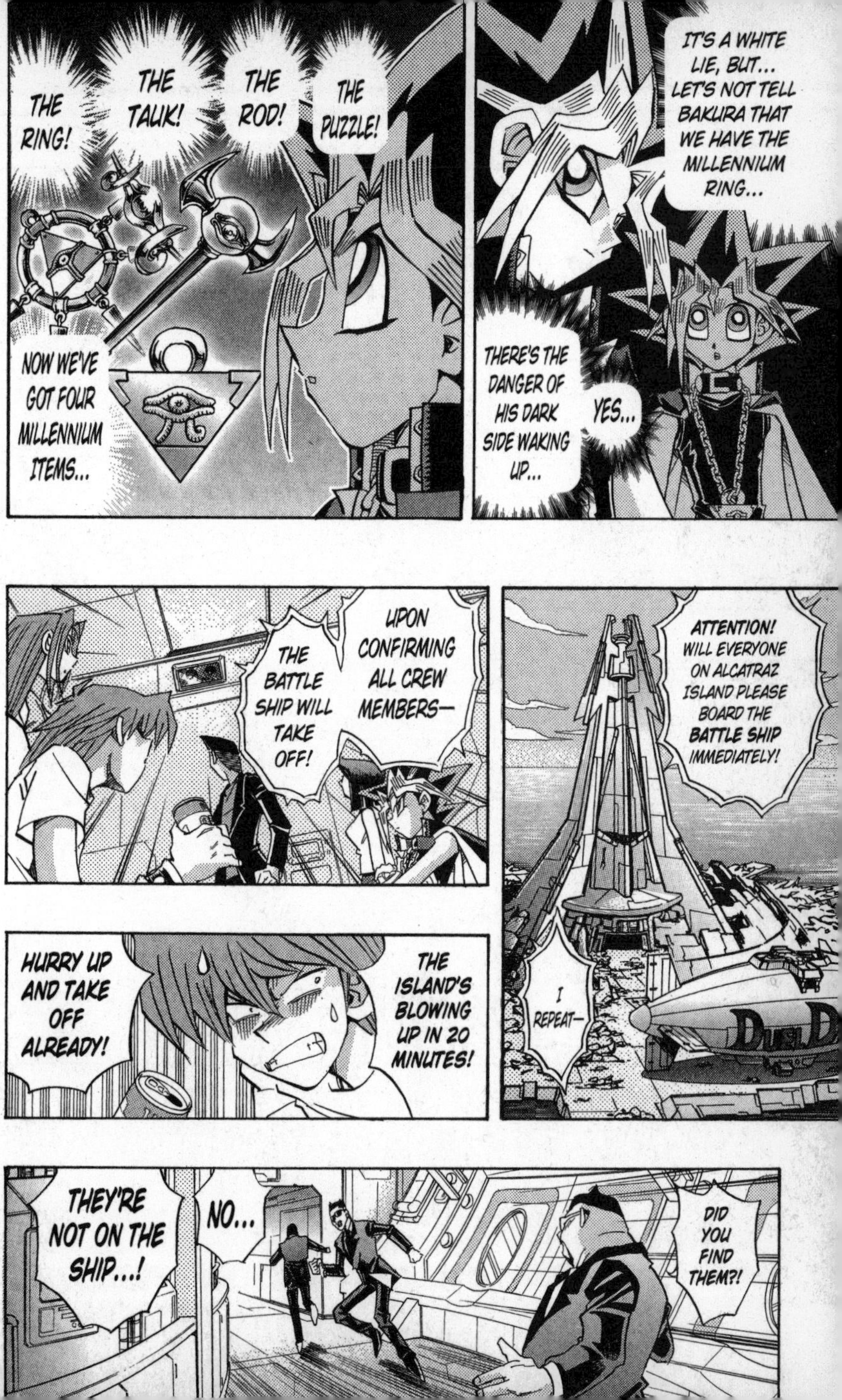
IT'S A WHITE LIE, BUT... LET'S NOT TELL BAKURA THAT WE HAVE THE MILLENNIUM RING...
THERE'S THE DANGER OF HIS DARK SIDE WAKING UP...
YES...
THE PUZZLE!
THE ROD!
THE TAUK!
THE RING!
NOW WE'VE GOT FOUR MILLENNIUM ITEMS...
ATTENTION! WILL EVERYONE ON ALCATRAZ ISLAND PLEASE BOARD THE BATTLE SHIP IMMEDIATELY!
I REPEAT—
UPON CONFIRMING ALL CREW MEMBERS—
THE BATTLE SHIP WILL TAKE OFF!
THE ISLAND'S BLOWING UP IN 20 MINUTES!
HURRY UP AND TAKE OFF ALREADY!
DID YOU FIND THEM?!
NO...
THEY'RE NOT ON THE SHIP...!

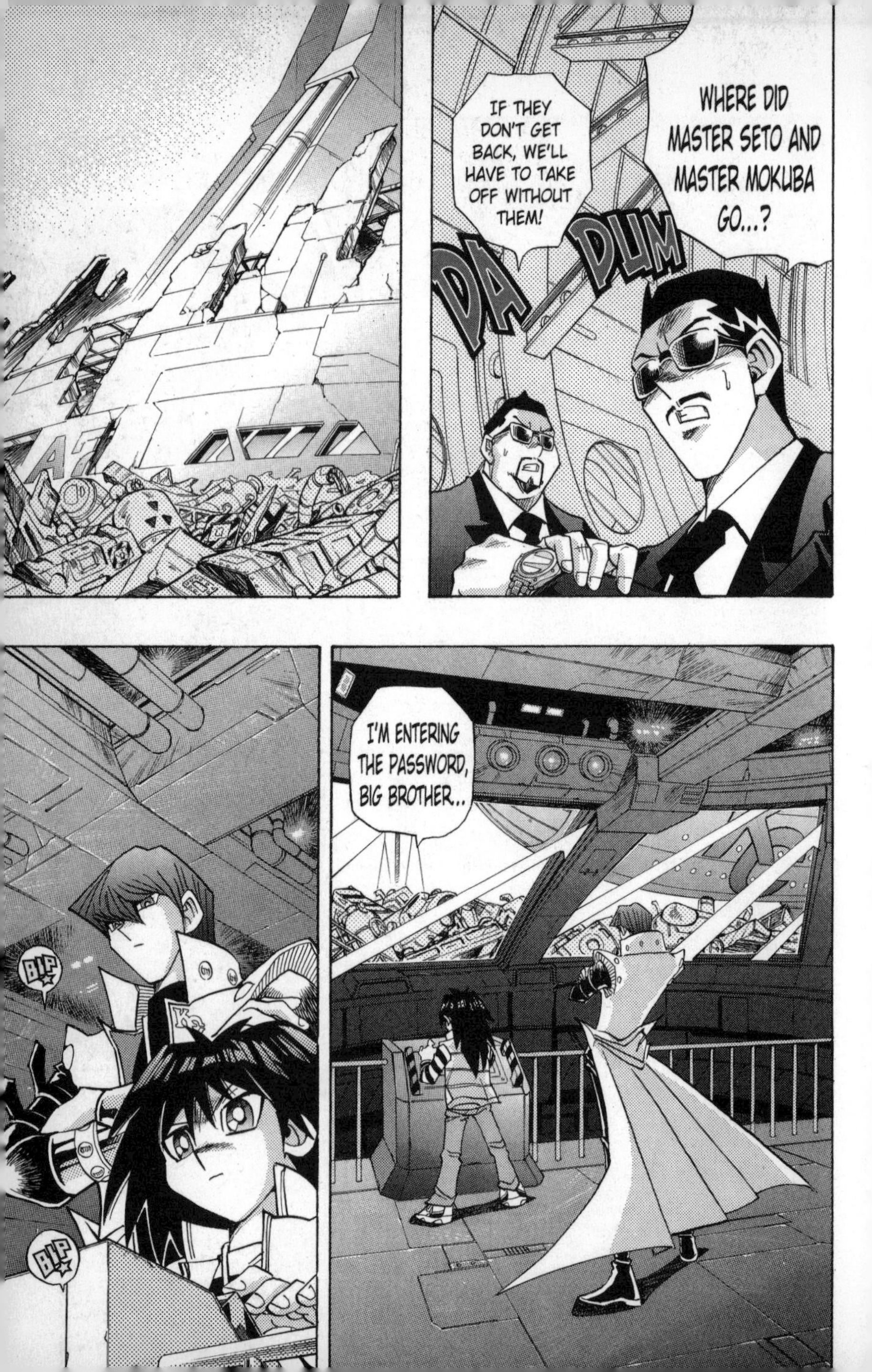
WHERE DID MASTER SETO AND MASTER MOKUBA GO...?
IF THEY DON'T GET BACK, WE'LL HAVE TO TAKE OFF WITHOUT THEM!
DA DUM
I'M ENTERING THE PASSWORD, BIG BROTHER..
BLIP
BLIP

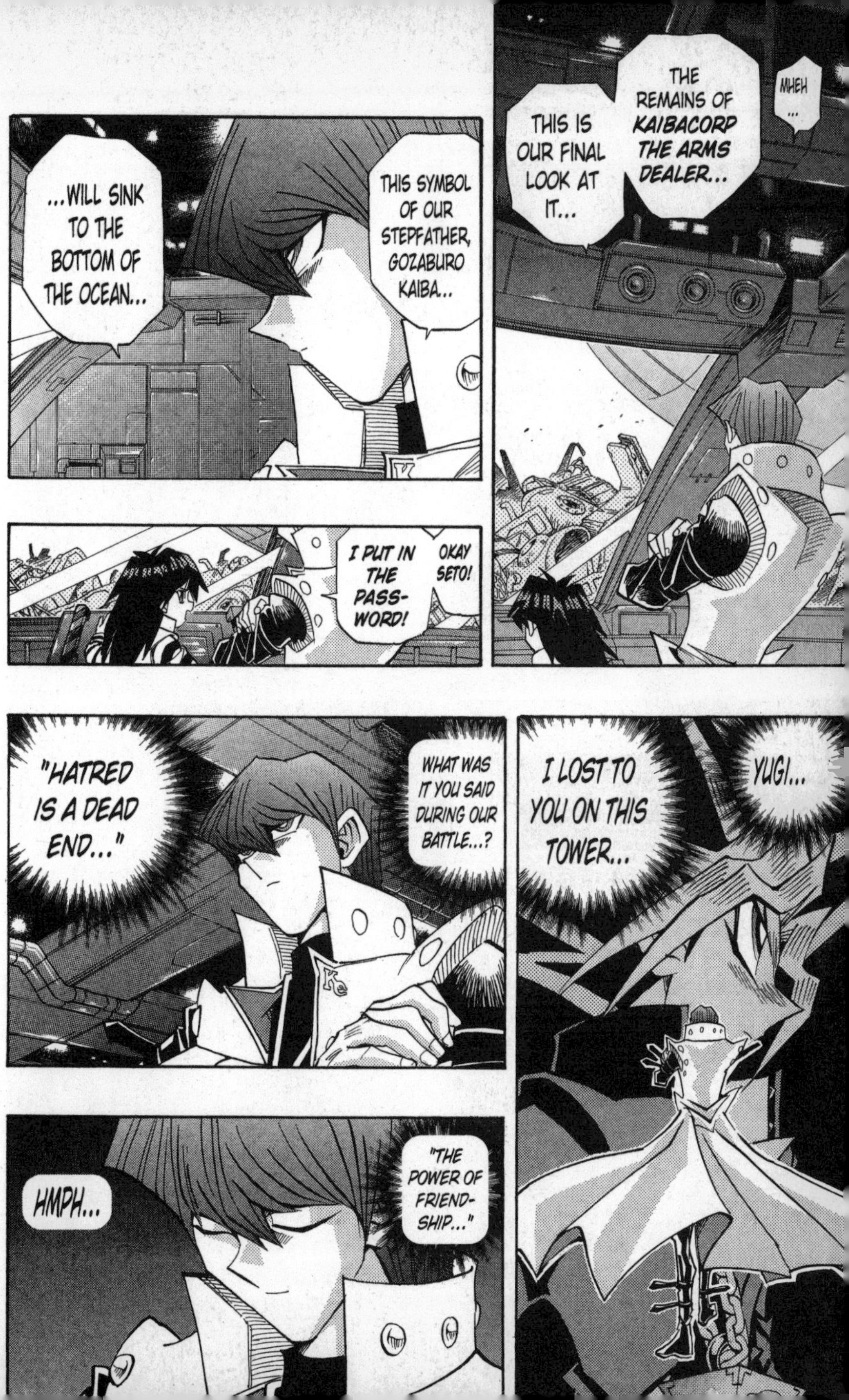
MHEH ...
THE REMAINS OF KAIBACORP THE ARMS DEALER...
THIS IS OUR FINAL LOOK AT IT...
THIS SYMBOL OF OUR STEPFATHER, GOZABURO KAIBA...
...WILL SINK TO THE BOTTOM OF THE OCEAN...
OKAY SETO!
I PUT IN THE PASS-WORD!
YUGI...
I LOST TO YOU ON THIS TOWER...
WHAT WAS IT YOU SAID DURING OUR BATTLE...?
"HATRED IS A DEAD END..."
"THE POWER OF FRIEND-SHIP..."
HMPH...

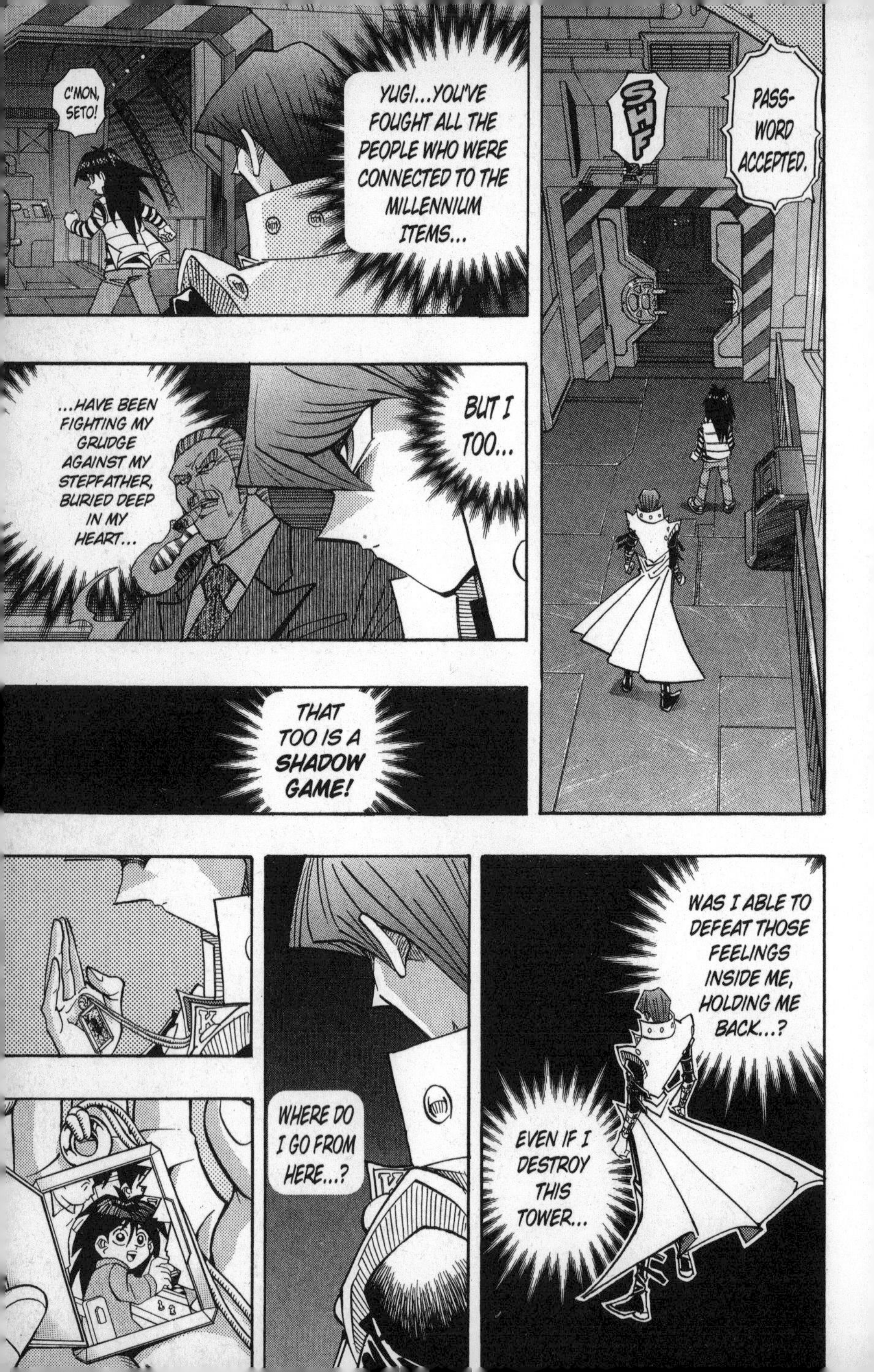
PASS-WORD ACCEPTED.
SHF
YUGI...YOU'VE FOUGHT ALL THE PEOPLE WHO WERE CONNECTED TO THE MILLENNIUM ITEMS...
C'MON, SETO!
BUT I TOO...
...HAVE BEEN FIGHTING MY GRUDGE AGAINST MY STEPFATHER, BURIED DEEP IN MY HEART...
THAT TOO IS A SHADOW GAME!
WAS I ABLE TO DEFEAT THOSE FEELINGS INSIDE ME, HOLDING ME BACK...?
EVEN IF I DESTROY THIS TOWER...
WHERE DO I GO FROM HERE...?

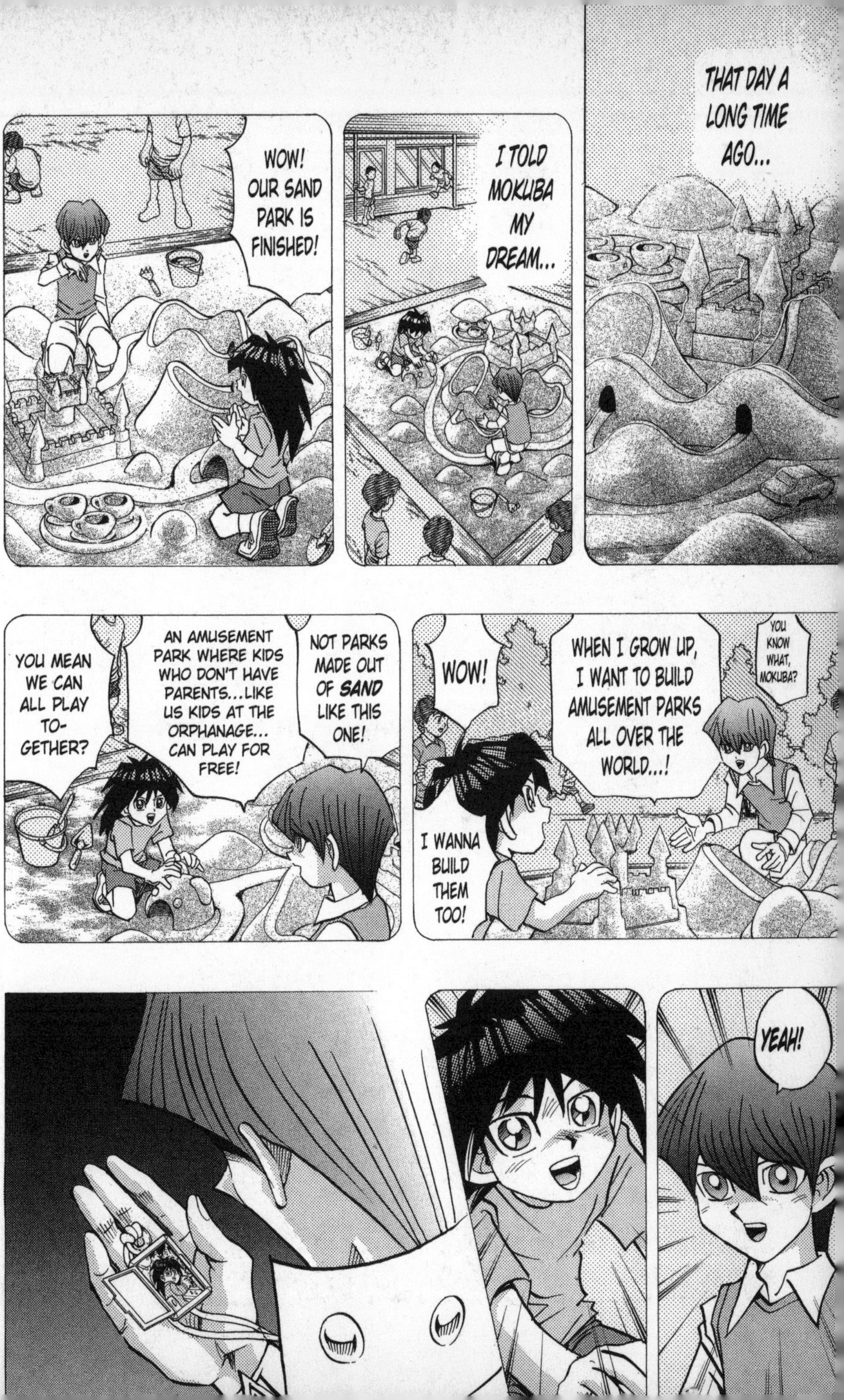
THAT DAY A LONG TIME AGO...
I TOLD MOKUBA MY DREAM...
WOW! OUR SAND PARK IS FINISHED!
YOU KNOW WHAT, MOKUBA?
WHEN I GROW UP, I WANT TO BUILD AMUSEMENT PARKS ALL OVER THE WORLD...!
WOW!
I WANNA BUILD THEM TOO!
NOT PARKS MADE OUT OF SAND LIKE THIS ONE!
AN AMUSEMENT PARK WHERE KIDS WHO DON'T HAVE PARENTS...LIKE US KIDS AT THE ORPHANAGE... CAN PLAY FOR FREE!
YOU MEAN WE CAN ALL PLAY TO-GETHER?
YEAH!

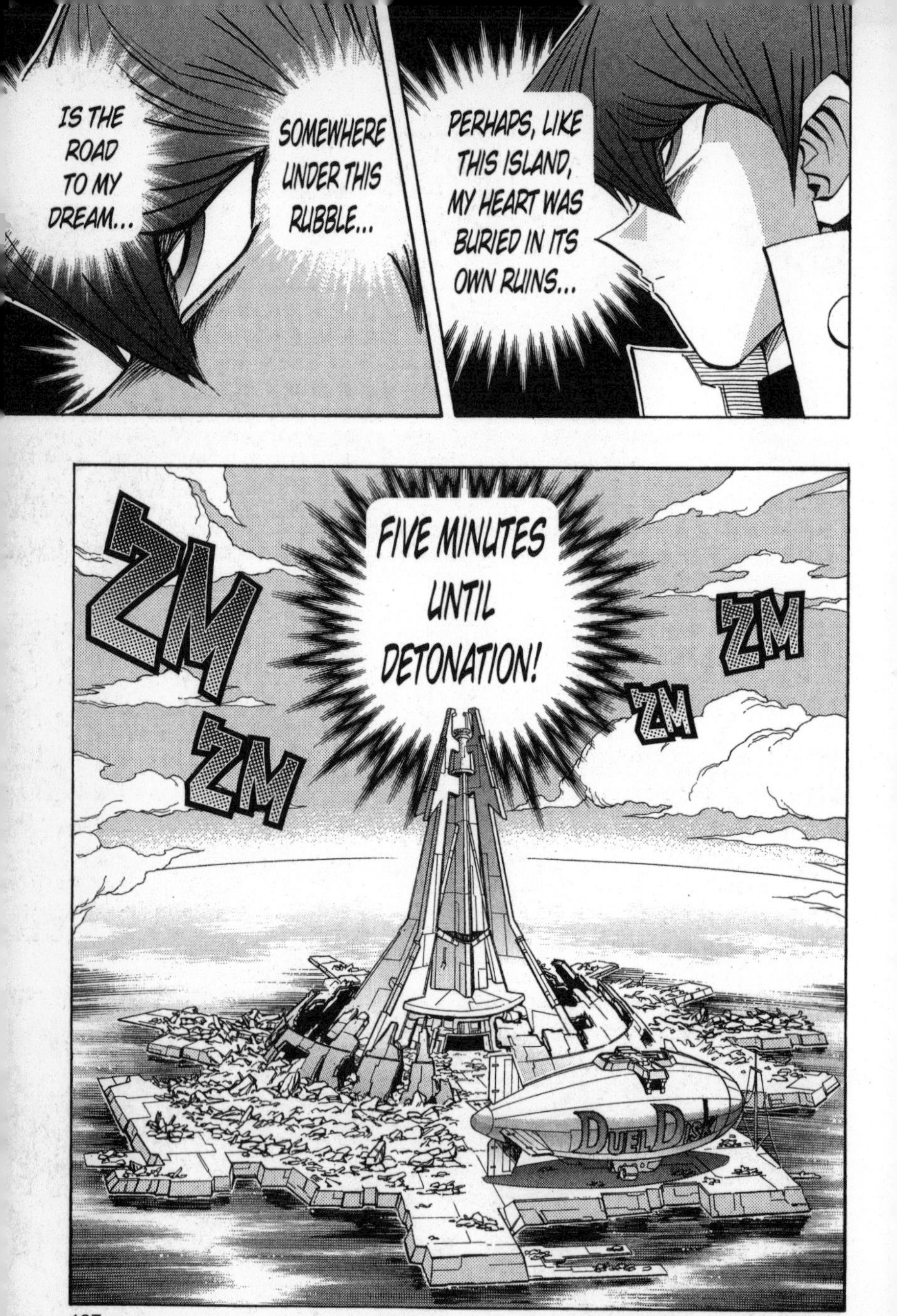
PERHAPS, LIKE THIS ISLAND, MY HEART WAS BURIED IN ITS OWN RUINS...
SOMEWHERE UNDER THIS RUBBLE...
IS THE ROAD TO MY DREAM...
ZM
ZM
FIVE MINUTES UNTIL DETONATION!
ZM
ZM
DUEL DISK

# Duel 219: A New Journey!

SPIRIT

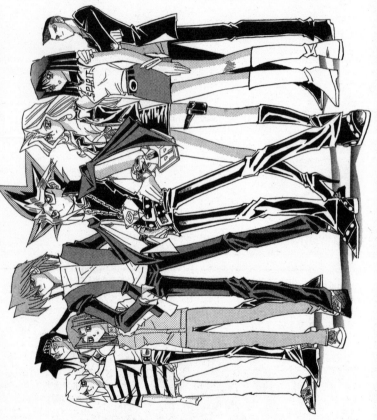

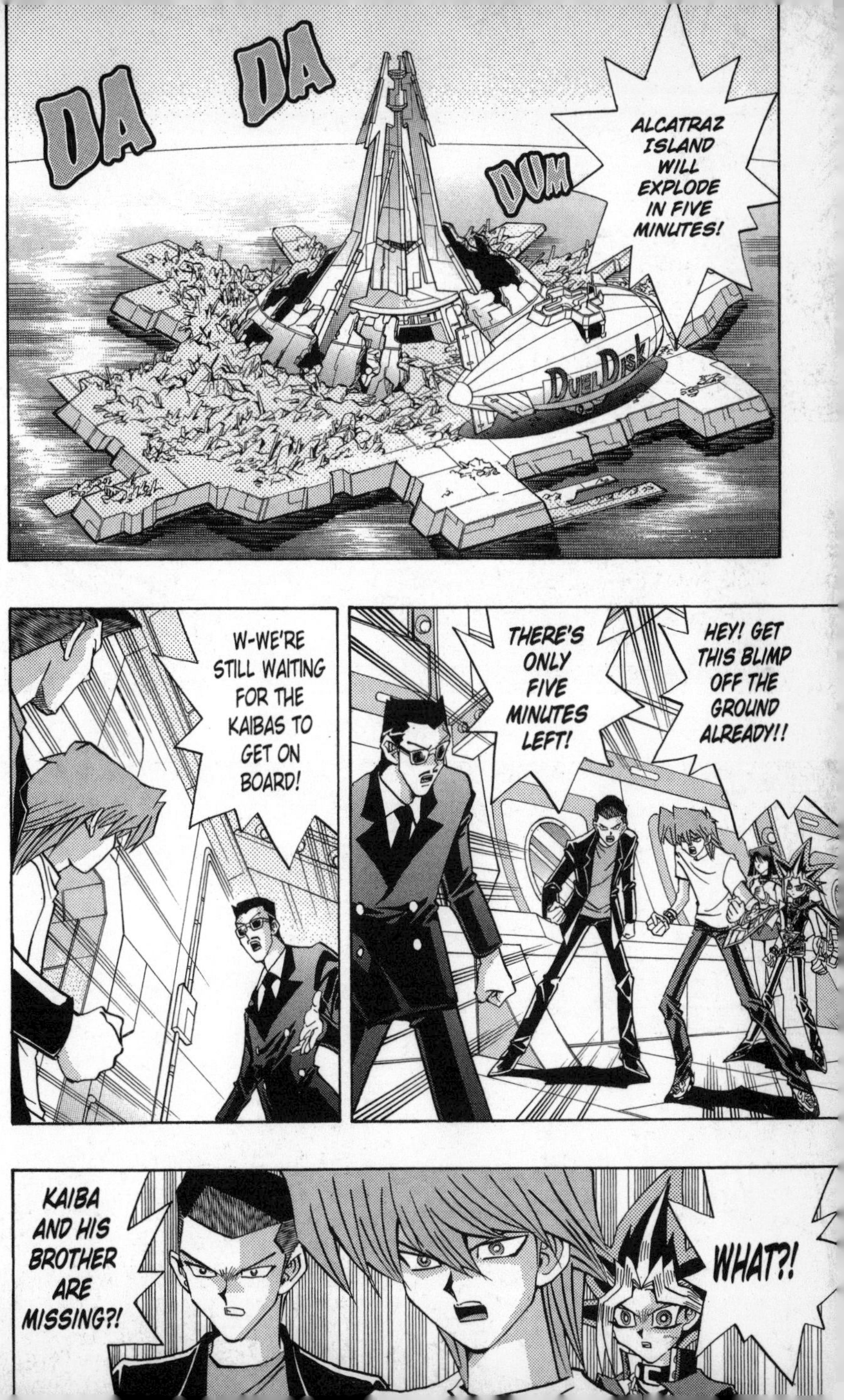
ALCATRAZ ISLAND WILL EXPLODE IN FIVE MINUTES!
DA
DA
DUM
DUEL DISK
HEY! GET THIS BLIMP OFF THE GROUND ALREADY!!
THERE'S ONLY FIVE MINUTES LEFT!
W-WE'RE STILL WAITING FOR THE KAIBAS TO GET ON BOARD!
WHAT?!
KAIBA AND HIS BROTHER ARE MISSING?!

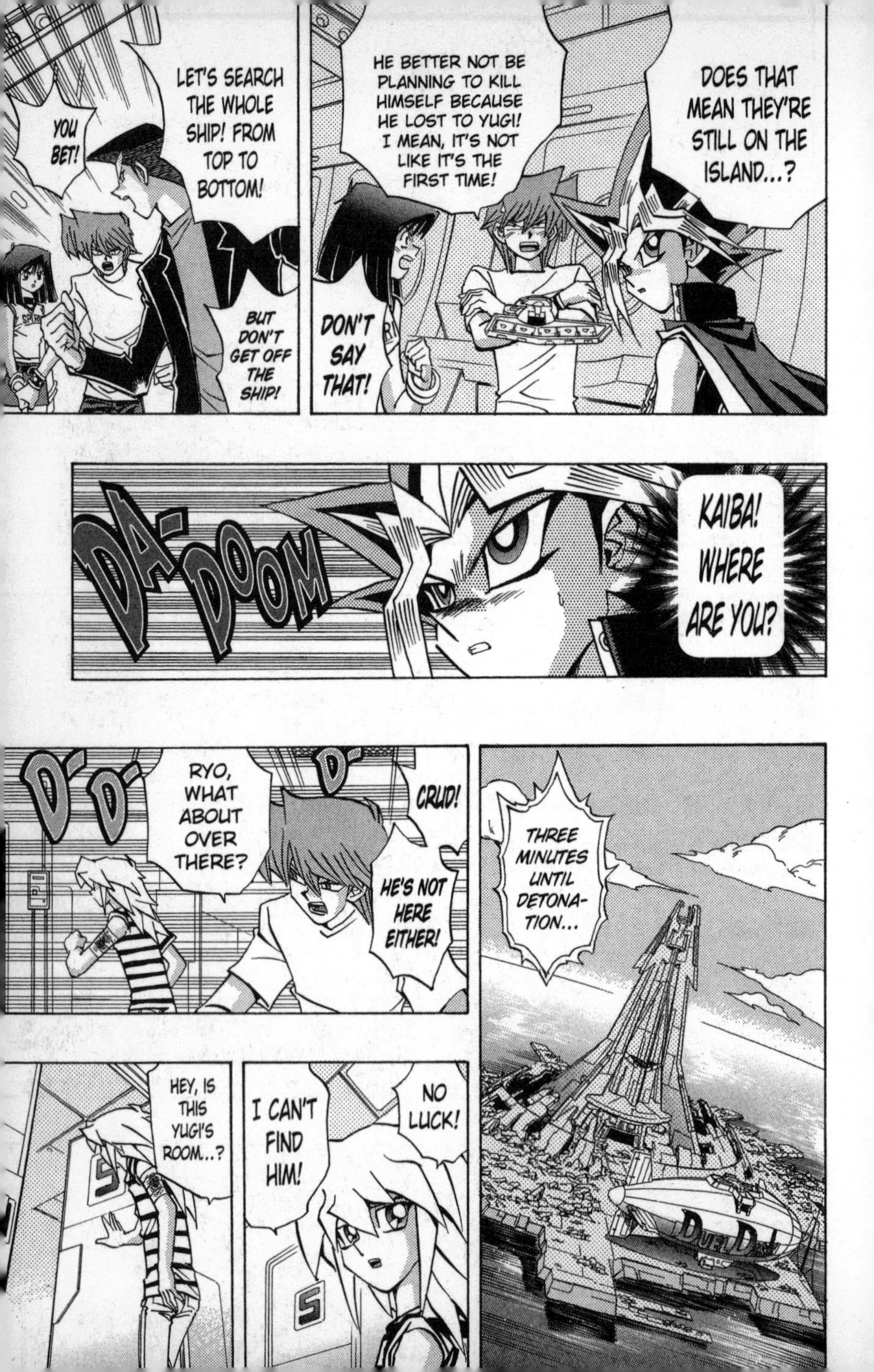
DOES THAT MEAN THEY'RE STILL ON THE ISLAND...?
HE BETTER NOT BE PLANNING TO KILL HIMSELF BECAUSE HE LOST TO YUGI! I MEAN, IT'S NOT LIKE IT'S THE FIRST TIME!
DON'T SAY THAT!
LET'S SEARCH THE WHOLE SHIP! FROM TOP TO BOTTOM!
YOU BET!
BUT DON'T GET OFF THE SHIP!
KAIBA! WHERE ARE YOU?
DA-DOOM
THREE MINUTES UNTIL DETONATION...
CRUD!
D-
RYO, WHAT ABOUT OVER THERE?
HE'S NOT HERE EITHER!
D- D-
NO LUCK!
I CAN'T FIND HIM!
HEY, IS THIS YUGI'S ROOM...?

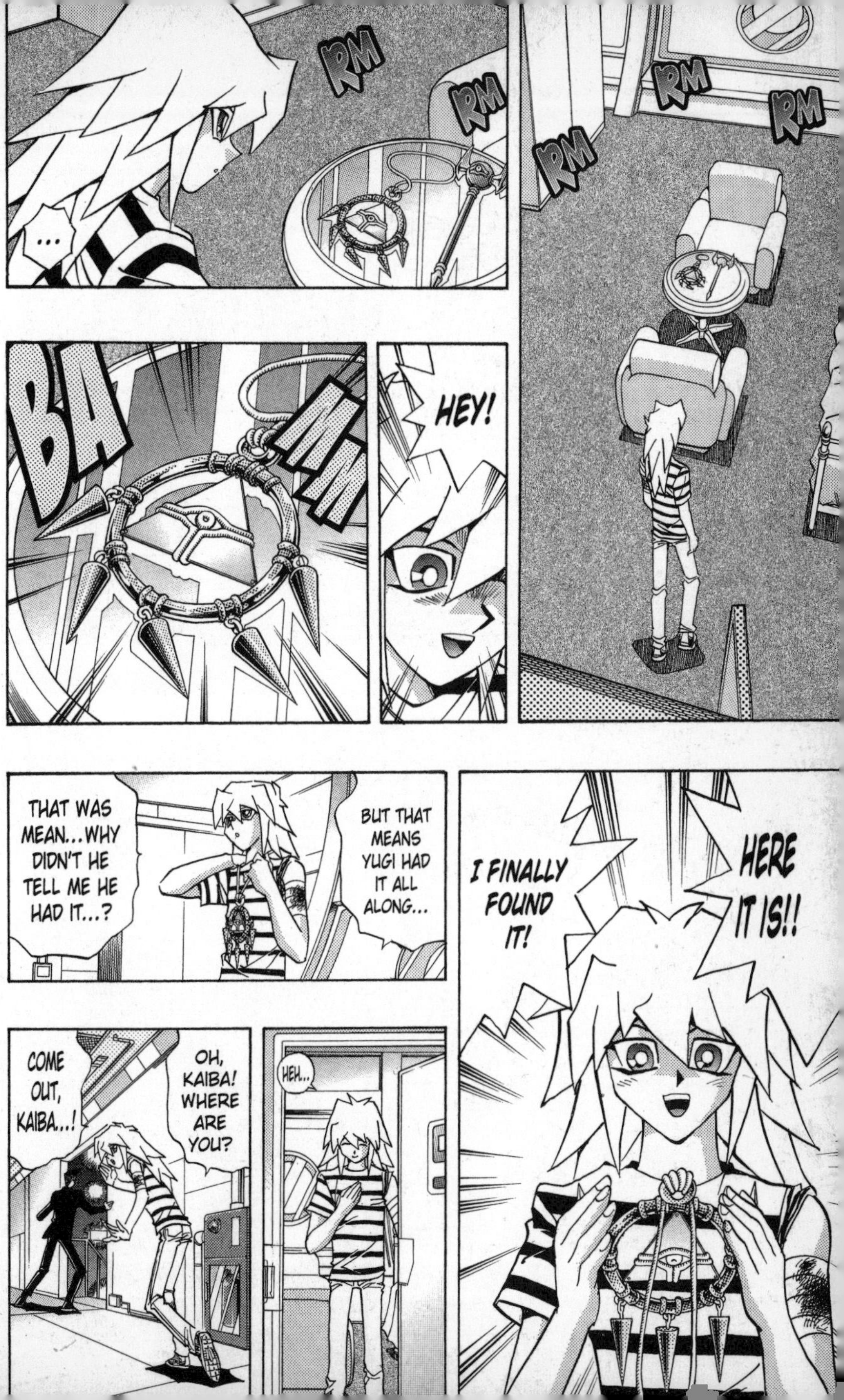
RM
RM
RM
RM
RM
...
HEY!
BAM
HERE IT IS!!
I FINALLY FOUND IT!
BUT THAT MEANS YUGI HAD IT ALL ALONG...
THAT WAS MEAN...WHY DIDN'T HE TELL ME HE HAD IT...?
HEH...
OH, KAIBA! WHERE ARE YOU?
COME OUT, KAIBA...!

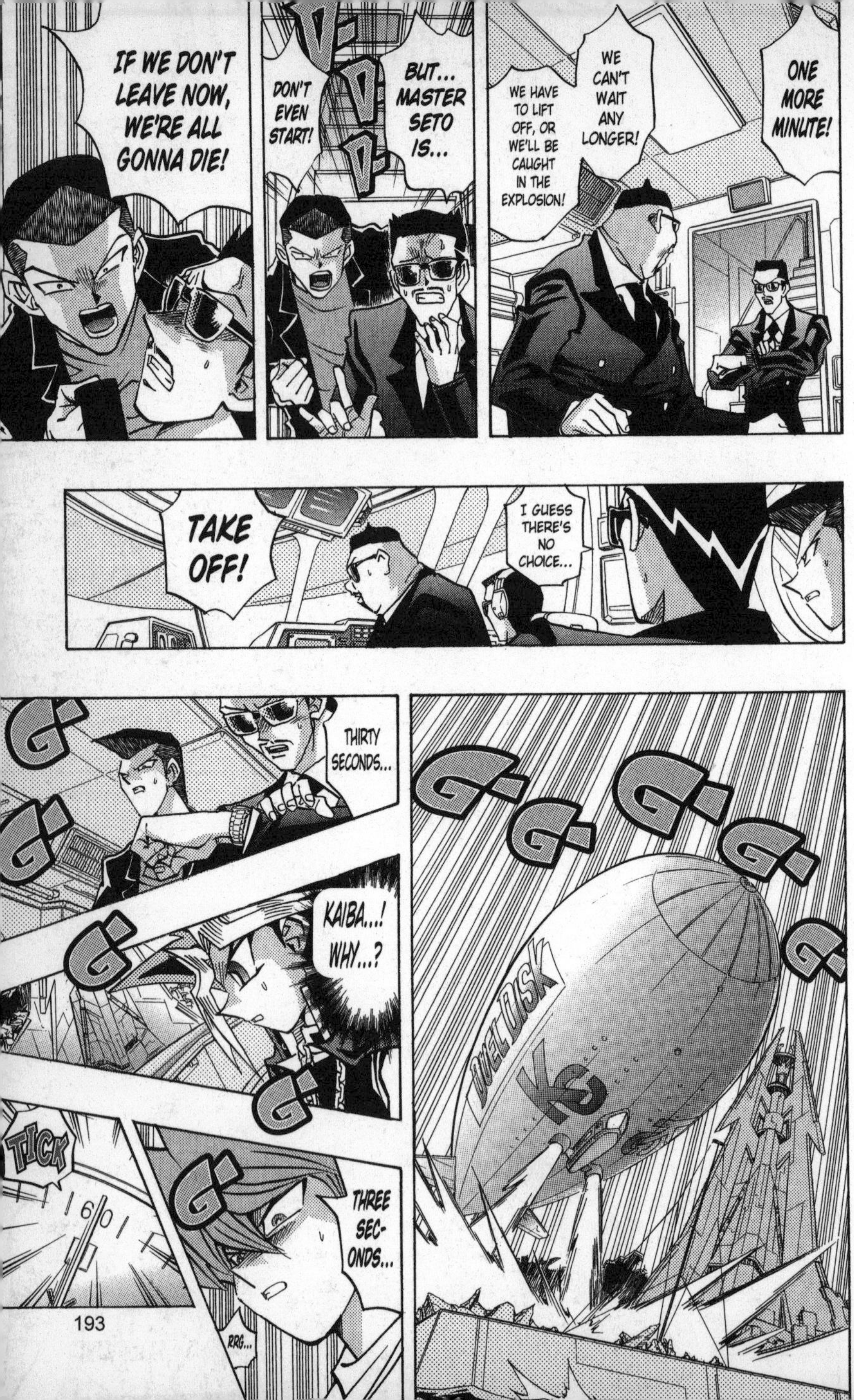
ONE MORE MINUTE!
WE CAN'T WAIT ANY LONGER!
WE HAVE TO LIFT OFF, OR WE'LL BE CAUGHT IN THE EXPLOSION!
BUT... MASTER SETO IS...
DON'T EVEN START!
IF WE DON'T LEAVE NOW, WE'RE ALL GONNA DIE!
I GUESS THERE'S NO CHOICE...
TAKE OFF!
G-G G-G-G-G G-
DUEL DISK
KC
THIRTY SECONDS...
KAIBA...! WHY...?
TICK
THREE SEC-ONDS...
RRG...

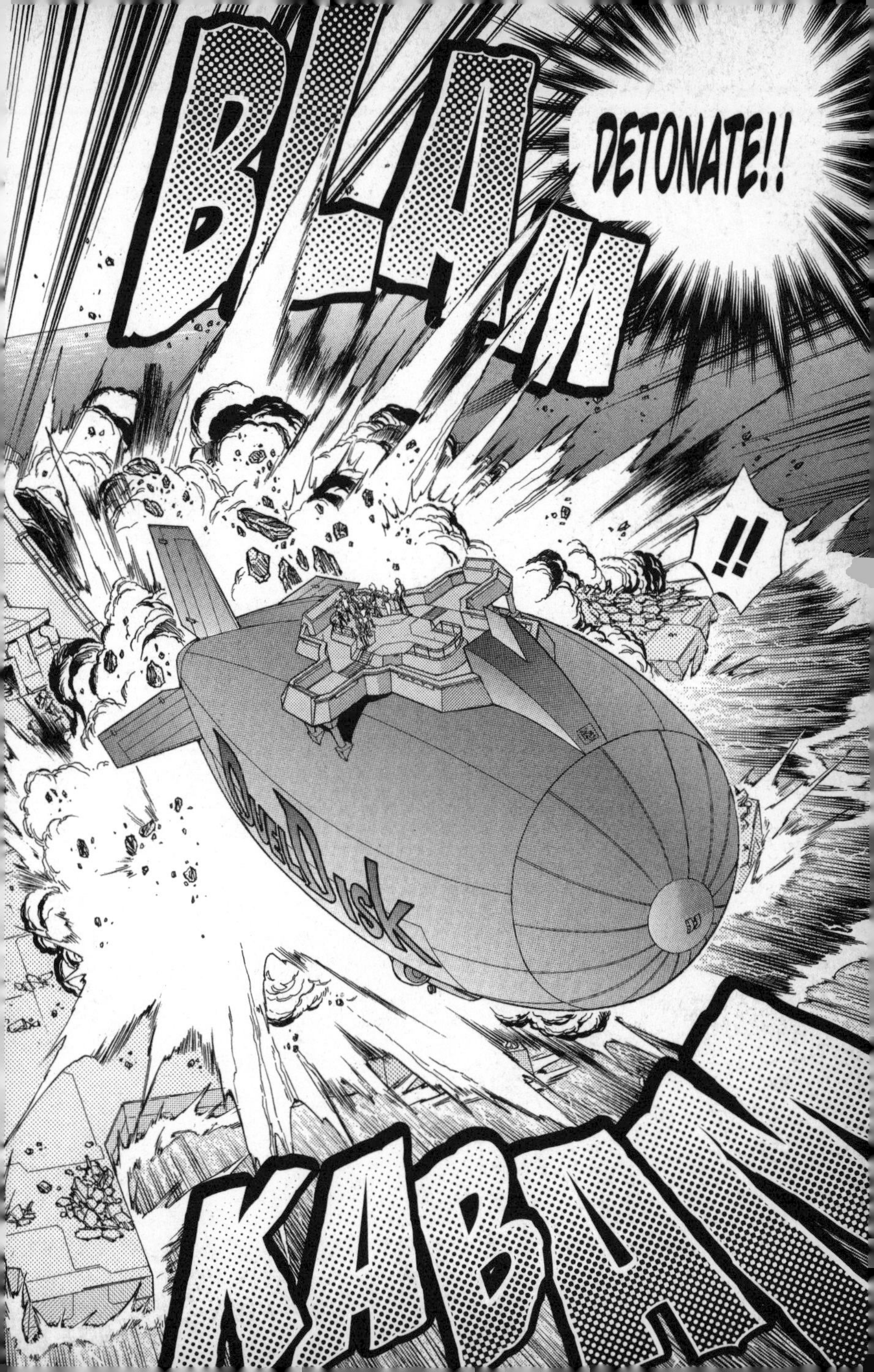
DETONATE!!
BLAM
!!
KABAM

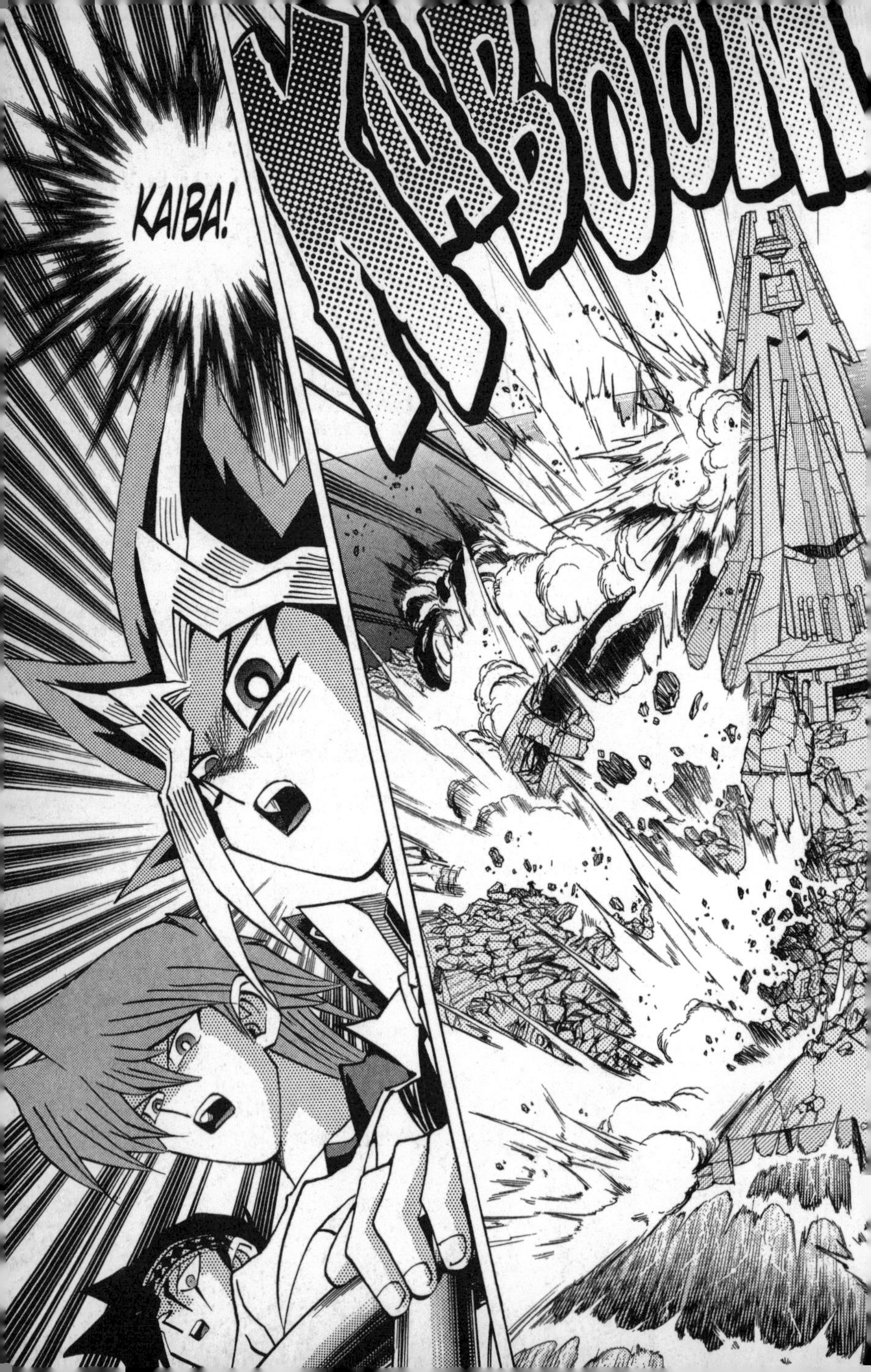
KABOOM
KAIBA!

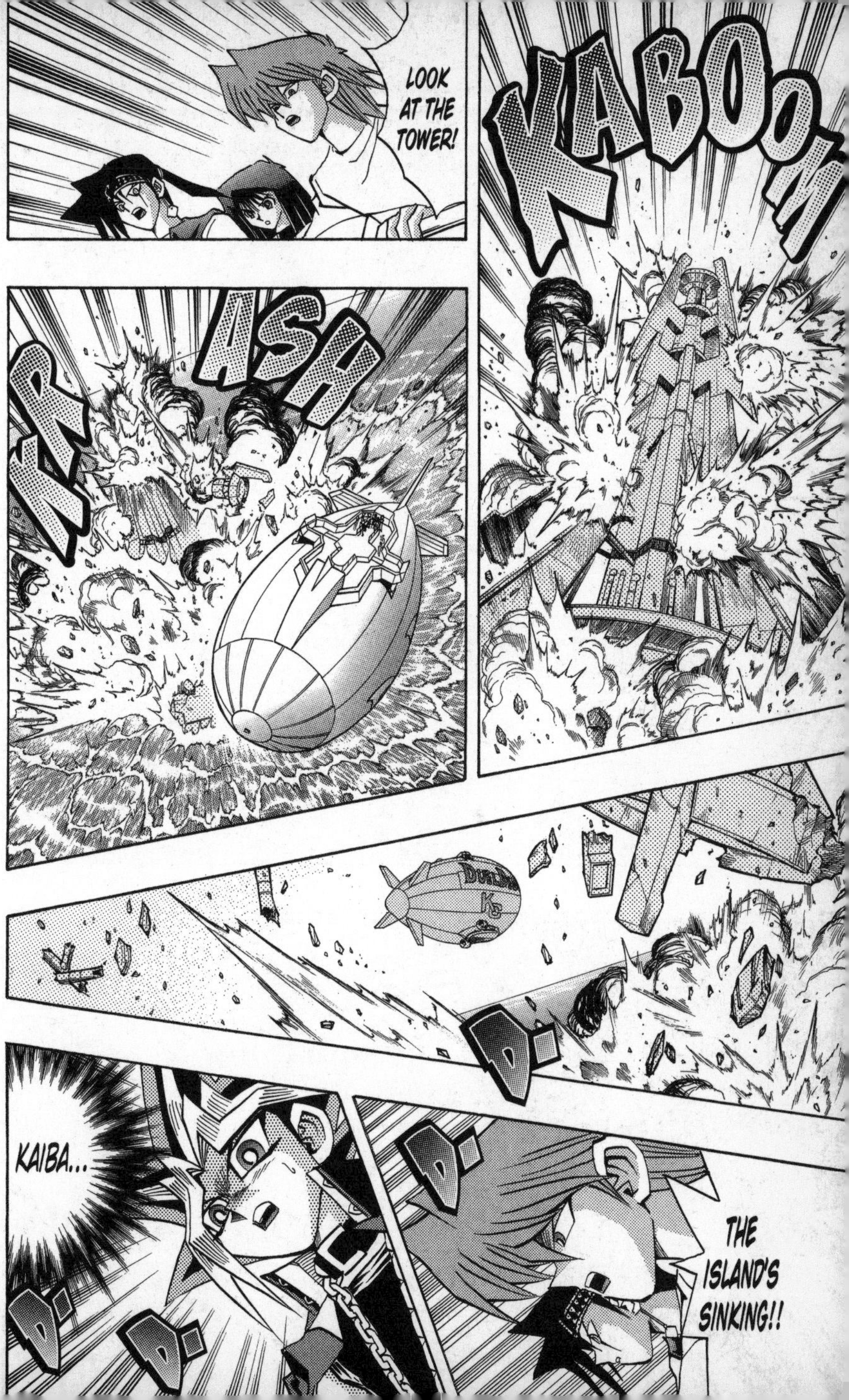
KABOOM
LOOK AT THE TOWER!
RASH
THE ISLAND'S SINKING!!
KAIBA...

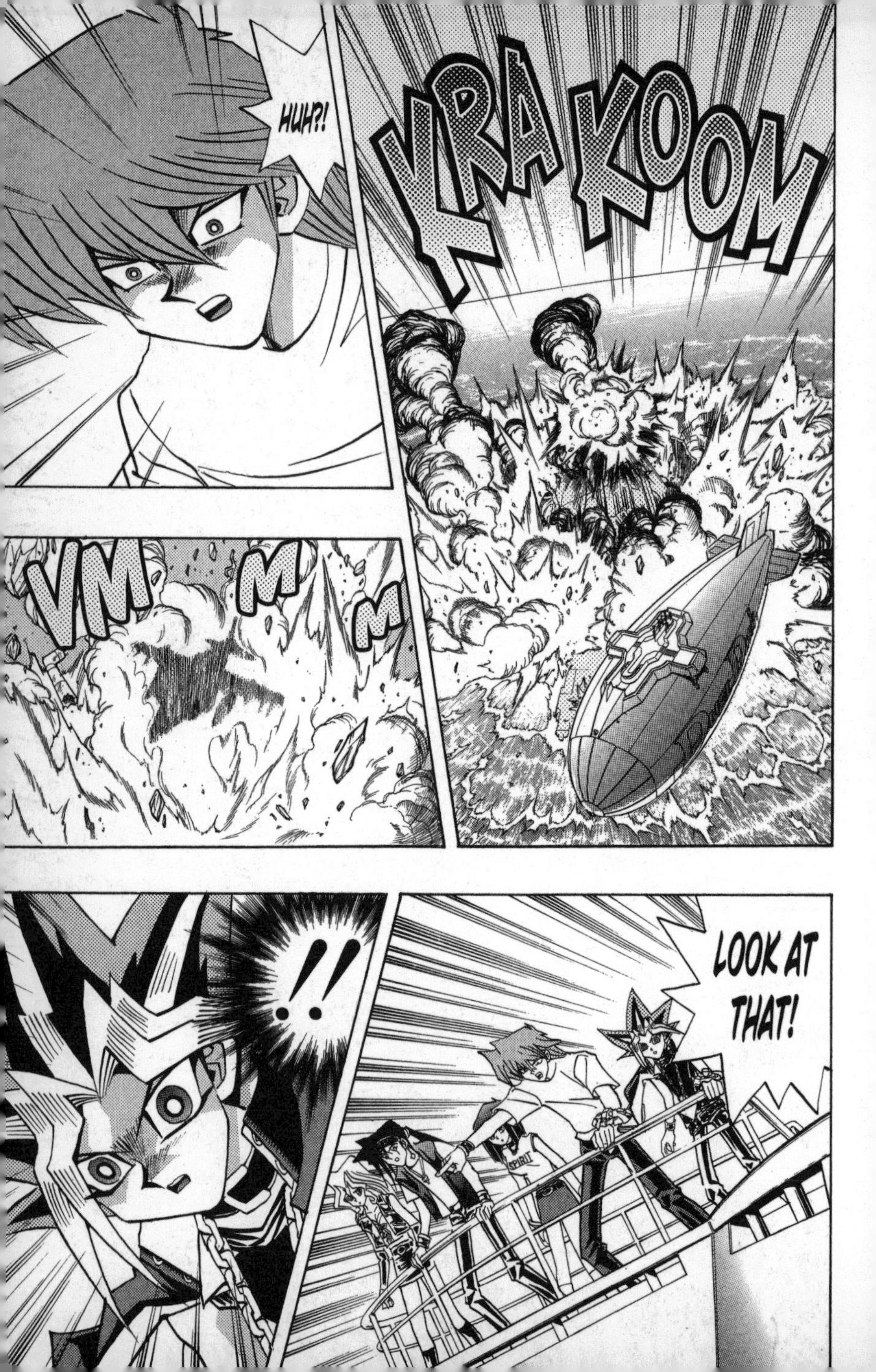
KRA KOOM
HUH?!
VM M M
LOOK AT THAT!
!!

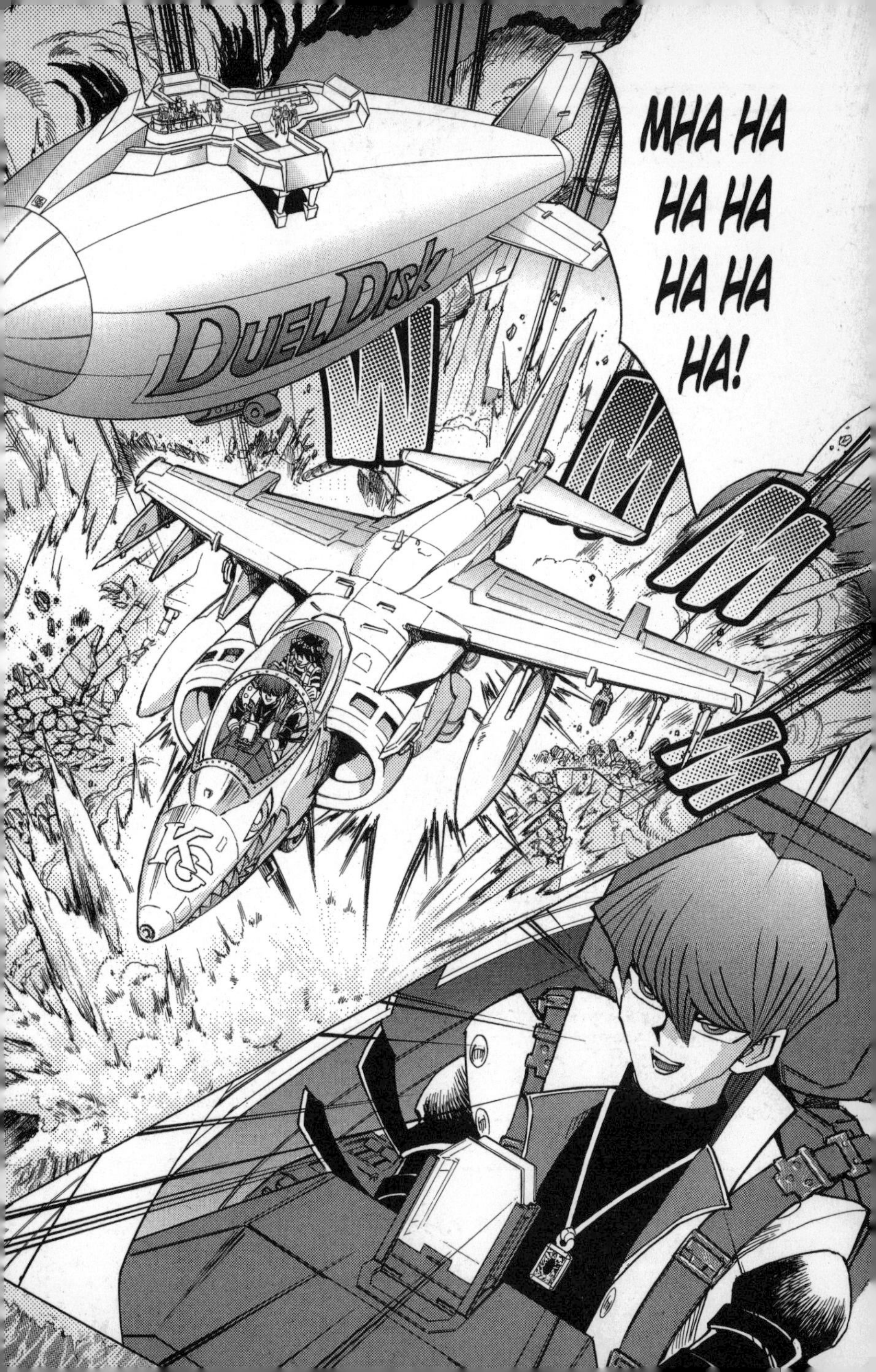
MHA HA
HA HA
HA HA
HA!
DUEL DISK

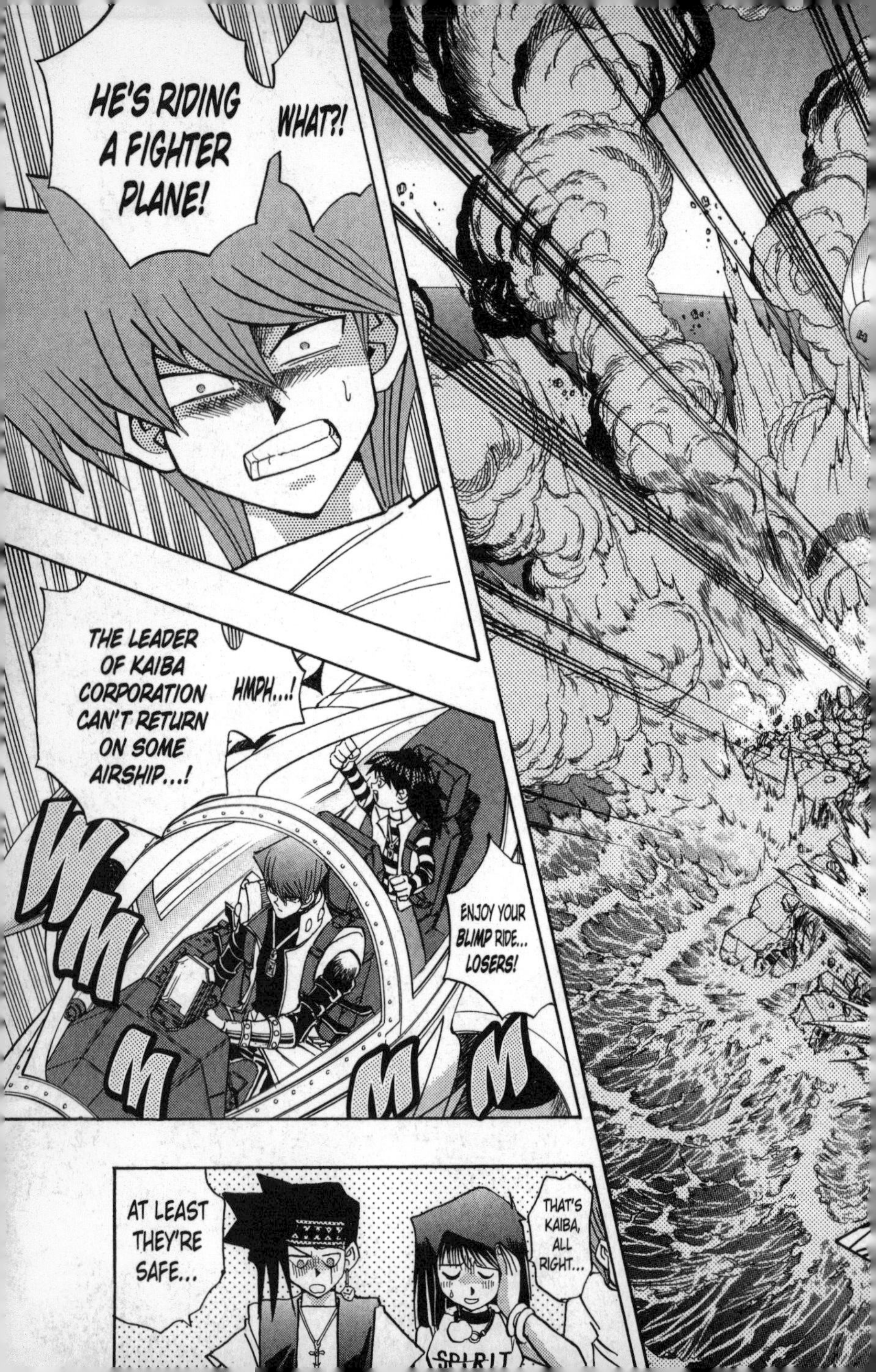
HE'S RIDING A FIGHTER PLANE!
WHAT?!
HMPH...!
THE LEADER OF KAIBA CORPORATION CAN'T RETURN ON SOME AIRSHIP...!
ENJOY YOUR BLIMP RIDE... LOSERS!
WMMMMM
THAT'S KAIBA, ALL RIGHT...
AT LEAST THEY'RE SAFE...

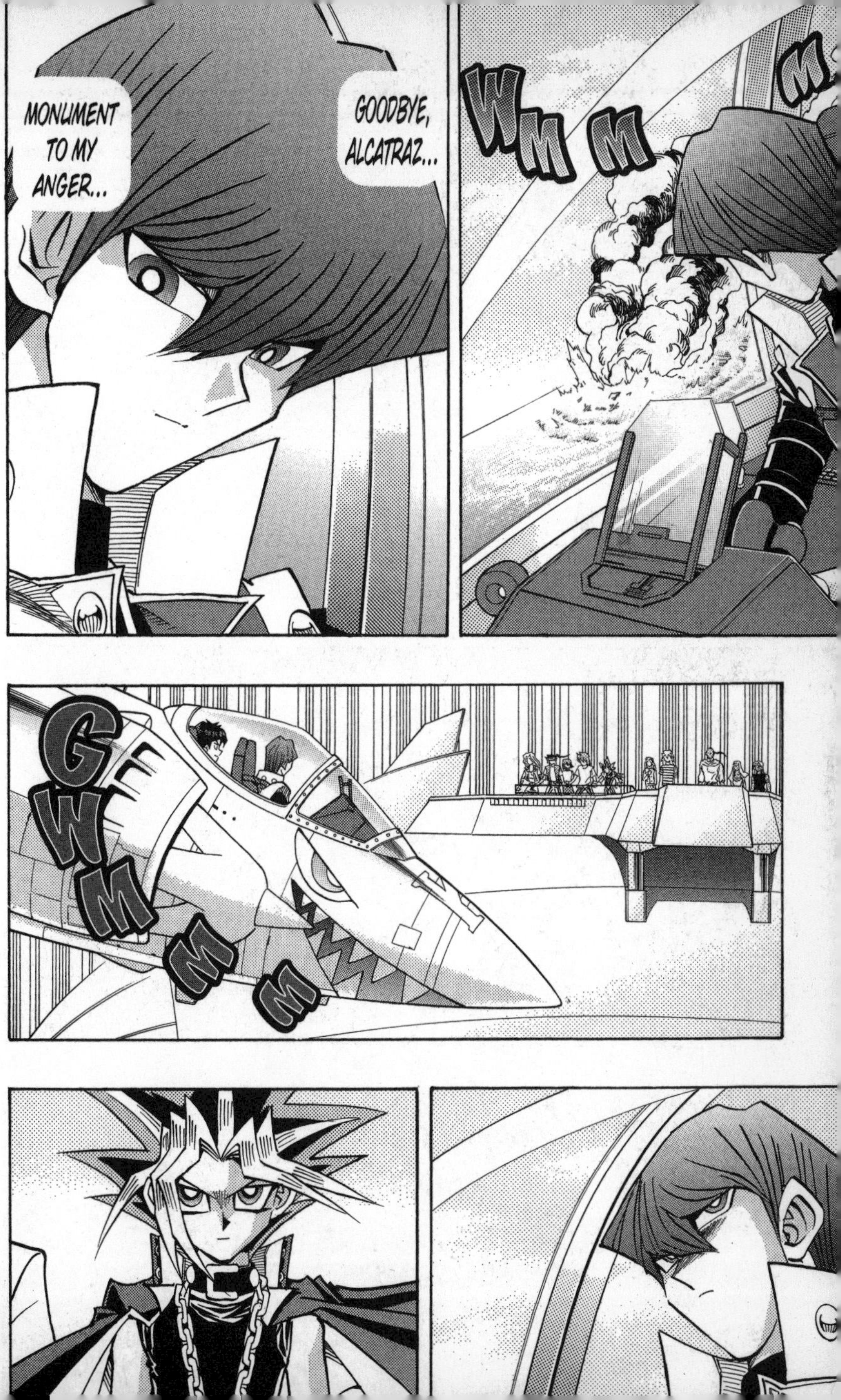
WMMMM
GOODBYE, ALCATRAZ...
MONUMENT TO MY ANGER...
GWMMM

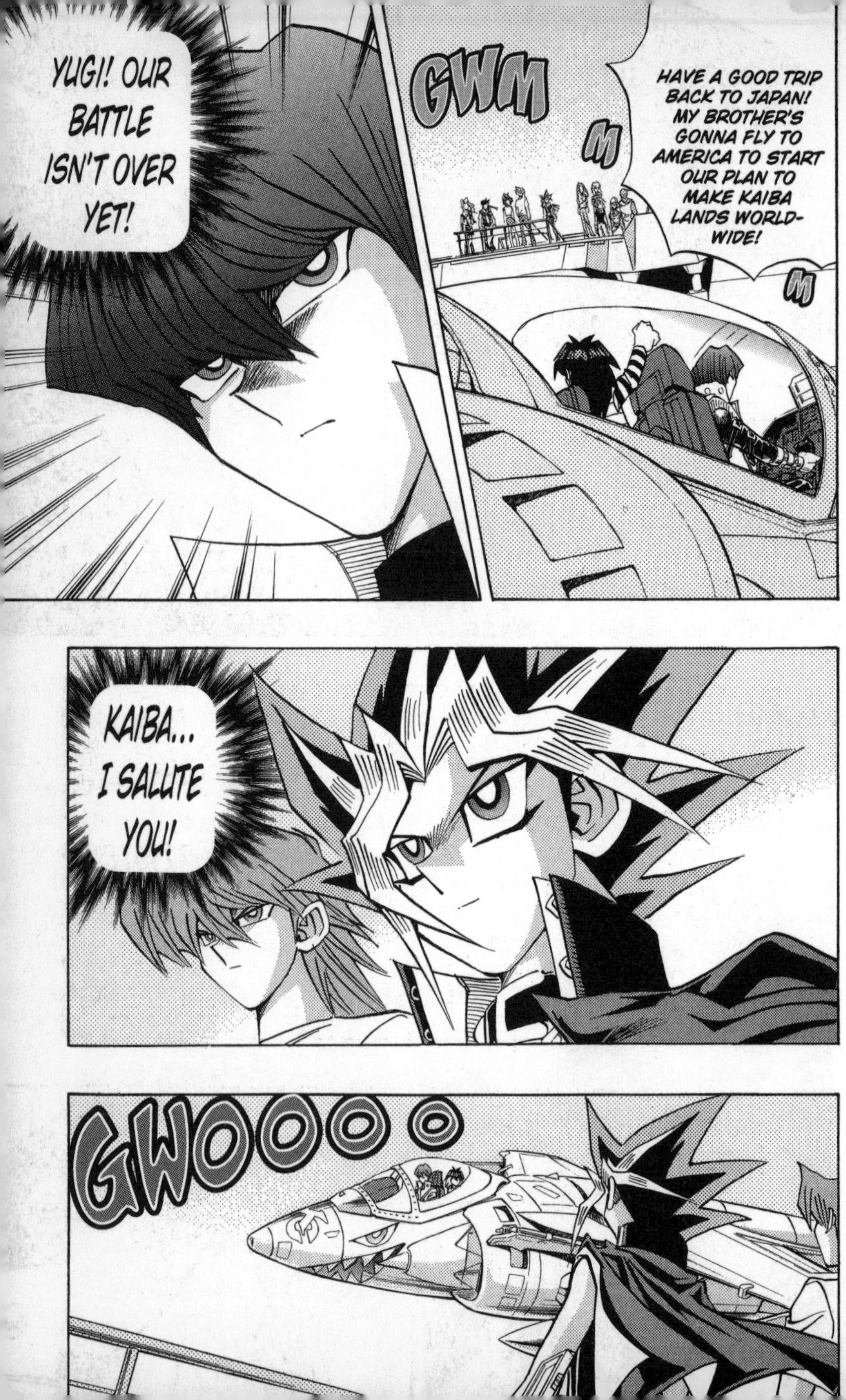
GWMMM
HAVE A GOOD TRIP BACK TO JAPAN! MY BROTHER'S GONNA FLY TO AMERICA TO START OUR PLAN TO MAKE KAIBA LANDS WORLD-WIDE!
YUGI! OUR BATTLE ISN'T OVER YET!
KAIBA... I SALUTE YOU!
GWOOOO

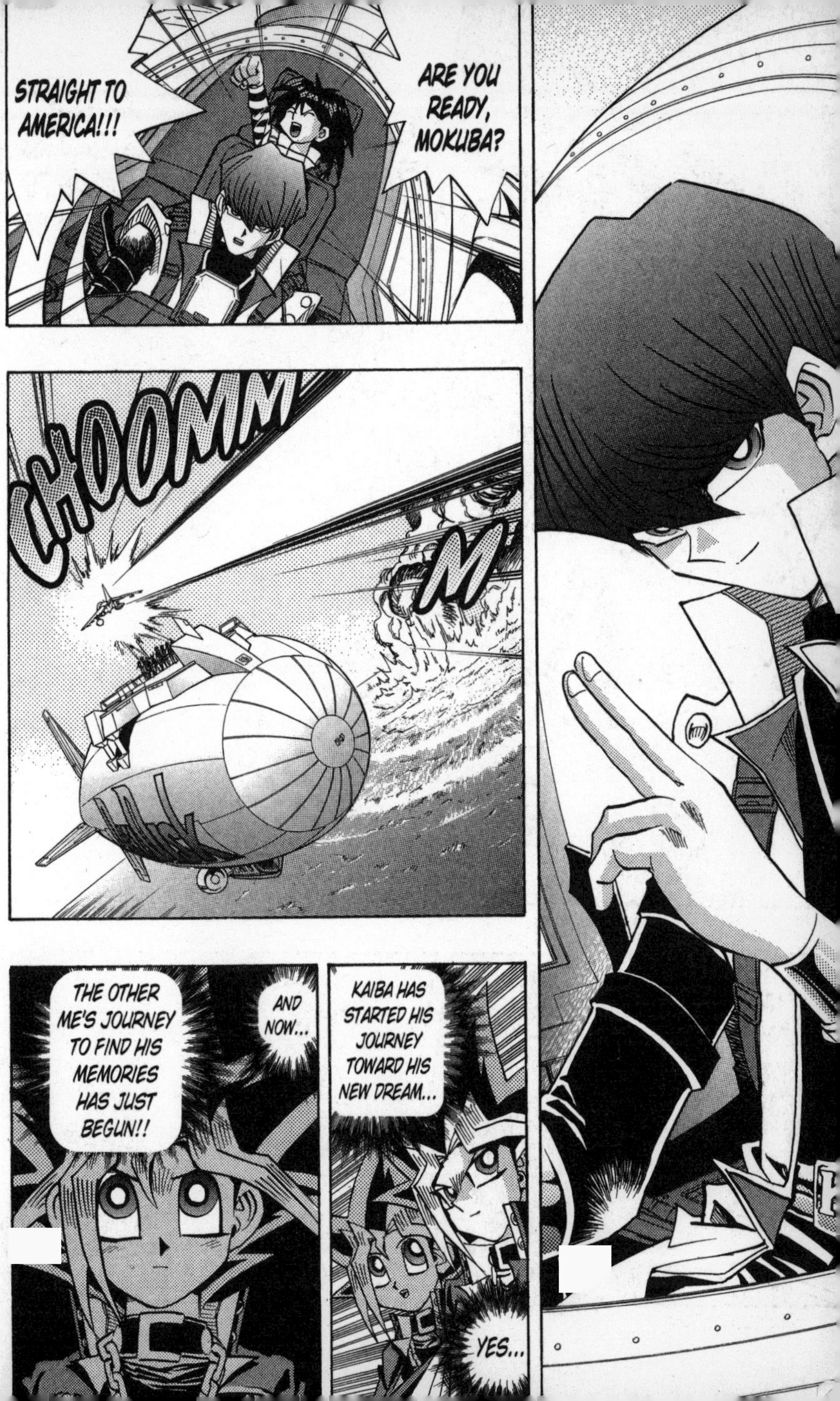
ARE YOU READY, MOKUBA?
STRAIGHT TO AMERICA!!!
CHOOMM
M
KAIBA HAS STARTED HIS JOURNEY TOWARD HIS NEW DREAM...
YES...
AND NOW...
THE OTHER ME'S JOURNEY TO FIND HIS MEMORIES HAS JUST BEGUN!!

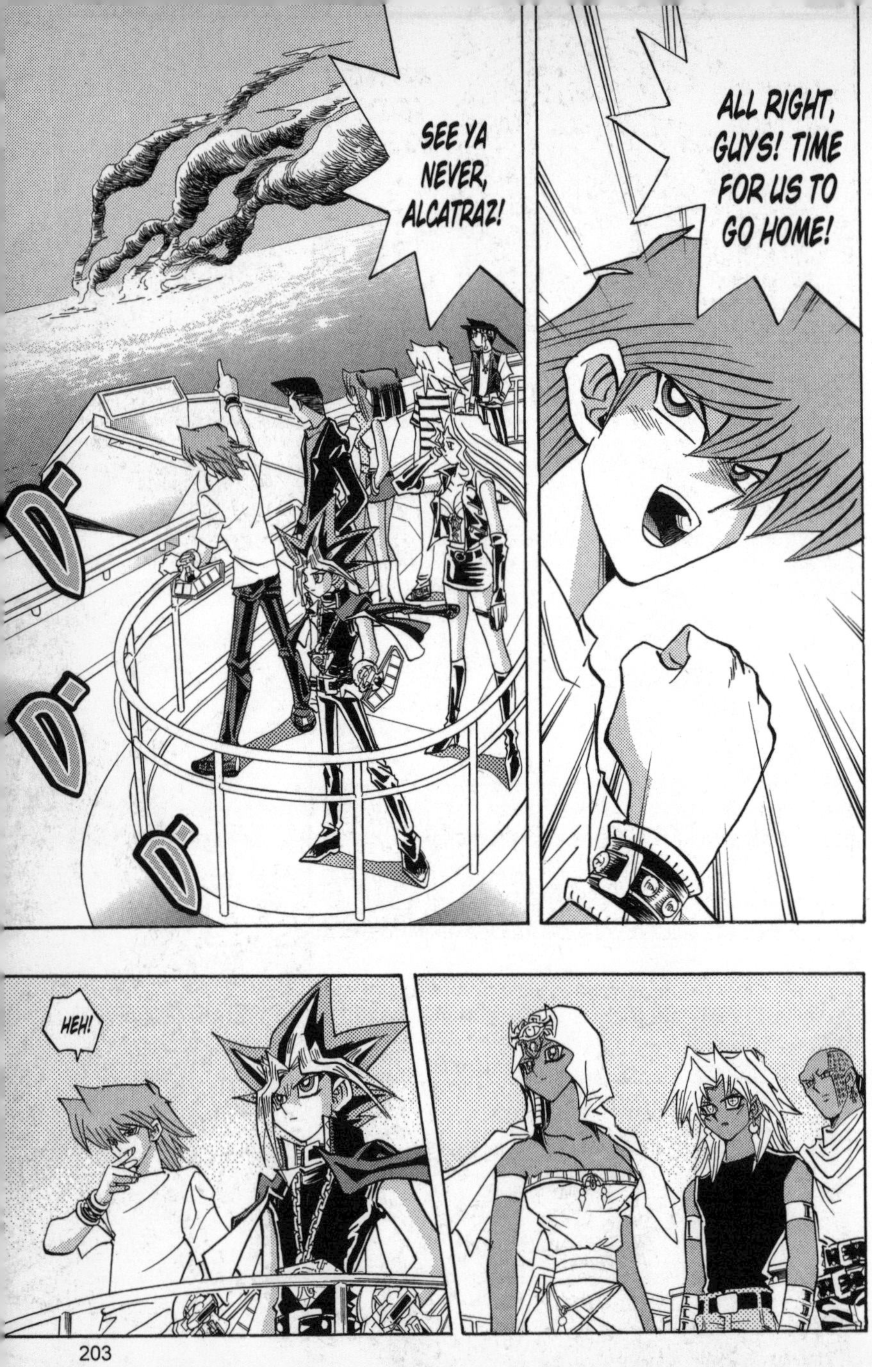
ALL RIGHT, GUYS! TIME FOR US TO GO HOME!
SEE YA NEVER, ALCATRAZ!
HEH!

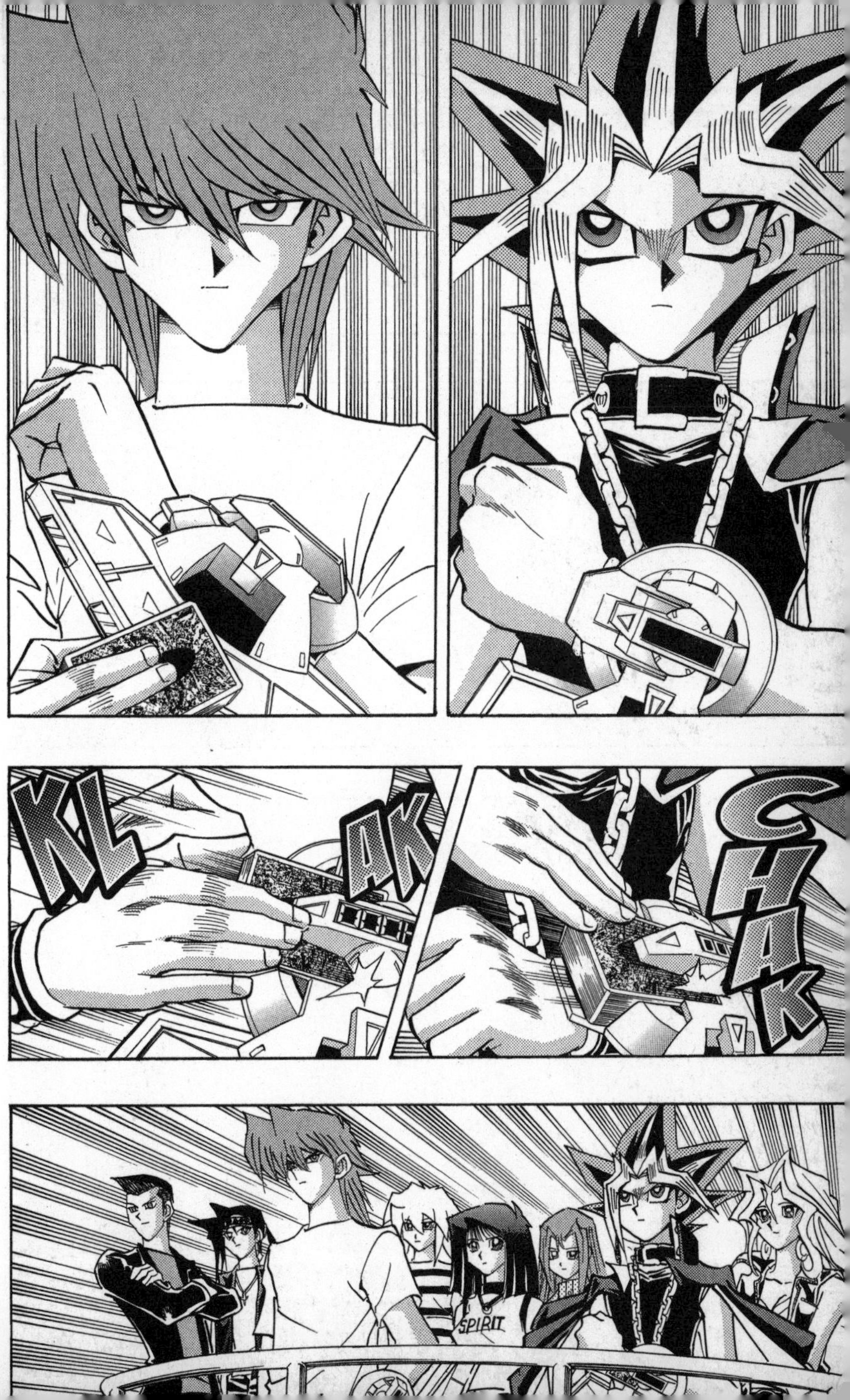
CHAK
KL AK
SPIRIT

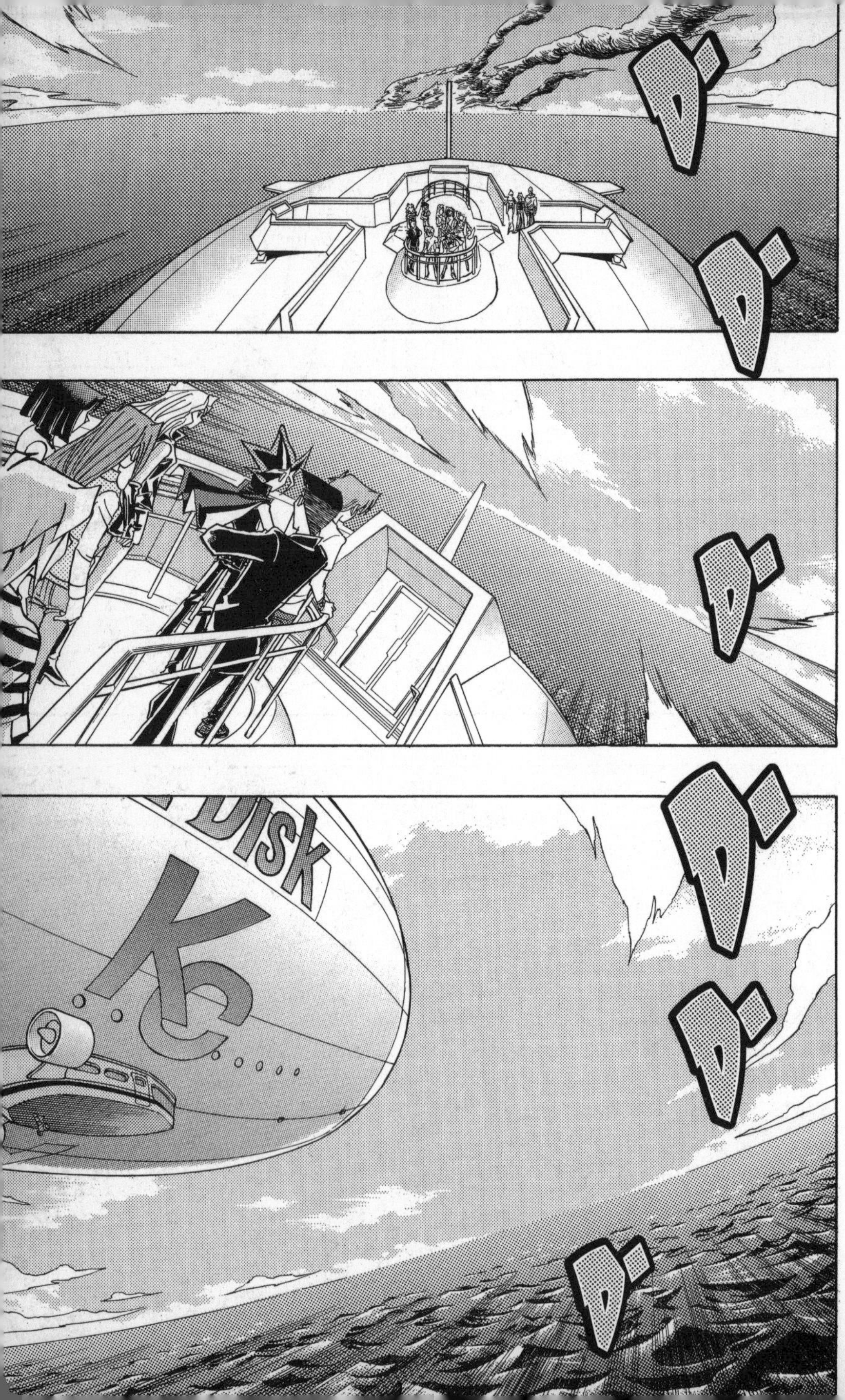
DISK
KC

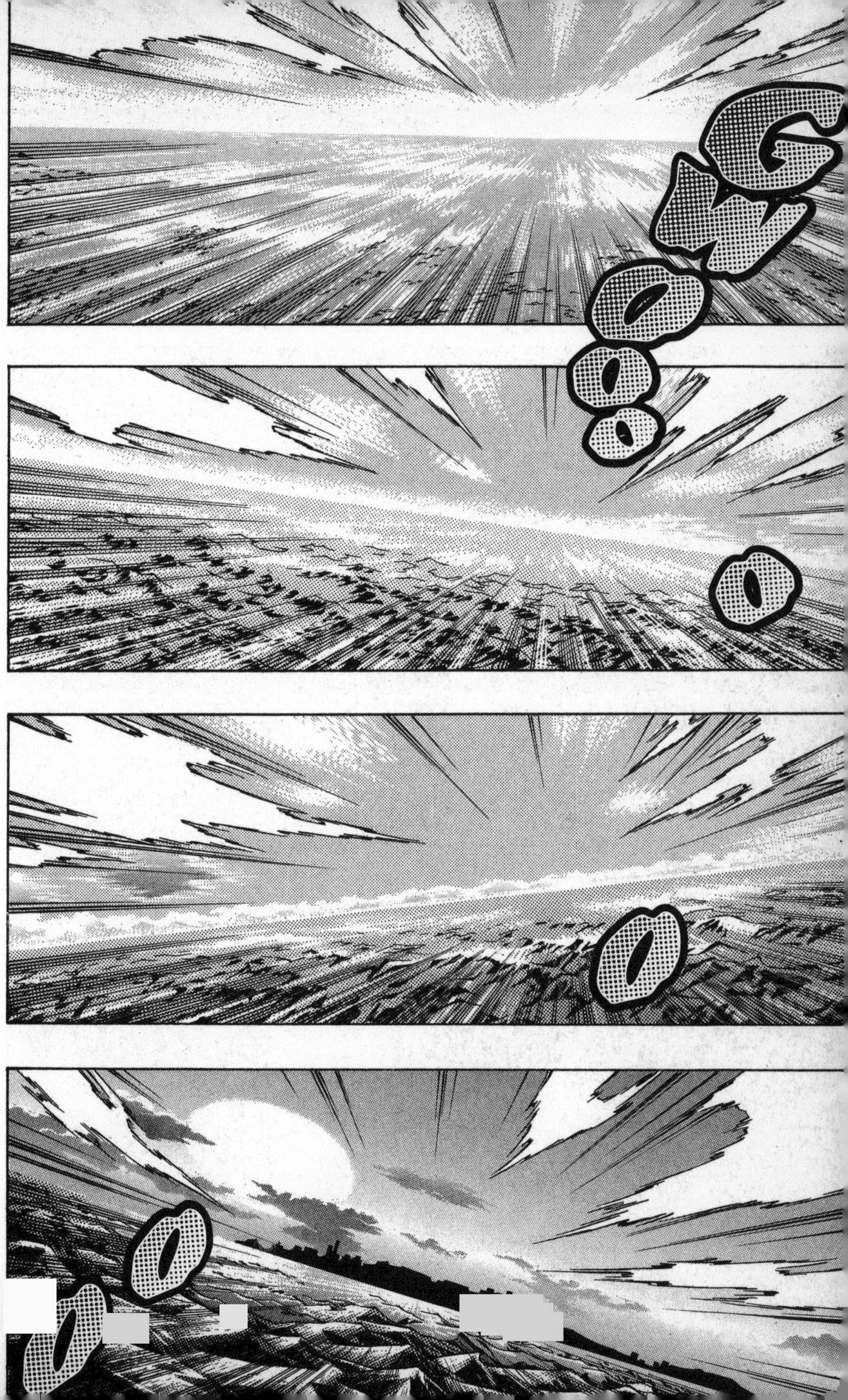
GWOOOOOOO

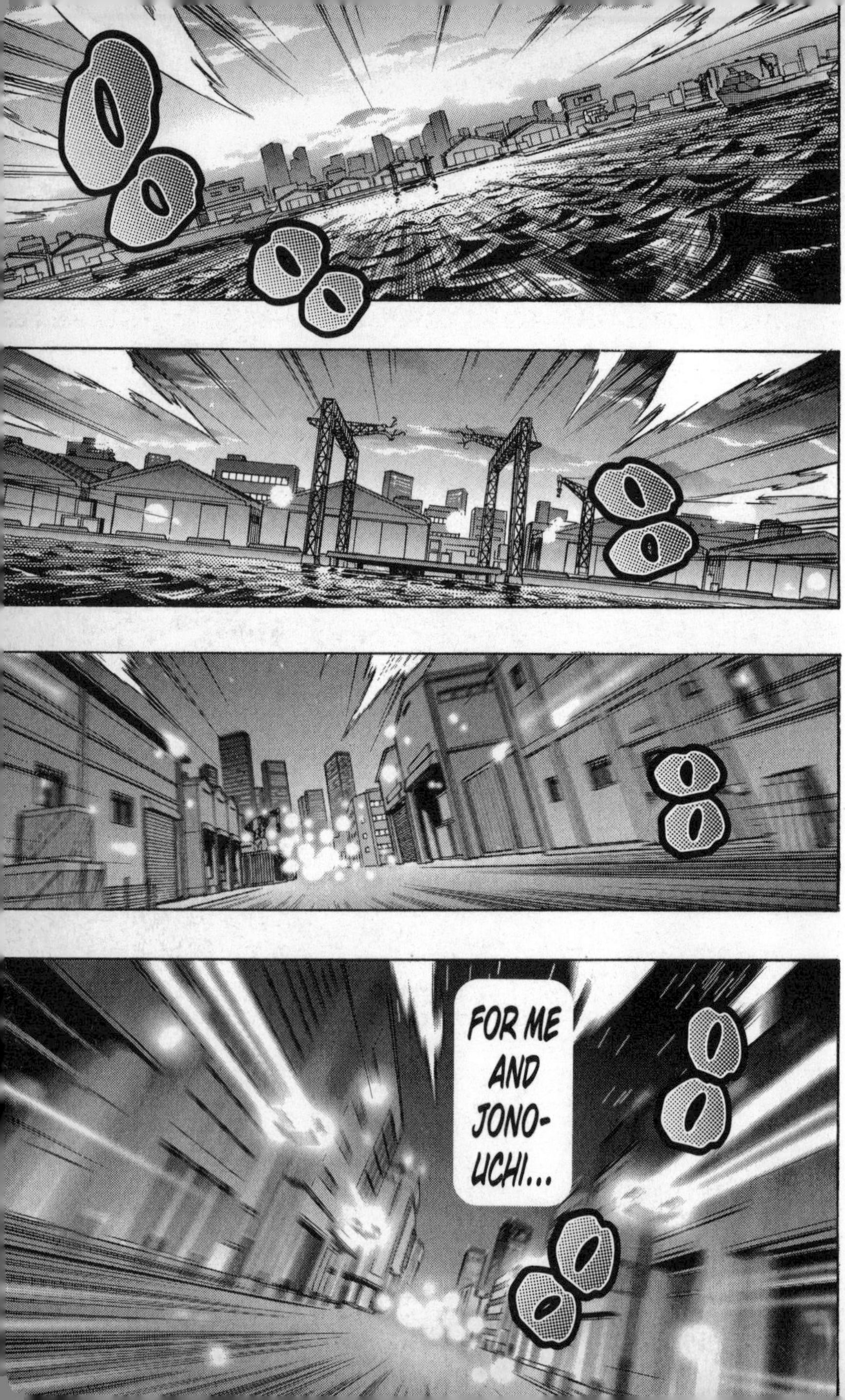
FOR ME AND JONO-UCHI...

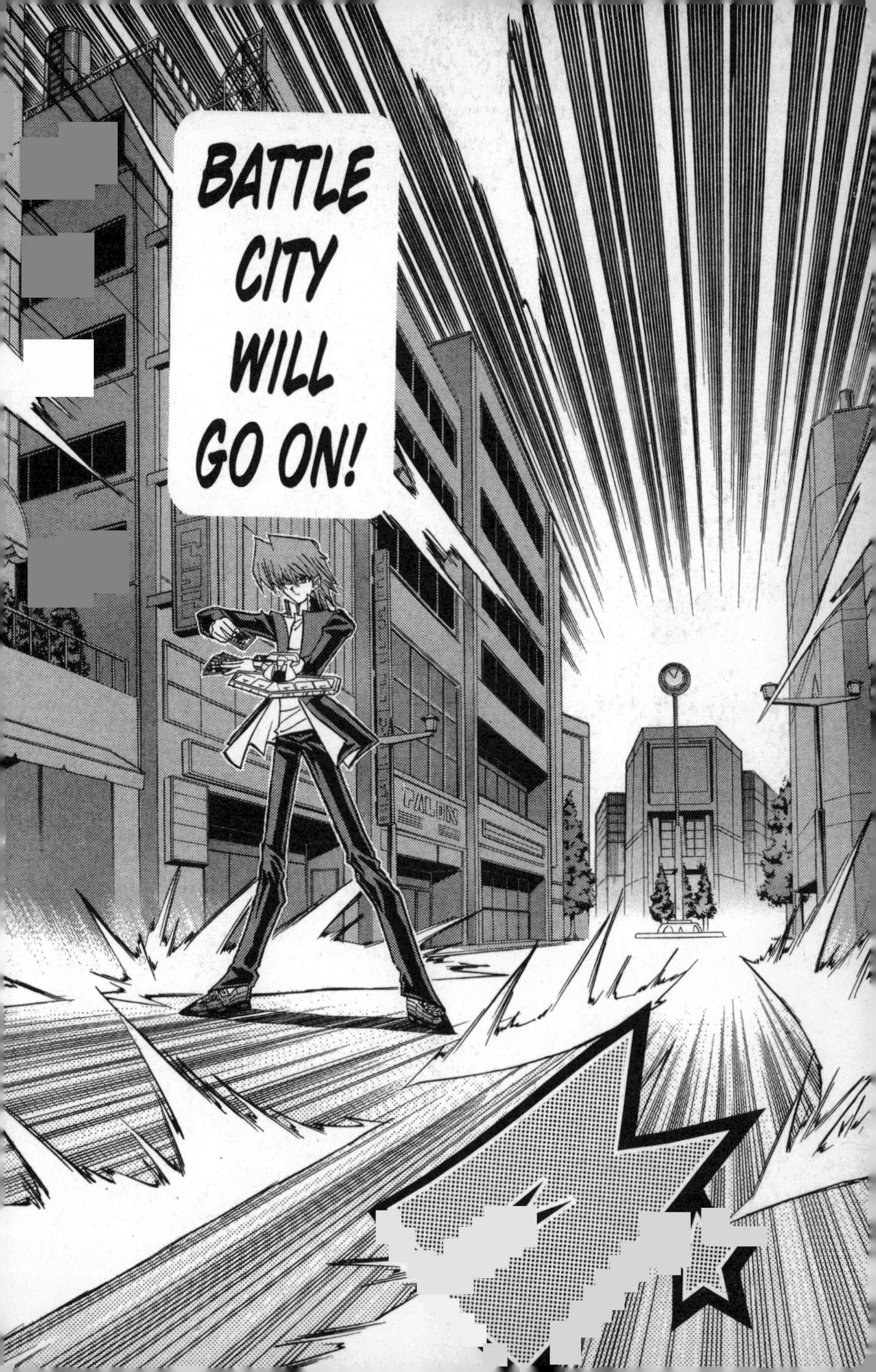
BATTLE CITY WILL GO ON!

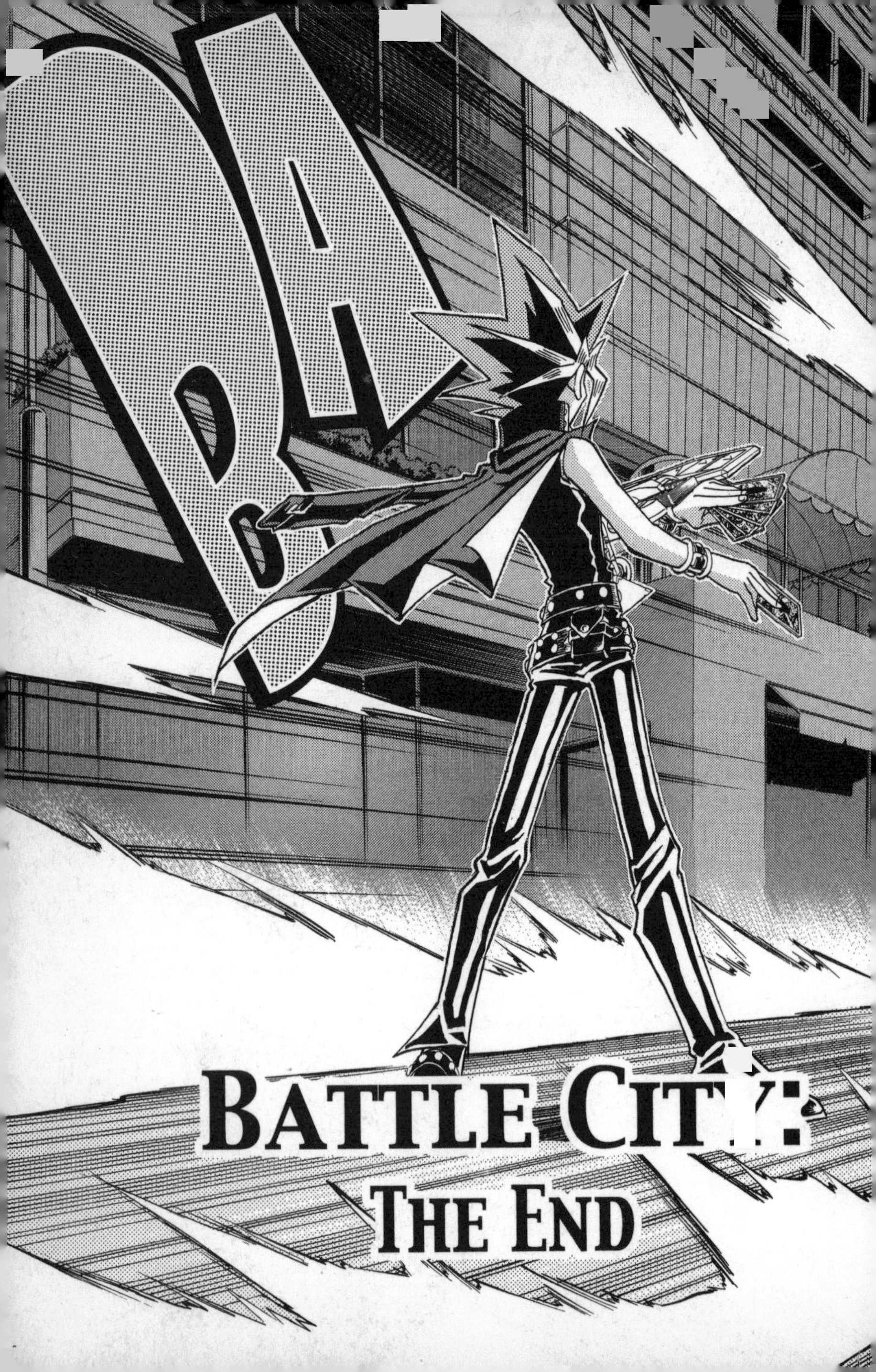
BATTLE CITY:
THE END

# MASTER OF THE CARDS

The "Duel Monsters" card game first appeared in volume two of the original **Yu-Gi-Oh!** graphic novel series, but it's in **Yu-Gi-Oh!: Duelist** (originally printed in Japan as volumes 8-31 of **Yu-Gi-Oh!**) that it gets really important. As many fans know, some of the card names are different between the English and Japanese versions. In case you play the game, or you're interested in playing, here's a rundown of some of the cards in this graphic novel. Some cards only appear in the **Yu-Gi-Oh!** video games, not in the actual trading card game.

| FIRST APPEARANCE IN THIS VOLUME | JAPANESE CARD NAME | ENGLISH CARD NAME |
|---|---|---|
| p.7 | *Juragedo* | Juragedo (NOTE: Not a real game card) |
| p.7 | *Ankoku no Masaisei* (Magic Revival of the Dark/Black Magic Regeneration) | Revival of the Dark (NOTE: Not a real game card) |
| p.7 | *Zombie no Hôseki* (Zombie's Jewel) | Zombie's Jewel (NOTE: Not a real game card) |
| p.7 | *Shisha Sosei* (Resurrection of the Dead) | Monster Reborn |
| p.12 | *Ra no Yokushinryû* (Ra the Winged God Dragon) (NOTE: The kanji for "sun god" is written beside the kanji for "Ra.") | The Sun Dragon Ra (NOTE: Called "The Winged Dragon of Ra" in the English anime and card game.) |

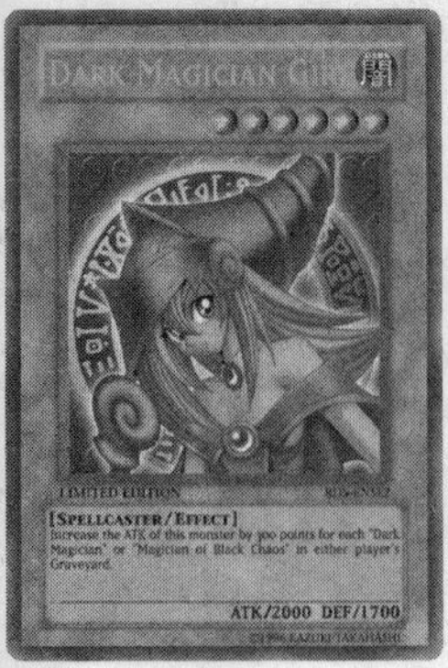
Dark Magician Girl
[Spellcaster/Effect]
ATK/2000 DEF/1700
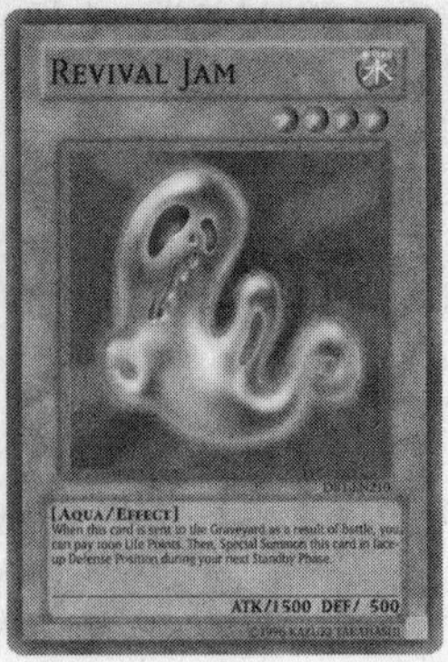
Revival Jam
[Aqua/Effect]
ATK/1500 DEF/ 500
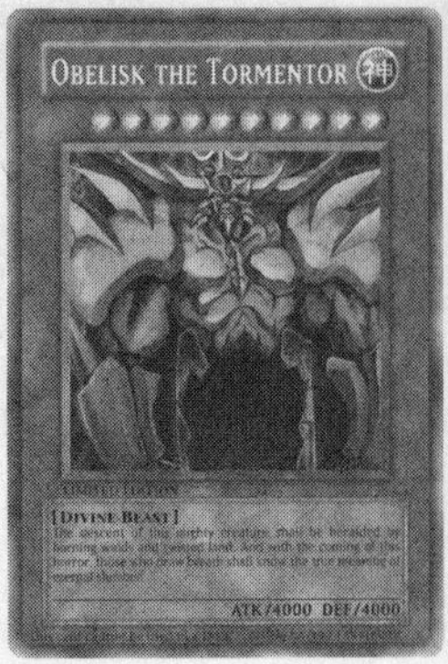
Obelisk the Tormentor
[Divine Beast]
ATK/4000 DEF/4000

| FIRST APPEARANCE IN THIS VOLUME | JAPANESE CARD NAME | ENGLISH CARD NAME |
|---|---|---|
| p.24 | *Devil's Sanctuary* | Devil's Sanctuary (NOTE: Called "Fiend Sanctuary" in the English anime and card game.) |
| p.35 | *Yûgô Kaijo* (Fusion Cancellation/Removal) | De-Polymerization |
| p.39 | *Zôshoku* (Multiply) | Multiply |
| p.39 | *Obelisk no Kyoshinhei* (Obelisk the Giant God Soldier) | The God of the Obelisk (NOTE: Called "Obelisk the Tormentor" in the English anime and card game.) |
| p.57 | *Metal Reflect Slime* | Metal Reflect Slime |
| p.62 | *Revival Slime* | Revival Jam |
| p.67 | *Yûgô (Fusion)* | Polymerization |
| p.71 | *Bowgunian* | Bowganian |
| p.72 | *Black Magician Girl* | Dark Magician Girl |
| p.74 | *Defend Slime* | Jam Defender |

THE WINGED DRAGON OF RA

[DIVINE-BEAST]
Spirits king of a powerful creature that rules over all that is mystic.

ATK/???? DEF/????

This card cannot be used in a Duel. ©1996 KAZUKI TAKAHASHI

MAGICAL STONE EXCAVATION

[SPELL CARD]

MAGICAL DIMENSION

[SPELL CARD]

| FIRST APPEARANCE IN THIS VOLUME | JAPANESE CARD NAME | ENGLISH CARD NAME |
|---|---|---|
| p.83 | *Mahôseki no Saikutsu* (Magical Stone Excavation/Mining) | Magical Stone Excavation |
| p.89 | *Granadora* | Granadora |
| p.95 | *Genjûô Gazelle* (Gazelle the Mythical Beast King) | Gazelle the King of Mythical Beasts |
| p.97 | *Yami kara no Kishû* (Surprise Attack from the Darkness) | Surprise Attack from the Darkness (NOTE: Not a real game card. Called "Surprise Attack from Beyond" in the English anime.) |
| p.102 | *Osiris no Tenkûryû* (Osiris the Heaven Dragon) | Slifer the Sky Dragon |
| p.117 | *Soul Taker* | Soul Taker |
| p.134 | *Dimension Magic* | Dimension Magic (NOTE: Called "Magical Dimension" in the English anime and card game.) |
| p.136 | *Black Magician* | Dark Magician |

# IN THE NEXT VOLUME...

*Yu-Gi-Oh!: Duelist* is over…but the adventure continues in *Yu-Gi-Oh!: Millennium World* volume 1! Yugi has gathered all the Egyptian God Cards, but his next journey will take his soul back in time to ancient Egypt, when the magic and monsters were real! Now Yugi and his friends must explore the world of Yugi's forgotten past…and fight an enemy who has been waiting for them for 3,000 years!

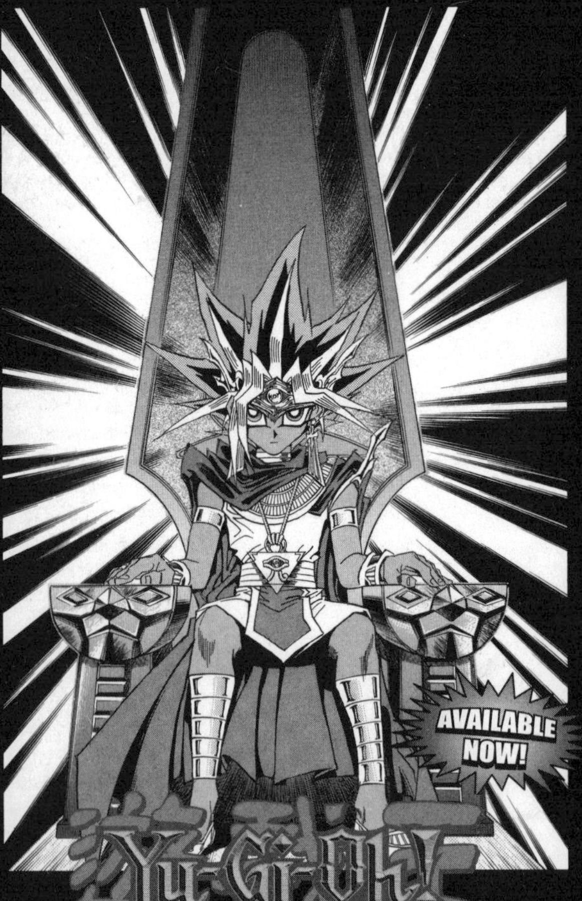
AVAILABLE NOW!
Yu-Gi-Oh!
Millennium World

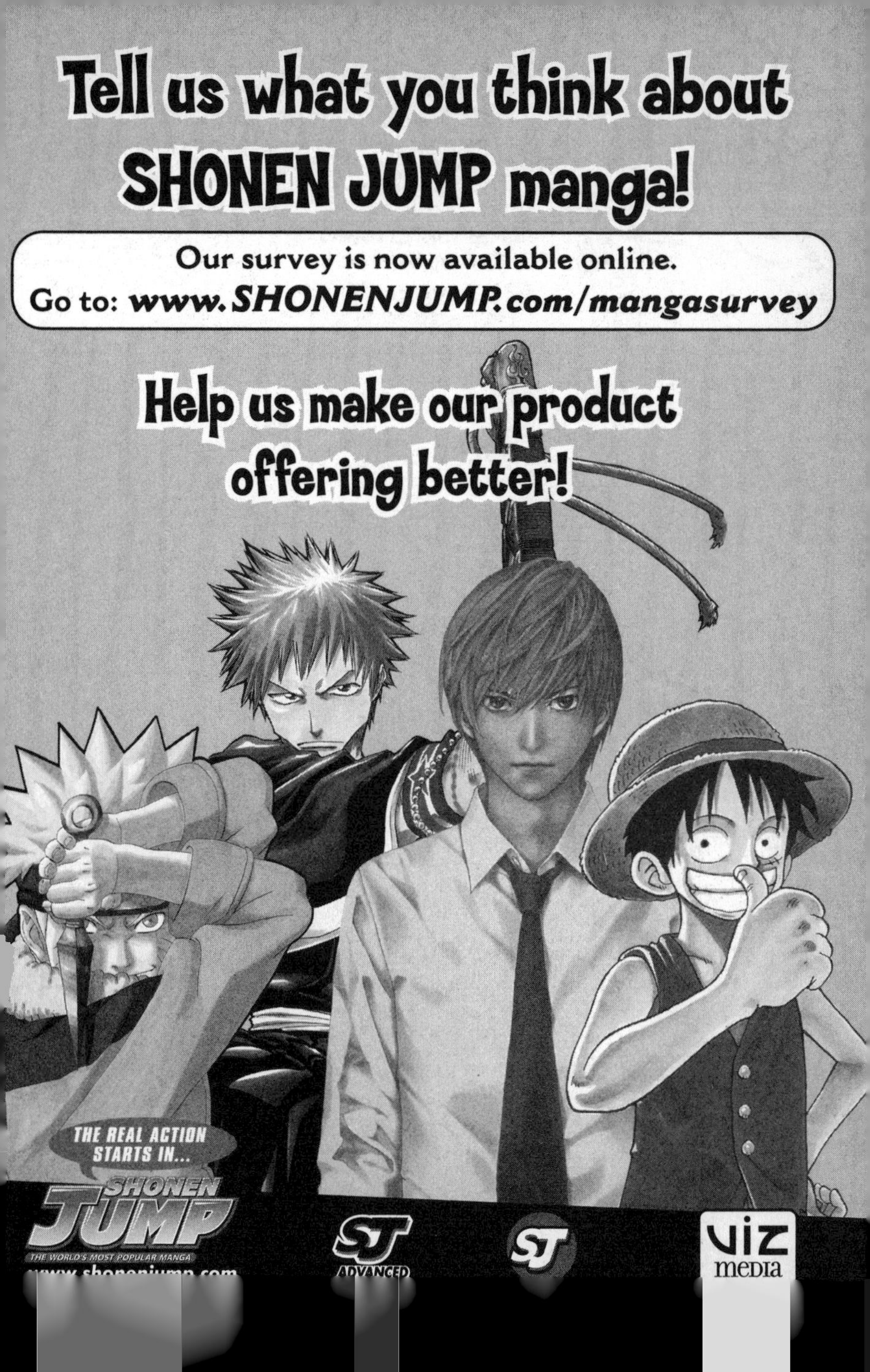
Tell us what you think about SHONEN JUMP manga!
Our survey is now available online.
Go to: www.SHONENJUMP.com/mangasurvey
Help us make our product offering better!
THE REAL ACTION STARTS IN...
SHONEN JUMP
THE WORLD'S MOST POPULAR MANGA
SJ ADVANCED
SJ
VIZ media

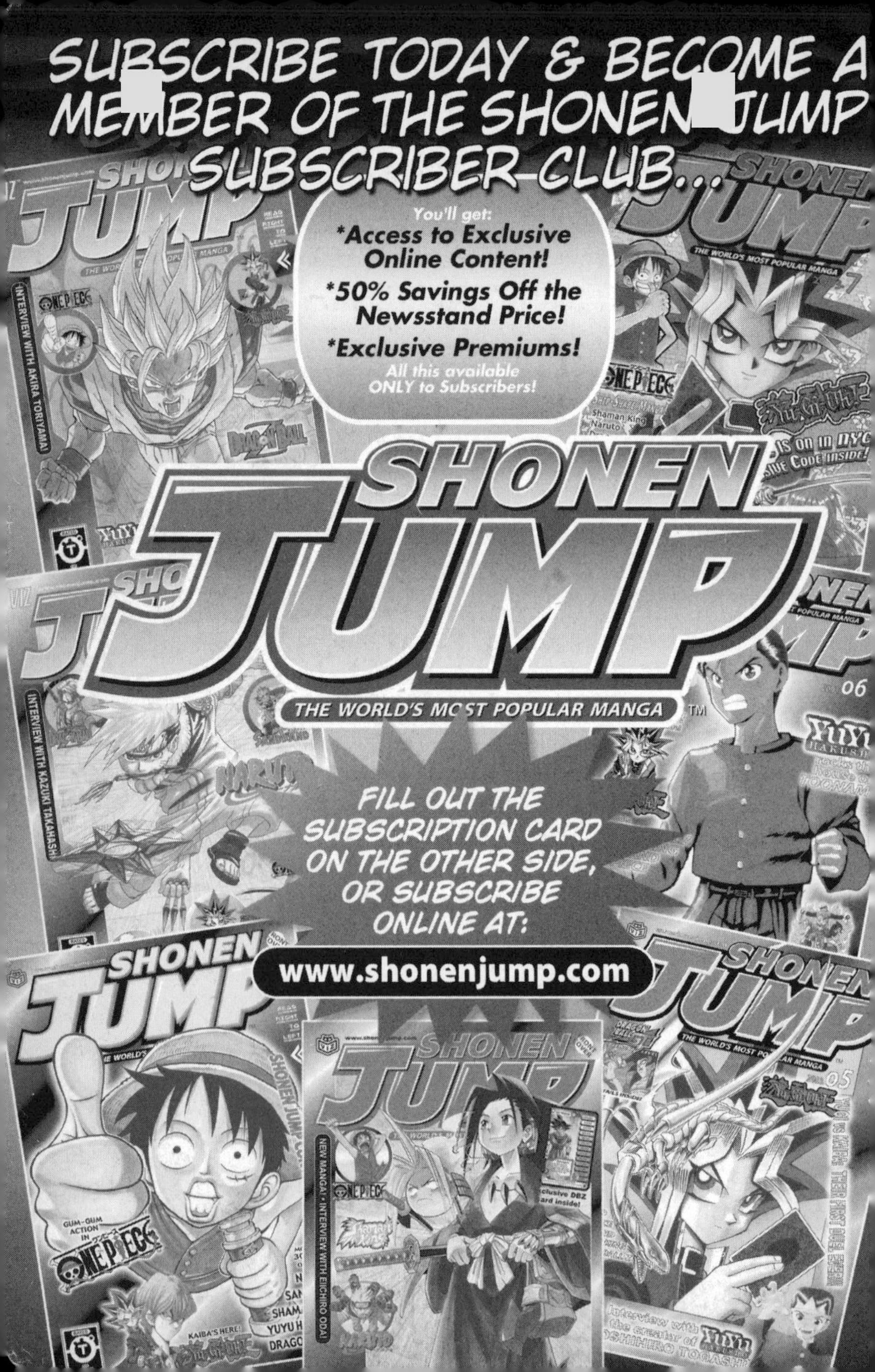
SUBSCRIBE TODAY & BECOME A MEMBER OF THE SHONEN JUMP SUBSCRIBER CLUB...
You'll get:
*Access to Exclusive Online Content!
*50% Savings Off the Newsstand Price!
*Exclusive Premiums!
All this available ONLY to Subscribers!
SHONEN JUMP
THE WORLD'S MOST POPULAR MANGA
TM
FILL OUT THE SUBSCRIPTION CARD ON THE OTHER SIDE, OR SUBSCRIBE ONLINE AT:
www.shonenjump.com